THE FAR ENEMY

Since September 11, Al Qaeda has been portrayed as an Islamist front united in armed struggle, or jihad, against the Christian West. However, as the historian and commentator Fawaz A. Gerges argues, the reality is rather different and more complex. In fact, Al Qaeda represents a minority within the jihadist movement, and its strategies have been vehemently criticized and opposed by religious nationalists among the jihadis, who prefer to concentrate on changing the Muslim world rather than taking the fight global. It is this rift that led to the events of September 11 and that has dominated subsequent developments. Through several years of primary field research, the author unravels the story of the jihadist movement and explores how it came into being, the philosophies of its founding fathers, its structure, the rifts and tensions that split its ranks, and why some members, like Osama bin Laden and his deputy Ayman al-Zawahiri, favored international over local strategies in taking the war to the West. This is an articulate and original book that sheds light on the tactics used by the jihadis in the last three decades. As more alienated young Muslims are seduced into joining, the author asks where the jihadist movement is going and whether it can survive and shed its violent character.

Fawaz A. Gerges holds the Christian A. Johnson Chair in International Affairs and Middle Eastern Studies at Sarah Lawrence College. He was educated at Oxford University and the London School of Economics and has previously been a Research Fellow at Harvard and Princeton universities. He is also a senior analyst and regular commentator for ABC television news. His books include *America and Political Islam: Clash of Interests or Clash of Cultures?* (Cambridge, 1999) and *The Journey of the Jihadis: A Biography of a State of Mind* (Harcourt Press, 2006). He has written extensively on Arab and Muslim politics, Islamist movements, American foreign policy, and relations between the world of Islam and the West. His articles have appeared in several of the most prestigious journals and newspapers in the United States, Europe, and the Middle East.

The Far Enemy

WHY JIHAD WENT GLOBAL

Fawaz A. Gerges

Sarah Lawrence College

CAMBRIDGE UNIVERSITY PRESS
Cambridge, New York, Melbourne, Madrid, Cape Town, Singapore, São Paulo

Cambridge University Press
40 West 20th Street, New York, NY 10011-4211, USA

www.cambridge.org
Information on this title: www.cambridge.org/9780521791403

First published 2005

Printed in the United States of America

A catalog record for this publication is available from the British Library.

Library of Congress Cataloging in Publication Data

Gerges, Fawaz A., 1958–
The far enemy : why Jihad went global / Fawaz A. Gerges.
p.   cm.
1. Jihad.   2. War – Religious aspects – Islam.   3. Islam and world politics.   I. Title.
BP182.G4   2005
297.7′2–dc22   2005020121

ISBN-13   978-0-521-79140-3 hardback
ISBN-10   0-521-79140-5 hardback

For all those who died on September 11
and the loved ones they left behind

Contents

Acknowledgments

This book has been in the making since 1999 and is based on hundreds of interviews with Islamists, former jihadis, activists, civil society leaders, and opinion makers throughout the Middle East. I benefited greatly from a generous MacArthur Foundation fellowship and a Smith Richardson Foundation grant, which enabled me to spend two years in the region conducting field research, traveling widely, and spending countless hours talking to the rank and file, not just leaders, of the Islamist and jihadist movements. The interviews I conducted inform my analysis throughout the book and complement recently acquired primary sources. This book relies overwhelmingly on original material.

When the United States was attacked on September 11, 2001, I decided to wait until the smoke had dissipated before I concluded the writing of the book. I am glad I did, because the aftershocks of the September 11 earthquake have shed more light on the internal dynamics, tensions, and struggles within the jihadist movement. I also did follow-up primary research to bring the story up to date. My hope is that the book makes a humble critical contribution, not to the polemical and charged foreign policy debate, but rather to understanding the road to September 11 and its aftermath: how and why transnationalist jihadis brought the war to American shores against the wishes of the bulk of their religious nationalist associates who wanted to keep the struggle focused on the home front. And to what extent is this global war a direct product of the internal strife among jihadis themselves?

In researching and writing this book, I have incurred many intellectual debts to friends, colleagues, and strangers who sat down with me for countless hours and shared with me their insights and views. In particular, I cannot do justice to the hundreds of activists, students, and opinion makers in Egypt, Yemen, Lebanon, Jordan, Palestine, and elsewhere who took the time to meet with me and enrich my education on the unfolding struggles in the region. They welcomed me in their homes and offices, put up with my nonsensical questions, and provided me with precious primary sources. This book is as much theirs as it is mine, although they might disagree with my conclusions and are not responsible for any existing errors of judgment or fact.

A partial list of the people who went out of their way to help me includes Hassan Hanafi, Al-Sayyid Yassin, Nabil Abdel Fattah, Mustafa Kamal al-Said, Hazem Amin, Kamal Salibi, Bahgat Korany, Walid Kazeha, Galal Amin, Mustafa Hamarneh, Ahmad Thabet, Adel Hammad, Yosri Mustafa, Emad Eldin Shahin, Ridwan al-Sayyid, Ahmad Sobhi Mansour, Gameel Matter, Abul Ela al-Madi, Esam Sultan, Ahmad Abdullah, Omar Morsi, Tariq al-Bashri, Manar El Shorbagi, Ali Fahmi, Seif al-Din Abed al-Fattah Ismail, Nadia Mahmoud Mustafa, Abdel al-Azeez Shadi, Gamal al-Banna, Dallal al-Bezri, Adel Hussein, Hassan Ahmed Abu Taleb, Mohammed Salah, Dia' Rashwan, Montasser al-Zayat, Mohammed al-Maitami, Nasr Taha Mustafa, Nemat Guenena, Saad Eddin Ibrahim, Enid Hill, Hala Mustafa, Anees al-Anani, Samir Marqus, Faisal Mokarram, Abdel al-Bari Taher, Wahid Abdel al-Majid, Abdu Mohammed al-Jundi, Hassan Zaid, Abdel Kareem Alkhwani, Mansour Azzandi, Gamil al-Ansi, Ghaleb al-Gershi, Najib Ghanem, Khaled al-Bojairi, Haseeb al-Oraiki, Mohammed Kahtan, Mohammed al-Yadomi, Yasin Abdel al-Aziz, Abdel Wahab al-Ansi, Ahmad al-Shami, Mohammed Mansour, Mohammed Mottahar, Mohammed Abdel Malak Almotawakel, Mohammed Abdel Wahab Jubari, Layth Shubaylat, Tariq al-Tal, Mohammed Suleiman, Rahil al-Gharaibah, Abed al-Lateef Araibat, Jameel Abu Bakr, Nahed Hattar, Muraywid Tal, Khair el-Din Haseeb, Nadim Mseis, Hicham Chehab, Haytham Mouzahem, Fares al-Sakkaf, Hani Hourani, Abdulwahab Alkebsi, Mona Makram-Ebeid, Nadia Abou El-Magd, and many others.

Colleagues and friends in the Middle East generously offered intellectual nourishment as well as friendship and hospitality. In particular, I would like to thank Tariq Tal and Jocelyn DeJong, Anees al-Anani,

Bahgat Korany, Mustafa Hamarneh, and Mohammed al-Maitami for hosting me in their homes and welcoming me with open arms. I remain grateful.

I owe a special thanks to London University Professor Charles Tripp, who read an early draft essay of the book and was not discouraged by its lack of refinement. His critical feedback and insights forced me to contextualize the analysis and be more comparative. Needless to say, any remaining shortcomings are mine. Yezid Sayigh of London University also furnished me with conceptual and practical suggestions that helped me in revising the book. Kamran Bokhari, senior analyst at Strategic Forecasting, Inc., read the entire manuscript and made extensive notes throughout. The book is better thanks to his diligent efforts. Over the years Avi Shlaim of Oxford University has been and remains a source of inspiration and friendship. I also want to thank my friend J. Michael Mahoney, whose moral support has sustained me. I am grateful to Julie Kidd of the Christian A. Johnson Endeavor Foundation, which has been a generous supporter of Middle East studies and my work at Sarah Lawrence. I also want to thank my research students, Marie Webb and Anthony Fleming, for their assistance.

Special thanks go to Ms. Marigold Acland, Senior Editor at Cambridge University Press, for her patience and commitment to this book. Although my contract stipulated that I complete the book by 2002, she just gently nudged me to plug along. More important, her critical feedback enriched the overall analysis. I also want to thank Ms. Shari Chappell, my editor at Cambridge, for shepherding the book from its early conception until birth; Shari's magical editorial touch has transformed the book. The entire team at Cambridge has been most helpful.

Finally, this book belongs to my family. They invested as much time and energy, if not more so, in making it happen as I did. I could not have traveled for long periods or written the book without Nora's love and encouragement; her intellectual feedback has guided the project since its inception. My children's tenderness and affection also kept me sane during those hectic days of travel and writing. Hannah never let a day go by without reminding me that I should hurry and be done with the book. Laith wandered in and out of my study showering me with kisses. From the outset Annie-Marie never tired inquiring about "why did

Al Qaeda attack America?" She motivated me to try to find intelligent answers to her question. Bassam helped me access key primary documents and listened closely and patiently to my chatter about the far enemy and the near enemy; he often had something critical to say. This book is a fruit of their love.

Fawaz A. Gerges
New York

Prologue

The Far Enemy, or al-Adou al-Baeed, is a term used by jihadis to refer to the United States and its Western allies. This book tells the story of the internationalization of jihad (armed struggle) and how and why in the late 1990s jihadis – who since the 1970s had focused their fight against the "near enemy," or al-Adou al-Qareeb (Muslim regimes) – shifted gears and called for a new global jihad against the far enemy. Jihadis (they invented the term and refer to themselves as such) are militant activists who feel estranged from the secular social and political order at home and intrinsically threatened by globalization and westernization.[1] Unlike mainstream Islamists who have given up on the use of force, since the 1970s jihadis have utilized violence in the name of religion and have sought to seize power and Islamize society by autocratic fiat from the top down. But their revolt is directed not only against the secular status quo, which they perceive as morally abhorrent, but also against the religious authority and the established canon of Islamic jurisprudence, scholarship, and history that they view as being subverted by corrupting Western influences.[2] In a sense, jihadis are practicing taqleed (emulating tradition) and are engaged in ijtihad (an effort of interpretation of the sacred texts) at the same time.

My study focuses on doctrinaire jihadis who have used violence against both their own governments (the near enemy) and Western targets (the far enemy); the most important of these jihadis are the Egyptian al-Jama'a al-Islamiya (Islamic Group) and Tanzim al-Jihad (Islamic Jihad); the Algerian Armed Islamic Group (GIA), which now seems to be defunct and replaced by the Salafist Group for Dawa and Combat; Al Qaeda; al-Tawhid wa al-Jihad, led by the militant Jordanian Abu Musab al-Zarqawi; and other smaller fringe groups.[3]

But I do not examine the so-called irredentist jihadis, who struggle to redeem land considered to be part of dar al-islam (House of Islam) from non-Muslim rule or occupation, like Palestinian Hamas and Jihad, Lebanon's Hizbollah or Party of God, and other groups in Kashmir, Chechnya, Mindanao, and elsewhere. Irredentist jihadism is sometimes the object of rivalry between nationalist forces, who may not conceive of it as jihad, and Islamists, and, within the latter, between local and global elements, as between the Afghan mujahedeen (Islamic fighters) and the "Afghan Arabs" who joined their struggle in the 1980s; similar nuances have been discernible in other irredentist conflicts, notably in Bosnia from 1992 to 1996, in Mindanao, and now in Iraq. There exist major differences among these three distinct strands of jihadism – internal, global, and irredentist – in terms of diversity of objectives, strategy, and tactics. For example, an important distinction is between the resort to armed struggle that is primarily determined by the context (foreign rule or military occupation) and that which arises primarily out of a radical doctrine expressing a preference for violence over nonviolent strategies despite the possibility of engaging in the latter: "Irredentist struggles are not as a rule the work of doctrinaire jihadis, whereas both internal and global jihads typically are."[4]

Another critical distinction is that my book does not deal with mainstream Islamists, that is, with Muslim Brothers and other politically independent activists who now accept the rules of the political game and emphatically embrace democratic principles and elements of a modernist outlook, although many observers still question their real commitment to democracy.[5] In the 1940s, 1950s, and 1960s elements of the Muslim Brotherhood flirted with violence and established the so-called al-Jihaz al-Sirri, or secret apparatus (an underground paramilitary unit within the political organization), which led Egyptian authorities to brutally suppress and persecute its rank and file.[6] But since the early 1970s, the Muslim Brotherhood – the most powerfully organized Islamist movement in the world of Islam, with local branches in the Arab Middle East and central, south, and southeast Asia – has moved more and more to the political mainstream, and now it aims to Islamize state and society through peaceful means.

Although Muslim Brothers are often targeted and excluded from politics by ruling autocrats, they no longer use force or the threat of force to attain their goals. Mainstream Islamists represent the overwhelming majority within the Islamist political spectrum, whereas jihadis, the focal point of this book, are a tiny – but critical – minority.

The New Definition of Jihad

Nowhere is jihadis' revolutionary challenge more evident than in their systemic effort to elevate the status of jihad in Muslim consciousness and make it equal with the five pillars of Islam (profession of faith, prayer, fasting, alms-giving, and pilgrimage). Since the time of the Prophet there has existed a consensus among Muslim ulema (religious scholars) on the status of jihad as a collective duty (fard kifaya), one that is determined by the whole community, not by individuals. They also agree that there are five pillars in Islam. Pious Muslims, and even mainstream Islamists, accept the existing consensus and may even take it for granted.

In contrast, jihadis of all colors consider jihad a permanent and personal obligation (fard 'ayn) and a vital pillar, though now absent, of Islam.[7] Osama bin Laden, the chief of Al Qaeda, subscribes to this definition of jihad as an "individual duty" for every Muslim who is capable of going to war.[8] As he put it, "jihad is part of our religion and no Muslim may say that he does not want to do jihad in the cause of God.... These are the tenets of our religion."[9] Bin Laden went further: "No other priority, except faith, could be considered before [jihad]."[10]

Among the five pillars, bin Laden ranked jihad second only to iman (belief), an astonishing judgment coming from a nonreligious authority. But we should not be surprised by that because the new ideologues of jihad contest the very foundation of the classical school, which laid more stress on the "defensive" and "collective" nature of jihad. The new ideologues claim that the old rules and regulations do not apply because Muslim lands are "occupied," by either local "apostates" or their American masters.[11] Under such conditions, jihad becomes obligatory to all Muslims, to defend their religion and its sanctuaries.[12] Thus the lines become blurred between "defensive" and "offensive" jihad as well as between "collective" and "individual" duty. The new ideologues portray jihad as an all-encompassing struggle that requires full and permanent mobilization of Muslim society against real and imagined enemies at home and abroad. In this context, bin Laden warns fellow Muslims against complacency and dereliction of duty:

> Fighting is part of our religion and our Shariah. Those who love God and the prophet and this religion may not deny a part of that religion. This is a very serious matter. Whoever denies even a very minor tenet of religion would have committed the gravest sin in Islam. Such persons must renew their faith and rededicate themselves to their religion.[13]

Jihad as a Permanent Revolution

More than anyone else, Sayyid Qutb, hanged by Egyptian authorities in 1966 for his alleged subversive preaching and plotting against the nationalist regime of Gamal Abdel Nasser, inspired generations of jihadis, including Al Qaeda's senior leaders, Osama bin Laden and his deputies – the two late military commanders, Abu Ubaidah al-Banshiri and Mohammed Atef (known as Abu Hafs al-Masri), theoretician Ayman al-Zawahiri, and thousands of others – to wage perpetual jihad to "abolish injustice from the earth, to bring people to the worship of God alone, and to bring them out of servitude to others into the servants of the Lord."[14] Far from viewing jihad as a collective duty governed by strict rules and regulations (similar to just war theory in Christianity, international law, and classical Islamic jurisprudence, or fiqh), jihad, for Qutb, was a permanent revolution against internal and external enemies who usurped God's sovereignty.[15] He attacked Muslim scholars and clerics with "defeatist and apologetic mentalities" for confining jihad to "defensive war." There is no such thing as a defensive, limited war in Islam, only an offensive, total war, Qutb asserted: "The Islamic Jihaad has no relationship to modern warfare, either in its causes or in the way in which it is conducted. The cause of Islamic Jihaad should be sought in the very nature of Islam, and its [universal] role in the world."[16]

Qutb was the first contemporary radical thinker who revolutionarized the concept of jihad and invested it with a new meaning – waging an "eternal" armed struggle "against every obstacle that comes into the way of worshipping God and the implementation of the divine authority on earth, hakimiya, and returning this authority to God and taking it away from the rebellious usurpers [rulers]."[17] In his legal summation in his own defense during the trial for the assassination of Egyptian President Anwar Sadat, sheikh Omar Abdel Rahman, former emir (prince) of al-Jama'a al-Islamiya (Islamic Group), indirectly utilized Qutb's idea of God's sovereignty to rationalize Sadat's murder: "God made hakimiya a matter of kufr [disbelief] or iman [belief] or kufr and Islam or jahiliya [ignorance of divine authority]. There is no middle way in this command and no solh [truce]. Believers govern according to God's laws and do not change or replace a single letter or word of them; kufar [infidels] are those who do not govern according to God's laws," a direct reference to Sadat.[18] That is a crime punishable by death, Abdel Rahman implied. In his closing arguments, he challenged the definition offered by the ruling and religious establishment regarding the defensive nature of jihad; Islam does not put any limits on jihad in the cause of God because it is a continous struggle against internal and external enemies. Like Qutb, Abdel Rahman sarcastically debunked this official heresy and asked the judges if the imperial expansion of the Islamic empire was "defensive"?[19]

In Zawahiri's memoir, which he began to write in 2000 and which he published immediately after September 11, he writes that Qutb's powerful ideas, particularly the sovereignty of God, along with his violent death, comprised the first spark that lit the jihadist fire.[20] Zawahiri credits Qutb with giving rise to the contemporary jihadist movement and dramatically and strategically changing its direction and focus. According to Zawahiri, Qutb convinced young activists that the internal enemy is as dangerous as, if not more dangerous than, the external one because it serves as a tool for the latter to wage a hidden war against Islam and Muslims. As a result, Zawahiri adds, the Islamic vanguard, who used to consider the external enemy as the enemy of Islam, began to fight local regimes, which he said are the real enemy of Islam.[21] Zawahiri does not appear to be aware of the irony and contradiction of his position. In his memoir, he heaps praise on Qutb for reminding jihadis of the urgent need to attack the near enemy as opposed to the far enemy. Yet it does not occur to Zawahiri that by targeting the United States, he and his Al Qaeda associates took their jihadist movement in a dramatically opposite direction from that recommended by Qutb, threatening its very existence. But he rationalized this pronounced dichotomy between his rhetoric and his action by saying the "battle today cannot be fought on just a regional level without taking into account global hostility," a reference to America's direct intervention against the Islamist movement.[22]

Adding a personal touch to his narrative of Qutb's contribution to the jihadist movement, Zawahiri, who was in his teens when Qutb was executed, said that Qutb personally inspired him to establish the first underground cell (composed of a few high school friends) of Egyptian "Jihad" in 1967.[23] Indeed, Zawahiri's radicalism is deeply influenced by Qutb's writings, and all his publications borrowed intellectually from Qutb's, particularly his commentary on the Qur'an, *In the Shades of the Qur'an*, considered by some jihadis to be his best for its accessibility and human dimension.[24] Qutb's *Milestones* targeted Zawahiri's generation – "this vanguard" – who, Qutb noted, should know the landmarks on the road toward their destination, which is to rid Muslim society and politics of jahiliya and to restore hakimiya to earth. As he said in the introduction, "I have written *Milestones* for this vanguard, which I consider to be a waiting reality about to be materialized."[25] Those fateful words, written in a prison cell before he was hanged, led thousands of young men on a violent journey to exact revenge on jahili rulers and jahili society in general.

Thus Zawahiri was not the only young jihadi to adopt Qutb's expansive definition of jihad as a perpetual war and a personal obligation. In the eyes of the new ideologues, jihad ceases to be a collective endeavor and is transformed into an individual journey and a path to self-realization and purification. In his trial, Abdel Rahman, a radical cleric who acted as the spiritual guide to Egyptian jihadis from the 1970s until the early 1990s, publicly lectured the judges that Sadat's killers had a duty, not just a right, to take matters into their own hands: "Any Muslim who observes his society not to be governed by the Shariah [Islamic law] must struggle hard [pursue jihad] to apply it, and he is not required to be a scholar."[26] Disputing the government's assertion, Abdel Rahman reminded his audience that there is no church and no hierarchy in Islam and that believers can directly interpret the texts with no recourse to the established authority; jihad is very much an individual obligation and does not need blessing by the clerical community.[27]

It would not be an exaggeration to say that jihadis look up to Qutb as a founding, spiritual father, if not the mufti, or theoretician, of their contemporary movement. Qutb's *Milestones* provided the religious justification for jihadist groups, like Egyptian al-Takfeer wal-Hijira (Excommunication and Hegira, or the Society of Muslims, led by Shukri Mustafa, an agronomist), Tanzim al-Jihad and Jama'a al-Islamiya, and Algerian Armed Islamic Group, which appropriated his concepts of hakimiya and jahiliya and used them as ammunition in their ideological and political struggle against Muslim rulers. In the eyes of Islamic activists, *Milestones* is symbolically powerful because it was the last book written by Qutb before his execution and so is seen as his final "will" to future generations. Ironically, Qutb's Arab biographers agree that of all his texts, *Milestones* is the weakest and the least rigorous intellectually, and that it includes one old idea, jahili society, which he rehashes in a long literary monologue form. But that is part of the strength and appeal of *Milestones* to young activists who hunger for radical, simplistic notions that challenge classical interpretations of the Islamic canon and allow them to go directly to the sacred texts without mediation or intervention by the religious authority. As one Arab writer said, Qutb's importance to jihadis lies in "daring" to neutralize the fiqh and providing jihadis with direct access to the original texts, which they utilized as absolute weapons against "impious regimes."[28]

Jihadis whom I interviewed in several countries said they were inspired by Qutb, who showed them the way forward and whom they referred to as a shahid, or martyr. They talked about the torture he endured at the hands of the Nasserist security apparatus and the dignity and courage he showed under duress. Zawahiri says that Qutb's words acquired a deeper resonance because of his defiance and refusal to appeal to President Nasser to spare his life, which provided activists with an example of steadfastness and sacrifice. For example, he cites the case of Salah Sirriya, a Palestinian Islamist who in the early 1970s assembled a group of young Egyptian college students to carry out a coup d'etat and kill President Sadat by seizing control of the Military Academy in Heliopolis in the Cairo suburbs. The coup failed, and Sirriya and his top aide were sentenced to death for leading what came to be known as the "Military Academy" group. Zawahiri heaped praise on Sirriya for his courage and not faltering in the face of death; when a group of political prisoners gathered around Sirriya and begged him to petition Sadat for leniency, he retorted with the conviction of a believer: "What powers does Sadat have to prolong and control my destiny? Look at this melancholic prison, and this awful food, and these clogged toilets in which we empty this food. This is the harsh reality of prison life, so why do we hold on to it?"[29] For dramatic effect, Zawahiri describes the last meeting in prison between Sirriya and his wife and nine children before his execution, in which he unequivocally told her: "If you petition for amnesty, consider yourself divorced."[30] The moral of the story, Zawahiri concludes, is that although Sirriya was killed and his group dismantled, other jihadis have carried the banner forward, including his own group – the Jihad organization – and have brought Sadat to justice by assassinating him.

In jihadis' eyes, Qutb appears bigger than life, a model to live up to and an example to be imitated. According to Zawahiri, Sirriya was one of the first jihadis to follow in Qutb's footsteps, and he, too, motivated other activists to travel the same road. Jihadism has gradually evolved into a living experience, not only an intellectual discourse. Although the senior echelon of the movement are versed with theory and doctrine, on the whole the foot soldiers are driven by the suffering of Muslim communities or specific individuals. In a strikingly revealing interview with the Arabic-language newspaper Asharq al-Awsat, the Moroccan widow of an Al Qaeda operative, Abd al-Karim al-Majati, who was killed in 2004 in a shootout with the Saudi security forces and who is accused of planning the Madrid train bombings, said her husband's baptism into jihad was purely natural and emotional, not doctrinal and intellectual. Asked about al-Majati's alleged disagreement with radical clerics, she answered: "I stress that educationally my husband was a simple man because he did not attend university and did not take lessons in the Shariah, and he even had problems with the Arabic language [more fluent with French]. ... Sometimes we received texts from the Internet, but my husband did not read them, his relationship to jihad was instinctual."[31] Al-Majati is the norm, not the exception.

After listening to jihadis' tales about Qutb and other martyrs, I realize that their movement is nourished on a diet of political persecution and suffering and that they are socialized into a siege mentality and driven by a powerful force to exact revenge against their ruling tormentors. The bloody history of official torture and persecution perpetuates a culture of victimhood and a desire for revenge and enables the movement to mobilize young recruits and constantly renew itself. Arab/Muslim prisons, particularly their torture chambers, have served as incubators for generations of jihadis. For example, Montasser al-Zayat – who in the early 1980s served time with Zawahiri in prison in the Sadat assassination case and who has since become the best-known attorney defending jihadis and Islamists in Egyptian trials – published two memoirs in Arabic titled *Ayman al-Zawahiri as I Knew Him* and *Islamic Groups: An Inside-Out View* that show that jihadis are terribly influenced by their experience of persecution and suffering and a deep-seated desire to seek revenge.[32] Qutb's Arab biographers also wondered if his words would not have been calmer had he not been mistreated in prison.[33] As long as Muslim governments violate the human rights of their citizens and sanction abuse, they will continue to breed radicalism and militancy. To summarize, Qutb popularized and legitimized the idea of making jihad a personal and permanent endeavor to confront "jahili leadership" and "jahili society" alike.[34]

Jihad Against the Near Enemy

If Qutb provided an overarching intellectual architecture for the contemporary jihadist movement, Mohammed Abd al-Salam Faraj (who coordinated the 1981 assassination of President Sadat and was the ideologue of the Jihad Group, which later evolved into Tanzim al-Jihad (widely known as Egyptian Islamic Jihad) translated the meanings of jihad into operational terms. While Qutb produced an ideological manifesto, Faraj was an activist who preached jihad in local mosques, recruited jihadis, and plotted underground to overthrow the regime along lines similar to those of the Islamic revolution in Iran. Faraj, whose colleagues describe him as a fiery and charismatic orator, defined jihad in a small booklet titled "al-Faridah al-Ghaibah," or "Absent (or Forgotten) Duty," which became the bible and operational manual of all Egyptian jihadis in the 1980s and 1990s, including the two leading organizations – Jihad and its much bigger sister, al-Jama'a al-Islamiya.[35]

Several points are worth highlighting about this critical document. To begin, the title of Faraj's booklet refers to the jihad duty, which is no longer observed and is even contested and denied by some ulema. He aimed at reviving jihad by reminding Muslims of the significance of this concept to the establishment of an Islamic government, to which all Muslims are obliged to strive. Here Faraj presented a new idea: that jihad was the way to establish an Islamic state, while the classical conception of jihad required the existence of an Islamic authority to do so. Next, Faraj makes the case for jihad as a personal, not just collective, duty because now the near enemy (Muslim rulers) occupies the country. Historically, the classical view held that jihad was a collective duty that could be activated only if outside enemies threatened or invaded Muslim lands. But Faraj turned the classical view on its head and asserted that present-day Muslim rulers, particularly Egyptians, forsake their religion by not applying the Shariah and by taking unbelievers as their allies: "The rulers of these days are apostate. They have been brought up at the tables of colonialism, no matter whether of the crusading, the communist, or the Zionist variety. They are Muslim only in name, even if they pray, fast, and pretend that they are Muslims."[36] Therefore, waging jihad against these apostates is a personal duty of every Muslim who is capable of fighting, until the former repent or get killed.

The importance of Faraj's operational dictum does not lie in defining jihad as an individual and permanent obligation and refuting the classical view regarding the collective and defensive nature of jihad. Qutb and others had already made that argument very eloquently and powerfully. Rather, Faraj posited a new paradigm, assigning a much higher priority to jihad against the near enemy than against the far enemy. According to Faraj, a young activist who came from a middle-class family and who graduated from Cairo University with a degree in electrical engineering, not even liberating Jerusalem (the occupied Palestinian capital and the most important place for Muslims after Mecca and Medina in Saudi Arabia) takes precedence over the struggle against local infidels. Why? Faraj advances three arguments in support of his position. First, "fighting the near enemy must take priority over that of the far enemy." Second, liberating Jerusalem must be waged under the banner of Islam, not the internal impious leadership, lest the impious leaders be the main beneficiary of such a victory. And finally, the colonial presence in Muslim lands is the fault of these Muslim rulers. Faraj concludes by saying that jihad's first and foremost priority must be to replace these infidel rulers with a comprehensive Islamic system. Any other external agenda would be a waste of time, Faraj said.[37]

According to an associate of Faraj, who knew him personally and listened to his sermons, Faraj was anxious that the liberation of Jerusalem would strengthen and consolidate impious Muslim rulers; he would rather that Jerusalem remain occupied by the Zionists than be liberated by apostate Arab states. "This shows the extent of flaw in Faraj's case," Zayat, the Islamist attorney adds, "even though this thinking resonated with us and expressed our psychological predicament."[38]

Faraj's call to jihad against the near enemy resonated with most jihadis and informed their rhetoric and action throughout the 1980s and 1990s. For lack of a better term, these jihadis, whom I will refer to as "religious nationalists," believed that seizing power at home by armed struggle was the swiftest and most effective way to Islamize state and society.[39] Pursuing jihad against the far enemy must and should await internal liberation and emancipation. For the next fifteen years, the bulk of the jihadist movement accepted Faraj's definition of the enemy as being the local regimes, and they waged an all-out war against them. Faraj left a deep imprint on leading contemporary jihadis, including familiar names like Karam Zuhdi of the Islamic Group and Zawahiri of Jihad. Zawahiri, who knew Faraj well and befriended him, bought into his notion that confronting the Egyptian regime superseded everything else, including confronting Israel and the United States. Until the late 1990s, when he joined bin Laden's World Islamic Front for Jihad against Jews and Crusaders, Zawahiri faithfully adhered to the strategic principle of making jihad against the near enemy and kept his focus on the big prize – overthrowing the Egyptian government. His former associates well remember Zawahiri's famous dictum that the road to Jerusalem goes first through Cairo.[40]

One of the distinctive characteristics of the contemporary jihadist movement is its stress on the centrality of jihad against internal enemies. The new ideologues of jihad, including Qutb, Sirriya, Shukri

Mustafa, Abdel Rahman, Faraj, Zawahiri, and Zuhdi, were first and foremost religious nationalists whose key priority was to dismantle the secular social and political order at home and Islamize it. From the 1970s until the mid-1990s the jihadist movement, with few exceptions, did not pay much attention to the far enemy and kept the heat on the near enemy. The war in Afghanistan was not an exception to this rule.

Jihad Against the Far Enemy?

Although the Afghan jihad against Russian military occupation ultimately bred a new generation of what I call transnationalist jihadis (who were emboldened by the Russian defeat and who decided to fully internationalize jihad and export the Islamist revolution worldwide), it did not constitute a shift by jihadis away from localism to globalism. The latter went to Afghanistan to find a "secure base" to train and conduct military operations against renegade rulers back at home, not to wage jihad globally. The fight against the foreign enemy was not as important as the existential struggle against "the corrupt, apostatic regime" in Kabul, Afghanistan, and elsewhere.[41] Zawahiri (a leader of Jihad Group in Egypt, who arrived in Afghanistan in the 1980s and who organized and transformed a collection of desperate cells into a formidable organization – Tanzim al-Jihad) expressed the sentiments of many jihadis by saying he went to Afghanistan to establish a safe haven for "jihadist action" from which to launch attacks against the Egyptian regime: "A jihadist movement needs an arena that would act like an incubator where its seeds would grow and where it can acquire practical experience in combat, politics, and organizational matters."[42]

Similarly, throughout the 1980s jihadis from Egypt, Algeria, Saudi Arabia, Yemen, Jordan, Pakistan, Iraq, Libya, and central and East Asia joined the Afghan jihad to acquire military skills that would assist them in their struggle against infidel regimes back at home. In the eyes of many jihadis, Afghanistan served as a military training camp and a fertile ground for new young recruits. It prepared them for the coming wars on their home fronts. My critical point here is that localism, not globalism, informed the thinking and action of jihadis who had initially fought in Afghanistan. The extent of their international ambition was to assist in expelling the Russian invaders from Afghanistan and in bringing about an Islamic government there. Well after the end of the Afghan war, jihadis developed no expansive vision or paradigm to internationalize jihad and "Islamize the world," notwithstanding spurious claims to the contrary.

For example, in his memoir released after the September 11 attacks on the United States, Zawahiri superimposed the present on the past to rationalize and justify his dramatically radical shift away from targeting the near enemy to targeting the far enemy. He makes it appear that the change in the definition of the enemy was natural and logical and that all along he and his associates had been training in Afghanistan for the final battle against the United States: "The jihad was a training course of the utmost importance to prepare Muslim mujahedeen to wage their awaited battle against the superpower that now has sole dominance over the globe, namely, the United States."[43]

Zawahiri does not seem to be aware of the flagrant contradictions in his position given in his memoir. On the one hand, he says he went to Afghanistan to find "a secure base for jihad activity in Egypt." Yet later in the same chapter, he claims that Afghanistan was no more than a training exercise for the "awaited battle" against America and Americans. Surely, Zawahiri could not take on the Egyptian "apostate" regime and the "leader of the criminals," the United States, simultaneously. A closer look at his rhetoric and action from the 1970s through the late 1990s shows clearly that the overthrow of the Egyptian government was his first strategic priority. More than any of his cohorts, Zawahiri was emphatic about the need to keep the fight focused on the near enemy and to avoid being distracted by external adventures, including helping the Palestinians. Like most jihadis, Zawahiri was bred on anti-Westernism and anti-Americanism, although the latter were not on his radar screen until the late 1990s. His words and deeds speak louder than his postmortem rationalization.

Likewise, neither bin Laden nor his spiritual guru, Abdullah Azzam, who initiated him into the jihad business and influenced his fateful decision to fully dedicate himself to the Afghan war, saw the struggle against the Russian occupiers as a way station to wage a total war against the West, particularly the United States.[44] At that stage jihadis possessed no such ambitious international agenda. In retrospect, it is easy to forget that throughout the 1980s the United States was not very high on jihadis' lists of targets. Jihadis found themselves in the same trenches with American foreign policy, a policy that was bent on turning Afghanistan into Russia's Vietnam. Despite subsequent denials by both jihadis and American officials, the two camps were in a marriage of convenience, united in opposition to godless Communism. They had a common enemy and a vested interest in joint coordination and collaboration, at least until the Russians folded their military tents and hurried back home in disgrace.[45]

I do not mean to imply that jihadis were not intrinsically opposed to the American military, political, and cultural presence in Muslim lands. Their rhetoric and discourse were highly inflammatory and hostile. But from the early 1970s until the mid-1990s, the far enemy, as represented by America and Israel, was not an operational priority for Sunni-oriented jihadis. The shift to globalism occurred much later, long after the end of the Afghan war around the mid-1990s, and reflected monstrous mutations within the jihadist movement itself. However, since the mid-1990s, a small minority of jihadis, transnationalists led by Al Qaeda, a network composed of several tiny militant groups, launched a systemic onslaught to hijack the whole jihadist movement and strategically change its direction and destination.

Now the very same jihadis, who had made the fight against the near enemy a key operational priority, shifted gears and called for a new "jihad" against the far enemy, particularly the United States and its Western allies. The road to Jerusalem no longer passed directly through Cairo, Algiers, Amman, or Riyadh but rather through a double-lane highway, including stops in Washington, New York, Madrid, London, and other Western capitals. The same arguments marshalled in support of jihad against the near enemy were dusted off and remade to fit that against the far enemy. In other words, the definition of jihad did not change; what did change was the definition of the enemy. The jihadist caravan took a new sharp and dangerous turn that would bring it into a total confrontation with the world community. Although transnationalist jihadis, like Al Qaeda, were a tiny minority within the jihadist movement, their actions plunged the whole movement into an existential crisis.

Since the late 1990s an intense struggle for the soul of the jihadist movement has unfolded and has largely escaped the attention of American commentators. With the exception of a few critical treatments by European and Arab scholars and analysts, the war raging within the jihadist movement has not received the scrutiny it deserves.[46] This book will remedy this shortcoming by delving deeper into the jihadist universe and highlighting the internal debates, critiques, tensions, and contradictions among jihadis. The goal is to understand how the events of September 11 occurred and the weight and importance of the social base, future prospects, and durability of transnationalist jihadis and religious nationalists alike.

One of the key questions addressed in this book revolves around the hows and whys behind the jihadis' fateful decision to internationalize "jihad" and dramatically shift their tactics and strategy. What explains this revolutionary change from localism to globalism? How and why did jihadis arrive at this critical juncture on their rocky journey? What does this radical metamorphosis say about the sociology of jihadis and new possibilities for a further radical transformation? Is this just a new cycle of jihadist activism, or does it signal a total rupture with historical patterns? Where do jihadis go from here, and how can they survive the raging two-pronged wars – the war within and the war without that is led by the United States and the international community?

Introduction

The Road to September 11 and After

The Semiofficial Narrative of September 11

The final report of the U.S. commission investigating the September 11 attacks offered a vivid portrait and dramatic details of how Osama bin Laden, leader of a transnationalist jihadist group, and a few of his close lieutenants painstakingly plotted and coordinated the multiple, spectacular suicide bombings on New York and Washington.[1] The independent commission presented a riveting account of the various phases of the menacing plot, the leading characters and villains who led it, the ups and downs of operational planning, and the last horrific moments of its execution. Bin Laden emerges as the indisputable leader and mastermind who gave Khalid Sheikh Mohammed, a terrorist operator-entrepreneur, the green light for the September 11 operation in the late 1990s. In mid-1996 the latter reportedly met with bin Laden in Tora Bora, a mountainous redoubt from the Afghan war days, and presented a proposal for an operation that would train pilots to crash planes into buildings in the United States. The proposal would eventually become the September 11 operation.

Bin Laden is portrayed as playing the most vital role in all stages of the plot, from selecting individuals to serve as suicide bombers to developing an initial list of targets. He reportedly wanted to destroy the White House and the Pentagon, and he was very anxious to strike hard inside the United States. According to Sheikh Mohammed, at various points bin Laden urged him to advance the date of the attack, even if that meant the hijackers simply downed the planes rather than crashed them into specific targets. Bin Laden was a driven man on a mission who wanted to see it through as soon as possible. One of his close associates reportedly heard him remark, "I will make it happen even if I do it by myself."[2]

The 9/11 report paints a picture of bin Laden as being blindly obsessed with attacking the United States, possessing a vendetta and an irrational, intrinsic loathing of America and Americans. His "grievance with the United States may have started in reaction to specific U.S. policies but it quickly became far deeper," the report said.[3] Although the report is footnoted and sprinkled with references to bigger and broader concerns and intentions, the underlying theme revolves around a driven man – bin Laden – who ran the show from its early inception through to its conclusion. Once or twice bin Laden's associates are quoted recalling bin Laden arguing that attacks against the United States needed to be carried out immediately to support the Palestinian armed intifada as well as to protest the American military presence in Saudi Arabia, his homeland. But these appeals are given no weight and are dismissed as "rhetorical."

The 9/11 report stresses the pivotal role of personality and religious-ideological factors over history, politics, and foreign policy. Everything revolves around the persona of bin Laden, his whims, predilections, and charisma, and nothing happens without his explicit orders and blessing. Thus the story of September 11 is reduced to that of an anti-Christ–hero – bin Laden – who saw himself as called "'to follow in the footsteps of the Messenger and to communicate his message to all nations,' and to serve as the rallying point and organizer of a new kind of war to destroy America and bring the world to Islam."[4]

The importance of the 9/11 report is that it fleshes out the technical and operational details of the plot and the top field commanders responsible for the planning and execution of the operation. These include bin Laden's military commander, Abu Hafs al-Masri, also known as Mohammed Atef, a close confidant; Sheikh Mohammed, the chief manager of the "planes operation"; Abd al-Rahim al-Nashiri, the mastermind of the 2000 bombing on the USS *Cole* in Yemen and the eventual head of Al Qaeda operations in the Arabian Peninsula; and Ramzi Binalshibh, a middleman between bin Laden and the hijackers.

Two clarifications are in order. First, all these men, with the exception of Abu Hafs, were field lieutenants with little knowledge of the internal workings of Al Qaeda and its political-strategic thinking. They belonged to the Al Qaeda military committee but did not sit on the Shura (consultative) Council, which constituted bin Laden's inner circle. Abu Hafs did, and he was unquestionably very close to and trusted by bin Laden (he was related to bin Laden by marriage) and the two, along with Abu Ubaidah al-Banshiri (who drowned in Lake Victoria in 1996 while on a mission with Abu Hafs to obtain basic materials to produce a dirty bomb), were founders of Al Qaeda. But the 9/11 report has very little to say about Abu Hafs's role in the conspiracy because it says he was killed by an American air strike in Afghanistan in November 2001. In fact, the report's silence on Abu Hafs is due to the lack of information provided about him by the few captured Al Qaeda operatives on whose extracted interrogations the independent commission relied excessively.

Although the 9/11 report introduces the origins of the plot and the mechanics of putting it in operation, it sheds little light on the Al Qaeda decision-making process or the leading actors in the militant network, like bin Laden's right-hand man Ayman al-Zawahiri, leader of Egyptian Tanzim al-Jihad, or Islamic Jihad. Zawahiri is mentioned just three or four times in the report, mainly in the footnotes, and the captured operatives contradict one another regarding his stance on attacking the American homeland. Thus the reader of the 9/11 report gets the mistaken idea that Sheikh Mohammed, who coordinated and managed the plot, played a more prominent role within Al Qaeda than did Abu Hafs or Zawahiri. Yet Zawahiri has served as the conceptualizer and theoretician of Al Qaeda and has shaped and deepened bin Laden's ideological-religious education. With the exception of the late sheikh Abdullah Azzam, who was considered the spiritual father of the so-called Afghan Arabs and who discovered bin Laden and inspired him to devote his time, energy, and resources to the Afghan jihad, Zawahiri has influenced the Saudi dissident the most.

But there is very little mention of Zawahiri in the 9/11 report because the plot is narrated mainly through the lenses of the few captured operatives – Binalshibh, Abu Zubaydah, and Sheikh Mohammed – who deceptively come across as primary drivers behind the conspiracy. One searches in vain for the names and roles of Zawahiri and the other pivotal political players in the militant network. The 9/11 report devotes more time and space to the technical and operational details than to the brains and captains steering the Al Qaeda ship and directing its strategic destination. The goal of the 9/11 report seems to be less to gain an understanding of Al Qaeda's inner circle and broader strategic goals and more to figure out what really happened on September 11, who the actors involved were, how the operation was planned, who made the preparations, and who executed those plans from a tactical point of view. For example, according to testimony secretly obtained from Sheikh Mohammed, when finally informed about the major attack against the United States, most senior members of the Al Qaeda Shura Council reportedly objected on religious and strategic grounds; bin Laden overrode the majority's decision, and the attacks went forward. We still simply do not know what transpired in the Shura Council or who said what because the only existing evidence is that of Sheikh Mohammed – who was neither a member of the council nor present at the meeting. However, although recent evidence does not contradict the 9/11 report, it does show intense struggles between the "hawks" and "doves" within the Shura Council and the organization as a whole. For example, the Arabic-language newspaper *Asharq al-Awsat* published a rare critical document titled "The Story of the Afghan Arabs: From the Entry to Afghanistan to the Final Exodus with the Taliban" written by Abu al-Walid al-Masri, a senior member of the Al Qaeda Shura Council who is considered a leading theoretician in the organization and who has participated in the most important moments of the drama. Abu al-Walid's memoir, coupled with other primary sources, reveals a network riven by ethnic, regional, and ideological rivalries (more on this point later).[5]

This leads to my second point: the 9/11 report is based largely on a series of interrogations conducted in secret locations by U.S. intelligence officers of two of the plot managers, Sheikh Mohammed and Binalshibh, who were captured in 2002 and 2003, respectively. The two lieutenants provided the most detailed account yet of the origins of the September attacks and the internal dynamics and challenges that they and the hijackers faced and had to overcome. In particular, the 9/11 Commission relied heavily on Sheikh Mohammed's testimony and confessions. It would not be an exaggeration to say that the plot described in the report is seen through the eyes of Sheikh Mohammed. Two problems arise.

The first has to do with the credibility and reliability of the accounts supplied by incarcerated Al Qaeda operatives. Senior American officials acknowledged that high-level Al Qaeda detainees – including Sheikh Mohammed, Binalshibh, Abd al-Rahim al-Nashiri, and Abu Zubaydah – have been the subjects of "highly coercive interrogation methods [inhumane torture?] authorized by the Bush administration...."[6] Some 9/11 commissioners themselves wondered about how "trustworthy" Sheikh Mohammed's information was and raised serious questions about the nature and substance of his testimony. For example, counterterrorism officials suspect that captured Al Qaeda operatives have exaggerated the input of bin Laden in commanding the September 11 plot in order to downplay their own roles in the conspiracy. Their analysis of communication traffic between the September 11 hijackers and their confederates, like Sheikh Mohammed, failed to show a close collaboration between them in the months before the attacks – and virtually no communication with bin Laden.[7]

We should not be surprised if the incarcerated lieutenants have been feeding their interrogators and torturers disinformation and lies; they would not be the first suspects to do so. Information gotten through coercion and torture is not necessarily useful or truthful. According to American and European intelligence officials, under harsh interrogation methods, Sheikh Mohammed and Binalshibh appeared to have been willing to provide elaborate accounts of past events but less eager to describe potential future operations. It is no wonder these officials raised serious questions about the truthfulness of some or all of their statements.[8]

Intelligence officials are not alone in questioning the credibility and reliability of the narratives forced out of the captured Al Qaeda field lieutenants. In a released staff report on the plot against the United States, the commission staff members wrote that they did not have direct access to any Al Qaeda detainee and had based their account on intelligence reports drawn from the interrogations. "Some of this material is inconsistent," one report said. *The New York Times* quoted officials as saying that much of the information cited in the reports as fact is actually "uncorroborated or nearly impossible to confirm."[9]

In light of the credibility problem of information obtained under duress, what are we to make of the story told by the 9/11 report? How seriously should we take its findings, and what useful lessons, if any, can be drawn from its conclusions? To what extent does the focus on the operational details of the plot obscure and cloud our vision of the Al Qaeda network? Does the investigation of the plot itself limit or distort the scope of analyzing and making sense of the new jihadis who finally decided to "move the battle to American soil."[10] In other words, does the report help us to understand the internal dynamics and forces within the jihadist movement that culminated in the September attacks? Does it shed light on leading jihadi actors, not just bin Laden, who played a pivotal role in the globalization of jihad?

These questions are not academic, but they address another critical shortcoming in the 9/11 report: it stops short of illuminating the big, historical-sociological questions of how and why jihadis decided to attack the United States. It does not mention, let alone examine, the revolutionary conceptual and operational shift that occurred among important jihadist elements in the late 1990s regarding the primacy and urgency of targeting the "far enemy" (al-Adou al-Baeed), the United States, as opposed to continuing the fight against the "near enemy" (al-Adou al-Qareeb), local Muslim rulers.

Throughout the 1980s and 1990s jihadis launched an all-out frontal assault on the near enemy (such detested pro-Western regimes as Hosni Mubarak's Egypt, Saudi Arabia, and Algeria) rather than the far enemy (the West in general and the United States in particular). But by the end of the 1990s, a critical mass of jihadis, including Al Qaeda, Egyptian Islamic Jihad, and smaller shadowy groups, shifted focus and turned their guns against what they labeled "the Zionist-Crusader alliance and their collaborators" – the United States and its Western allies. Why did they do so, and what explains this dramatic shift in their thinking and action? Did all jihadis follow suit and declare war on the United States, or did they split into two competing camps – religious nationalists and religious transnationalists – and part ways?[11] Does fleshing out the internal tensions and contradictions within the jihadist movement illuminate significant milestones on the road to September 11 and the current nature of the threat facing the United States and the international community?

The 9/11 report hardly touches on these substantive questions and concerns and instead focuses solely on the origins of the plot against the United States and its alleged masterminds. The actual plot could have originated with Sheikh Mohammed and been approved by bin Laden and Abu Hafs, but the road to carrying it out was much more complex than that, and unraveling it requires a deeper understanding of the jihadist universe. Unmasking the hideous conspiracy is a noble task that matters greatly to the families of the victims and the nation at large. Of course, Americans want to know the identity and character of the killers who visited death and horror on their shores on September 11, 2001. But they also want to know why they were brutally attacked and why their security institutions failed to forewarn them.

The 9/11 report approaches the September attacks like a criminal investigation, trying to piece together the various threads of the plot, such as when the orders were given, who gave them, who were the leading conspirators behind the plot, if Al Qaeda operatives received advice and assistance from neighboring states, and the challenges faced by the group's top lieutenants. These questions represent an important chapter in the September 11 narrative, but they are technical and narrow and miss the big picture: internal mutations within the jihadist movement and the splitting up of jihadis into religious transnationalists on one side and religious nationalists on the other. The story of September 11 cannot be fully comprehended without untangling the layers of these internal mutations whose violent reverberations reached the American homeland.

At the outset of their investigation, the commissioners promised to look "backward in order to look forward" and to make an earnest effort to examine the foundation of the new terrorism and the rise of bin Laden and Al Qaeda. Had the commissioners done so by fully examining the context behind the rise of religious transnationalists and the consequent shifts in their operational thinking, they would have unraveled the Al Qaeda phenomenon, not just the September 11 plot, significant as it is. But the report makes only a halfhearted effort at delving deep into the structure of the new global jihad. Instead, it devoted a great deal of time and space to the criminal investigation of the conspirators, including the thoughts and motivations of the hijackers, which are nearly impossible to confirm.[12] Acting like prosecutors, the commissioners delineated the plot's top leaders, particularly Sheikh Mohammed and Binalshibh, and tried to reconstruct the crime scene and the steps and actions taken to execute the planes operation.

This approach suffers from three shortcomings: (1) the accounts are built largely on information obtained from Sheikh Mohammed and Binalshibh under extreme circumstances; (2) the broader context of jihadism is glossed over; and (3) the scope and focus of the inquiry are too narrow to warrant the sweeping policy generalizations arrived at. It is one thing to define and specify the enemy as the "Al Qaeda network, its affiliates, and its ideology," as the 9/11 report does, but it is another thing to delineate the new threat in broad ideological terms:

> Our enemy is two fold: al Qaeda, a stateless network of terrorists that struck us on 9/11; and a radical ideological movement in the Islamic world, inspired in part by al Qaeda, which spawned terrorist groups and violence across the globe. The first enemy is weakened, but continues to pose a grave threat. The second enemy is gathering, and will menace Americans and American interests long after Usama Bin Ladin and his cohorts are killed or captured. Thus our strategy must match our means to two ends: dismantling the al Qaeda network and prevailing in the longer term over the ideology that gives rise to Islamist terrorism.[13]

The 9/11 report seems to imply that all Islamists, not just transnationalist jihadis like bin Laden, Abu Hafs, Zawahiri, and the militant Jordanian Abu Musab al-Zarqawi, leader of Al Qaeda in Iraq, are potential enemies of the United States, and thus they all need to be confronted and defeated. The commissioners call on the United States to wage an all-out war measured in "decades," not "years" to defeat the very ideology of "Islamist terrorism." If by "Islamist terrorism" is meant the Al Qaeda network and its affiliates, that is understandable and legitimate. But if it is an open-ended war to restructure Arab and Muslim societies and politics, it could backfire. Moreover, the commissioners' forensic-like investigation of the complex Islamist phenomenon does not warrant such sweeping generalizations. There is a disconnect between the 9/11 report's narrow analysis and its ambitious conclusions. There exists an urgent need to revisit and reexamine the September 11 story within the broader context of the evolution, fragmentation, and mutation of the jihadist movement as a whole.

The War Within the Jihadist Movement

This book will argue that the globalization of jihadist tendencies and the road to September 11 were directly related to the internal upheaval within the jihadist movement as well as to changing regional and international conditions. Al Qaeda emerged as a direct result of the entropy of the jihadist movement in the late 1990s and as a desperate effort to alter the movement's route, if not its final destination, and to reverse its decline. It represented a monstrous mutation, an implosion from within, not just another historical phase in the movement's evolution.

In the last few decades a bloody power struggle for the soul of Islam has roiled the Muslim world. This struggle was – and is – being fought on multiple levels. On the one hand, jihadis have battled local regimes along with their secular allies. On the other, an internal struggle existed between jihadis and mainstream Islamists, both of whom used religion as a source of mobilization and recruitment. Finally in the late 1990s, another upheaval broke out among jihadis themselves over tactics and strategy, the nature of the enemy, and the most effective ways and means to target their imagined or real enemies.

Of all these fault lines, the tug-of-war among jihadis themselves has received the least attention and has escaped serious analytical scrutiny. This book will rectify this shortcoming by examining the tensions, contradictions, and dissensions among various jihadist leaders and groups.

My main argument is that the September 11 attacks were not just a product of the civil war within the House of Islam[14] but a direct result of the civil war within the jihadist movement itself. In this sense, the United States was a secondary, not a primary, target of jihadis' military escalation, and the bulk of jihadis (religious nationalists) remained on the sidelines and did not join the onslaught by their transnationalist counterparts. If my thesis holds, then Al Qaeda represents more of a national security problem to the United States than a strategic threat, as the conventional wisdom in the American foreign policy establishment has it.[15]

Therefore, it is critical to highlight the internal turmoil among jihadis because it brought about dramatic shifts in their thinking and action and caused further splits in their ranks. From the 1970s until the mid-1990s militant Islamists or jihadis launched an all-out frontal assault to dismantle the secular social and political order and replace it with a theocratic one. By the mid-1990s their insurrection lost momentum, and they were dealt mortal blows by Muslim government security services. But as jihadis met their waterloo on homefront battlefields in Egypt, Algeria, and elsewhere, they split up into two main factions: (1) transnationalist jihadis, like bin Laden, Abu Ubaidah al-Banshiri, Abu Hafs, Zawahiri, and others, who were emboldened by the defeat of the Russians in Afghanistan and wanted to fully internationalize jihad and export the Islamist revolution worldwide; and (2) religious nationalists, whose chief goal was to make sure that the Islamic revolution succeeded at home.

Military defeat at the hands of detested local regimes (the Algerian military junta and Hosni Mubarak) left transnationalist jihadis with few bitter options. They could have closed the jihadist shop, as many of their counterparts did, and tried to rejoin society and live by its rules. Instead, bin Laden and his cohorts rethought their business after the Afghan war and turned their guns against the West in an effort to stop the revolutionary ship from sinking. Frustrated in their attempts to topple "impious" Muslim rulers and incapable of sustaining their costly confrontation with the near enemy, transnationalists wrongly and naively reckoned that confronting the United States militarily would reverse their declining fortune and bring about the destruction of local apostates. For example, in his memoir released immediately after September 11, Zawahiri said that one of the lessons learned from his confrontation with the Egyptian regime over three decades is that the jihadist movement cannot isolate itself from the ummah (the Muslim community worldwide) and turn into an elite pitted against authority. The jihadist vanguard, he said, must be fully integrated into Muslim society's social fabric and must be attentive to its aspirations and concerns. The implication is that jihadis lost the struggle against the near enemy because they had isolated themselves from the ummah and failed to mobilize it. Therefore, Zawahiri offers an alternative solution: taking the war global against Islam's enemies. He says that the slogan understood by the ummah and to which it responds is waging jihad against Israel and the American military presence in the region: "The jihadist movement finally assumed leadership of the ummah after it adopted the slogan of liberating the ummah of its foreign enemies and portrayed it as a battle between Islam and kufr [impiety] and kufar [infidels]."[16]

A few months after the 1998 announcement establishing the so-called World Islamic Front for Jihad against Jews and Crusaders, Zawahiri sent a confidential letter to the Islamic Group's imprisoned leaders in which he said that the Front had expanded the fight against "the biggest of the criminals, 'the Americans,' to drag them for an open battle with the nation's masses ..."[17]

These transnationalist jihadis internationalized an essentially internal conflict and set the world on fire. By doing so, they transformed the nature of their confrontation against local rulers and hoped to reenergize and invigorate the rank and file of their followers. Transnationalists led by bin Laden, Abu Ubaidah al-Banshiri, Abu Hafs, and Zawahiri embarked on a dangerous long-term adventure to expel American influence from Muslim lands.

Ironically, until the end of the 1990s, Zawahiri was a staunch advocate of revolution first at home, and he rejected all calls from his associates to regionalize, let alone internationalize, jihad. Throughout the 1980s and most of the 1990s he held fast to the idea that overthrowing the near enemy (Mubarak's Egypt) took priority over the far enemy. But in his memoir published after September 11, Zawahiri says that by the end of the 1990s, he came to the inevitable conclusion that "we must take the battle to the enemy to burn the hands of those who ignite fire in our countries." It was no longer possible, writes Zawahiri, to keep the fight focused on the near enemy because "the Zionist-Crusader alliance," led by the United States, will not allow Islamists to reach power anywhere in the Muslim world.[18]

Zawahiri's tirade leaves many questions unanswered. Why did he and his globalist associates finally and unexpectedly turn their guns against the United States after two decades of waging war at home? What fueled their anger and rage "to make jihad against the criminal nation" – the United States? What explains the operational shift by jihadis away from targeting the near enemy to attacking the far enemy?

Or was this revolutionary shift natural given their blindly entrenched anti-Westernism? Providing convincing answers to these vital questions will help us to fully understand the context of September 11 and the road to war as well as to assess the future prospects of jihadis.

One of the most neglected aspects of the September 11 story and its aftermath is the position and role played by religious nationalists, who represented the overwhelming majority of jihadis (see the distinctions described later). Understandably, since the September attacks, all eyes have focused on Al Qaeda, its ideology, and its operational tactics. But it is misleading and counterproductive to lump all jihadis under the rubric of Al Qaeda and its affiliates, because they account for only a tiny minority within the jihadist movement (I will provide evidence of this in subsequent chapters). To say this is not to underestimate the lethal nature of Al Qaeda and its destructiveness. As they have recently shown, a few thousand Al Qaeda members, who are blindly committed to waging global jihad, can wreck international peace and threaten the world community. The number of Al Qaeda members is not as important as their asabiya (group or tribal solidarity) and willingness to die for the global jihad cause. No one doubts the asabiya ties that bind the Al Qaeda rank and file.

All of this is true. But the fact remains that religious nationalists – a huge block within the jihadist movement – vehemently rejected Al Qaeda's strategy and methods and broke with their transnationalist counterparts for good. Religious nationalists opposed both the globalization and expansion of jihad outside of Afghanistan and the waging of war on Western nations. They also are in the process of questioning the very usefulness and efficacy of their own strategy, that of fighting the near enemy. For a short while, Al Qaeda's attacks on the United States diverted attention from existing fissures and divisions among jihadis. But long before September 11, a tug-of-war ensued between transnationalist jihadis and religious nationalists over the future of the jihadist movement. Since then, the rivalry has intensified, and the divide between the two camps has grown wider. It can no longer be swept under the carpet and kept under control.

The subsequent reverberations and military developments unleashed a storm of protest by the old jihadist guard, who publicly criticized and condemned Al Qaeda's recklessness and shortsightedness. The dominant narrative among the majority of jihadis was that opening a second front against the United States endangered the very survival of the whole movement and harmed the ummah's vital interests. Bin Laden and his chief theoretician, Zawahiri, are portrayed as irresponsible, reckless adventurers who risked bringing the temple down on their followers' heads and the heads of other jihadis.[19]

Old simmering and hidden disagreements among militant jihadis burst into the open with a vengeance. For the first time, jihadis publicly criticized one another and engaged in a heated debate and public relations campaign to sway Muslim public opinion in their favor. They have written books and pamphlets and given media interviews to advance their viewpoints and discredit their rivals. The media war among jihadis is important in that it sheds light on their states of mind and the nuanced differences in their tactics regarding the use of force, terrorism, and political strategies.

A full-fledged struggle for the leadership of jihadism is unfolding in the world of Islam. Yet media and academic commentary continue to treat jihadis as one undifferentiated constituency with no substantive differences in rhetoric and action. Critics may ask, where are the religious nationalists, and why are they silent while Al Qaeda monopolizes jihadist actions and the airwaves? Do they offer a nonviolent path that has defined and scarred the jihadist movement since birth? Does their opposition to Al Qaeda make a difference in reducing the flow of new recruits to its ranks? What does their denial of revolutionary legitimacy to Al Qaeda mean to the latter's long-term survival and prospects? These are not just theoretical questions or a policy formula to draw distinctions between "bad jihadis" and "good jihadis"; I do not subscribe to such a simplistic dichotomy. Rather, delineating operational and conceptual differences between the two schools of thought is essential to understanding how September 11 occurred as well as the future direction of the jihadist movement as a whole, not just Al Qaeda. The book will address these questions and emphasize the internal dynamics, development, and evolution of leading jihadist groups in the last three decades. The goal is not just to tell the story of September 11 in all of its complexities but also to throw light on the emerging trends and patterns among jihadis. In other words, to determine whether the jihadist movement has a future.

Since the late 1990s I have interviewed jihadis of all colors and stripes, and I have formed a fairly critical idea of the kinds of tensions, second thoughts, and self-criticism that have been taking place within various elements of the movement. These interviews, coupled with access to jihadis' primary documents and their unpublished manifestos, will inform and enrich my analysis throughout the book.

In particular, I will flesh out the subtle and dramatic shifts in jihadis' rhetoric and action and discuss how they perceived and interacted with the secular, pro-Western regimes at home (the near enemy) and the great powers, particularly the United States (the far enemy). I will revisit key documents put out by jihadis since the 1970s and compare and contrast their positions across time and space, particularly Egyptian al-Jama'a al-Islamiya and Tanzim al-Jihad, Al Qaeda, and other small fringe groups. The goal is to show the complexity and diversity of the jihadist phenomenon and to highlight salient features that brought about the September 11 attack. In addition to reconstructing how September 11 occurred, I will examine its aftermath. I will analytically review responses and critiques by religious nationalists and transnationalists alike; by mainstream Islamists, clerics, and scholars; and I will assess the balance of power between religious nationalists and transnationalists. Special emphasis will be given to the war within the jihadist movement, or what remains of it.

Splitting Up of Jihadis: Religious Nationalists versus Transnationalists

Since the burst of jihadism onto the scene in the 1970s, the overwhelming majority of jihadis have been religious nationalists whose fundamental goal was to effect revolutionary change in their own society. Their overriding goal revolved around confronting the secular, pro-Western Arab rulers as a first strategic step before engaging Israel and the United States. Fighting the near enemy took priority over fighting the far enemy, including the Zionist enemy, because young militants wanted to establish an Islamic base or a safe haven at home. In fact, there existed very little operational thinking, let alone conceptualizing, about the primacy of engaging the far enemy. At this early revolutionary stage, unlike leftists and Marxists who dreamt and theorized about world revolution and systemic transformation, jihadism was a local, not a global, phenomenon.

Religious nationalists aimed at violently overthrowing the secular state at home and Islamizing politics and society from the top down as opposed to from the bottom up. They believed that by capturing the state, they could transform society and build a utopian moral order. The very raison d'etre of religious nationalists revolved around the near enemy and ways and means to bring about its downfall. In their eyes, all politics are local. Even the establishment of the caliphate (centralized Islamic authority) or the liberation of Palestine, dear to all jihadis' hearts, had to await the destruction of "apostate" local rulers. Islamic revolution starts first and foremost at home, with no delineated program or vision for the morning after. Ironically, mainstream Islamists (the Muslim Brotherhood) possess a much more developed transnational apparatus and consciousness than that of religious nationalists, and their powerful branches in many Muslim countries testify to their global reach and ambition.

Like their secular nationalist counterparts before them, religious nationalists hoped to either climb on the shoulders of the military or use brute force to seize power and install themselves at the helm. Separated from their moralizing zeal, the ideas and tools utilized by religious nationalists were similar to those of junior army officers who, in the second half of the twentieth century, destroyed the old regime and replaced it with bloated bureaucratic authoritarianism. They were statist and disposed to use violence and shock tactics, not political struggle, to gain power. In this sense, religious nationalists, like other revolutionary liberation movements, had a limited objective and were not antisystem. They just wanted to capture the state and remake it in their own Islamist image. Their armed onslaught against the secular Muslim state was not aimed at state institutions per se but rather against its secularism, moral corruption, and subservience to the West.

However, by the end of the 1990s, a dramatic change had occurred within the jihadist movement: from localism to globalism. The underlying context behind this momentous change included: (1) the withdrawal of Russian troops from Afghanistan and the subsequent collapse of the Soviet Union; (2) the 1991 Gulf war and the permanent stationing of American forces in Saudi Arabia; and (3) the defeat of religious

nationalists on their home turf by the end of the 1990s. A paradigmatic shift among a tiny segment of jihadis gave birth to a new breed of
transnationalist jihadis led by Al Qaeda.

This book utilizes a nuanced approach informed by historical sociology, which locates the causes and sources of the rise of transnationalist
jihadis within the volatile jihadist soil and the changing regional and
international conditions. Although the intellectual genealogy of globalist jihadis is deeply rooted in the movement's traditional discourse, their
birth culminated in a dramatic conceptual shift away from localism and
toward globalism and marked a striking departure from the movement's
dominant wing. The operational shift by transnationalist jihadis had
implications for the way they viewed the world as well as for the effect
it had on their tactics and strategies.

For example, transnationalists broke away from their religious nationalist counterparts and stated that the most effective means to create an
Islamic polity and to defeat the near enemy would be to attack its superpower patron, the United States. More than anyone else, bin Laden and
Zawahiri articulated the new globalist paradigm.

In his 1996 "Declaration of War Against the Americans Occupying the Land of the Two Holy Places," bin Laden called on Muslims
"to hit the main [far] enemy who divided the ummah into small and
little countries and pushed it, for the last few decades, into a state of
confusion. The Zionist-Crusader alliance moves quickly to contain and
abort any 'corrective movement' appearing in the Islamic countries."
Therefore, expelling the American enemy – "the greatest kufr" – out of
Muslim lands is much more important than engaging the "lesser kufr"
(Saudi and other Arab regimes), according to bin Laden. He advised
fellow Muslims: "Utmost effort should be made to prepare and instigate
the ummah against the enemy, the American-Israeli alliance, occupying
[Saudi Arabia and Palestine]."[20]

After the 1998 bombings of the U.S. embassies in Kenya and Tanzania, bin Laden reiterated his conviction that the fight against world
infidels – "the biggest enemy" – should take priority over the fight
against pro-Western Muslim rulers: "Our enemy is the crusader alliance
led by America, Britain, and Israel."[21]

As to tactics and strategy, bin Laden counseled young Muslims, who,
in his words, long for martyrdom to redeem the honor of the ummah and

to liberate its "occupied sanctities" not in a conventional war against Americans "due to the imbalance of power between our armed forces and the enemy forces...." Rather, the goal, according to bin Laden, is "to initiate a guerrilla warfare, where the sons of the nation, and not the military forces, take part in it."[22] Surprisingly, bin Laden also envisions an active role for women, which revolves around "boycotting" American goods and supporting jihadis, to expedite the defeat of the enemy. His is a total war that mobilizes all Muslims (men and women), particularly in his homeland, Saudi Arabia.[23]

In his memoir, *Knights Under the Prophet's Banner*, Zawahiri echoed bin Laden's call to arms against the far enemy:

> The struggle to establish the Islamic state cannot just be fought on a regional level.
> It is clear from the above that the Jewish-crusader alliance, led by the United States, will not allow any Islamic force to reach power in any of the Muslim countries. It will mobilize all its power to hit it and remove it from power. Toward that end, it will open a battlefront against it that includes the entire world. It will impose sanctions on whoever helps it, if it does not declare war against them altogether. Therefore, to adjust to this new reality we must prepare ourselves for a battle that is not confined to a single region, one that includes the apostate domestic enemy and the Jewish-crusader external enemy. It is no longer possible to postpone the struggle against the external enemy...because the Jewish-crusader alliance will not give us time to defeat the domestic enemy...[24]

Like bin Laden, Zawahiri freely dispenses minute and detailed operational advice to the sons of the ummah on how to wage an effective jihad against the far enemy:

> Tracking down the Americans and the Jews is not impossible. Killing them with a single bullet, a stab, or a device made up of explosives or killing them with an iron rod is not impossible. Burning down their property with Molotov cocktails is not difficult. With the available means, small groups could prove to be a frightening horror for the Americans and the Jews....[25]

Yet in 1995, the very same Zawahiri dismissed Muslim critics who called on jihadis to shift their focus away from targeting the near enemy at home to targeting the far enemy, Israel, and assisting their besieged

Palestinian counterparts, Palestinian Hamas and Jihad. Zawahiri wrote an essay titled "The Road to Jerusalem Goes Through Cairo," that appeared in *Al-Mujahidun* (26 April 1995), a newsletter published by Egyptian Tanzim al-Jihad, in which he clearly stated that "Jerusalem will not be liberated unless the battle for Egypt and Algeria is won and unless Egypt is liberated." In jihadis' eyes, the real enemy was the apostate political system at home that is not governed by the Shariah (Islamic law).[26]

In 1987 Tanzim al-Jihad in Upper Egypt distributed an important internal document, "The Inevitability of Confrontation," which listed four tasks (in order of priority) that were "religiously sanctioned" and must be accomplished:

(1) toppling the impious ruler who has forsaken Islam;
(2) fighting any Muslim community that deserts Islam;
(3) reestablishing the caliphate and installing a caliph (pan-Islamic ruler); and
(4) liberating the homeland, freeing the captives, and spreading religion.[27]

Notice that the Jihad Group's priority list focused primarily on internal, not regional or international, enemies. There is hardly any mention of the need to fight the far enemy, whether it is considered Israel or the United States.

This book will address a set of critical questions in order to explain what propelled some jihadis, particularly Zawahiri and his cohorts, to alter their operational priorities at this late stage of the struggle. Did they succeed in hijacking the jihadist movement, one that had been in business for more than four decades and whose history is written in blood? How did they accomplish this feat – taking the war global – against the wishes of the movement's rank and file? By the late 1990s, to what extent was the movement in tatters, ready to be hijacked by new strong-willed and charismatic leaders like bin Laden, Abu Hafs, and Zawahiri? Or was the change from localism to globalism natural in light of the Afghan jihad against the Russians and jihadis' deeply entrenched anti-Westernism?

Another set of critical questions will deal with the response by religious nationalists to the secession engineered by some of their counterparts and the declaration of war on the West, particularly on the United States. Do religious nationalists blame transnationalists for their current predicament? Is there any critical thinking or soul searching taking place among the old guard (religious nationalists)? What remedies and solutions do they prescribe to overcome their crisis? What is the likelihood of another paradigmatic shift by nationalist jihadis toward embracing human rights and the rule of law? Could the putsch by Al Qaeda serve as a catalyst, a wake-up call for the majority of jihadis to rejoin Muslim civil society as law-abiding citizens?

Many people do not realize that for almost a decade transnationalist jihadis and religious nationalists have been engaged in a bitter struggle for control of the jihadist movement. Thus, at the risk of redundancy, one of the book's central theses is that the establishment of Al Qaeda reflected internal mutation and fragmentation of the jihadist movement. It was not just an indication of weakness, decline, and decay, as several analysts have clearly shown, but it also reflected the war within the jihadist movement. Jihadis did not just wake up one day and decide to take on the only surviving superpower after they expelled Russian troops from Afghanistan. They did so when they reached the end of their rope and could no longer battle the security services at home, after they had splintered into rival factions. The root causes of September 11 lie deep in the internal turmoil pulling and pushing jihadis in different directions.

Understanding the tensions, differences, and shifts among jihadis will shed light on how September 11 occurred as well as on the relative weight of transnationalist jihadis and religious nationalists. It will also illuminate the rise of Al Qaeda, its influence within the jihadist movement, and its potential long-term durability.

The Primacy of Charismatic Personalities

In my conversations with former jihadis, one of the critical lessons I have learned is that personalities, not ideas or organizations, are the drivers behind the movement. It is a personality-driven animal that devours idealistic and alienated young Muslims.

The most lethal and violent jihadist factions and cells were led by highly charismatic, aggressive, and daring personalities who captivated and inspired followers to unquestionably do their bidding. Loyalty to the emir (prince) supersedes everything else, including young jihadis' own families. In fact, the emir assumes the role of the father and the big brother that young jihadis look up to and aspire to please. Many of these young jihadis, including the September 11 hijackers, rebelled against their own families, only to find religious-ideological nourishment, sustenance, and comradeship by joining underground paramilitary groups and cells.

For example, according to Abdelgahni Mzoudi, a close friend of Mohammed Atta, the leader of the September 11 suicide bombers, who was acquitted of charges linking him to an Al Qaeda cell in Hamburg, Germany, Atta told him he did not belong to any organizations because his father prohibited him from joining any political or paramilitary group.[28] Atta was not unique. We have a great deal of testimony from jihadis and their families that indicates that the families are often kept in the dark about their sons' journeys underground. In a rare interview with Asharq al-Awsat, the Moroccan widow of an Al Qaeda operative, Abd al-Karim al-Majati, who in 2004 was killed in a shootout with the Saudi security forces, said her husband never told his parents he traveled to Afghanistan to join Al Qaeda and had concealed his secret from them. Although she would have liked to let them know, she conceded she could not tell them.[29] In his diaries, recently published in the Arabic-language newspaper Al-Quds al-Arabi, Nasir Ahmad Nasir Abdullah al-Bahri (known as Abu Jandal), bin Laden's senior "bodyguard" and lieutenant, who held dual Saudi-Yemeni citizenship, described his first journey of jihad at the age of 21: "I traveled from Saudi Arabia to Yemen in October 1994. I ran away from home without the permission of my family ... I then started to plan my trip to Bosnia. I stayed in Yemen around one year, until the battles in Bosnia escalated in the summer of 1995, so I left for Bosnia. My goal was to win martyrdom and to win what God has in store for me. This was my strong motivation for going to jihad there, and that was my first jihad station."[30] One year later, al-Bahri ended up in one of bin Laden's Afghan training camps and was subsequently promoted to be part of bin Laden's personal security entourage.

Atta, al-Majati, and al-Bahri all were captivated by bin Laden's charisma and admired his austerity and courage – for turning his back

on a life of wealth and comfort. Those traits, which bin Laden nourished, resonated with young Muslim men, mostly Arabs, who reviled the
political and moral decadence and corruption of the Arab ruling elite;
they found in bin Laden a heroic, fatherly figure who inspired them to
sacrifice their lives for a worthy cause. Al-Majati's widow describes her
disappointment when her husband did not get to meet bin Laden immediately after their arrival in Afghanistan a few days before September 11;
they went to great trouble to see him before they settled in Kabul but
it was not to be, she said, because bin Laden had just left Qandahar in
anticipation of the September 11 attacks.[31] According to al-Bahri, the
more time he spent with his boss, the more he fell in love with him: "I
loved sheikh Osama deeply and, indeed, after a while I stopped calling
him sheikh and started calling him 'Uncle.'"[32]

In my interviews with former jihadis, I was often told of the fundamental role played by charismatic figures in influencing and shaping
the conduct and action of the movement or parts of it. The jihadist
movement is pregnant with the memories of these celebrity figures that
continue to retain their hold on the imagination of former and current jihadis. Bin Laden and Zawahiri are the latest embodiments of
a long line of revered (mostly martyred) heroes like Egyptian pioneer
Sayyid Qutb and his disciples Mohammed Abdel Salam Faraj, Aboud al-
Zumar, Essam al-Qamari, Abdullah Azzam, Abu Ubaidah al-Banshiri,
Abu Hafs, and many others. If and when they are killed, they will likely
join this venerated list of shuhada' (martyrs) and will provide inspiration to future generations of jihadis.

The 9/11 Commission Report describes the inner core of Al Qaeda as a
"hierarchical top-down group with defined positions, tasks, and salaries.
Most but not all in this core swore fealty (baiya) to bin Laden."[33] In
his memoir al-Bahri, whose unit was composed of dozens of Saudis and
Yemenis who agreed to join the Al Qaeda network, writes that each
of them swore fealty to bin Laden secretly: "Sheikh Osama met with
each of us separately, and many of us swore allegiance to him immediately. Of course, the swearing of allegiance was very secret. No one
knew who swore allegiance to him and who did not."[34] Asked if everyone who stayed with bin Laden or worked with him was a member of
Al Qaeda, al-Bahri said that not all the people who were around bin
Laden were members of his organization. The requirement for formal

membership, he added, was a secret ceremony of swearing fealty to bin Laden: "Sometimes we used to hear that one of the young men [around bin Laden] had carried out a martyrdom operation. It was only then that we were sure he had sworn allegiance to Al Qaeda. The execution of martyrdom operations was a kind of proof that enabled us to identify those who had sworn allegiance to Al Qaeda."[35]

Although the 9/11 report correctly stresses the paramount role of bin Laden as the driver behind Al Qaeda, it significantly underestimates the input of other strong members, like Abu Ubaidah al-Banshiri, Abu Hafs, and Zawahiri, all of whom are "hawks" who were powerful actors in the militant network. In his book, Abu al-Walid, a senior member of the Al Qaeda Shura Council, relates the secret details of the internal struggle between the "doves" and "hawks" in the organization regarding weapons of mass destruction and expanding the war beyond national borders. Although this first-hand account shows bin Laden to be the final arbiter, he had to balance the demands of the two camps and keep internal peace. According to Abu al-Walid, who witnessed and participated in Al Qaeda's most important moments, Abu Hafs, then bin Laden's defense minister and leader of the hardliners, had tried to resign from his position on several occasions in protest against bin Laden's delaying and accommodationist methods; Abu Hafs compared bin Laden's conduct to that of autocratic Arab rulers who promise to be responsive to the aspirations of the young people only to gradually empty them of their substance and move in a completely different direction. In Abu Hafs's opinion, bin Laden was not radical enough or daring enough and acted more like a politician than a revolutionary. Yet ironically, bin Laden sided with the hawks against the doves, even ignoring the warnings that once provoked the United States would not show mercy on its enemy. Abu al-Walid's conclusion is very damning of bin Laden, whose autocratic style of leadership proved to be "catastrophic" and brought Al Qaeda to the brink of the abyss.[36] It is only by fleshing out these internal debates and struggles that we gain a real portrait, not just a sketch, of Al Qaeda and its fateful decisions like the September 11 attacks.

My argument is that personalities in jihadist circles are more important than organization in instilling a sense of comradeship, esprit de corps, and asabiya. Al Qaeda is no exception to this rule. From the outset, bin Laden and his senior confidants, particularly Abu Hafs and Zawahiri, impressed on their followers the need to blindly trust the leadership and be loyal. Loyalty and obedience took precedence over institutional transparency and democratic decision making. "Trust us to lead because we know what is better for you and the ummah," is a line of thinking used by the jihadist movement, including Al Qaeda. In his best-selling post–September 11 memoir, Zawahiri dispenses free advice to the rank and file of Al Qaeda and young Muslims in general about the importance of loyalty and gratitude to the jihadist leadership, meaning himself and bin Laden, without investing it with any holiness and sacredness.[37]

In the case of Al Qaeda's decision making, blind loyalty to "sheikh" bin Laden not only stifled free debate but also encouraged fatal hubris. Abu al-Walid, a leading theoretician of the organization, draws a comical picture of the organization whereby junior operatives sought to please bin Laden and fed him stories that reinforced his perceptions or misperceptions; for example, bin Laden thought that the United States was a paper tiger and that it "would not be able to sustain more than two or three of his painful blows." To flatter bin Laden and confirm his "illusions," Abu al-Walid adds, young Saudis who had visited America told bin Laden that the United States could be taken down with a few blows and would be forced to leave Arab lands. Senior members of the Shura Council, including Abu al-Walid himself, knew that whatever bin Laden wanted, he got; accordingly, they decided not to swim against this powerful current and learned the art of pleasing and flattery. For example, after heated discussions in which the results were already known, according to Abu al-Walid, a senior member of the Shura Council would smile despondently and say in summation, "'you are the emir' and then everyone bends to his will and takes his orders, knowing full well they are catastrophic errors."[38]

Notwithstanding this belated post-mortem, almost everyone around bin Laden, including Abu al-Walid, acted their part and paid homage to the undisputed leader, sheikh Osama, or Abu Abdullah, as they fondly addressed him. But bin Laden's genius does not just lie in stamping his imprint on recruits and followers but in establishing and financing an organizational umbrella that provided tiny jihadist factions with a base (Al Qaeda is an Arabic term that means the base or foundation) to pursue jihad. Asked about the goals behind his 1998 launching of the World Islamic Front for Jihad against the Jews and Crusaders (referred to hereafter as the World Islamic Front), bin Laden said "this front has been established as the first step to pool together the energies and concentrate efforts against the infidels represented in the Jewish-crusader alliance, thus replacing splinter and subsidiary fronts."[39]

But the statement announcing the establishment of the World Islamic Front was signed by leaders of fringe militant factions who were beholden to and dependent on bin Laden for financial support and could not bring the rank and file of their organizations into the new alliance. In addition to bin Laden, the signatories included Zawahiri of the Egyptian Islamic Jihad; Rifa'i Ahmad Taha (alias Abu Yasir) of the Egyptian Islamic Group (al-Jama'a al-Islamiya); sheikh Mir Hamzah of the Jamiat ul Ulema e Pakistan; and Fazul Rahman of the Jihad Movement in Bangladesh.[40]

Of all these factions, the Egyptian Islamic Group was the largest. But Taha, a hardliner who was present at the creation of the World Islamic Front, did not speak for the incarcerated senior leadership of his group and was subsequently forced to disclaim being part of the World Islamic Front. After the 1998 bombings of the U.S. embassies in Kenya and Tanzania, Taha released an official statement in which he denied that al-Jama'a al-Islamiya was a founding member of bin Laden's World Islamic Front: "We are not a party in any front that confronts Americans."[41] By fully joining bin Laden, Zawahiri even precipitated a rupture within his own organization, Islamic Jihad. The rank and file of Islamic Jihad outside Afghanistan expressed their shock at Zawahiri's reckless move and kept their distance. Several members whom I interviewed in Egypt (in 1999 and 2000) said they could not understand how and why Zawahiri would take on the United States, the sole surviving superpower, and open a second front after suffering major military and operational setbacks at the hands of Egyptian authorities. "It was like Zawahiri committed political suicide," a former senior associate of Islamic Jihad told me.[42]

In the end, Al Qaeda was – and still to a lesser extent is – synonymous with bin Laden and his close confidants, with no independent institutional anchor. It is not a transnational version of the Muslim Brotherhood's defunct al-Jihaz al-Sirri, or secret service, and it has no parallel supporting social, political, or educational institutions. In comparison with the Brotherhood, Al Qaeda is a skeleton of an organization. Now it has been reduced to an ideological label, a state of mind, and a mobilizational outreach program to incite attacks worldwide.

Al Qaeda operatives swore baiya to bin Laden – not to Al Qaeda – and developed no institutional links with the organization itself. As an organization, Al Qaeda did not exist apart from its creator, and it is unlikely to survive his demise, even though since September 11 bin Laden and his associates have succeeded in branding Al Qaeda as a revolutionary idea to new recruits. But even if Al Qaeda as a revolutionary idea and a brand takes off, it will retain no centralized organizational infrastructure of any effective global reach. It is critical to make distinctions between the existence of desperate, local affiliates and cells, which have proliferated since 2003, and a global organization with a centralized leadership and decision making and an ambitious agenda. The latter appears to have suffered major strategic blows and is being gradually and systemically dismantled. Al Qaeda has become more decentralized, amorphous, diffuse, and difficult to locate; it no longer represents as big a threat as it once did, and its global reach has diminished considerably. Although Al Qaeda–inspired or –directed cells can still wreak havoc in London, Madrid, and Sharm el Sheik, Egypt, their ability to carry out spectacular operations like on September 11 has been weakened. We should not lose sight of the important distinction between the nature of the threat represented by local jihadist affiliates and networks and the threat posed by a centralized global network, which since September 11 has been degraded. But one point must be made clear: personalities will continue to drive the new brand, as seems to be the case with Zarqawi in Iraq and Al Qaeda operatives in Saudi Arabia and elsewhere. To say so is not to write the obituary of Al Qaeda as a centralized global paramilitary organization or to discount its ability to recover in the long term if appropriate conditions arise, as the case seems in Iraq today.

However, we must be careful not to exaggerate Al Qaeda's organizational attributes just because it succeeded in carrying out audacious attacks and hiding its two top leaders – bin Laden and Zawahiri – so far. A close reading of the testimony of key captured Al Qaeda operatives shows that the September 11 plot was troubled and improvised and could have easily gone awry. Its success was not due to complex organizational skills but rather to individual tenacity, commitment, and luck. Yes, luck. Several hijackers first assigned to the plot lost their nerve and dropped out, and other volunteers had to be recruited to take their place. The lineup of suicide bombers changed throughout the two years (1999–2001) of preparation, and there was reportedly infighting between Mohammed Atta, the mission leader, and another pilot, Ziad al-Jarrah. According to the plot's manager, Sheikh Mohammed, bin Laden became very restless and impatient with the preparations and wanted the planes operation to proceed as soon as possible regardless of its efficacy. In 2000, for instance, amid the controversy after then–Israeli Likud opposition party leader Ariel Sharon's visit to the Temple Mount in Jerusalem, Sheikh Mohammed claimed that bin Laden told him "it would be enough for the hijackers simply to down planes rather than crash them into specific targets."43

All this petty squabbling and amateurism and the obsession with revenge have more in common with criminal mafias than with structured and complex organizations. Thus it is very surprising that the bombings were carried out successfully. The malfunctioning of American institutions partially explains the success of Al Qaeda's audacious and spectacular attack. Thus it is misleading to view Al Qaeda through the prism of its September 11 feat and endow it with a complex organizational structure.

One of the major failings of all jihadis, not just Al Qaeda, is their inability or unwillingness to construct formal institutions and organizations, as opposed to informal committees and networks, that could survive the incarceration of their founding charismatic emirs. Like their ruling tormentors, jihadis are addicted to the cult of personality. But unlike ruling autocrats, jihadis possess neither the resources nor the bureaucracies to keep them afloat. They remain deeply dependent on a narrow core of charismatic leaders who have mastered the art of blunders, to navigate their loyal followers through stormy seas.

This structural handicap does not bode well for jihadis' future prospects because of the lack of institutional continuity and renewal and the difficulty of nourishing a broad social base. The problem lies in their paramilitary and underground character and their overwhelming reliance on armed means and shock, as opposed to a more comprehensive strategy, to attain their goals. In such a secretive and self-enclosed environment, powerful personalities dominate the jihadis' decision-making process at the expense of institution building. All jihadist groups fall into this personality trap and become self-imposed prisoners.[44]

This book will highlight the role of jihadist leaders within both the transnationalist and the religious-nationalist camps who served as the drivers behind their groups. For example, the rise of transnationalist jihadis cannot be understood without contextualizing the alliance between bin Laden and Zawahiri and the merging of their assets – Al Qaeda and Zawahiri's loyal contingent within Tanzim al-Jihad. The coming together of these two men, who were estranged from their countries and without an anchor, played a decisive role in the formation of the World Islamic Front. In June 2001 they cemented their marriage by merging their two groups – Al Qaeda and elements of the Tanzim – into one, Qaeda al-Jihad. The experience and character of the two complemented each other and fueled their unholy alliance with missionary zeal.

I will discuss the development and evolution of their relationship and their interaction with associates within their own organizations as well as with religious nationalists. In particular, I will flesh out the power struggle and personality clashes between the leaders of the two camps, particularly bin Laden and Zawahiri on the one hand, and their religious-nationalist rivals, on the other.

To summarize, the book will not just tell the story of the rise of transnationalist jihadis; it will also delve deeper into the structure of the jihadist movement as a whole. For example, why did jihadis neglect and disregard low politics in favor of high (and international) politics? Why the obsession with the use of force to capture the state? What went wrong with the jihadist movement? How deep has entropy settled in its body politic? Where does it go from here? Does it have a future? Could it overcome its existential crisis and transform itself into a nonviolent religious and social-political movement?

ONE

Religious Nationalists and the Near Enemy

Throughout the 1980s and the first half of the 1990s jihadis devoted most of their resources to dislodging the near enemy and establishing theocratic states governed by Shariah (Islamic law). A review of their documents, manifestos, and actions indicates a preoccupation with the internal conditions of Muslims in disparate countries compared to those of the ummah as a whole. Little attention was paid to the need to confront the far enemy, particularly the United States. Since September 11, the received wisdom in the United States and the West generally has it that jihadis had always possessed an ambitious and expansive global agenda and had patiently waited for an opportune moment to execute it. Ironically, transnationalist jihadis, including Zawahiri, bin Laden, and Abu Musab al-Zarqawi, would also like us to believe this. The weight of evidence indicates otherwise, however, and the situation is much more complex than that.

Jihad Goes Local

Clearly, jihadis deeply mistrusted international arrangements that, in their eyes, discriminated against Muslims and kept them militarily impotent and politically and economically dependent. They also suspected the United States and the Soviet Union of being intrinsically hostile to dar al-islam, or the House of Islam, and more specifically to their revolutionary Islamist project. But throughout the 1970s, 1980s, and the first half of the 1990s the dominant thinking among leading jihadis was that the ability of the international system, dar al-harb, or the House of War, to dominate and subjugate dar al-islam depended on the collusion and submissiveness of local ruling "renegades."[1] As one influential jihadist manifesto put it in 1986, the latter are a "fifth column that gnaws the bones of Muslim society at the behest of foreign powers. They lost their will and sold their honor and dignity.... They paved the way for colonialism and exploitation."[2]

During this period, almost all the documents written or distributed by jihadis stressed the treacherous, destructive role played by the near enemy in facilitating the penetration of the Muslim ummah by the far enemy as well as the elimination of Islam from public life. They also called for a total mobilization and confrontation against jahili society and rule rather than taking jihad global. At that time fighting the far enemy was neither a priority nor even a goal for the overwhelming majority of jihadis. Until the mid-1990s jihadist theory and practice focused almost exclusively on the domestic agenda and the need to replace the state of kufr (disbelief or rejection of divine guidance) with God's governance or sovereignty. The war against Islam and Muslims was considered to be as much perpetrated by secular rulers and their intellectual and religious allies at home as it was by the West or the East. Thus the first priority was to create Islamic polities as the first step to reinstall the caliphate that would make the Shariah the law of the lands. However, to achieve this worthy goal, according to jihadis, the overthrow of Muslim leaders, the guardians of the corrupt status quo, was required.[3]

In particular, two important jihadist documents deserve special mention. The first is "The Absent Duty," written in the late 1970s by Mohammed Abd al-Salam Faraj (who played a vital role in the 1981 assassination of Egyptian President Sadat and was subsequently executed by Egyptian authorities).[4] As noted in the Prologue, Faraj coined the terms "near enemy" and "far enemy" and assigned the highest priority to militarily confronting the former. According to Faraj, everything else, including liberating occupied Jerusalem, took a back seat to the fight against local apostates. Faraj's former associates whom I interviewed said that "The Absent Duty" became the operational manual of the jihadist movement in the 1980s and remained so through the first half of the 1990s, influencing the general direction of senior leaders, like Zawahiri, who for 15 years employed Faraj's hierarchy of enemies.

A decade later another pamphlet widely circulated by the Jihad Group in Upper Egypt, "The Inevitability of Confrontation," ranked four vital tasks that were considered "religiously sanctioned" in terms of importance:

(1) toppling the impious ruler who has abandoned religion;
(2) fighting any Muslim community that deserts Islam;
(3) reestablishing the caliphate and installing a caliph (pan-Islamic ruler); and
(4) liberating the homeland, freeing the captives (prisoners), and spreading religion.[5]

Notice that this list of priorities given by the Jihad Group centered primarily on internal, not regional or international, goals and concerns. There was hardly any mention of the need to fight the Zionists or the Americans. In the 1970s, 1980s, and early 1990s, jihadis did not articulate, let alone entertain, a paradigm of taking jihad global. Their politics were decidedly domestic. They were religious nationalists par excellence.

A close reading of jihadis' writings, unlike that of other social and political activists, shows an overwhelming emphasis on local affairs at the expense of foreign policy and the Arab-Israeli conflict, a highly emotive issue in Arab and Muslim politics. Activists of differing ideological colors and persuasions often use the Palestinian predicament to mobilize the masses and garner public support. Not so initially with doctrinaire jihadis, as opposed to irredendist ones in Palestine and Lebanon, who hardly invested any practical resources in assisting their Palestinian brethren. Jihadis' apparent lack of operational interest in the Palestinian trauma, framed mainly in terms of a nationalist, not religious, identity, reflected a set of domestic priorities as opposed to regional and international ones.[6]

In my conversations with scores of former jihadis, they said they were driven by a religious fervor to institute divine authority on earth and to rid their countries of ruling apostates. Regardless of their real motivations for rising up against the ruling elite, which are very complex, they all come across as religious nationalists with no global blueprint transcending their individual countries.[7] At the heart of their grievances lie a repulsion for and rejection of the moral decadence that is prevalent in society, not concern for foreign policy. It was fascinating and enlightening to listen to Egyptian jihadis, who were directly or indirectly involved in the assassination plot against Sadat, explain why they turned against the "pious president" (Sadat referred to himself as such). The most common response I heard from jihadis was that Sadat did not deliver on his promise to apply the Shariah, and that he insulted clerics who sympathized with their revolutionary project. Time and again jihadis expressed their rage over Sadat's wife's "immoral conduct," such as her frequent public appearances with no headscarf or headcover and a widely seen televised image of her dancing with President Jimmy Carter at a White House reception. They did not accept the explanation given by Sadat's men: that it was Carter who took Jihan Sadat's hand and led her to the dance floor and she could not refuse. In jihadis' opinion, the moral symbolism and lesson of the story was that Sadat and his "influential" wife violated deeply held Islamic values and the prescribed code of conduct for Muslim leaders.

Although all jihadis I interviewed said they vehemently opposed Sadat's signing of the 1978 Camp David peace accords with Israel and his offering a refuge for the deposed Shah of Iran, they reserved their harshest criticism for his supposed "deception" and "lies" about applying the Shariah and his mistreatment and incarceration of radical Islamic figures. I got the impression that jihadis could have quietly tolerated Sadat's peace treaty with Israel and his opening up to the West, particularly to the United States, had he delivered on his pledge to symbolically Islamize the state and played the part of the "pious president," that is, if he had kept his alliance with Islamists and showed humility and religiosity in public pronouncements.

In their eyes, the "pious president" became a "pharaoh" marked for assassination after he violated what they considered to be the moral compass of an Islamic polity. At the risk of simplification and exaggeration, jihadis were particularly enraged by Sadat's not honoring his promise to make the Shariah the only source of legislation and his distancing of his administration from Islamists. It was this, not his foreign policy, that drove jihadis to think the unthinkable: that they should kill Sadat, who had released the Islamist genie and who portrayed himself as a patron of Islamists, and make a move to seize power.

I do not mean to suggest that regional and foreign policies did not matter to jihadis. That would be misleading because their documents and publications were littered with references to external threats and regrets about the recolonization of Muslim countries by Western powers, particularly the United States. Two points are worth mentioning. Until the mid-1990s the dominant thinking among jihadis was that Muslim rulers' subservience to and collusion with Western powers enabled the latter to dominate the world of Islam. Therefore, jihadis argued that the most effective means to terminate Western hegemony over their societies was by replacing the secular local order with an Islamic one. They also correctly reckoned, as many subsequently acknowledged, that they did not have the resources to militarily confront Western states.[8]

For example, in the early 1980s an important document written by Egyptian Jihad entitled "America, Egypt, and the Islamist [Jihadist] Movement" ranked the United States as number one on its list of enemies. It listed three reasons for that. The first lies in the unholy strategic alliance between America and Arab states, which led to the latter's loss of "political, economic, and military independence." The second has to do with the special relationship the United States shares with Israel, which was built at the expense of Muslim interests and rights. Finally, the Jihad document asserts that American global hegemony represents a direct threat to the jihadist and Islamist movements.[9]

Even at this early stage jihadis defined their struggle with the United States not just in political and economic terms but also as a zero-sum game. The document claims that all American citizens, not just politicians, are socialized into an anti-Muslim mind-set and tend to bless their government's war against Muslims and to support and incite minorities in Muslim countries. By not making distinctions between the American people and their government and by holding both equally accountable for injustices perpetrated against Muslims, jihadis could easily justify targeting American civilians.

Although it was written by a small Egyptian jihadist faction, the importance of this internal document stems from its shedding light on jihadis' thinking and worldview toward the far enemy, the United States. Two decades later, jihadis, like bin Laden and Zawahiri, used similar references to sell their war, not just their enmity and hostility, against America and Americans. Therefore, the political and moral rationalization of the September 11 attacks was laid long before Al Qaeda was officially born in the late 1990s. Jihadis of all political persuasions possessed a dangerously distorted and antagonistic view of American civil society, even though they held different opinions on how to deal with it. There is a historical and philosophical continuity to jihadis' hostile perceptions of America, which has proved to be durable thanks to the simmering regional conflicts and the political and social turbulence sweeping through Arab and Muslim societies.

Over the years I have interviewed scores of former jihadis or militant Islamists and I am yet to meet a single jihadi – or read an account by one – who has anything positive to say about America and Americans or even the West generally. Unlike their secular pan-nationalist, leftist, and enlightened Islamist counterparts who, while being highly critical of U.S. foreign policies, are fascinated with and attracted to American society and culture, jihadis are as much opposed to Western liberal ideas as to Western foreign policies. Their antipathy toward everything Western is an extreme form of Orientalism, which misrepresents and distorts the complex reality and humanity of the other – the East. There is no space here to delve deeper into the intellectual and philosophical genealogy behind jihadis' anti-Westernism.[10] Suffice it to say that anticolonialism, coupled with absolute raw religious moralism, lies at the heart of their antipathy to the West. This deeply embedded anti-Western genealogy facilitated and paved the way to September 11. The doctrinal seeds had been planted long before.

"America ... and the Islamist Movement" advanced a two-pronged explanation for America's hostile stance toward Islamists and jihadis. First, American foreign policy is driven and informed by religious and ideological considerations: "crusading hatred is the real source behind all American positions toward the Islamist [jihadist] movement." Egyptian Jihad also criticizes those Muslims who see the struggle between Islam and the Christian West as being one of interests and politics, rather than of culture and religion. Second, the document asserts that America views the growing strength of the jihadist movement as a threat to its presence in the region and, as such, the United States is determined to attack and weaken the Islamic revival.

Although this critical document is loaded with anti-Americanism and explicitly calls for expelling corrupting Western influences from the world of Islam, it did not advocate a direct armed clash with the United States, at least not yet. There was no call to war against the far enemy. Rather, Egyptian Jihad urged Muslims to attack America's secular Arab and Muslim clients – those "traitors" who serve its interests in the region and are apostates and thus must be destroyed. Accordingly, the most effective means to deter this "crusading enemy" (the United States) is "to shed more blood and to offer more martyrs and to carry the banner of Islam in order to restore the caliphate or face martyrdom."[11] The fight against America could be thus won by overthrowing its ruling Muslim allies that do its bidding. But overthrowing local apostates was the only intended end; it was not merely a first step, a way station to attacking the far enemy.

The document clearly placed much higher priority on attacking the near enemy (pro-Western Muslim rulers) and establishing an Islamic polity ruled by a caliph than on attacking the far enemy. This leads to the second point. From the mid-1970s until the mid-1990s, jihadis' key fundamental goal was to capture the state and Islamize it – along with society – from the top down. Unlike mainstream Islamists (Muslim Brothers, for example), who belatedly discovered the importance of Islamizing society from the bottom up, jihadis had no patience or faith in al-da'wa (call). They also considered democracy to be nizam al-kufr (a deviant system) and, unlike mainstream Islamists, they eschewed participation in electoral politics because they view democracy as a rival religion supplanting the rule of God with that of a popular majority. Jihadis were literally obsessed with controlling state bureaucracies and using them to advance their Islamic project, which was not fully developed. Their view of the state as a strategic tool to restructure society and politics put them squarely in the religious nationalist (statist) camp alongside their secular nationalist opponents, and it highlighted their poverty of ideas – the absence of a new radical social contract. At this stage jihadis put everything on the back burner, including regional and foreign policy questions, until they completed infiltrating and seizing the state. They were faithful disciples of Faraj's dictum regarding the primacy of the near enemy as opposed to the far enemy.

It could also be argued that there existed no tidy distinction in the minds of jihadis' leaders between confronting the near enemy and confronting the far enemy. The fight was one and the same because the end result would be to construct an Islamic state and expel Western influence. But most jihadis of the religious nationalist camp whom I interviewed said that assigning operational priority to the near enemy stemmed from practical, commonsensical reasons: "Why should we take high risks by militarily attacking the United States, the unrivaled superpower, if we can achieve our goal by targeting ruling Muslim apostates?" They viewed the matter less in ideological and religious terms and more in terms of material capability and necessity.

For example, Zawahiri, whose views on the importance of the near enemy reflected those of most jihadis, firmly believed that the road to Arab Jerusalem must pass through Cairo, and that priority should be given to overthrowing the pro-Western "renegade" regimes in such Arab countries as Egypt, Saudi Arabia, and Jordan. In 1995, Muslim ulema (religious scholars) feared that the new emphasis on Afghanistan could come at the expense of Palestine and criticized jihadis for not assisting their Palestinian counterparts (Hamas and Jihad) and for squandering Muslim strength in internal squabbles and strife. For example, sheikh Yusuf al-Qardawi, an influential Egyptian-born cleric who works in Qatar, warned against the tendency to place Afghanistan ahead of even Palestine: "Palestine remains the first Islamic issue, and it is not true that the movement has forgotten Palestine for the sake of Afghanistan."[12] Zawahiri had already made up his mind and wrote a rebuttal in which he stated that "Jerusalem will not be liberated until the battle for Egypt and Algeria is won and until Egypt itself is liberated."[13]

Thus as late as 1995 there existed no ambiguity about Zawahiri's prioritizing the fight against the near enemy. Islamic Jihad's spectacular military operations against the Egyptian regime testified to the high value Zawahiri placed on targeting the near enemy over the far enemy. He sent waves of militants to Egypt to destabilize its government and soften its defenses. His words and actions were consistent. He and his religious nationalist cohorts had no second thoughts about the character and nature of the real enemy being the secular order at home that was not governed by the Shariah.[14]

Yet in his 2001 memoir, Zawahiri tried to portray and package himself as having been a transnationalist jihadi long before he established his unholy alliance with Osama bin Laden in the late 1990s. He claims that in the 1980s the Afghan "jihad was a training course of the utmost importance to prepare Muslim mujahedeen to wage their awaited battle against the superpower that now has sole dominance over the globe, namely, the United States."[15] This is very difficult to believe because Zawahiri is imposing the present on the past in an attempt to justify his recent change of heart regarding the importance of attacking the far enemy. This rationalization does not hold up because Zawahiri cannot erase historical memory and empirical evidence by sleight of hand. The rise of transnationalist jihadis must be understood as a product of the internal social upheavals and mutations that occurred within the jihadist movements in the 1990s. Although transnationalist jihadis grew out of the wombs of religious nationalists and sought to inherit their slogans and legacy, they underwent a dramatic metamorphosis and further radicalization, which marked a critical rupture in the movement. The divide between the two camps (religious nationalists and transnationalists) became wider and deeper.

Zawahiri's Tanzim al-Jihad or Islamic Jihad, one of the most aggressive and violent jihadist organizations, was the norm, not the exception to the rule. Jihadis everywhere limited their attacks to the near enemy and avoided targeting Western powers. To be more precise, until the mid-1990s the modern jihadist movements had not developed a transnationalist paradigm or a corresponding operational armada or network capable of initiating qualitative attacks abroad. It is true that in the early 1990s Egyptian and Algerian jihadis attacked soft Western targets at home, including the tourist industry and foreigners. But a heated internal debate among jihadis exposed critical fault lines in their thinking and stance. For example, although Egyptian Islamic Group, the largest jihadist organizations in the Arab world, sanctioned and initiated assaults against soft Western targets in Egypt, its sister group, Tanzim al-Jihad (led by Zawahiri), considered them politically, as opposed to morally, counterproductive because they would play into the hands of the regime, which they did.[16]

Similarly, the terrorist attacks carried out during the 1990s by Algerian Armed Islamic Group (GIA) in France did not represent a qualitative or quantitative shift from its strategy of targeting the near enemy (Algerian regime) to targeting the far enemy (France, the leading ally of the Algerian government). The GIA aimed at punishing Paris for its logistical and political support of the military junta in Algiers and at deterring France from any further active intervention in the Algerian civil war. But brutal and deadly as they were, these terrorist attacks had a limited goal and did not signal an expansion of jihad outside Muslim frontiers. It is also worth mentioning that leaders of the Algerian Islamic Salvation Front (FIS) and its armed wing, AIS, the largest paramilitary organization confronting the Algerian regime, publicly denounced the GIA's "excesses" against Algerian and Western civilians as well as the increasing manipulation and penetration of militant factions by the security services.

By the mid-1990s a further splintering and radicalization of the GIA, coupled with the complicity of the Algerian security and military apparatus, caused a violent rupture and costly civil war within the Algerian Islamist movement. The assassination of several heavyweights of the FIS in Algeria and France was a case in point. As Francois Burgat, a leading French scholar on Islamist movements in North Africa, noted, the FIS and Algerians in general were caught between "two terrorisms," one of the radical wing of the Algerian military junta, and "Islamic terrorism," which was a derivative of that.[17] The Algerian war was a classic case of civil strife pitting a tyrannical wing of the military apparatus that suspended the constitutional process against a powerful popular Islamist movement that was radicalized and splintered after its electoral victories had been rescinded and subjected to a formidable offensive of repression.

The point I'd like to stress here is that until the mid-1990s jihadis in two pivotal Arab states, Egypt and Algeria, who represented by far the largest active number of militants in the Muslim world (tens of thousands of active operatives), confined their confrontations to the near enemy and did not internationalize jihad. Their attacks against nonregime targets were limited in scope and did not greatly expand beyond national borders. On the whole, jihadis were still bogged down in civil wars at home and had not yet fully developed a transnationalist paradigm.

Early Warnings of Transnational Jihad

Nonetheless, in the early 1990s a wave of terrorist attacks against Western, particularly American, interests in Africa, the Middle East, and inside the United States was an omen of bigger and deadlier operations to come. Although it would be misleading to link all these desperate attacks together and hold bin Laden and his jihadist cohorts account-able, evidence subsequently emerged that the bin Laden terrorist net-work had infiltrated many countries and established informal, tacit alliances with other similar-minded jihadist cells and factions. Some of bin Laden's associates later took credit for those attacks and boasted that their assistance led to the October 1993 shootdown of two U.S. Black Hawk helicopters by members of a Somali militia and the subse-quent withdrawal of American troops from that country in early 1994.[18]

For example, a senior "personal guard" of bin Laden, Nasir Ahmad Nasir Abdullah al-Bahri (known by his nom de guerre Abu Jandal), who spent several years by bin Laden's side, claimed that "the U.S. forces were met with fierce resistance from the Somali mujahedeen and Al Qaeda organization, which managed to expel them from Soma-lia in humiliation and ignominy after teaching them a harsh military lesson."[19] Regardless of the real military input of Al Qaeda in the Somali skirmishes, bin Laden and his senior associates subsequently exagger-ated their role in order to recruit young Muslims into their organization and to convince them that American soldiers were vulnerable and could be easily defeated. Listen to bin Laden's use of Somalia in his pre-2001 recruitment videotapes: "We believe that America is much weaker than Russia; and our brothers who fought in Somalia told us that they were astonished to observe how weak, impotent, and cowardly the American soldier is. As soon as eighty American troops were killed, they fled in the dark as fast they could, after making a great deal of noise about the new international order."[20]

Thus lines became blurred between fiction and nonfiction regarding Al Qaeda's role in Somalia. One gets the impression that Al Qaeda's supermen, not Somali militiamen and fighters, fought the October 1993 costly, pitched battles that, for all intents and purposes, ended the American military mission there. But propaganda matters because it sheds light on efforts by the Al Qaeda leadership to portray itself as possessing a strategic vision designed to preempt and deter Amer-ica's encroachment over Arab and Muslim territories long before September 11.

In a series of lengthy interviews and recollections with the Arabic-language newspaper *Al-Quds al-Arabi*, bin Laden's bodyguard and senior lieutenant, al-Bahri, says that before American forces deployed to Somalia in late 1992, Al Qaeda had built a base there for Arab jihadis to use as a staging arena into the Arabian Peninsula, mainly Saudi Arabia, with the aim of overthrowing the pro-American royal families. Al-Bahri, a dual Saudi-Yemeni national who spent 20 months in a Yemeni prison, adds that "Al Qaeda viewed the entry of the Americans into Somalia not as a move that is meant to save its people from what happened to them, but to control Somalia and then spread U.S. hegemony over the region."[21] He also credits Abu Ubaidah al-Banshiri, general field commander of Al Qaeda until his death in 1996, who set up the cell that later carried out the 1998 bombings of the two U.S. embassies in Nairobi, Kenya, and Dar es Salaam, Tanzania, with establishing a foothold in Africa in general and the Horn of Africa in particular. According to the recollections by bin Laden's personal guard, Banshiri used to say: "The United States will certainly control the Horn of Africa, and therefore we must establish ourselves in the Horn of Africa close to the Arabian Peninsula."[22]

This self-serving narrative endows Al Qaeda operatives with a "far-reaching" transnationalist foresight that predates the 2001 attacks on the United States by almost a decade. But the account must not be taken at face value and must be scrutinized because it colors history with a contemporary brush and deposits much more strategic credit in Al Qaeda's account than it deserves.

In the first half of the 1990s, similar attacks against American interests could also be interpreted as heralding a new dramatic shift from local to global jihadism. For example, in December 1992 bombs exploded at two hotels in Aden, Yemen, where U.S. troops stopped en route to Somalia, killing two people, but no Americans. According to The 9/11 Commission Report, the perpetrators are reported to have had connections with bin Laden's Al Qaeda.[23] In November 1995 a car bomb exploded outside a joint Saudi-U.S. facility in Riyadh for training the Saudi National Guard. Five Americans and two officials from India were killed. Almost a year later an enormous truck bomb detonated in the Khobar Towers residential complex in Dhahran, Saudi Arabia, which housed U.S. Air Force personnel. Nineteen Americans were killed and 372 were wounded.

The weight of evidence indicates that the Khobar operation was carried out by Saudi Hizbollah, an organization that had received support from the Iranian regime. Although *The 9/11 Commission Report* insinuates that Al Qaeda may have played a role in the Khobar bombing, it stops short of assigning principal blame to the terrorist network. When asked if Al Qaeda was behind the Riyadh and Khobar explosions, al-Bahri, who had boasted about the organization's feat in Somalia, said he later learned from his boss that he "had nothing to do with these operations." Saudis dissatisfied with the royal family carried out the attacks, bin Laden informed his associates.[24]

Yet in a widely disseminated recruitment videotape in 2001, bin Laden heaped praise on the Khobar perpetrators by name because they responded "positively to our incitement." "We incited, and they responded. We hope that they are in heaven," bin Laden added.[25] It is possible that bin Laden was trying to take credit for the Khobar bombing without having been directly involved because he wanted to appeal to young Saudis to rise up against the ruling royal family. Otherwise, why had bin Laden conceded privately to some of his close subordinates that he had no direct role in the Khobar attack?[26]

Al-Bahri (who was privy to secrets, had an insider's view within Al Qaeda, and supported the attacks on the United States) adds that the Riyadh and Khobar bombings had more to do with domestic politics in Saudi Arabia than with international affairs or American foreign policy. In the first half of the 1990s there existed no centralized structure for transnational jihad, and Al Qaeda, as a formal organization, had not been activated yet. It would be misleading to talk about Al Qaeda as a formal organization before 1996; its official birthday is widely recognized as the 1998 announcement establishing the World Islamic Front. In the first half of the 1990s bin Laden was still in the process of formally setting up his network under the rubric of Islamic Army Shura, composed of his own Al Qaeda Shura together with representatives of other independent jihadist groups from various Muslim countries. The latter's principal target was the near enemy, not the far enemy.[27]

The 9/11 Commission Report lists other prominent attacks that occurred during the first half of the 1990s in which it says that bin Laden's involvement was also at best "cloudy."[28] These include the 1993 bombing of the World Trade Center, a plot that same year to destroy landmarks in New York, and the 1994–5 Manila Air plot to blow up a dozen U.S. airliners over the Pacific.

Regardless of whether bin Laden's role was "cloudy" or crystal clear in these attacks, the "new terrorism" constituted a qualitative escalation by targeting the American homeland and aiming to kill thousands of civilians. Freelance jihadis, not just bin Laden and his professional associates, frequently turned their guns against the United States and its citizens, whom they characterized as the oppressor of Muslims worldwide.

Why Did Jihad Go Global?

By the mid-1990s a new shift of focus away from localism and toward globalism began to take shape among some jihadis. A few critical factors contributed to this dramatic shift. To begin, the Afghan war and the humiliating withdrawal of Russian troops planted the seeds of transnationalist jihad and emboldened Arab veterans, in particular, to embark on ambitious military ventures both back at home and abroad. (For the effects of the Afghan war on jihadis, see Chapter Two.) Next, just as the Russians cut their losses in Afghanistan and went back home, the United States found itself entangled in the shifting sands of the Arabian Peninsula (Saudi Arabia) after the 1990 Iraqi invasion of Kuwait. The decision to station American forces in Saudi Arabia after the liberation of Kuwait inflamed the religious sensibilities of many Saudis, including bin Laden and like-minded radicals, and reinforced their convictions that the United States possessed hegemonic designs on their countries.

Overnight, the United States, the sole surviving superpower, went to the top of the list of bin Laden's enemies. More than any other variable, bin Laden frequently used the American military presence in the "land of the two holy places" (Islam's two holiest cities in Mecca and Medina) as a rallying cry and an effective recruitment tool to lure young Muslims to join his anti-American network: "Do people not believe that the home of the prophet and of his grandchildren is occupied and under American-Jewish control? Thus to fight Americans is fundamental to the Muslim faith and tawhid [affirmation of the oneness of God]. We have incited the ummah against this angry occupier [the Americans] to expel it from the land of the two holy places."[29] Since then bin Laden has been obsessed with expelling American troops from "our most sacred places in Saudi Arabia," and he has made a fateful, strategic decision to take on what he called "the head of the snake," the United States. (Chapter Three elaborates further on the reasons and causes behind the rise of transnationalist jihadism.) Suffice it to say that the Gulf war in 1991 and the permanent stationing of U.S. forces in Saudi Arabia played a decisive role in the globalization of jihad, particularly in the ideological incitement and mobilization of anti-Americanism.[30]

Furthermore, the early 1990s witnessed the emergence of a new generation of freelance roaming jihadis (I do not mean mercenaries), who traveled from one front to another in support of their persecuted and oppressed Muslim brethren worldwide. For example, after the withdrawal of Russian troops from Afghanistan in 1989, thousands of Afghan veterans and other seasoned jihadis, along with young Muslims from many countries, felt compelled to defend their coreligionists in Bosnia-Herzegovina, Chechnya, the Philippines, Kashmir, Eritrea, Somalia, Burma, Tajikistan, and elsewhere and to wage jihad on their behalf. On the one hand, seasoned Afghan veterans and other jihadis effectively used these new theaters to stay in the jihad business and keep in touch with one another as well as to consolidate and expand their jihadist networks and numbers. The new jihad caravan proved to be a godsend to many Afghan veterans, who could not go back home for security reasons and who were able to utilize their rich operational experience to make further inroads into Muslim societies.

Take the case of Saudi commander of the "Arab mujahedeen" in the Caucasus, known by the nom de guerre Ibn al-Khattab (his real name was Samir Saleh Abdullah al-Suwailem), who was killed in 2002. According to recent diaries by Abu al-Walid al-Masri, a senior member of Al Qaeda's Shura Council, Khattab, who was strongly supported by one of the leading Saudi religious scholars, who provided him with money and a steady stream of fighters, succeeded in establishing an economic and financial base in the Gulf states as well as in controlling the flow of Arabs into Chechnya. Khattab also built his own media apparatus that linked him with the outside world. The result, Abu al-Walid adds, is that Khattab's position and status in Chechnya until the 1999 Russian military campaign were stronger than bin Laden's in

Afghanistan. In the 1990s the two Saudi jihadis communicated with each other and tried to pull each other to their own battle plans; but Khattab and bin Laden had defined the enemy differently and both were too ambitious to accept a subordinate role. To Khattab, Abu al-Walid notes, Russia was the real enemy and his goal was to free Muslim people and the lands of the former Soviet Union (Central Asia) from Russian control.[31]

In contrast, bin Laden wanted to fight the United States and expel its forces from Saudi Arabia. Abu al-Walid notes that bin Laden was interested in wooing Khattab to his side not just because Khattab had gained a large following and a reputation for courage and successful military exploits against Russian troops but also to obtain dirty bombs from the Russian arsenal through his contacts; bin Laden believed that Khattab joining in jihad against the Americans was a religious obligation because he was from Hijaz, a region in Saudi Arabia controlled by U.S. forces (which was not true). Bin Laden also believed that Khattab was a newcomer mujahid (Islamic fighter), whereas he was commander-in-chief of the Afghan Arabs and thus had earned the right to the leadership slot. But Khattab, Abu al-Walid reports, was not impressed and asked bin Laden to join him because he had a comprehensive program to liberate Central Asia from the Russian yoke.[32]

Although by the end of the 1990s the correspondence between the two Saudis had not produced any practical results, it is important for several reasons. First, it sheds light on the stiff competition between differing jihadist poles and perspectives and the intense drive to take charge of the jihadist caravan and control its speed and destination. Khattab not only competed on equal footing with bin Laden but assembled a more powerful contingent of jihadis than the latter. Second, the correspondence shows clearly the emergence of new transnationalist jihadi pockets and networks in Afghanistan and elsewhere. By the end of the 1990s the jihadist caravan had gone global with full speed. Third, regional conflicts in the Middle East, the Caucasus, Bosnia, Kashmir, and other places supplied a steady stream of Arab and Muslim recruits, most of whom became foot soldiers in the brigades of jihadis like bin Laden, Khattab, and Zawahiri. Fourth, by the end of the decade Saudis played a vital role in this transnationalist jihad caravan as top chiefs and operatives, and they equalled, if not surpassed, their Egyptian counterparts who had founded and pioneered the jihadist movement; the bulk of the money was also Saudi. Equally important, Saudi religious clerics and scholars provided the doctrinal justification for this large migratory movement of men and resources to many corners of the world. Fertilized and fused with a new militant sensibility imported from Egypt and elsewhere, the traditionally introvert Salafi-Wahhabi genie is out of the bottle and can't be put back in. Khattab, bin Laden, the fifteen hijackers who crashed into the World Trade Center and the Pentagon on September 11 are a direct product of this recent marriage between conservative, local Salafism-Wahhabism and revolutionary Egyptian Islamism.

Fifth, despite the asymmetry of power between transnationalist jihadis and their foreign powers, they were willing and prepared to take on the two most militarily powerful nations in the world without regard to repercussions, and they believed they could prevail. For example, as mentioned previously, bin Laden often lectured his associates that "America would not be able to sustain more than two or three of his painful blows," a reference to the attacks on the USS *Cole* in Yemen, the 1998 bombings of the two American embassies in East Africa, and September 11; similarly, Khattab reportedly said that the Muslim lands in Central Asia "would eventually fall into his hands" as soon as he operationalized his plans. Both also sought, Abu al-Walid reports, to obtain and use weapons of mass destruction (WMD), or at least dirty bombs, in their confrontation with the great powers. One of the major reasons for bin Laden's contacts with Khattab was a quest for WMD because Al Qaeda hawks were convinced, Abu al-Walid says, that their Chechen counterparts could acquire these weapons ready-made from the scattered arsenal of the former Soviet Union, or by seeking help from experts, who worked during the Soviet era and are now suffering unemployment.[33]

According to the author, after the failure of the Khattab–bin Laden correspondence, Al Qaeda hawks in Afghanistan wrote to Khattab and warned him against complacency and overconfidence in his fight with the Russians, who would militarily persevere until they prevailed and punished the Chechens: "The only way to protect the Chechens against this danger is to obtain WMD.... They also drew his attention to the point that Chechen mujahedeen are by law Russian citizens and that the Chechen mafia is able to obtain anything in Russia."[34] But Khattab paid little attention to the warning from the Al Qaeda hawks,

Abu al-Walid tells us, and when in 1999 the Russians struck militarily in retaliation for Khattab's failed attack on Daghistan, the mujahedeen government in Grozny, Chechnya, fell and the fighters met defeat; had Khattab planned for the worst-case scenario and listened to the free advice proffered by Al Qaeda hawks, he would have been more cautious and reluctant to do battle with Russia. Ironically, Abu al-Walid reports that after Grozny's fall, a Chechen mujahedeen delegation visited Afghanistan and sought assistance from the Taliban and the Afghan Arabs there; delegation members even asked if there were any WMD available in Afghanistan so that they could use them in Chechnya against the Russians to stop the mass killing of the Chechens. The moral of the story, Abu al-Walid concludes, is that neither bin Laden nor Khattab had reflected critically about their confrontation with America and Russia and, instead, had a superficial plan to win a quick and easy battle that would not require WMD: "Two years later, Afghanistan was lost and so was Chechnya. As for the ambitious plans of the Saudi jihadist leadership, they too failed."[35]

A qualification is in order here. Thousands of young Muslims, who were genuinely moved by the plight of their coreligionists and who had no previous links to militants, left their secure homes and families and traveled the world to fight for what they perceived to be a just cause. These young Muslims cannot be considered either religious nationalists or transnationalists. I interviewed several of them, who said they felt enraged by the suffering of Muslims worldwide, which they watched on their television screens, and this motivated them to leave everything behind and migrate to defend fellow believers.[36] But many of these zealous young men were transformed by the baptism of blood and fire and the comradeship of arms with other activist Muslims and jihadis alike. In the process, they acquired a new transnationalist consciousness and sensibility that made them vulnerable to radical calls by militants like bin Laden.

In his recent diaries and recollections in *Al-Quds al-Arabi*, al-Bahri retraced his jihad journey, which in 1995 took him first to Bosnia:

My first station for jihad was Bosnia-Herzegovina. My journey for jihad at that time was not organized; it was an emotional trip to wage jihad. I was watching the tragedies of Muslims in Bosnia; the slaughtering of children, women, and old people; the violation of honor and mass rape of girls; and the huge number of widows and orphans left by the war. Therefore, I decided to go to jihad as a young man who was raised on religious principles and chivalry and who is full of zeal about religion and care for Muslims. Before that, I had wanted to take part in the jihad in Afghanistan, but God willed that I miss that opportunity. The arena of jihad in Bosnia-Herzegovina was an opportunity for me.[37]

Al-Bahri (who was 21 years old when he said he "ran away from my home without the permission of my family" to join jihad in Bosnia) says that his generation closely followed political developments in Muslim countries and greatly interacted with and responded to them: "I recall a picture that is still printed in my mind to this day. It is of a Jewish soldier breaking the limbs of a Palestinian child with a stone, in front of the eyes of the world. No one moved for his sake. I cried at that sight."[38] A similar version of al-Bahri's story is often told by religious activists, who, time and again, list injustices inflicted on Muslims worldwide as a contributing factor behind their decision to join in jihad.

But there is more to al-Bahri and his generation's story than the simple emotional reaction to social and political upheaval in distant Muslim lands. There also existed a fertile religious environment and a large group of radical clerics who exercised profound impact on the impassioned youths and who instigated, not just enjoined, them to migrate and participate in jihad in those distant lands. For example, al-Bahri says that "our motivation in going forward and defending the honor of Muslims was not only chivalry and courage; there was a stronger religious drive. Add to that the instigation and call to jihad in the Friday sermons, the tape cassettes, the magazines that covered such events, and other media. I was greatly influenced by that, and I wished I was one of those mujahedeen, defending Muslim lands."[39]

Particularly critical was the role of the religious sheikhs who materially and morally prepared young men for jihad. Al-Bahri cites a hardliner cleric, Salman al-Awdah (along with 25 prominent Saudi religious scholars, in November 2004 Awdah posted an open letter on the Internet urging Iraqis to support fighters waging jihad against "the big crime of America's occupation of Iraq"),[40] who was highly active and effective in preparing and materially equipping many youths to go to

Afghanistan, Bosnia-Herzegovina, Tajikistan, and elsewhere. According to al-Bahri's personal encounters, clerics had access to huge charitable sums of money to nourish and finance the jihad caravan: "There were astronomical sums available for equipping the youths for jihad. There was no religious sheikh who stood against the jihad trend at all. This is because all of Saudi Arabia, starting with the government, the religious scholars, and the ordinary people, was on the side of driving the youths toward jihad...."[41]

In the 1980s and early 1990s, according to al-Bahri, the landscape was in total harmony regarding the value of waging jihad in support of Muslims worldwide. Religious scholars, the Saudi ruling elite, and society at large fully supported the migration of young men to pursue jihad overseas. Private donations filled the coffers of mosques and sympathetic charitable foundations, financing the jihad. This fact partially explains the presence of a large number of Saudi men among the volunteers for jihad throughout the world. According to inside accounts by Al Qaeda members, the Saudi contingent was also the biggest within Al Qaeda.

Although in a way Saudi Arabia was an ideal case, it was not unique. In this period, young Muslims, not just Saudis, were bombarded with calls and pleas by the religious establishment to militarily support their beleaguered Muslim brethren all over the world. Governments either turned a blind eye to this systematic recruitment and indoctrinational drive of the youths or indirectly blessed the effort. They wanted to direct and divert jihad outside their own bloody borders and to counterbalance the powerful influence of revolutionary Shiite Iran among their citizens. It was a short-term tactic designed to buy time and absorb the jihadist shocks threatening their rule. Money was not in short supply, thanks to contributions from the Gulf, particularly Saudi Arabia and Kuwait, which subsidized the initial expenses of young Muslims heading abroad.

The tacit encouragement and support given by the religious and ruling establishment to the pursuit of jihad by young men had profound unexpected repercussions. A new transnational generation of young warriors was born. These warriors got a taste of freedom and military triumph. Muslim men of various national and social backgrounds met on the battlefield and shed blood in defense of an imagined community. They lost their innocence and were exposed to jihadis' radical ideas, and they built enduring ties cemented by toil and blood. The old rules no longer applied or mattered to the new warriors, who viewed themselves as the vanguard of the ummah, not as citizens of separate countries.

For instance, al-Bahri's personal journey into jihad had a transformative, ideological effect on him. He says that before running away from home to go to Bosnia, "I used to consider jihad and carrying arms a kind of voluntary work. I did not view jihad as a religious duty prescribed to every individual (fard 'ayn, or a personal obligation) [as jihadis do], but a collective duty (fard kifaya), i.e,. if it is carried out by some, then others are exempt from it, albeit with their parents' consent."[42] By the time he left Bosnia, al-Bahri said he was a changed young man, and his definition of jihad mirrored that of jihad being a permanent and personal obligation and a pillar of Islam "like profession of faith, prayers, fasting, alms-giving, and pilgrimage."[43] Equally important, his brief stay there turned him into a committed pan-Islamist:

> We began to have real contact with the other trends, the enemies of the ummah, and the ideology of the ummah began to evolve in our minds. We realized we were a nation [ummah] that had a distinguished place among nations. Otherwise, what would make me leave Saudi Arabia – and I am of Yemeni origin – to go and fight in Bosnia? The issue of [secular] nationalism was put out of our minds, and we acquired a wider view than that, namely the issue of the ummah. Although the issue was very simple at the start, yet it was a motive and an incentive for jihad.[44]

Far from being unique, al-Bahri's experience is typical of a generation of young Muslims that was morally and emotionally transformed by the jihad journey. When he left Saudi Arabia and Yemen to fight in Bosnia at the age of 21, he possessed no jihadist tendencies of either localism or globalism. A year later al-Bahri sounded like a pan-Islamist on an eternal mission to fight and die for an imagined ummah. After Bosnia, he spent a few weeks in Somalia and Tajikistan, hoping to join in jihad with fellow Muslims there, but he was unsuccessful. Disappointed and frustrated, in 1996 al-Bahri went to Afghanistan and ended up swearing baiya (fealty) to bin Laden and becoming a trusted member of his inner circle and clan.

Recognizing his strong muscular build and his blind commitment to jihad, not to mention the fact that he was not yet married and did not have much family responsibility, bin Laden coopted al-Bahri as a senior "personal guard," which meant being with bin Laden until bedtime every day. From 1996 until 2000 al-Bahri served as bin Laden's bodyguard and confidant, performing sensitive tasks and missions for bin Laden both inside and outside Afghanistan. This gave al-Bahri access to bin Laden's entire circle of associates and subordinates. It also made him privy to vital secrets and information within Al Qaeda in the second half of the 1990s, a formative period in the terrorist network's development and evolution (I will cite his lengthy diaries in subsequent chapters).

Al-Bahri's dual Saudi-Yemeni nationality also helped. Bin Laden had been born to a Yemeni family that migrated to Saudi Arabia and made its fortune there. He was trying to balance ethnically the large contingent of Egyptians within his organization by recruiting Saudis, Yemenis, and other young men from the Arabian Peninsula (the Gulf). According to al-Bahri, bin Laden told him this when he tried to recruit him and other young men from the Gulf. Ethnicity mattered and was a nuisance and complicating factor within Al Qaeda. Bin Laden was conscious of the criticism that Egyptians, including Zawahiri, Abu Ubaidah al-Banshiri, Abu Hafs, Seif al-Adl, and many others, dominated his circle, and for several years he worked hard to rectify the ethnic imbalance among his men. By 2001 he had succeeded in surrounding himself with more recruits from the Arabian Peninsula, like al-Bahri and most of the September 11 suicide bombers, than from Egypt and elsewhere.

In less than two years, the terribly young al-Bahri underwent a metamorphosis and became a transnationalist jihadi, not just a pan-Islamist. He and his new generation of young warriors traveled a long distance in a short period of time. When he swore allegiance to bin Laden (a secret, private ceremony that includes only the new member and bin Laden), he said he knew he consciously embarked on a dangerous venture that would pit him against the might of the United States. There was no ambiguity about the new enemy being targeted: America and Americans. When bin Laden recruited al-Bahri and his companions to his network, according to al-Bahri, bin Laden tried to "convince us of the justification for his call to wage jihad against America."[45]

Although it took bin Laden a few days to sell his new call to these young men, they signed on with their eyes wide open. They bought into his sales pitch wholeheartedly and believed that they possessed the will and tenacity to force the United States to leave Arab lands. Listen to al-Bahri's enthusiasm and inflated zeal when he and his young companions finally decided to join Al Qaeda:

> In view of our military experience and our experience in carrying arms, we said: What is America? If we had succeeded in many armed confrontations and military fronts against the Serbs, the Russians, and others, America will not be something new. We often sat down with the brothers who fought the Americans in Somalia, and we used to hear about the brothers who struck the Americans at the Aden Hotel in the early 1990s and about the brothers who blew up American residences in Riyadh and al-Khobar. We reached the conclusion that America is no different from the forces we have fought because it has become a target for all and sundry. All of its foes have dealt blows to it. So I decided to join sheikh Osama bin Laden. That was the beginning of my work with Al Qaeda.[46]

Al-Bahri's story captures the predicament and odyssey of a new generation of ideal young warriors who left their homelands to defend their Muslim brethren worldwide. But the jihad journey radicalized them and transformed them into hardened jihadis. They supplied the foot soldiers and suicide bombers for transnationalist jihadist groups, like Al Qaeda and Khattab's legion of Arab mujahedeen, as well as operated as militant freelancers.

Finally, the shift from localism to globalism occurred after pro-Western Muslim rulers militarily suppressed the uprising launched by religious nationalists during the second half of the 1990s. Jihadis in Egypt, Algeria, and elsewhere had to choose between surrender and a new mission that would keep their sinking ship afloat. They lost the battle against the near enemy and had few options at their disposal. From the early 1990s until the late 1990s government security services inflicted heavy losses on jihadis by killing and arresting tens of thousands of them and brutally cracking down against their families, friends, and potential supporters. After a brief initial hesitation, they adopted a systematic policy of collective punishment and military preemption that brought jihadis to their knees. Jihadis proved to be no match against the powerfully entrenched security apparatus and could not withstand its counteroffensive. By the second half of the 1990s jihadis' internal revolt withered away.

In private conversations, jihadis, who were direct or indirect participants, acknowledged the asymmetry of power between themselves and their ruling nemesis and said they miscalculated horribly by plunging into an armed uprising against a militarily superior foe. Their inflamed passions and tribal desire to exact revenge against their ruling tormentors got the best of them, they added. They conceded that they possessed no strategy or program of reaching out to society at large and building a strong social base and foundation. But regardless of the reasons and causes for the operational defeat of jihadis on their domestic battlefields by the second half of the 1990s, they faced existential choices. At home, leaders of religious nationalists called for an unconditional unilateral ceasefire and decided to reassess the efficacy and utility of the strategy of armed struggle against the near enemy. A consensus existed in society that jihadis had reached a dead end, and a majority of jihadist leaders at home and abroad also arrived at a similar conclusion, even though they did so out of logistical and practical necessity, not good will or moral repulsion against the use of force and violence (more on the internal debates later).

Not all jihadis agreed with the call to lay down their arms and rethink the strategy of armed struggle. A vocal, strong, and determined minority of jihadis – residing overseas, mainly in Afghanistan, Europe (in the 1980s and 1990s senior jihadi leaders sought and obtained asylum status in European capitals), and elsewhere – dissented and went its separate way. A big schism developed within the jihadist movement and Zawahiri, leader of Tanzim al-Jihad, led the intrajihadist coup and stoked its flames. Unable to steer the jihadist ship in his direction in the late 1990s, Zawahiri broke away and joined forces with transnationalist jihadis like bin Laden and others. The irony is that while an overwhelming majority of religious nationalists at home agreed to the ceasefire call and suspension of military operations, a minority overseas, represented by the Al Qaeda network, escalated the confrontation and took jihad global.

Thus in the late 1990s, as jihadis' conflict with the near enemy was winding down, it was replaced by a deadlier one against the far enemy, the United States. Bin Laden's Al Qaeda, along with other fringe jihadist groups, spearheaded this transnationalist war and discarded the views and attitudes of the bulk of jihadis, who as religious nationalists had no interest in fully internationalizing jihad. But this transnationalist generation of jihadis did not arise in a social and political vacuum and thrust itself on the world scene. Its journey was complex, full of ironies and dramatic turns and shifts. It is a tale that speaks volumes about political manipulation by Muslim authoritarian rulers and their Western, particularly American, patrons, as well as fatal miscalculation by jihadis whose thirst and hunger for power blinded their vision and led them into reckless adventures.

Nonetheless, it is worth stressing that the shift from localism to globalism did not occur until after the mid-1990s. From the mid-1970s through the first half of the 1990s, the modern jihadist movement was inward-looking and fully engaged in a costly internal struggle to overthrow entrenched local rulers. On the whole, jihadis, most of whom were religious nationalists, possessed little appetite to expand their jihad against the far enemy and go beyond their national borders. Their overriding goal was to keep the battle lines as close to the home front as possible. In my conversations with jihadis, they said that it was not in their interest to internationalize jihad because not only did they not want to give Western powers, particularly the United States, a pretext to actively join the fight against them but also, in the 1970s, 1980s, and early 1990s jihadis were satisfied with their political prospects and felt that they had made inroads into society. By the 1980s and early 1990s their ranks, they added, had swelled with thousands of highly motivated young recruits. As a senior jihadi leader put it, "we were on a roll, while powerful Arab rulers were fighting for their political survival."

Muslim Rulers Flirt with Jihad

In the early 1990s pro-Western Muslim regimes aimed at internationalizing the confrontation and more deeply committing Western powers to their side. They hoped to obtain Western material and political support, particularly to ensure that their great power patrons remained committed to their survival. As hostilities between jihadis and government security forces intensified in the first half of the 1990s, pro-U.S. Arab rulers became very anxious about being abandoned by their superpower patron and lashed out angrily against supposed plots by their reluctant, ungrateful partner. For example, Egyptian and Algerian leaders frequently criticized American and European governments for allegedly appeasing mainstream Islamists by initiating secret contacts with their rank and file and granting asylum to the "terrorist" leaders of the jihadis. The Algerian military junta also expressed its displeasure with its French ally for not doing enough to tip the civil war in its favor.

But pro-Western Muslim rulers had a short memory of their own complicity and shortsightedness in letting the jihadist genie out of the bottle. After the Russian invasion of Afghanistan, Saudi Arabia, Pakistan, Egypt, Jordan, Morocco, the Gulf shiekdoms, and others collaborated with the United States in facilitating – or at least they turned a blind eye to – the recruitment and flow of young Muslims to wage jihad against the Russian occupiers. Their goals were to please their superpower patron, divert the threat of potential jihadis and militants away from their own thrones, and capitalize on their support for jihad against Communist invaders to gain public legitimacy at home. Although since September 11 the role of the United States in financing and arming the jihad caravan in Afghanistan has received considerable critical scrutiny, analysis of the full weight and input of Muslim rulers remains incomplete and shrouded in mystery.

According to recent memoirs, diaries, and private conversations with the so-called Afghan Arabs, Muslim political and religious authorities played a vital role in creating a fertile environment in support of the Afghan jihad. Young Muslims were bombarded with calls to join in jihad against the atheist occupiers. Mainstream and radical clerics alike urged and incited the youths to migrate to Afghanistan to help their Muslim brethren. Official media coverage also brought the message home regarding the importance of making jihad in support of Muslims worldwide. In his recollections, al-Bahri, who was in his teens at that time, said that the Saudi media "played a big role in stoking the fire of jihad among the people through coverage of the arenas of jihad, particularly the press interviews that were held with some of the leading mujahedeen figures."[47] As mentioned previously, al-Bahri painted a picture of the Saudi scene whereby the royal family and clerics fully supported the Afghan jihad with words and deeds. It is little wonder that of all their Muslim counterparts, the Saudi contingent was the largest and that the ruling house of Saud contributed more financially to the Afghan war effort than the United States did.

In his memoir, a senior veteran of the Afghan jihad, Abdullah Anas, an Algerian and a son-in-law of sheikh Abdullah Azzam, leader of the Afghan Arabs, writes that Saudis donated millions of dollars to sheikh Azzam's Maktab al-Khadamat or Services Bureau, which housed and trained thousands of Muslim volunteers in Peshawar, Pakistan. Saudi Arabia, according to Anas, also became a ferrying port and station for Arab veterans and jihadis, like Zawahiri, who were journeying to Peshawar on their way to Afghanistan, and the country provided a 75 percent discount on airline tickets for young Muslims wishing to join the jihad there. Other veterans and jihadis confirm Saudi Arabia's centrality in supplying men and materiel to the Afghan war, as did neighboring Gulf states.[48]

Although Saudi Arabia and Pakistan led the way in supporting the Afghan war, other pivotal Muslim states, such as Egypt, Algeria, Indonesia, Turkey, Morocco, and Jordan, contributed their share. For example, Arab rulers profusely praised the Afghan mujahedeen and called on their subjects to join the jihad against the Russian occupiers. According to a first-hand account by an official of the Egyptian Muslim Brotherhood who spent time in Afghanistan, President Sadat met with the leader of the Brothers and encouraged them to help the Afghanis and send volunteers there. He added that the Brothers did so during Sadat's reign and after his 1981 assassination. Sanctioned officially and blessed by the religious authority, materiel and men, including both militants and seasoned jihadis, flowed freely into Afghanistan.[49]

Muslim rulers were as guilty of miscalculation in Afghanistan as their superpower patron, the United States, was; the United States had no monopoly on foreign policy blunders. In their eyes, the Afghan war briefly enabled Muslim rulers to export their troubles to distant lands, and it gave them a short respite. The patron-client relationship also required collaborating with Washington and performing useful functions for their superpower ally. But like the United States, Muslim autocrats gave little thought to what would happen after the Afghan jihad. What was to be done with the hardened and radicalized Afghan returnees? How would these fighters and militants affect the already widening Islamist-secular divide in Muslim countries? How could they be fully reintegrated into restive and turbulent political structures? Would they channel their paramilitary experience and religious-ideological indoctrination to tip the internal balance of power in Muslim societies and turn their guns against their original sponsors and financiers?

Indeed, Muslim rulers' active support of the Afghan jihad helped to create a transnational army of jihadis, who felt emboldened by the Russian defeat and who subsequently attacked former local and external backers. Although in the 1980s Arab dictators unknowingly played a vital part in planting the seeds of transnationalized jihad, in the 1990s they desperately sought to internationalize the fight against those very same jihadis whom they helped to create. In both cases, American politicians took fateful decisions based on short-term, not long-term, calculations.

America Flirts with Political Islam

Since September 11, relations between the United States and Islamic activists, not just jihadis, have been portrayed as having always been on a collision course and fated to militarily clash. A dominant paradigm has gained momentum regarding the historical inevitability of confrontation between the two camps given their divergent values and interests. Thus the September 11 attacks are seen as a natural product of the intrinsic hostility and enmity that all Islamists and jihadis have against the West, particularly the United States. Similarly, mainstream Islamists accuse the United States of exploiting September 11 to launch a total war against the entire Islamist movement, not just jihadis, and the ummah. Their publications and pronouncements echo those of their hardliner American counterparts, who posit a hypothesis of hostility and inevitable confrontation. Both camps overlook and neglect history and substitute ideology and propaganda for critical analysis and reflection on a highly complex subject.

Far from being a one-way street leading to the September 11 attacks, the relationship between American foreign policy and political Islam is highly complex and nuanced, fraught with misunderstandings, contradictions, and bad judgments. Although I have written a book on the dynamics of this relationship, it is worth briefly highlighting its salient features here.[50] Throughout the second half of the twentieth century, the Cold War defined world politics. The United States and the Soviet Union fought war-by-proxy to avoid direct confrontation with each other and to reduce the risks of a nuclear holocaust. Both powers were in league with shadowy groups, trying to gain a comparative advantage over each other. As the Cold War rivalry in the 1950s and 1960s intensified, the United States viewed political Islam as a useful and effective defense mechanism against the rising local forces of revolutionary nationalism and socialism. Having failed to coopt these local forces, the United States turned to traditionalist Islamism – being a powerful legitimizing symbol – and hoped to build, as President Dwight Eisenhower said, an alliance of Islamic states with sufficient prestige to counterbalance "godless communism" and its secular nationalist allies as represented by Egyptian President Gamal Abdel Nasser.[51]

This marriage of convenience between American foreign policy and political Islam was designed to prevent the further expansion of the radical secular, socialist-nationalist tide. As beneficiaries of the status quo, American officials and traditionalist Islamic forces, such as Saudi Arabia, Pakistan, the Muslim Brothers, and other Islamists, found it beneficial to cooperate against the new common menace. American policy was driven by Cold War considerations and strategic calculations, not by culture, values, or religious fervor. Washington did not possess a hidden agenda but took a hard, calculating, pragmatic stance to maximize its own interests.

Similarly, although Salafis-Wahhabis (ultraconservatives) and traditionalists, like the Muslim Brothers, deeply mistrusted American foreign policy, they were much more ideologically hostile toward world communism and secular Arab nationalism. Islamic activists were also engaged in a bloody power struggle against secular-nationalist rulers, who were tactically allied with the Soviet Union and who harshly suppressed and stifled Islamists' political ambitions. Forced to choose between either the pro-Western camp or the pro-Soviet one, Islamic traditionalists and fundamentalists chose the former – the lesser of the two evils. But deep down, mainstream Islamists were disposed toward Western capitalism, which resonated among their rank and file. It is worth mentioning that the Islamist movement was socially and economically very conservative and had more in common with the capitalist West than with the socialist East. The Islamists' decision, like that of the United States, was based on pragmatic calculations of gains and losses. They cooperated with the Western powers because they considered them to represent no immediate danger to their values and interests, and they considered them as states with whom they could do business. Therefore, from the 1950s until the 1970s Islamic activists and American officials suspended their reservations and doubts about one another in order to confront the common enemy – Soviet communism and its local nationalist and socialist allies.

This mutual perception of the common enemy also partially explains the tactical alliance reached between the United States and revolutionary Islamists in Afghanistan. The 1979 Russian invasion of Afghanistan reminded American decision makers that their strategic struggle against the communist camp dwarfed their recent feud with the radical Iranian mullahs who had just toppled the pro-U.S. Shah of Iran and seized power. As President Carter said, the Russian invasion "could pose the most serious threat to the peace since the Second World War."[52] It is no wonder that United States actively supported the Afghan mujahedeen and turned a blind eye to, if it did not actually encourage, the recruitment and flow of foreign fighters and jihadis into that war-torn country. In American eyes, the rivalry with the Soviet Union took precedence over everything else, including the possibility that revolutionary Islamism and jihadism could spill over the Afghan borders and destabilize neighboring Muslim states, including Pakistan, Saudi Arabia, Egypt, and Turkey. Equally important, the trauma of the Islamic revolution in Iran did not leave deep scars on the official psyche of the United States, even though initially Ayatollah Ruhollah Khomeini's assault on America's moral authority had a "profound effect" on American policy toward the broader Middle East.[53] Never before had a Muslim leader used the pulpit to denounce America as the epicenter of evil. In the American mind, populist, revolutionary Islam came to be associated with terrorism and the promotion of subversive activities. But in the hierarchy of strategic threats, communism was still seen as more potent and real than revolutionary Islamism.

Thus when Russian troops marched into the Afghan minefield, U.S. officials, who were caught off guard, swiftly seized this opportunity to mobilize Islamic resistance and to tap into the anticommunist feelings of the now-dominant "fundamentalist clergy" in Iran and elsewhere in Muslim countries. Containing Soviet communism, said Zbigniew Brzezinski, Assistant for National Security Affairs for President Carter, dictated an avoidance of anything that could split Islamic opposition to the Russians, especially an American-Iranian military confrontation: "It now seemed to me more important to forge an anti-Soviet Islamic coalition," Brzezinski stressed.[54]

As in the 1950s and 1960s, the United States hoped to use religion and political Islam as a counterweight to radical, secular local forces and their atheist ally – the Soviet Union. The Carter and Reagan administrations recognized the new possibilities for cooperation with Islamist activists and hoped to harness their religious and ideological fervor against communist expansionism. Because they were obsessed with the struggle against godless communism, American leaders were naturally inclined to flirt with and align their country with the soldiers of God in the Muslim world. They paid little attention to the potential militarization of Muslim politics and the rise of a new generation of young warriors who could wreck the existing order. Nothing could distract the Americans from this engrossing game that great powers play.[55]

For more than three decades, the American foreign policy establishment got socialized into an anticommunist mind-set. Originality and nonconventional thinking were not nourished or encouraged. In official U.S. eyes, Islamic resurgence was a temporary distraction from the Cold War and was simply viewed through the lenses of the Cold War. Khomeini and his revolutionary ideologues were seen more as a nuisance than as a viable threat to U.S. security interests. American policy still revolved around the containment and rollback of "the evil empire" and remained wedded to supporting conservative religious elements against Third World nationalist-socialist forces. In a way, Afghanistan represented a continuity, not a rupture, in American foreign policy in the Muslim world during the second half of the twentieth century.

American officials viewed the fielding of a mujahadeen army in Afghanistan, including foreign veterans and jihadis, as an extension of their war-in-proxy against the Soviet Union.[56] They gave little thought to the aftermath of the Afghan struggle: what to do with tens of thousands of hardened fighters baptized into a culture of martyrdom and emboldened by victory over a rival superpower. How could these warriors be demobilized and reintegrated into their societies as law-abiding citizens? Could the jihad genie be put back into the bottle? With hindsight, one would have expected American policy makers to reflect on these questions before throwing caution to the wind and plunging into the shifting sands of Afghanistan and Islamic politics. But no systematic assessment of the potential repercussions of the Afghan jihad seems to have been undertaken. Obviously, American officials reckoned that the mujahedeen and foreign guests and veterans could be contained and kept under control by their local clients once the Afghan conflict was over.[57]

Jihadis' Revisionist History

The Afghan war was full of ironies and contradictions. It brought out an unlikely convergence of interests between the United States and Muslim authoritarian regimes, on the one hand, and mainstream Islamists and jihadis, on the other. For expedient reasons, the latter set aside their deep suspicions of the United States and its local allies and collaborated against an immediate common enemy, the Russian occupiers. In particular, Afghanistan provided jihadis with a safe haven to regroup and gain field experience, recruit new foot soldiers, and build networks among other jihadis from various Muslim countries (see Chapter Two for further analysis). Both camps temporarily needed one another and cynically used each other. But they did join ranks and they found themselves fighting in the same trenches.

Although a marriage built on such a shaky foundation was bound to come to a bitter end, it lasted for a decade. Regardless of what occurred subsequently, history cannot be erased or suppressed. More than their former local and external sponsors, transnationalist jihadis, who underwent a metamorphosis in the second half of the 1990s, have tried to rewrite history and deny having had relations or getting financial and logistical support from the United States and its pro-Muslim partners. The jihadis want to portray themselves as having always been implacable enemies of the "head of the snake" (America) and its Muslim apostates. Retracing their journey, with its many dramatic turns and shifts, will show the many faces and colors of the jihadis and the pronounced contradictions in their words and deeds. Taking stock of their entire record will bring these "warriors of God" down to earth, which they deeply dread.

In his post–September 11 memoir, Zawahiri, official historian and theoretician of transnationalist jihadis, labors hard to convince his Muslim audience that Arab veterans and jihadis in Afghanistan neither dealt with America and its local cronies nor received any financial assistance from them. According to Zawahiri, Arab jihadis relied on their own resources and societal, as opposed to official, support by Muslim publics. It is worth quoting Zawahiri at length to bring his point home:

> While the United States backed Pakistan and the [Afghan] mujahedeen factions with money and equipment, the young Arab mujahedeen relationship with the United States was totally different.
>
> Indeed, the presence of those Afghan Arabs and their increasing numbers represented a failure of American policy and new proof of the famous U.S. political stupidity. The financing of the activities of the Arab mujahedeen came from aid sent to Afghanistan by popular organizations. It was substantial aid. The Arab mujahedeen did not just finance their own jihad but also carried Muslim donations to the Afghan mujahedeen themselves. Osama bin Laden informed me of the size of the popular Arab support for the Afghan mujahedeen that amounted, according to his sources, to $200 million in the form of military aid alone in ten years. Imagine how much aid was sent by popular Arab organizations in the nonmilitary fields such as medicine and health, education and vocational training, food, and social assistance (including sponsorship of orphans, widows, and the war-handicapped). Add to all this the donations that were sent on special occasions such as Id al-Fitr and Id al-Adha feasts and during the month of Ramadan.
>
> Through this unofficial popular support, the Arab mujahedeen established training centers and centers for the call to the faith. They formed fronts that trained and equipped thousands of Arab mujahedeen and provided them with living expenses, housing, travel, and organization.[58]

Zawahiri's revisionist account flies in the face of empirical evidence, which shows that Saudi Arabia and other Gulf governments, not just Muslim masses, provided much of the money that financed the Afghan jihad. Between 1979 and 1988, like their American allies, the Saudis supplied billions of dollars worth of secret assistance to rebel groups in Afghanistan fighting the Russian occupation.[59] The Saudis partially financed sheikh Abdullah Azzam's Services Bureau, or guest house, which housed and trained thousands of the so-called Afghan Arabs. Azzam and other Arab jihadis heaped praise on the ruling Saud family for its generous financial and moral contributions to the Afghan jihad. So did bin Laden before his estrangement from the Saudi regime after the 1990 deployment of American forces in the kingdom following Saddam Hussein's invasion and occupation of Kuwait.

Ironically, bin Laden was the middleman between the Saudis and Azzam's guest house, and he became the financier of the latter's activities, thanks mainly to official Saudi funds and donations flowing through charities or other nongovernmental organizations (NGOs). Although bin Laden used a small fraction of his own family's huge fortune, he also relied on a complex network of charities, personal contacts, and official Saudi contributions.[60] Bin Laden was a frequent visitor to the Saudi embassy in Pakistan, which funneled financial assistance through the Pakistan military intelligence service (Directorate for Inter-Services Intelligence, or ISI, which played a pivotal role in supplying weapons and ammunition and in training Afghanis and other volunteers during the Afghan war years; it also served as a bridge between American intelligence services and Afghanis but its input went beyond that which fostered and nourished the jihadist internationale); and he also became very familiar with the Saudi intelligence chief, Prince Turki bin Faisal, who was in charge of the Afghan portfolio. By virtue of being one of the first prominent Saudis to go to Afghanistan and due to his family's standing as one of the wealthiest in the kingdom, Osama bin Laden became Saudi Arabia's point man during the Afghan jihad. There was no conspiracy involved. The United States and Saudi Arabia financed the Afghan resistance against the Russian occupation. But it is very important to register that arms and aid were flowing to the Afghan mujahadeen long before the Russian intervention in December 1979 and, in some measure, helped to bring it about. Since September 11, and after initial hesitation, Saudi officials came clean and publicly acknowledged that they, along with their American partner, financed the Afghan jihad but stopped doing so when the war ended. However, evidence shows that although between October 1989 and October 1990 the United States reduced its aid to Afghanistan by almost 60 percent, Saudi Arabia increased funding during the same period. The point to stress is that both the United States and Saudi Arabia invested heavily in Afghanistan. President Ali Abdullah Saleh of Yemen, a pro-American ally who supported the U.S. project in Afghanistan, was less charitable, holding the United States accountable for creating the terrorist phenomenon in that war-torn country.[61]

The belated effort by Zawahiri and bin Laden to deny the official Saudi, Pakistani, and Arab connection can only be explained by their subsequent change of heart and their decision to internationalize jihad and target the United States and its local allies, including Saudi Arabia. Zawahiri is correct to reject the claim that the Afghan Arabs were funded (even "one penny") or trained by the United States. Azzam and bin Laden had access to a broad network of official and semiofficial Gulf funds as well as to donations from Arab and Muslim NGOs. They did not need American money to wage jihad, even though their network raised funds in the United States. But their mission and journey were facilitated by official Arab and Muslim support and American knowledge and agreement. They were part of the same diverse desperate team haphazardly assembled to roll back the Russian advance. For a decade, they willingly concurred in this arrangement and actively played by the rules of the game.

As a theoretician of transnationalist jihadis, Zawahiri sells a particular version of events and developments that serves his own network's interests. His sales pitch is that jihadis have always possessed independent and rebellious spirits and have been above politicking and making deals with the enemies of the ummah. Zawahiri devotes a whole section of his memoir to rebutting charges that jihadis had been America's "mercenaries" who subsequently turned against their master. If this is true, he sarcastically asks, "why cannot America bribe them once more? Are not they considered, particularly Osama bin Laden, danger number one that threatens American interests? Would not their purchase be less costly than the astronomical security and preventive budgets which America spends to defend itself against jihadis?"[62] Ironically, in the early 1990s the very same Zawahiri, who now denies having had any dealings or contacts with America, visited California's Silicon Valley and met with Muslims to raise funds for his local, not global, jihad. Although the FBI closely monitored his visit and movements, at this stage neither the FBI nor the CIA considered Zawahiri a menace to

American security; he had not theorized or called for targeting the far enemy yet.

Zawahiri goes for the overkill to disprove the existence of any prior link between jihadis and the United States in Afghanistan. He wants his jihadist base, and Muslims in general, to know that he and his associates never cooperated with America and have been intrinsically hostile to its designs in the region. As usual, Americans, Zawahiri writes, exaggerate and distort the historical record by claiming that bin Laden was on their payroll:

> How could bin Laden, who in his 1987 lectures called [on Muslims] to boycott American goods in support of the Palestinian Intifada, be an agent for Americans in Afghanistan? America was shocked to discover that its cooking in Afghanistan was spoiled by the "Afghan Arabs" and those good ones of the Afghan mujahedeen. America wanted a war-by-proxy against Russia in Afghanistan, but Arab mujahedeen turned it into a call to revive the neglected duty, jihad, for the sake of God.[63]

Zawahiri revisits and revises the history of the jihadist movement to avoid explaining the dramatic shifts that occurred within one of its constituencies – the Al Qaeda network. His is a selective, post–September 11 reading that does not take into consideration the tensions and differences that have shaken the movement to its foundation. It imposes the present on the past and fails to account for the dramatic turns and shifts in the journey of jihadis. Zawahiri also wants to project an image of jihadis as having all along had a master plan to join the Afghan jihad caravan, defeat the Russians, and then launch a two-pronged assault against the far enemy and the near enemy simultaneously. Zawahiri's memoir implies that the jihadis' entire plot was hatched in advance and that they had a strategic vision and strategy to cleanse Muslim lands of the local apostates and of corrupting Western influences.

No one doubts jihadis' enmity toward westernization, globalization, and secularism. But their selective ahistorical narrative overlooks critical questions and vital junctures in their journey. Why, for example, did jihadis take jihad global at this late stage in their march (the second half of the 1990s)? Why did they spend the first two decades of their existence (from the mid-1970s until the mid-1990s) targeting the near enemy, as opposed to the far enemy? What brought about this dramatic shift in tactics and strategy? How do jihadis explain the fact that religious nationalists (the majority of jihadis) stayed on the sidelines and did not join the new crusade against the far enemy? Do they have anything to say about the internal mutation within the jihadist movement? And is it useful to deny their participation in the tactical alliances and coalitions built by Muslim states and the United States to resist the Russian occupation of Afghanistan?

TWO

The Afghan War

Sowing the Seeds of Transnational Jihad

Initially, in the early 1980s, the Afghan war provided jihadis with a "secure base" to train and prepare for the coming jihad (armed struggle) against the "near enemy" (Muslim rulers). But it ultimately bred a new generation of transnationalist jihadis, who felt empowered by the Russian defeat and who decided to go fully global with their Islamist revolution. The 1979 Russian military intervention in Afghanistan, which coincided with the Islamic revolution in Iran and the rise of militant political Islam in general, radicalized Muslim politics and societies further and played directly into jihadis' hands; one of the very first acts by a proto-jihadist group was the 1981 assassination of President Sadat by the Jihad group in Egypt.[1] The Afghan war became a rallying cry and recruiting ground for many religiously inclined Muslims, and it fueled jihadis' ambitions.

The Afghan Jihad as Defensive War

Leaving their families and homes, young and old pious Muslims migrated into Afghanistan to defend their coreligionists and the faith and to resist aggression against the dar al-Islam (House of Islam). Over the years I met scores of the so-called Afghan Arabs, those who spent months or years either fighting or providing other forms of support to the Afghan mujahedeen (Islamic fighters). They came from all walks of life and were driven by the plight and predicament of their Afghan counterparts who were seen as struggling against an atheistic enemy. I heard heart-wrenching stories of men who sacrificed their jobs, economic well-being, and comfort and went to Afghanistan to do their "duty" and partake in what they saw as a sacred struggle. Some said they could not afford to purchase airline tickets to fly to Pakistan (a vetting and resting station for foreign fighters and volunteers heading to Afghanistan), and their mothers, wives, and sisters had to sell their jewelry to send them off. Others used their meager life savings to get to Afghanistan, while Islamic charities and pro-Western Muslim regimes in Saudi Arabia and the Gulf subsidized the journey of many.

Now, in light of the subsequent monstrous distortion of the Afghan jihad, it is easy to forget that many Arab and Muslim volunteers who traveled to Afghanistan and fought there did so to defend a Muslim community, which in their opinion was occupied by an infidel, atheist power. They joined the Afghan jihad for a specific limited purpose: to expel the Russian invaders from Muslim lands. Many of these Afghan volunteers cannot be classified as doctrinaire jihadis who, in their drive to establish an Islamic polity, express a preference for violence over nonviolent strategies despite the possibility of engaging in the latter; rather, they are irredentist jihadis, who struggle to redeem land considered to be part of dar al-islam from non-Muslim rule or occupation. On the whole, irrenditst jihadis possess no political ambition to wage jihad against either their own goverments or Western nations.

In my conversations with several former Afghan volunteers in Egypt, Yemen, Jordan, and elsewhere, they stressed that they had not been Islamic activists or jihadis before migrating to Afghanistan, and they did not join a jihadist organization while they were there or after. Some even expressed shock at how radical jihadis like bin Laden, Zawahiri, and other associates hijacked the Afghan jihad for their own political purposes. Memoirs written by several former Arab Afghan veterans bemoan the terrorist label that has been slapped on the so-called Afghan Arabs that lumps them with Al Qaeda. They talk about their unique and diverse experiences that brought them to Afghanistan, particularly how the plight of the Afghanis moved them to leave their families and everything behind to join in jihad against the Russians.[2]

It is worth mentioning that a consensus then existed among Muslim clerics and scholars that doing jihad against the Russian invaders was legitimate (defensive) and could be considered a "collective" duty. Leading mainstream religious figures in Saudi Arabia, Egypt, Pakistan, and elsewhere issued fatwas (religious edicts) calling on Muslims to join their Afghan coreligionists in resisting Russian aggression. Tens of thousands of Muslims responded to the jihad call from their religious authority. Thousands of radical Islamists and jihadis also migrated to Afghanistan to train and prepare for the coming wars against "impious" Muslim rulers.

Never before in modern times had so many Muslims from so many lands who spoke different tongues separately journeyed to a Muslim country to fight together against a common enemy. There were Egyptians, Saudis, Yemenis, Palestinians, Algerians, Sudanese, Iraqi Kurds, Kuwaitis, Turks, Jordanians, Syrians, Libyans, Tunisians, Moroccans, Lebanese, Pakistanis, Indians, Indonesians, Malaysians, and others. Although their actual numbers (tens of thousands) were minuscule in comparison with the Afghanis, who did most of the fighting and suffered most of the casualties, the presence of such a widely representative section of Muslims transformed the Afghan war into a religious struggle between the ummah (the community worldwide) and godless Communism.

In the eyes of mainstream Islamists and conservative Muslims, for a fleeting moment in Afghanistan in the 1980s there existed a community of believers united in arms against infidel encroachment and aggression that dreamed of past glories and victories. Afghanistan was a crucible in which diverse Muslims heeded the call of religious clerics, kings, and presidents and came to the aid of fellow believers to wage jihad to expel the Russian invaders out of the House of Islam.[3] As a Yemeni Afghan volunteer confided to me, "Afghanistan reminded Muslims of all colors and races that what unites us [the Islamic faith] is much more important than the superficial differences wrought by colonialism and secular nationalism. We felt we were on the verge of reenacting and reliving the Golden Age of our blessed ancestors."

On the whole, however, an ideological and a cultural gulf existed between the Afghani fighters and their foreign guests. The ideology of the Afghan Arabs, both practicing Muslims and militant Islamists, who migrated to Afghanistan was more rigid, scripturalist, and diehard than that of their Afghan counterparts. Many of the Arabs who went to Afghanistan adhered to a Salalfi-Wahhabi understanding of Islam, which is ultraconservative and textualist, whereas the Afghans were mostly of the Deobandi subschool of the Hanafi school of thought – more relaxed and less conservative. Despite their rhetorical pronouncements of Islamic solidarity and unity, some of the Afghan Arabs looked with contempt and shock at the localized "primitive" and "diluted" religious practices of the Afghanis. Traditional Wahhabism has no tolerance for mazhabiya (confessionalism or sectarianism). An air of moral superiority colored some of the Afghan Arabs' attitudes toward their hosts, and deep tensions existed between the allies under the surface. Although foreign veterans and Afghanis were united to fight the common enemy (the Russians), they disagreed on almost everything else, including politics and religion. The two sides frequently came to armed blows over praying over the body of a fallen comrade or visiting cemeteries and praying and honoring the dead. Foreign fighters, particularly Afghan Arabs, considered some of the Afghanis' religious practices "sacrilegious" and tried to show them "the correct Salafi" (ultraconservative) way. At the heart of these differences lay a bigger moral clash between Afghanis' homegrown, nuanced traditions of worship and that of an absolutist, textualist, and fundamentalist interpretation that denies context-oriented local customs. Even after the Russians went home in the late 1980s and the Taliban took over in the 1990s, many Arab jihadis never warmed up to Afghanistan, and they resented bin Laden and Zawahiri's decision to return there (more on this point later).

Furthermore, unlike foreign veterans who journeyed to Afghanistan to take part in an ideological battle on behalf of an imaginary or real ummah, Afghanis possessed a more mundane and limited goal: liberating their homeland from the yoke of Russian occupation and fighting the local communists of the People's Democratic Party, which in 1978 seized power in a military coup and subsequently invited the Russians to send troops to Afghanistan. They had no intention or desire to turn their country into a theater or camp from which to wage global jihad against either other Muslim governments or Western states.[4] Throughout the confrontation with the Russians in the 1980s, leaders of the Afghan mujahedeen requested financial and technical assistance, not men, from their Muslim counterparts in order to train, arm, and feed their own fighters, whose numbers were plentiful. There was no need for foreign veterans to replenish the ranks of the mujahedeen, and there exists no evidence pointing to any vital role played by foreign veterans in the Afghan victory over the Russians. Despite efforts by foreign veterans, particularly the Afghan Arabs, to exaggerate their armed input, the war would have been won with or without them. Militarily, they represented a tiny and inconsequential factor in the Afghan battle.

The Law of Unintended Consequences: Nourishing Transnational Jihad

The major contribution of the Afghan veterans, particularly militant Islamists, was felt outside the borders of Afghanistan, in many Muslim countries and beyond. Although never conceived or intended as a way station to global jihad, the Afghan war gave birth to a new mobilized, seasoned, and professionalized transnational force composed of Muslim fighters and freelancers who became addicted to the jihad business. My conversations with nonjihadi Afghan veterans indicated that they were radicalized by their war experience, especially by their interaction with paramilitary organized jihadis like Egyptian Islamic Jihad, and al-Jama'a al-Islamiya (Islamic Group), militant Algerian Islamists, Pakistani Jamaat-i-Islami, Kashmiri Harakat ul-Ansar, and others. Afghanistan had an overall radicalizing impact on foreign combatants and served as a transformative experience on both hardened jihadis, like Abdullah Azzam, Abu Ubaida al-Bansihiri, Abu Hafs, Seif al-Adl, Zawahiri, and their cohorts, as well as on unseasoned ones, like bin Laden. Bin Laden, who subsequently took jihad global against the "far enemy," the sole surviving superpower, the United States, felt empowered and drew vital, if misleading, lessons from the Afghan war.

For example, Zawahiri, one of the first senior jihadis to go to Afghanistan, devoted an entire chapter in his 2001 memoir, *Knights Under the Prophet's Banner*, to the effect of the war on the jihadist movement: "the jihad battles in Afghanistan destroyed the myth of a (superpower) in the minds of young Muslim mujahedeen. The Soviet Union, a superpower with the largest land army in the world, was destroyed, and the remnants of its troops fled Afghanistan before the eyes of the Muslim youths and with their participation."[5]

The Afghan experience also went to bin Laden's head; he concluded that poorly armed but dedicated men can confront better-equipped adversaries. In a 2000 recruitment video, bin Laden used the Afghan war as a model to terrorize the other surviving superpower – the United States:

> Using very meager resources and military means, the Afghan mujahedeen demolished one of the most important human myths in history and the biggest military apparatus. We no longer fear the so-called Great Powers. We believe that America is much weaker than Russia; and our brothers who fought in Somalia told us that they were astonished to observe how weak, impotent, and cowardly the American soldier is. As soon as eighty American troops were killed, they fled in the dark as fast as they could, after making a great deal of noise about the new international order [a reference to then–President George H. W. Bush, who spoke of a "new world order" after the 1991 Gulf wars]. America's nightmares in Vietnam and Lebanon [referring to the suicide attacks on the U.S. embassy and Marine barracks in the 1980s] will pale by comparison with the forthcoming victory in al-Hijaz.[6]

It is doubtful that transnational jihad would have materialized without the prolonged Afghan war and its socializing and mobilizational effects on Arab jihadis. It is worth noting that when militant Arab Islamists, as opposed to just volunteers, came to Afghanistan in the 1980s, they were mainly interested in acquiring the necessary skills and tools to confront the near enemy at home, not to unleash a campaign of terror against a faraway enemy that did not figure prominently on their radar screen. Although their rhetoric and discourse were littered with anti-Western diatribes and they were socialized into an anti-Western mind-set, they assigned the highest priority to unseating local rulers who did not apply the Shariah (Islamic law) and who allied themselves with Islam's foreign enemies. They had neither the commitment nor the resources and means to internationalize jihad. In his memoir, which he began writing in 2000 but did not release until immediately after September 11, Zawahiri said that the Afghan war changed all that and provided the jihadist movement with an arena that served as an "incubator" for its seeds to grow and where it acquired "practical experiences in combat, politics, and organization."[7]

Equally important, Zawahiri says that the Afghan jihad years nourished a kind of esprit de corps among veterans from various backgrounds and nationalities, one that subsequently helped them survive the devastating military campaign launched by the United States against Al Qaeda and the Taliban jihadis in October 2001. Afghanistan, he writes, "gave young Muslim mujahedeen – Arabs, Pakistanis, Turks, and Muslims from Central and East Asia – a great opportunity to get acquainted with each other on the land of Afghan jihad through comradeship-at-arms against the enemies of Islam."[8] Jihadis, who trained and fought together in Afghanistan, have shown an exceptional tenacity and loyalty to one another that has proven to be lethal. Thus the Afghan war experience infused the jihadist movement with new global sensibilities and ambitions and a small but cohesive army of converts to transnational jihadism with a strong asabiya (group or tribal loyalty). But ironically, by challenging the operational hegemony of localism and paving the way for globalism, the Afghan experience shattered the supposed unity of the jihadist movement and fed the centrifugal forces within.

The law of unintended consequences works in mysterious ways. Although it was not until the mid- to late 1990s that transnationalist jihadis burst on the scene and began to articulate an operational blueprint to justify attacking the far enemy, the doctrinal seeds of transnational jihadism had been planted in the volatile and fertile Afghan soil in the 1980s. Particularly pivotal was the fusion of puritanical Salafism-Wahhabism with a militant internationalist strand of the Muslim Brotherhood. More than anything else, this marriage between introvert, ritualistic Salafism and militant Egyptian Islamism occurred during the Afghan jihad years and lay the foundation of bin Ladenism. Global jihad was a product of the fertilization between two opposite currents of Islamism – the Egyptian Nile and the Saudi desert (more on this point in Chapter 3).[9] In the end, it is safe to say that the Afghan war fueled and unleashed global jihad, even though neither jihadis nor their patrons and sworn enemies had conceived of such a revolutionary metamorphosis.

Initially, the Afghan war served as a training and recruiting ground and safe haven for radical Islamists from Egypt, Algeria, Saudi Arabia, Pakistan, Yemen, Iraq, Libya, Chechnya, and elsewhere. Few had thought of the Afghan theater as a first step in a long journey that would take them to New York, Washington, Madrid, and London. At that stage, there existed no such expansive vision or function of jihad. But to say so is to miss the law of unintended consequences in politics and to underestimate jihadis' ambitions, recklessness, and deeply entrenched anti-Western attitudes. Once set in motion, political actions and decisions cannot stop, and they tend to have a life and logic of their own. The Afghan jihad began as a defensive, limited war against the Russian occupiers and their client stratocracy in Kabul, but it transformed not only state and society in Afghanistan but also the very jihadis who shifted gears and launched unlimited, offensive war against the far enemy.

The Case of Zawahiri: The Transformation of a Religious Nationalist

In this context, the case of Zawahiri, emir of Egyptian Islamic Jihad, is instructive. For Zawahiri and his cohorts, the Afghan jihad was a God-sent opportunity to heal their wounds and replenish their depleted ranks after being hunted down by government security services. They could plot and conspire against their ruling archenemies in safety and infiltrate hardened fighters back home to foment instability and disorder. In his memoir, which was written to justify the dramatic shift from localism to globalism and which was smuggled out of Afghanistan at the peak of the American invasion, Zawahiri wrote that for a long time he had been very preoccupied with the problem of finding a secure base for jihad outside Egypt because that country's flat terrain made it inhospitable to underground guerrilla warfare: "the River Nile runs in its narrow valley between two deserts that have no vegetation or water. Such a terrain made guerrilla warfare in Egypt impossible and, as a result, forced the inhabitants of this valley to submit to the central government and to be exploited as workers and compelled them to be recruited into its army."[10]

Zawahiri notes that in the summer of 1980 his connection with Afghanistan began by a twist of fate. While in a colleague's clinic, he was asked to accompany him to Pakistan to tend to the Afghan refugees, who were fleeing by the thousands across the border because of the Russian invasion; Zawahiri writes that he "immediately agreed." He spent a few months in Peshawar, Pakistan, tending to the refugees and went back to Egypt full of heroic stories about the Afghan resistance. That experience, Zawahiri asserts, left its mark on his character and paved

the way for his 1986 return to Afghanistan, not just to provide medi-
cal care to suffering Afghanis but to rebuild and reorganize a network
of jihadist cells (which had received crippling blows from the Egyptian
authorities after the 1981 assassination of President Sadat) into a new
lethal paramilitary group – Islamic Jihad.[11]

Between 1986 and 1989 Zawahiri succeeded in making Islamic Jihad
a power to be reckoned with in the jihadist movement, thanks to the
new freedom and resources afforded to him in Afghanistan. Analysts
commit a common error by thinking that since the 1970s the Egyptian
Jihad Group existed as a unified organization; it did not. Former senior
and junior members told me that until the mid-1980s the Jihad group
included a motley crew of loosely linked cells and networks and did not
constitute a unified structure like its bigger sister, the Islamic Group.
Afghanistan enabled Zawahiri to mold and shape Islamic Jihad in his
own image and to unify it under his command. According to Hani al-
Sibai, a fugitive jihadi leader who knows Zawahiri and lives in exile in
Britain with a life sentence hanging over his head (the Egyptian government wants him repatriated), Zawahiri was greatly assisted in his efforts
to restructure and to make Islamic Jihad operational by enthusiasts from
the Gulf (Saudi Arabia, Kuwait, United Arab Emirates, and others) who
in the 1980s visited Afghanistan and contributed financially to jihad.[12]

The bottom line is that Zawahiri went to Afghanistan, as he noted, to
"establish a secure base from which to continue to wage jihad in Egypt,"
not against the United States, or even Israel. To this militant jihadi,
Afghanistan provided a political refuge, combat experience, and fresh
recruits of young Egyptians journeying to fight alongside their Afghani
coreligionists. Afghanistan also afforded Zawahiri an opportunity to
assert his leadership over Islamic Jihad by mobilizing, indoctrinating,
and leading his followers to do battle with the "apostate" regime in
Cairo. He could finally emerge out of hibernation and escape the powerful shadow of more charismatic fellow jihadis and lead the way forward.

In a book that is highly critical of Zawahiri, Montasser al-Zayat (who
in the early 1980s served time with Zawahiri in prison in the Sadat
assassination case and who has since become the best-known attorney defending jihadis and Islamists in Egyptian trials), asserts that by
going to Afghanistan Zawahiri hoped to establish an effective underground jihadist organization that could help him realize his dream of

overthrowing the loathed Egyptian government through a military coup d'etat. Zayat says that Zawahiri's experience in Afghanistan influenced him fundamentally and made him more ambitious and self-serving.[13] Despite his forced restraint, Zayat's personal testimony indicates that the Afghan experience had a transformative impact on Zawahiri and that power went to his head and distorted his vision and rationality. Keep in mind that Zayat and other former associates of Zawahiri, while heaping praise on the man for his commitment and dedication to the jihadist cause, are at a loss when trying to make sense of the dramatic shift in his thinking and action.

The Young Revolutionary

To understand the substance and depth of Zawahiri's metamorphosis after his departure to Afghanistan, it is critical to trace from the beginning his journey within the jihadist movement in Egypt. Traveling back in time with Zawahiri will shed light on the development, evolution, and changes in his ideas and actions. More than any other jihadi, Zawahiri knew that a frontal attack on the entrenched Egyptian state would not succeed and would likely end in defeat. Like his secular nemeses in the 1950s and 1960s (the young army officers who launched coups d'etat and destroyed the ancien regime and replaced it with a military dictatorship), he wanted to seize power through a military coup, which he perceived to be more effective and less costly than a prolonged head-on confrontation with the powerful security apparatus. He concentrated his efforts on infiltrating the armed forces and recruiting officers into his Jihad cell, creating a core of loyal jihadis in the military who, when conditions ripened, would rise up and destroy the secular order. In 1981, after his arrest in the Sadat assassination case, an Egyptian security interrogator quizzed him on how he planned to topple the government. "By an armed coup and with collaboration by civilians and the military," Zawahiri retorted.[14]

Unlike other jihadis, who were reckless and impatient and could not wait to pick a fight with the regime, Zawahiri believed that the struggle was bound to be prolonged and costly and that jihadis would need staying power and stamina for the long haul. According to former comrades and associates, he opposed rushing into armed clashes with the state or falling into its trap. He thought it was better to concentrate on building and consolidating jihadist cadres and to deepen links and connections with the military. Notice the absence of any strategic blueprint to mobilize the youth and harness their political energy and passion. Zawahiri seemed to be uninterested in social and political mobilization, because such a course of action would have required bargaining, give-and-take, and open participation in the political process.[15] In his memoir released after September 11, Zawahiri indirectly acknowedged this structural flaw by calling on jihadis to integrate, not separate or disconnect, into society and mobilize and lead the ummah. The problem with Zawahiri's new thinking is that taking the war global, as bin Laden and Zawahiri and their associates have done, is not one of the ummah's prioritities, and transnationalist jihadis never consulted the ummah about such a dangerous undertaking. The shift from localism to globalism is bound to complicate, not ameliorate, jihadis' relations with ordinary Muslims, who have paid dearly for the former's infatuation with violent change.

None of Zawahiri's contemporaries remember him as a political or religious activist. Zawahiri did not even use the mosque for recruiting and mobilizational purposes, only as a meeting place for his cell. The politics of the underground shaped his character. He had no faith in normal political processes, and he relied exclusively on subversive means to overthrow the secular system. He was an underground revolutionary who secretly plotted against the Egyptian regime by trying to infiltrate its most powerful institution, the army, and recruiting and coopting Islamist-leaning junior officers into his militant network. His colleagues say that in his eyes, the military represented the fastest and easiest means to capture the state, and to do so only required meticulous planning, organization, and a deep penetration into the officers corps.[16]

In several private conversations, a former leader of an Islamic Jihad cell, Kamal al-Said Habib, who played a key operational role in the assassination of Sadat, confided to me that living underground is not just politically "unhealthy" but it also distorts reality and leads to hasty and reckless decisions. In a way, Habib, who spent ten years in an Egyptian prison and who learned the pitfalls of an underground life the hard way, was describing the predicament and existential crisis of the whole jihadist movement, not just of Zawahiri.

For most of his life, Zawahiri hibernated under the surface and plotted methodically to rid Egypt of its secular government. In 1967, as a fifteen-year-old in a high school in Ma'adi, Cairo, he established an underground cell, Jama'a al-Jihad, or Jihad Group, which was subsequently absorbed into Tanzim al-Jihad. In his memoir, Zawahiri wrote that his decision to go underground and to target the near enemy (the Egyptian regime) was inspired by the 1966 hanging and martyrdom of Sayyid Qutb, whom jihadis in general, including Zawahiri and bin Laden, view as the founding father of the contemporary jihadist movement. Far from stifling the Islamic revival, Zawahiri said that the killing of Qutb and the brutal crackdown by the Nasserist regime were "the first spark to ignite the jihadist movement in Egypt against the government."[17] He recruited a few classmates and some of his best friends. Although it was only a tiny amateur operation, the Jihad Group was one of the first jihadist cells in the Arab world and a harbinger of bigger things to come. Unlike the Military Technical Academy group led by Salah Sirriya and the al-Takfeer wal-Hijra (Excommunication and Hegira, or the Society of Muslims) headed by Shukri Mutafa in the early 1970s, Zawahiri's al-Jihad remained underground and did not go operational. But Sadat's assassination, which Zawahiri reportedly did not fully endorse but did provide tactical assistance for, exposed his jihadist links and connections and let the Egyptian authorities in on his long-held secret.

Former associates who knew Qutb well and who spent time in prison with him in the early 1980s, say that he, more than any other religious or political figure, shaped Zawahiri's mind-set and led him on this dangerous path. Zawahiri also told his colleagues that he felt a sense of "shame and humiliation" for Israel's 1967 defeat of the Arabs, one that Islamists and jihadis ascribed to the absence of the Shariah from government. In his memoir, Zawahiri notes that the Arab naksa, or setback, "added a dangerous factor that influenced the awakening of the jihadist movement."[18]

Unlike other jihadis, who were in a hurry to rise up against the state, Zawahiri displayed resilience and cunning. He warned his jihadist counterparts to be patient, not to be provoked, to prepare for D-Day, and to remain focused on the big prize – infiltrating the military and using it as a vehicle to seize power and Islamize state and society from the top down. Throughout his memoir, Zawahiri recounts specific historical incidents and events in which he tried to dissuade his associates from rushing into military action without taking into account the operational and strategic contexts. He sounds like a shrewd calculator and patient operator. But because Zawahiri shunned political participation and activism, his ideas did not register on jihadis' radar screen. Jihadis, mostly young men in their twenties and thirties, were restless and in a hurry to impose a strict uniform morality consistent with their Islamic utopia regardless of the costs incurred. They were less concerned with the questions of how and when and of the means and the tools and the internal balance of power than with taking immediate and swift action against ruling apostates.

When in October 1981 Zawahiri was informed about a plot by a few jihadist cells to kill President Sadat and incite a public uprising, he reportedly shrugged his shoulders and said that this action had not been properly thought through: "In fact, I was astonished and shaken," Zawahiri told his interrogators. He did not think that jihadis, on their own, could resist the regime's security apparatus, let alone overthrow it. According to Zayat, the Islamist attorney, who was imprisoned with Zawahiri, the latter told him he hadn't wanted the assassination to take place because he thought "they [jihadis] should have waited and plucked the regime from the roots through a military coup." That would have been swifter and less costly in blood, he added.[19]

Zawahiri correctly feared that jihadis' revolt would be drowned in bloodshed and would fail. Zayat quotes Zawahiri to show that he was not as "bloodthirsty" as the post–September 11 narrative portrays him to be. The truth, however, is that Zawahiri's ambivalence about the use of force had more to do with efficacy and probability of success than with any moral qualms obout doctrinaire jihadist ideology in its nascent formative phase. Other jihadis belatedly arrived at a similar conclusion. Kamal al-Said Habib told me that luck played a crucial part in killing Sadat, and that his group was far from equipped to topple the Sadat regime and establish a viable Islamic government. This fact became clear to Kamal and other members of his generation (many of whom I have interviewed since the late 1990s) after spending years in prison and reflecting on their reckless conduct and violent deeds. Jihadis with whom I talked now appear to appreciate the futility and high cost of using blood and iron to remake society in their image, even though they do not critically and philosophically question the morality of transforming state and society by force.

In fact, according to a senior lieutenant in the Egytian Islamic Group, Osama Rushdi, who also spent time in prison with Zawahiri, after being imprisoned, Zawahiri and his cohorts dissolved their jihadist cell and he reportedly uttered his famous statement: "We have been defeated."[20] Zayat agrees with Rushdi's conclusion. In his recently published diaries, Zayat writes that in 1984 he met his former cellmate in a courtroom and recounts a conversation in which Zawahiri informed him that he was leaving for Afghanistan soon, and that he feared that the aggressive conduct by the Islamic Group would lead to a confrontation with the authorities. "All leaders are in prison," Zayat remembers Zawahiri telling him, "and there are no leaders left to see the jihadist project through. My program is secret and my journey is not with you."[21] So when in the mid-1980s Zawahiri embarked on his Afghan voyage, he did not seem poised to declare war on either the near enemy or the far enemy. He indirectly conceded, by words and deeds, that the Sadat assassination had reinforced his belief that only a swift military coup, not jihadis' armed skirmishes with local rulers, is the most effective means to replace jahiliya (state of ignorance) with hakimiya (God's sovereignty).

But the prison years left deep scars on Zawahiri and changed him forever – making him a man on a revenge mission. In their attempt to make sense of Zawahiri's subsequent descent into confrontation with the Egyptian regime, his former associates say that ultimately the prison experience, particularly abuse and torture, had a lasting effect on his future conduct. After his release in 1984, one would have expected Zawahiri, as he told his prison mates, to have become disillusioned with jihadis' blind recklessness and dismal failure to weigh benefits and costs. He paid dearly for their miscalculation and spent three years in hard labor, not to mention being tortured and forced under harsh interrogation by security officers to betray the closest members of his Jihad cell and to reveal their identities.

In his memoir, Zawahiri writes about the "humiliation" of imprisonment and how the mujahid (Islamic fighter), under torture, is forced to betray his comrades and destroy his movement with his own hands. Torture was not just physically and psychologically brutal, Zawahiri says, but it included particularly degrading and shocking methods in a traditional conservative Muslim society, such as locking up women, sexual violation, and humiliating men by giving them female names. He also argues that the widespread torture of young jihadis marked another bloody chapter in the history of their contemporary movement and poured more fuel on their raging fire. According to Zayat, who observed Zawahiri closely in prison and afterward, Zawahiri could not forgive himself for betraying close comrades to his official tormentors.[22] In my conversations with former jihadis, many said they were tortured in prison, and that far from breaking their spirit and will, torture stiffened their resolve and filled them with rage.

To keep the story short, Zawahiri left prison a hardened man with even more grievances against the Egyptian regime than when he went in. He could not forgive and forget those secular Muslim authorities that, in his words, inflicted pain and humiliation on believers at home, like himself and other associates, while forsaking their fundamental duty to defend the homeland against foreign enemies. According to the version advanced by Zawahiri's former associates, a thirst for vengeance took hold of his soul. He became more convinced than ever that overthrowing the near enemy must take priority over everything else; ending secular tyranny at home was a prerequisite for freeing the ummah from its bondage and empowering it to resist external aggression.

After the Egyptian authorities had exposed his secrets and plots, Zawahiri could not stay in Egypt, particularly if he still wanted to subvert the existing order. Accordingly, in 1986 he says he emigrated to Afghanistan to rebuild Tanzim al-Jihad and prepare anew to overthrow the Egyptian regime. Everything else paled in comparison with this goal, including the Afghan jihad itself and the more theoretical ambition of expanding the armed struggle against the far enemy, which was not even in his thoughts yet.[23] Zayat, the Islamist attorney, recounts another encounter with Zawahiri in 1986 after Zawahiri had left Egypt and worked in Saudi Arabia for a year – from 1985 to 1986 – just before he moved permanently to Afghanistan. Zayat says that Zawahiri's views had hardened regarding Islamic Group's stance and he reiterated his conviction that a military putsch is the way to proceed rather than a direct clash with the authorities; Zawahiri also said his migration to Afghanistan would be temporary, to prepare the ground for a military takeover in Egypt. Zayat adds that Zawahiri mentioned he had met bin

Laden in Saudi Arabia and did not utter a word about attacking the United States: "but he did talk about the liberation of Palestine, saying the road to Palestine goes through Cairo!"[24]

There is nothing new or original in Zayat's first-hand account because as late as the mid-1990s Zawahiri's pronouncements and actions remained focused on the near enemy and had not shifted to targeting the far enemy. As I have stressed before, the shift from local jihadism to global jihadsim occurred in the late 1990s. But what Zayat's personal diaries do is to show that by the second half of the 1980s Zawahiri had not critically reflected on the far enemy, let alone contemplated a direct confrontation with it; even Israel was not a priority because, as he put it, the liberation of Cairo takes precedence over everything else. Therefore, as soon as he arrived in Afghanistan in 1986, the cold, calculating, and patient underground revolutionary openly plotted his revenge in the mountains and valleys of Afghanistan. The Afghan jihad, as he makes clear in his memoir, supplied him with an operational cover and considerable resources to wage war against enemy number 1: the secular Egyptian government.

However, Zawahiri appears to have fallen into the deadly trap against which he had warned other jihadis earlier: rushing into an uneven fight against the Egyptian authorities and using "shock tactics." Thus he lost sight of one of his key strategic principles – infiltrating the military – as the most effective means to overthrow the regime from within.[25] It is not convincing to argue, as some jihadis and their apologists do, that while in Afghanistan Zawahiri could not control his zealous foot soldiers and lieutenants, who were anxious to do battle against the "apostate" regime in Cairo.[26] Zawahiri is portrayed as being swept away by this powerful tide without being able to stop or control it. Nonsense! By the early 1990s, after Zawahiri finished reorganizing and rebuilding Islamic Jihad, far from restraining his followers, he sent waves of fighters from Afghanistan, Yemen, Sudan, and elsewhere to retaliate and attack official targets inside and outside Egypt. According to Zayat, these insurgency operations were an extension of Zawahiri's broad strategy to destabilize the Egyptian government.[27] The Afghan experience emboldened Zawahiri and other jihadis, who launched an all-out offensive against Muslim rulers because they hoped that the entire ruling structure would collapse under their heavy blows. Power led them to miscalculate monstrously; for instance, Zawahiri boasted that "the Afghan arena, especially after the Russians had withdrawn, became a staging theater of jihad against renegade [Muslim] rulers who allied themselves with the foreign enemies of Islam."[28]

Former jihadis with whom I talked blame the military escalation in the early 1990s on Arab regimes that, they claim, provoked them and forced them into an uneven and unfair fight. But this rationalization misses the big point: jihadis' dismal failure to correctly assess the internal balance of power and their relative weight and capability vis--vis the state apparatus. Surely, Arab and Muslim rulers, who mastered the art of political survival, could not wait for the jihadis' gathering storm to attain full speed. They had a vested interest in preempting the rising threat. The question is not whether government security agencies provoked jihadis into retaliation, which they did, but rather why the latter fell into their trap. And what was the jihadis' own responsibility in this violent drama?

Psychologically, jihadis had been fully prepared to rise up against the ruling elite, whom they viewed as un-Islamic and morally corrupt and bankrupt; they believed that existing Muslim rulers had committed kufr (impiety) and therefore were illegitimate. But this tendency is a product of a deeply entrenched takfeeri (the practice of excommunication of Muslims) ideology whose roots were sowed by Sayyid Qutb in the 1960s and blossomed operationally, particularly in Egypt, in the 1970s. It all began with Qutb, who claimed that both Muslim society and politics had forsaken hakimiya (God's authority) and fallen into jahiliya (ignorance of divine authority). This jahili state must be righted by any means, including migration, severing of links from family and society, and the use of force. In the early 1970s Shukri Mustafa was one of the first Egyptian militants who tried to operationalize this takfeeri tendency (too ready to excommunicate Muslims) by preaching uzla, or withdrawal from society, and leading his al-Takfeer wal-Hijra group on a violent journey that culminated in its annihilation and his own execution. The takfeeri ideology has colored jihadis' worldviews not only of the non-Muslim other but also of the nonjihadi Muslim; they have set themselves on a higher pedestal as the absolute moral police armed with a literal interpretation of the sacred texts and determined to impose this raw, textualist interpretation on state and society.

For example, leading Islamists and some of Zawahiri's former associates accuse him of being a takfeeri. A close reading and study of Zawahiri's writing and career, particularly after he arrived in Afghanistan in 1986, show him to have fully embraced the takfeeri ideology and used it against Muslims, not just rulers, who have a different take on the sacred texts (see his attack on the Muslim Brothers, discussed later). In an informative testimony on the influences that shaped Zawahiri's Tanzim al-Jihad, Osama Rushdi (in charge of al-Jama'a al-Islamiya's media or propaganda committee and a former member of its Shura Council; Holland granted him political asylum) writes that the most dangerous changes that occurred during the Afghan jihad years, were doctrinal. In particular, Rushdi ascribes the descent of Islamic Jihad into a takfeeri path to the role played by Dr. Abdel Aziz bin Adel Salam (known as Dr. al-Sayyid Imam), one of Zawahiri's oldest associates and a founder of the Tanzim who from the late 1980s until 1993 was its emir and who published an influential book titled *Al-Umdah fi Idad al-Uddah* (*The Main Issues in the War Preparation*) in 1989.[29]

In *Al-Umdah*, Sayyid Imam wrote that Muslims who do not join the fight against "apostate" rulers are themselves "impious" and must be fought. According to Rushdi, the effects of this blanket takfeeri judgment was devastating because it supplied justification for militants everywhere, particularly in Algeria, to commit attrocities against civilians, including women and children, in the name of defending the faith. In the mid-1990s the Algerian Armed Group and its supporters utilized *Al-Umdah* to issue fatwas sanctioning the killing of tens of thousands of civilians because they had stayed on the side lines in the unfolding civil war in the country. "Therefore, the takfeeri discourse authenticized by Dr. Sayyid Imam was operationally translated in the real world," Rushdi sadly concluded.[30]

In 1993 jihadis say that Sayyid Imam resigned his official duties in protest against Zawahiri's rush to armed confrontation with the Egyptian authorities; Sayyid Imam was of the opinion that the Tanzim or Islamic Jihad should focus on recruiting competent cadres within the military and wait until conditions ripened for a swift coup d'etat. His idea sounds like that of the old Zawahiri. Ironically, Sayyid Imam lectured Zawahiri, who had previously warned his associates against a direct clash with the state, on the need to show patience and restraint in the face of provocation by the Egyptian regime. Zawahiri had traveled a long journey and had been transformed by the Afghan experience.

Although in 1993 Sayyid Imam severed his official links with Islamic Jihad and concentrated on writing books that surpassed *Al-Umdah* in militancy, his takfeeri ideas fertilized Islamic Jihad's soil and left their imprint on other jihadis as well. The takfeeri ideology gained a large following among leading jihadis, including Zawahiri, bin Laden, Abu Hafs, and Abu Ubaidah. For a long while, jihadis thought that Zawahiri, not Sayyid Imam, authored *Al-Umdah*, a testament to the fertilization of ideas among jihadis and the radical transformation of Zawahiri.[31]

Therefore, jihadis played a pivotal part in igniting the spark that lit regional fires in the early 1990s. They were not innocent bystanders and victims of the brutality perpetrated by the state security apparatus. Although the latter had blood on its hands, jihadis also let themselves be provoked because they had been eager to wage jihad against "renegade" rulers. The challenge facing jihadis was how to exercise restraint and show wisdom, which were in short supply, in the face of official provocation. No, the battle was not forced on jihadis against their will. They welcomed the opportunity to flex their military muscle and escalated the confrontation by targeting not only "jahili leadership" but also "jahili society," including secular intellectuals, liberal practices and sensibilities, the tourist sector, and, in the Algerian case, the Muslim community at large.

Long before the outbreak of hostilities between jihadis and Muslim rulers in the early 1990s, the former, particularly Egyptians, Algerians, Saudis, Yemenis, Libyans, and Pakistanis, trained and readied themselves in Afghanistan for the inevitable clash against local apostates. The Afghan war was a rehearsal for the real battle to come, against the near enemy, not the far enemy. Senior jihadis with first-hand knowledge note that throughout the 1980s thousands of volunteers flooded to Afghanistan to gain experience and learn insurgency techniques to subvert the existing order back at home. (Those militants should not be confused with ordinary Muslim volunteers who went to Afghanistan to partake in a sacred duty to defend Muslim land from external aggression.) In other words, jihadist leaders – particularly Zawahiri, Sayyid Imam, Abu Hafs, Seif al-Adl (a field lieutenant who in 2001 succeeded Abu Hafs as Al Qaeda's defense minister), and many others – viewed Afghanistan as preparation for this more important fight to come.[32]

The Rivalry Among Jihadis

Not all jihadis thought alike and acted in unison, however. Far from joining ranks and pooling their resources in the 1980s and 1990s, jihadis were deeply splintered and segmented along charismatic personalities and regional affiliations, not institutional hierarchies and ideologies. There existed considerable competition and rivalry among various jihadist factions, whereby each set up its own shop and guest houses and tried to recruit more men and expand further. Rhetoric aside, jihadis lacked unity and possessed separate local identities and differing goals. There existed no jihadist superstructure with a well-delineated program and leadership representative of the diverse shades of opinion within the movement. Throughout the 1980s and 1990s, the most common thread unifying jihadis was the priority assigned to expelling the Russian invaders from Afghanistan and fighting the near enemy. But there was little else on which jihadis could agree, especially in terms of tactics and strategies needed to replace "jahili leadership" with hakimiya, or God's sovereignty and an acceptable qualified leadership to unite them in a common front to further the jihad cause.

The irony is that if jihadis could not jointly collaborate against their common near enemy, how would they be able to administer and interpret divine authority on earth? It is one thing to say, as all jihadis do, that God's law and rule must be made supreme. It is another to translate this moral ideal into concrete political currency. In this life, there is no escaping from human agency and sociopolitical contestation. In my interviews with former jihadis since 1999, they conceded that they were institutionally and politically unequipped to govern and to build viable Islamic states and societies. They said they were socialized into an underground paramilitary existence and fully preoccupied with seizing power at all costs. They hardly reflected on the morning after and the complex requirements of governance and economic planning.[33]

Furthermore, jihadis' prolonged costly confrontation with government security agencies led to their further splintering and fragmentation. Short periods of cooperation and coordination were the exception to the rule; separate, unilateral actions were the norm. The two largest jihadist movements in Egypt and Algeria are cases in point. Throughout the 1980s and 1990s, all attempts to merge and unify Egyptian Jihad and Islamic Group failed because of the unwillingness and inability of their senior leaders to put personal differences aside and transcend vested interests. There also existed hidden regional and social differentiations between the rank and file of the two groups that impeded efforts at merger and unification. Like their secular nemesis, jihadis could not overcome the urban-rural divide (Cairo versus Upper Egypt), which cast its divisive shadow over their conduct and actions.

For example, in the early 1980s discussions about unification among the incarcerated leaders of Egyptian Jihad and Islamic Group ended in disagreement over whether sheikh Omar Abdel Rahman (often called the "Blind Sheikh" in the United States, he is serving a life sentence for his role in the 1993 plot to bomb major New York landmarks, including the Holland and Lincoln tunnels, which was disrupted by the FBI) was eligible and qualified to serve as the spiritual guide of Islamic Group. Jihadis who were in prison then say that Zawahiri and the Jihad Group contingent vehemently opposed wilayat al-darir, or "rule of the blind," on operational and doctrinal grounds. Although they respected Abdel Rahman, who shared their worldview regarding the centrality and primacy of rising up against the near enemy, Zawahiri and his associates did not think that the sightless sheikh could navigate the labyrinth of underground insurgency activities and lead the jihadist movement to victory.

Regardless of the pros and cons of wilayat al-darir, the fact remains that jihadis failed to close ranks during one of the most difficult moments in their history: killing Sadat in 1981 and then being brutally suppressed by the Egyptian authorities. Facing the powerful might of the state and an existential threat to their survival, one would have expected jihadis' incarcerated leaders to rise to the challenge and put aside their petty personal and ideological differences and unite. Centrifugal forces proved to be more insurmountable than combining the power would have been. In his diaries, Zayat, who was in prison in the Sadat case and who witnessed petty quarrels and rivalries among incarcerated jihadis, draws an unsavory picture whereby tribal and regional biases superseded religious-nationalist loyalties and poisoned the atmosphere. Even sheikh Abdel Rahman, the emir of al-Jama'a al-Islamiya, acccording to Zayat, who was a member of al-Jama'a, was not immune to this deadly disease; at one point he says despite his admiration and respect for the sheikh he felt obliged to disagree with his judgment because "that would have meant the return of al-jahiliya 14 centuries after it vanished."[34]

In the 1990s leaders of Islamic Jihad and Islamic Group transferred their intense rivalry to the Afghan theater. Hani al-Sibai, an Islamist insider with access to jihadis, tells the story of how attempts to unify the two organizations fell victim to mutual suspicion and the cult of personality. Top leaders feared loss of control if the merger occurred, he confides.[35] But by the end of the 1990s, as jihadis met defeat at the hands of the government security apparatus in Egypt, Algeria, and elsewhere, turf infighting and internal rivalry escalated into a tug-of-war. The rise of Al Qaeda was a direct product of military defeat and internal mutation within the jihadist movement.[36]

Similarly, in the 1990s Algerian jihadis did not fare better than their Egyptian counterparts. The Armed Islamic Group (GIA) in Algeria, one of the most radical jihadist networks in the Muslim world, fractured into several factions and descended into internecine warfare. Emirs of differing extremist persuasions and various regions hunted and butchered one another and committed hideous massacres against civilians, government officials, and foreign nationals. The sad tale of Egyptian jihadis pales when compared with that of the Algerians. In contrast to Egypt, the prolonged confrontation in Algeria, which broke out in the early 1990s, was more of a civil war than a clash between jihadis and the secular state. The ruling elite, not just the jihadist network, was itself fragmented, and it cultivated Islamists and militants in its curiously violent internecine games.[37]

Thus it is misleading to view jihadis through the narrow lens of September 11. The jihadist universe was – and is – ripe with internal strife and rivalry. Although jihadis do not like to hang their dirty laundry in public, they tend to be as prone to infighting and power struggles as other local and international political forces. In a parallel way, the infighting among jihadis bears a strong resemblance to the intense power struggle and tensions that tore the revolutionary European world apart. Viewing jihadism in this comparative light helps to dilute the specificity of this political phenomenon as a way of raging against "the system." There is nothing unique about the jihadist movement, which has much in common with similar-minded social-political and paramilitary organizations in the Muslim world and elsewhere.

Since the advent of jihadism into the Muslim political scene in the 1970s, jihadis have been divided along charismatic personalities and minor ideological points. Like their secular, nationalist, and socialist nemeses, jihadis proved to be vulnerable to the cult of personality and regional and socioeconomic segmentation. Scores of recently published primary documents in Arabic show multiple fault lines tearing jihadist groups apart. Although jihadis often attempt to mask internal disagreements in doctrinal terms, the direction of contemporary jihadism can be seen as primarily coming out of power positioning, personality clashes, and ethnic and nationalist differences (I will elaborate on this conceptual point in subsequent chapters).

For example, neither the shift from localism to globalism nor the emergence of Al Qaeda can be fully understood without contextualizing the complex relationship among Osama bin Laden, Ayman Zawahiri, Abu Ubaidah al-Banshiri (who drowned in Lake Victoria in 1996), Mohammed Atef (also known as Abu Hafs al-Masri, military chief of Al Qaeda until his death by an American air bombing in November 2001 in the Afghan city of Jalalabad), and other charismatic personalities, such as sheikh Abdullah Azzam, spiritual guru of the Afghan Arabs, including bin Laden (more on this later). In his diaries, Abu al-Walid al-Masri, a senior member of Al Qaeda's Shura Council and its leading theoretician, said that bin Laden used the organization as his own tribal fiefdom and everyone "carried out his orders faithfully and with bitterness," although everyone knew their leader was leading them to the "abyss"; he stood above the rest and the hawks and doves competed for his ear and attention. In the end, Abu al-Walid, who participated in Al Qaeda's decision making, adds that bin Laden did not listen to either camp and had his whims and illusions validated by pliant associates: bin Laden's cult of personality proved to be "catastrophic" to Al Qaeda, the Taliban, and the ummah.[38]

Another related fault line within Al Qaeda revolved around ethnic and nationalist differences, which led to infighting and rivalries among its members. A common complaint voiced by many was that the Egyptian contingent around bin Laden was dominant and controlled most of the key sensitive committees in the organization. In his diaries, Nasir Ahmad Nasir Abdullah al-Bahri (known as Abu Jandal), bin Laden's "personal bodyguard" and senior lieutenant, concedes he often had to intervene and mediate among various nationalist groups within Al Qaeda. According to al-Bahri, bin Laden was troubled by the depth of the nationalist gulf and feared that his enemies would sow divisions and disagreements among his followers. Non-Egyptian members resented the dominance of their Egyptian counterparts and occasionally implored bin Laden to rectify the imbalance. Although bin Laden gently reminded operatives and lieutenants that they were all Muslims contributing to "the cause of God," al-Bahri's narrative showed clearly that his boss labored hard to recruit Saudis, Yemenis, and others from the Arabian Peninsula to counterbalance the "hegemony" of the Egyptians.[39]

In a revealing question-and-answer exchange from the U.S. court testimony of Jamal Ahmad al-Fadl, an Al Qaeda operative from Sudan who in 1996 defected to the United States because of financial disagreements with the organization, the issue of the "hegemony" of the Egyptians was highlighted as being very divisive. It is worth quoting in full the exchange between al-Fadl and the government attorney in order to shed light on the importance of nationalist rivalries among Al Qaeda members (although al-Fadl's English is poor and grammatically flawed, it is quoted here without correction):

Q. Did the people within Al Qaeda, people in Al Qaeda who were not Egyptian, ever complain about the number of Egyptians who were in Al Qaeda?
A. Yes.
Q. When did that occur?
A. The first time happened when we are in Peshawar in Pakistan.
Q. And where was it discussed?
A. I remember in a guest house we got meeting with Abu Ubaidah al-Banshiri and Osama bin Laden and Abu Hafs al-Masri.
Q. Abu Ubaidah al-Banshiri, you mentioned Osama bin Laden and Abu Hafs al-Masri. Abu Ubaidah al-Banshiri, was he part of the Jihad group [Zawahiri's]?
A. Yes.
Q. Abu Hafs al-Masri, was he part of the Jihad group?
A. Yes.
Q. What was said when the peple complained about how many Egyptians were members of Al Qaeda?

A. I remember we tell bin Laden and we tell Abu Hafs on the way to
– we told them –

Q. The reporter didn't hear what you said.

A. We told Abu Ubaidah and Abu Hafs and bin Laden in that meeting
that the camp run by Egyptian people and the guest house, emir
from the guest house is Egyptian and everything Egyptian people
and from the Jihad Group, and we have people from Nigeria, from
Tunisia, from Siberia, why is Egyptian people got more chance than
other people run everything?

Q. Now the people you mentioned this to, you said Abu Ubaidah, Abu
Hafs, and bin Laden. What was their reaction to this comment?

Q. Did anyone say anything in response to that comment?

A. I talk.

Q. What did you say?

A. I say, I tell them the people complain about that, but the people
embarrassing to tell them, to tell you face-to-face, but most of the
people, they complain about that. And another guy, his nickname
Abu Tamim Libby, also he talk.

Q. And his name Abu?

A. Tamim Libby.

Q. What did Abu Tamim Libby say?

A. He say why everything run by Egyptian people?

Q. And did any of the three you mentioned before, bin Laden, Abu
Hafs, or Abu Ubaidah, say anything in response?

A. First, I remember bin Laden, he talk, and he say, we do that for
God and we shouldn't complain about that, and when the people,
the emir, the emir run the guest house or train them just because
he's good, he be emir because he responsible for that and we trust
him. If somebody from another nationality, he can run the camp,
nobody cared.[40]

As this exchange shows, Al Qaeda, like other bureaucracies, was sus-
ceptible to internal rivalries along ethnic, nationalist, and regional lines
and financial and petty quarrels stemming from favoritism and penny-
pinching. These issues are interesting for two reasons; first, they debunk
the notion that Al Qaeda is a unique organization whose members stand
above the fray of bureaucratic and political infighting, self-interests, and
jealousies. At the heart of members' resentment against the Egyptians
lies the fact that the latter managed Al Qaeda's expanding bureaucracy
and controlled key positions in the organization; they made choices and
decisions that affected the lives and well-being of hundreds of members.

Second, internal rivalries had an impact on the performance and security of this underground, paramilitary network; it was not just a theoretical question.

Documents obtained from captured Al Qaeda computers in Kabul, Afghanistan, immediately after the fall of the city show intense infighting among various jihadist factions, including Al Qaeda, and major security loopholes that could have handicapped the organization's paramilitary activities. For example, in 1998, fed up with Al Qaeda's penny-pinching and the uncertainties of life in the Islamist underground, a veteran Egyptian jihadi walked into the heavily guarded offices of Yemen's feared intelligence agency, the Political Security Organization, and disclosed the hiding places of foreign militants in Yemen. Keep in mind that in the 1980s and 1990s, Yemen served as a major operational base for Al Qaeda, Egyptian Islamic Jihad and Islamic Group, and other militants. Luckily for Al Qaeda, Yemen security services were infiltrated by bin Laden and his associates (more on jihadis' internal infighting in subsequent chapters).[41] Al-Fadl is a case in point. Before his defection in 1996, he was a trusted Al Qaeda operative who had performed critical functions in Pakistan, Sudan, the United States, and elsewhere. One of the reasons for his estrangement and defection from Al Qaeda, he claims, was that he felt he was not compensated fairly and justly, and that other members received much higher salaries than his own; accordingly, he scammed tens of thousands of dollars from Al Qaeda (he was a money carrier for the organization) and when he was caught and ordered to return the stolen funds, al-Fadl walked into an American embassy and offered his services. Regardless of the particular pieces of al-Fadl's case, it illuminates how socioeconomic issues projected and manifested themselves in a highly secretive, supposedly egalitarian structure. Al Qaeda could not overcome social reality, and its members were as ambitious, power-driven, and corrupt as members in other social and political organizations. Again, it is worth citing an exchange during the trial between al-Fadl and the U.S. attorney to drive this point home (original transcript preserved):

Q. When you were a member of Al Qaeda in Afghanistan, did the members of Al Qaeda in Afghanistan all receive the same amount of money or did the salaries vary?

A. No, there's a difference. Some people, they got more. Some people, they got a little.

Q. And that was in Afghanistan?

A. Yes.

Q. When you got to Sudan, were the salaries of Al Qaeda members the same for everyone or did they vary?

A. No, it's different.

Q. And did you ever have a conversation with anyone about the different salaries for Al Qaeda members in the Sudan?

A. Yes, we have discussions why is difference, why not all the same.

Q. Did you ever have a conversation with Osama bin Laden about the difference in the salaries for different members of Al Qaeda?

A. Yes.

Q. And did you talk to them about one person's salary in particular?

A. Yes.

Q. Can you tell the jury about your conversation with Mr. bin Laden?

A. When I tell him, some people complain because some people, they got high salaries, some people, they got a little and they want to know if we all Al Qaeda membership, why somebody got more than others?

Q. How much money were you making at the time that you had this conversation?

A. I made from Al Qaeda membership $300 and from Kahlid Ali Waleed around $200.

Q. And did you know of anyone who was making more money per month?

A. Yes. I know few people they make more money than me.

Q. Who were they?

A. Abu Hajer al-Iraqi and Abu Fadhl al-Makkee and Abu Abdullah Lubnani and other people.

Q. Why don't we stop there. First, just focusing on the word "Lubnani," does that mean the person is from a particular place?

A. Yes, he's Lebanon.

Q. Can you tell us how much was Abu Hajer al-Iraqi making at the time?

A. It's around $1500

Q. And how much was Abu Fadhl al-Makkee making at the time?

A. I don't remember now, but I believe more than Abu Hajer.

Q. How about Abu Abdullah Lubnani?

A. $800

Q. Can you tell us what you said to Osama bin Laden about those salaries compared to yours?

A. I tell him the people complain about that and myself, too, I complain about that.

A. I tell him the people complain about that, some members, they complain about that, and me, too, I say why not the members together that same salary.

Q. Now, Abu Abdullah Lubnani, do you know his true name?

A. Yes.

Q. What's that?

A. Wadih El Hage.

Q. What did Osama bin Laden say to you when you complained about the salaries of Abu Fadhl al-Makkee, Abu Hajer, and Abu Abdullah Lubnani?

A. He say some people, they traveling a lot and they do more work and also they got chance to work in the country. Some people, they got citizenship from another country and they go back over there for regular life, they can make more money than in group. And he says that's why he try to make them happy and give them more money.[42]

Like their junior counterparts, senior jihadist leaders also suffered from personal rivalries and jealousies. Take the case of Hassan al-Turabi, then head of the Islamic National Front, who in the early 1990s hosted bin Laden, Zawahiri, and their families and associates in Sudan and welcomed them as fellow revolutionaries. But far from showing appreciation to Turabi, who was maligned by the United States and its allies for turning Sudan into a terrorist den, bin Laden and Zawahiri do not buy the Western image of Turabi as an authentic revolutionary; they suspect him of being an overambitious politician influenced by corrupting Western ideas. In his memoir, bin Laden's senior personal bodyguard, al-Bahri, says that his boss blamed Turabi for his expulsion from Sudan in the mid-1990s:

So the ruling Islamic Front in Sudan, under the leadership of Dr. Hassan Turabi, asked sheikh Osama to leave the country. For bin Laden, al-Turabi was always a nuisance, although he was an Islamic thinker, contrary to President Omar Hassan al-Bashir, who displayed all the good Sudanese qualities of courage and help. He would not accept the pressure because he considered bin Laden his guest and a refugee in his country. As for al-Turabi, it seems that his studies at the Sorbonne and his previous political background had a great impact on him. So al-Turabi became the tool to pressure sheikh Osama to leave the country.

Bin Laden praises General Bashir, the military dictator of Sudan, and disparages Turabi, an "Islamic thinker," who could not be trusted. Asked if Turabi played any role in convincing the Bashir regime to expel bin Laden and his entourage, al-Bahri noted accusingly:

Al-Turabi himself exerted a great deal of pressure on sheikh Osama to make him leave Sudan. He visited him for three consecutive days, holding long meetings and heated discussions with him, until late at night, to convince him to leave Sudan. Sheikh Osama tried to convince him of the opposite: that there was no need to expel him, that they had not committed any armed acts against Sudan, and that there was no other country ready to receive them. But al-Turabi told him that he had two options: either to keep silent or to leave the country. He was very determined that bin Laden leave the country. That was when sheikh Osama decided to leave Sudan. He said: as long as many young men have been detained and imprisoned in Saudi Arabia and the Sudanese want me to keep silent, I will leave Sudan. He made arrangements with the Sudanese to leave the country with his followers and moved to Afghanistan.

And how was the personal relationship between bin Laden and Turabi? Al-Bahri said his boss did not care much for the Sudanese Islamist, who felt threatened by bin Laden's rising stardom within the jihadist movement worldwide:

Yes, there were some sensitivities between them. Their biggest problem . . . was sheikh Osama's practical program and his success in defeating the American forces in Somalia, in cooperation with the Somali Islamic groups. They also defeated the American troops in Sudan [what troops?], where Sudan was supposed to be the Americans' entrance to their control over Somalia and the whole Horn of Africa. That was why bin Laden's success in defending Sudan was a sensitive spot, which caused al-Turabi's jealousy. Al-Turabi relies mainly on theories. Maybe he was afraid sheikh Osama would take over the leadership of Sudan someday in the future, at his own expense, especially because bin Laden was at that point looking at Sudan as the backbone of the international Islamic movement, as an important extension of the Islamic movement in the Horn of Africa and East Africa, in general.

So much for Islamist and jihadist brotherhood and solidarity. In bin Laden's eyes, Turabi's "jealousy" explains his decision to expel him from Sudan. Whether that is true or false, that was how bin Laden, a Salafi, perceived Turabi, whose roots were in the Muslim Brotherhood. Behind a faade of Islamic solidarity lie clashes of personalities and personal ambitions. Islamists and jihadis are no different from other political actors except that personalities play a pivotal role in their politics and dynamics; more than their secular opponents, they failed to create formal institutions and fell victim to "autocratic" charisma. At the risk of exaggeration, the history of the Islamist and jihadist movements can be written through the lenses and actions of dozens of patriarchical leaders. I do not mean to suggest that intrajihadist rivalries hindered the ability of Al Qaeda to carry out its attacks; they did not. But internal fissures and rivalries prevented jihadis from creating a unified, cohesive movement that could have represented a strategic threat to regional and international security.

Differences and divisions existed not only among jihadis but also between the jihadis and mainstream traditional Islamists, particularly the Muslim Brotherhood. Jihadis looked with contempt and derision on mainstream Islamists, who seem to have accepted the rules of the game set by "apostate rulers." Throughout the 1970s and 1980s, a fierce rivalry between jihadis and mainstream Islamists played itself out on university campuses; this rivalry served as the bastion and springboard for the modern jihadist movement (originally called al-Jama'a al-Islamiya, or Islamic Group) on the streets, in mosques, and in Afghanistan.[43] Initially, young jihadis of Islamic Group trained in the summer camps organized by the Muslim Brothers, which included physical fitness, paramilitary skills, and religious indoctrination. They also collaborated at the university level against Nasserist and socialist elements.

But former jihadis who were present at the creation of their movement in the 1970s tell me that they were deeply suspicious of the Muslim Brothers' efforts to coopt them and recruit them into their powerful organization. Although many did join the Muslim Brotherhood and play an important role there, the overwhelming majority maintained their independence and were fiercely protective of their separate and more puritanical identity. Jihadis defined their religious mandate and role in direct opposition to mainstream Islamists, who were willing to participate in the political process and who eschewed the use of violence. Both camps whom I interviewed said they sometimes came to violent blows, with jihadis harassing the Muslim Brothers and attacking fellow students with clubs and sticks. They fought over the control of mosques in poor neighborhoods in Cairo, Upper Egypt, and elsewhere, and they competed for the same constituency. Of course, jihadis could not compete on an equal footing with mainstream Islamists, who were powerfully organized and possessed considerable resources. But what jihadis lacked in material assets and organizational skills, they made up for with dogged determination and fanaticism. They were as intolerant of mainstream Islamists as they were of nationalists and socialists, whom they harassed, intimidated, and marginalized, thanks to the early support lent by the authorities. The rivalry between mainstream Islamists and jihadis was as intense as that between jihadis and secularists. In fact, to discredit their Islamist rivals, jihadis accused them of being secular and beholden to the existing authorities. Two decades later, on both sides the wounds have not yet healed. A close study of the discourse and actions of both camps shows a widening gulf of mistrust and suspicion. The notion of a super-Islamist structure or a superjihadist structure is a myth that does not withstand the test of history. The intra-Islamist struggle has not received its share of critical scrutiny and its understanding is vital to shedding light on the inner dynamics and complexities of Islamist and jihadist networks.

Senior jihadis of the 1970s' generation acknowledge that they made mistakes and "slightly abused" the relative freedom of action afforded to them by the Sadat regime, even though they deny receiving any direct official support. They refer to this period (the late 1970s) as one of lost opportunity because they did not build up coalitions and alliances with other political forces and did not nourish a broad social base to provide them with a safe societal anchor. Some jihadis acknowledge they felt intoxicated with the allure of power and driven by an immature fervor that proved to be their undoing, even though they shy away from publicly admitting that. Otherwise, what are we to make of this going-it-alone mind-set that pitted jihadis against both the state and society? From their early days, the writing was on the wall.

The Afghan war did not reduce the tensions or the power struggle among jihadis, let along between jihadis and mainstream Islamists. For example, Egyptian Islamic Jihad and Islamic Group launched a vehement ideological and public relations campaign to discredit the Muslim Brothers, who were actively engaged in humanitarian and other activities in Afghanistan, and lump them together with the loathed ruling elite. In Peshawar, Pakistan, Islamic Jihad distributed a booklet written by its chief, Zawahiri, entitled "The Bitter Harvest, the Muslim Brotherhood in Sixty Years," in which he railed against democracy, a rival religion that must be resisted and defeated. Zawahiri went so far as accusing the Muslims Brothers everywhere, not just in Egypt, of blasphemy because, in his eyes, they "substituted the democracy of dark ages to God's rule [the Shariah] and gave up on jihad." He also claimed that mainstream Islamists sold out their faith to the corrupt secular regimes in return for partial recognition and participation in the sociopolitical process: "Know that democracy means 'government by the people,' which is a new religion founded on worshiping the people by authorizing them to legislate without being limited by any other authority," a reference to hakimiya (God's sovereignty). Likewise, Islamic Group circulated a manifesto criticizing the Muslim Brothers for saying that sovereignty resides in and stems from the people whose representatives could not even legislate. The manifesto accused the Brotherhood of substituting man's law for that of the Shariah, which is tantamount to being blasphemous.[44] Two points: first, witness the anger and rage in jihadis' critique of the Muslim Brotherhood, an Islamist organization that has given birth to the jihadist movement; and second, Zawahiri and his associates use the takfeeri ideology against their Islamist counterparts, not just "impious" rulers and secularists.

Those inflammatory tirades were not uttered in the heat of the Afghan battle, but they reflected a pattern of infighting, rivalry, and fragmentation within jihadist factions and between the latter and mainstream Islamists. In his memoir, Zawahiri goes further in his attacks on the Muslim Brotherhood and asserts that by accepting the rules of the political game and by being passive in the face of disasters befalling the ummah, it "sheds its heritage and turns into a new creature divorced from its origins and so indulged in the present moment that it loses its vision for the future."[45] Although they may prosper organizationally in the short term, Zawahiri adds, in the long term the Brothers are "definitely committing ideological and political suicide."[46]

What disturbs Zawahiri the most is that the Muslim Brothers did not heed his earlier warning about the dangers of ijtihad (an effort at interpretation of the sacred texts) – he derogatively refers to this as "new jurisprudence" – and have since committed even greater doctrinal errors and sins. Particularly shocking in his opinion is that the Muslim Brotherhood made public pronouncements giving equal citizenship rights to minorities. How dare the Muslim Brothers, Zawahiri admonishes, say that Egyptian Christians have the right to serve in all official positions except the presidency? And if they do, he adds sarcastically, "why not also have an Egyptian Jew be a prime minister? Are not there Jewish citizens in Egypt?" He hastens to add that the pronouncements by the Muslim Brothers are a publicity stunt and have nothing to do with high-minded principles, as they pretend.[47] The implication is that the Muslim Brothers are engaged in a public relations campaign to ingratiate themselves with the powers that be and that they are self-serving and cynical to the core. In his view, there can be no equality between Muslim citizens and non-Muslim citizens because the litmus test is not citizenship, a decadent liberal Western concept, but a selective puritanical scripturalist reading of the religious texts.

Zawahiri's stand raises alarming questions about the whole jihadist enterprise being divorced from Muslim reality. In his memoir, Zawahiri, a theoretician of jihadism, devotes an entire chapter to attacking the Muslim Brotherhood and refuting the notion that all citizens are equal before the law. He does not recognize, let alone accept, the emerging consensus on this issue among almost all mainstream Islamists and former jihadis, and it sounds as if he slept through two decades of important developments and debates among his coreligionists. His language and reasoning seem to be frozen in time and space, preaching and appealing to a dwindling number of converts who are removed from their familiar environment and have few ties with the dominant Islamic culture.

For the last three decades, the mainstream Islamist caravan has slowly been moving forward, while jihadis, like Zawahiri and his associates, go round and round in a circle. The jihadis have conceptually reached a

dead end and no longer possess radically original ideas of any consequence. On the whole, jihadis and their followers are subsisting on an
old stale diet that provides no intellectual or moral nourishment. This
partially explains why jihadis turned their guns against the far enemy
– and one another. The only vocabulary left in the jihadist dictionary
is paramilitary action. They try to compensate for the paucity of original ideas by marching to war. They seem to be making a last stand
against an alien world, including Muslim reality and society, that does
not fit into their narrow textualist reading of the sacred texts, one that
is detached and divorced from that of the Muslim community. In the
name of applying the Shariah and reclaiming identity and authenticity, jihadis lost the very people – those who possess different historical
sensibilities and understandings of Islamic law – whom they had originally struggled to emancipate. Thus the validity and authority of their
literal interpretation of the religious texts take precedence over Muslim
society and the Shariah as distilled by ulema throughout the centuries.

For example, in his critique of mainstream Islamists, Zawahiri does
not proffer any creative ideas or a new vision. He rehashes old arguments
and, as in the past, indicts the Muslim Brothers for their treachery and
opportunism. But now Zawahiri goes beyond polemics and declares all-
out war on the Muslim Brothers. He calls on their shabab, or young
members, to rebel against the traditional leadership, which abandoned
jihad, a vital pillar of Islam, and to "join their mujahedeen brethren
[jihadis] everywhere."[48] He tries to incite the shabab of the Brotherhood
by saying that Islam and Muslims are under attack, and that they, unlike
their passive and pliant elders, must redeem their honor and defend the
faith.

Thus Zawahiri adds the Muslim Brothers to his long shopping list
of enemies and sees no need to politically engage and negotiate with
the Muslim Brotherhood. War becomes the ultimate arbiter of differences and contradictions, even among religiously oriented groups; but,
as argued previously, it is a much bigger confrontation pitting jihadis
against Muslim reality, society, and traditional fiqh (jurisprudence). It
is a war of one against all. In Zawahiri's universe, the sounds and drums
of war drown everything else out because there is nothing left except
doing battle. This is a testament to the existential crisis in which jihadis
find themselves and of the paucity of ideas at their disposal.

The jihadis' attack on the Muslim Brotherhood, the oldest and most powerful Islamist organization in the world, shows clearly the extent of polarization, splintering, and fragmentation of Islamists and jihadis alike. The latter launched an onslaught not only against secular local rulers and their superpower patrons, but also against mainstream traditional Islamists, who theoretically could have been their allies. Jihadis viewed their mission in revolutionary terms as a struggle for the soul of Islam, not just for political office or power. In their eyes, there existed one truth and one Islam, and there is no room for compromise. Interests, classes, ideologies, and complexities were and are dismissed as products of either internal or external kufr and jahili leadership and jahili society. Jihadis, most of whom are deeply influenced by Sayyid Qutb's ideas of "eternal" jihad, advance permanent revolution as a magical wand to pluck the decadent system from its root and replace it with God's sovereignty.

Therefore, engagement and participation in the existing order tend to be seen as treachery, prolonging, not ending, the state of kufr. Part of Zawahiri's anger against the Muslim Brothers stems from the Brothers' decision to participate in the political process and to shun the use of violence. In his memoir, Zawahiri admonishes the Brothers for not living up to the legacy and courage of Qutb, who was a senior member of the Brotherhood, and for not exacting revenge for his execution by the Egyptian authorities in 1966. They are no longer worthy of Qutb's name, Zawahiri adds, because they bought into the very system that hanged him.

On the other hand, mainstream Islamists consider jihadis' insurgency at home and taking jihad global as counterproductive to the prospects of the Islamist movement and the interests of the Muslim ummah. In particular, the Muslim Brothers found themselves in a terrible bind between a rock – jihadis' accusations of selling out their faith and being in cahoots with authorities – and a hard place – governments' accusations of being in league with jihadis' violence. They faced a critical crisis of authority and credibility and a serious challenge to their hegemony. Being patriarchical and authoritarian, leaders of the Brotherhood did not respond swiftly to the threat posed by jihadis by publicly and vocally condemning their bloody deeds and actively resisting their propaganda. They buried their heads in the sand, hoping that the violent storm would pass by and leave them unscathed.

But there is more to the story than the Brotherhood's historical inertia and preference for inaction. The old patriarchs guiding – or misguiding – the Brotherhood reasoned that the jihadis' armed uprising would indirectly serve their own interests by making them appear moderate and enabling them to act as mediators, which they tried to do in the 1990s, between the besieged regime and the jihadist rebels. They also assumed that after the dust settled on the battlefield at home jihadis would see the folly of their ways and return to their senses by joining the Brotherhood like many of their earlier comrades had done. In Algeria, Egypt, and elsewhere, the Brotherhood patriarchs waited and hoped to cash in on the deadly confrontation between the ruling establishment and jihadis by providing a nonviolent mainstream Islamist alternative.

In 1999 and 2000 I interviewed the Brotherhood's two top senior sheikhs, Mustafa Mashour and Hassan Hudaibi, who vehemently denied a widespread perception that they cynically exploited the confrontation and tried to inherit the spoils. They insisted that they condemned jihadis' armed tactics in the strongest possible terms and that the government distorted their stand and lumped them together with the jihadis in order to undermine them and exclude them from the political space. In response to my questions regarding the lack of clarity and the ambiguity in their political pronouncements, they became defensive and dismissed all concerns and criticisms as official propaganda and unwarranted accusations and inventions. I detected no hint of self-criticism or soul-searching in their answers.

But there is no denying that leaders of the Brotherhood miscalculated and underestimated the resilience of entrenched Arab rulers and their determination to punish the Brotherhood for its supposed complicity with jihadis and to clip its wings. They also did not appreciate that jihadis could drag all Islamists, radical and mainstream alike, to the brink of annihilation. Nor did they fully recognize the gravity of jihadis' onslaught against the canon of Islamic fiqh and the religious authority.

For example, jihadis viewed the religious establishment as an extension of the secular ruling order and as serving at its pleasure and consent. A recurrent theme in jihadis' diatribes is the supposed complacency and collusion of the religious authority with the dominant political establishment. They challenge the very cozy relationship between mainstream religious clerics and authoritarian regimes and try to discredit the former in the eyes of pious and practicing Muslims. In his memoir,

Zawahiri lambastes the most senior and distinguished Islamic figure in Egypt (the country's grand mufti, Jad al-Haq), who was used by the authorities to legitimize their cruel sentences against Sadat's assassins. Jihadis were "butchered," thanks to al-Haq's fatwa, Zawahiri said sarcastically.[49]

Bin Laden used a more diplomatic tactic than Zawahiri's by saying that the religious establishment lost its voice and calling because it had been silenced and tamed by ruling "apostates" at home and their masters abroad. He bemoans the fact that "the fiqh of defeat" is prevalent in Muslim lands. Accordingly, bin Laden anointed himself a leader fighting on behalf of all Muslims and inciting young men to join in his global jihad "to lift the iniquity that had been imposed on the ummah."[50]

Compounding the difficulties of the religious establishment is that ulema (religious scholars) are often called upon to justify good government relations with the Western powers, particularly the United States. Given the widespread suspicions of American foreign policies in Arab and Muslim lands, jihadis' challenge of the religious authority becomes insurmountable, or at the very least difficult to overcome. The dependency of the former on the ruling elite makes the religious authority vulnerable to criticism by dissenters, including jihadis, and limits its influence and efficacy.

The truth is that at the moment the religious and ruling elites are two sides of the same coin, and both are responsible for the crisis and vacuum of legitimate governance in Muslim countries today. Religious scholars are unlikely to serve as a counterweight to militants as long as they are appointed by government officials and lack an independent anchor in civil society. Reforming conservative religious institutions is a much more complex process than instituting socioeconomic and political reforms, because it involves sensitive cultural questions and risks a popular backlash. It requires time, sensitivity, and a genuine national dialogue about the most effective means to empower ulema and redefine their functions and roles in society, but it is a vital undertaking that is worth the inherent risks.

An enlightened religious authority could prevent the hijacking of Islam by false prophets like bin Laden and Zawahiri, as well as shield it from political use and abuse by authoritarian rulers. Although a consensus exists on the first task – protecting religion from extremism and militancy – the debate on political manipulation and abuse of Islam has just begun. However, the two tasks are intertwined and cannot be separated, because the politicization of religion often serves as an incubator for militants and distorts and subverts religious and political sensibilities. The ruling elite is fundamentally responsible for the marginalization and dilution of the religious authority's influence. By making the latter an extension of the state bureaucracy, Muslim rulers softened civil society's defenses against the jihadist takfeeri tide.

Contrary to the conventional wisdom, there has been no Islamist or jihadist "Comintern," or "Islamintern" similar to that of international Communism that was set up after World War I in 1919. As the previous debates, tensions, and rivalries clearly show, Islamists and jihadis were deeply divided and estranged from one another. Equally important, since its inception in the 1970s, the modern jihadist movement fragmented along strong-willed personalities whose own priorities defined its agenda and direction. From the 1970s through the mid-1990s, a rough consensus existed among jihadis over the definition of jihad as a permanent and personal obligation (fard 'ayn); the primacy of confronting the near enemy, as opposed to the far enemy; and the need to fight and expel the Russian occupiers from Afghanistan. Yet despite these general agreements, jihadis could not unite in a common front and overcome their differences. They could not even agree on an authoritative leadership to navigate the jihadist ship in rough seas.

Like their secular nationalist and socialist foes, jihadis splintered into competing and rival factions, each of which waged its unholy war against local "apostates." Not even the Afghan war, which attracted thousands of jihadis from many Muslim countries and which represented the height of the jihadist moment, succeeded in bridging the personality and social and regional divides among the leaders. They preserved their separate organizational labels and identities and bickered over turf, recruits, and material resources.

The tug-of-war among jihadis in the 1970s and 1980s escalated into a civil war in the late 1990s. The clash of personalities hardened into doctrinal and ideological differences. As jihadis dispersed after the end of the Afghan war and as religious nationalists met their waterloo at their homefronts in Egypt and Algeria, the partial consensus that existed over fighting the near enemy shattered. The jihadist movement fractured horizontally and vertically, and by the end of the 1990s, it seemed to be a spent force politically and militarily.[51]

But a small coalition of jihadis, who spent years in Afghanistan, launched a systemic campaign to shift the direction of the movement away from localism to globalism; they wanted to salvage the sinking jihadist ship. Far from reflecting a new consensus, transnationalist jihadis, who internationalized jihad and who represented a minority within the movement, failed to coopt religious nationalists, an overwhelming majority, into their network – Al Qaeda. The latter's emergence marked a deepening and widening of the internal mutations within the jihadist movement and an acceleration and intensification of the strife between the transnationalist and religious camps.

THREE

The Rise of Transnationalist Jihadis
and the Far Enemy

The rise of transnationalist jihadis and the shift from localism to globalism cannot be understood without contextualizing the alliance between
two men, Osama bin Laden and Ayman al-Zawahiri, and the merging
of their resources and talents. The experience and character of these
two senior jihadis were complementary, and their combination was vital
in the internationalization of jihad. Retracing the jihadist journey of
bin Laden and Zawahiri and the evolution of their ideas and actions
over time and space will illuminate the dramatic changes that occurred
within the jihadist movement in the second half of the 1990s.[1]

Since September 11, memoirs, diaries, and interviews with jihadis
clearly point to the bin Laden–Zawahiri connection as the driving force
behind the formal birth of Al Qaeda and its strategic decision to take
jihad global. Although Zawahiri was not one of the three founders of Al
Qaeda – bin Laden, Abu Ubaidah al-Banshiri, and Abu Hafs – by the
second half of the 1990s he played a pivotal role in the rising network
and had developed a close partnership with bin Laden.[2] It is true that
after the drowning of Abu Ubaidah in Lake Victoria, Abu Hafs became
bin Laden's most trusted aide and defense minister, but Abu Hafs was
bin Laden's military man, with no militia of his own and no intellectual
or scholarly religious capital. In contrast, Zawahiri was leader of Tanzim
al-Jihad, one of the oldest and deadliest existing jihadist organizations,
and he became a leading theoretician of jihadism.

Recent primary accounts show that Tanzim al-Jihad members, who
were highly experienced militarily, trained and groomed bin Laden's
men in the art of war and underground subversion; Tanzim al-Jihad
was operationally integrated with the bin Laden network, long before

the establishment of Al Qaeda, so that it was difficult to separate Zawahiri's men from those of bin Laden. But there was more to the Zawahiri–bin Laden relationship than the military or finance angle. Testimony by jihadis indicates a relationship that was much more complex and dynamic than the banker-theoretician dichotomy described in the media, including recently published secondary monographs on Al Qaeda. It is a relationship of equals, although, ironically, bin Laden is the one who decisively influenced the ideological and operational direction of the jihadist movement based in Afghanistan. One would have expected Zawahiri, one of the most seasoned jihadis among bin Laden's cohort and a fervent believer in attacking ruling Muslim "renegades" (the near enemy), to sway the attitudes of his junior partner, bin Laden, and slow down the jihadist march against the United States (the far enemy).

Instead of trying to slow or redirect bin Laden's speeding jihadist caravan, Zawahiri wholeheartedly joined it and pressured the leaders of religious nationalist jihadis to defect to Al Qaeda. He even led a putsch within the religious nationalist camp and attempted to redirect the entire jihadist movement toward bin Laden's transnationalist path. In the late 1990s more than any other leader, Zawahiri fired the first shot in the intrajihadist battle and as a result, he widened the divide that already existed within the religious nationalist camp itself and between the latter and globalist jihadis.

As Chapters One and Two show, Zawahiri's case is fascinating – and puzzling as well. He spent a lifetime preaching the merits and necessity of targeting the near enemy, plotting and conspiring to overthrow the secular Egyptian government. From the late 1960s through the mid-1990s, Zawahiri was unequivocal in assigning the highest priority to overthrowing ruling Muslim apostates and rejecting any diversion of the struggle toward regional or international enemies. He invested considerable capital in the confrontation against the Egyptian authorities, and he never lost sight of the primacy and hierarchy of this goal. His heart was set on effecting radical change by violent means at home, not abroad in other countries.

Zawahiri traveled to Afghanistan in 1986 to rebuild the Jihad organization, with the aim of making it a power to be reckoned with on the Egyptian scene. He did not go to Afghanistan to internationalize jihad but rather to develop strategic plans to overthrow the pro-Western government in Egypt. Afghanistan was supposed to serve as a detour and a staging arena to nip at the edges of the Mubarak regime. Zawahiri's colleagues, who knew him well, say that his long-term goal was to infiltrate the Egyptian military and engineer a coup d'etat from within. He was willing to wait and to recruit Egyptian army officers to the Islamist cause. But by the end of the Afghan war in the late 1980s, Zawahiri, his former associates say, came under tremendous pressure from Islamic Jihad's rank and file to launch attacks in Egypt, and by the early 1990s he obliged. Young operatives, we are told, were impatient and dying to do battle and exact revenge against their tormentors, Egyptian authorities; they had the training and the will to take the fight into Egypt and did not want to wait years to make inroads into the military. According to this logic, Zawahiri was forced, against his best judgment, to carry out paramilitary operations against the Cairo government.

Whatever the rationale behind Zawahiri's decision to reactivate hostilities against the Egyptian authorities in the early 1990s, it was consistent with the basic principle of battling the near enemy to which he had subscribed since his early days underground. Former associates criticize his rush into armed confrontation with a superior foe and lament the fact that he did not continue to concentrate his efforts on infiltrating the military to engineer a coup d'etat. They also fault him for not learning from the mistakes made by Egyptian jihadis in the late 1970s and 1980s. But these associates reserve their harshest criticism for Zawahiri's alliance with bin Laden, and for the dramatic change in his worldview regarding the centrality and urgency of attacking the United States. They seem completely unable to account for the unexpected rupture in Zawahiri's thinking and action in the second half of the 1990s.

Zawahiri's former associates and jihadis whom I interviewed ascribe the revolutionary shift in Zawahiri's views and goals in the 1990s to his increasing financial dependence on bin Laden and bin Laden's overall influence on him. They draw a portrait of Zawahiri as being financially bankrupt and anxious to ensure the survival and independence of his organization, Tanzim al-Jihad; he was squeezed and cornered with nowhere to go and no sponsor to keep him afloat. They tell me that he had to take care of the "martyrs' families," particularly in Egypt, and pay the salaries of his lieutenants and foot soldiers. According to Hani al-Sibai, an alleged leader of the Jihad Group, who knows Zawahiri well and who resides in exile in Britain (the Egyptian government sentenced him to death), with the end of the Afghan war Zawahiri's financial health worsened because enthusiasts from the Gulf, who used to visit Afghanistan and donate millions of U.S. dollars to jihad, stopped their contributions. Zawahiri's Islamic Jihad faced a serious financial crisis that worsened with time. After Zawahiri and bin Laden left Sudan for Afghanistan in 1996, the former had no access to funds and was at the mercy of bin Laden, who controlled the purse strings.

This version of the story suggests that a causal link exists between Zawahiri's deteriorating financial situation and his dramatic shift toward bin Laden's worldview; in other words, this is an unusual case of interests being shaped by ideology. Material interests usually cause an actor to moderate his views and actions over time. In the Zawahiri case, the reverse happened; all one has to do, we are told, is to follow the money trail to understand the reasons behind Zawahiri's transformation from a religious nationalist to a transnationalist jihadi. There is no denying that the political economy of jihadism, including Zawahiri's organization, is vital to understanding its ebb and flow; like other soldiers, jihadis cannot march on empty stomachs. By the 1990s the stomachs of Zawahiri and his men were empty, and the soldiers took desperate measures to generate revenue. Junior and senior members of the organization residing in Yemen and the Gulf were told to find employment and send funds to hard-pressed families in Afghanistan and elsewhere. Many did, but the sums were paltry and could not feed, house, and support hundreds, let alone thousands, of families. Zawahiri had no choice, his former associates say, but to turn to bin Laden to bankroll Islamic Jihad and keep it afloat.

Indeed, internal documents obtained by reporters for *The Wall Street Journal* and *Asharq al-Awsat* from Al Qaeda computers in Kabul after the retreat of the Taliban show Islamic Jihad members in a terrible financial bind even after Zawahiri joined bin Laden's World Islamic Front in 1998. Money, or the absence of it, not plotting against internal and external enemies, dominated the correspondence between the headquarters in Afghanistan and various stations in Yemen, London, and elsewhere. Zawahiri constantly reminded members to tighten their belts and freeze spending and reprimanded those who accumulated high telephone bills or purchased new computer hardware. A starved organization could not afford such luxury items, he indirectly scolded the rank and file. In fact, Zawahiri's penny-pinching and strict financial oversight bred resentment and led to some resignations and even defections to the enemy side. The following exchange between Zawahiri and one of his operatives in Yemen throws light on the organization's desperate finances, which critically affected the performance and interaction of members with one another and with Zawahiri:

> To: Ezzat (real name unknown)
> From Ayman al-Zawahiri
> Folder: Outgoing Mail – To Yemen
> Date: February 11, 1999
> Noble brother Ezzat...
> Following are my comments on the summary accounting I received:
> ...With all due respect, this is not an accounting. It's a summary accounting. For example, you didn't write any dates, and many of the items are vague.
> The analysis of the summary shows the following:
> You received a total of $22,301. Of course, you did not mention the period over which this sum was received. Our activities only benefited from a negligible portion of the money. This means that you received and distributed the money as you please...
>
> 1. Salaries amounted to $10,085 – 45 percent of the money. I had told you in my fax...that we've been receiving only half salaries for five months. What is your reaction or reponse to this?
> 2. Loans amounted to $2,190. Why did you give out loans? Didn't I give clear orders to Muhammed Saleh to...refer any loan requests to me? We have already had long discussions on this topic...
> 3. Why have guest house expenses amounted to $1,573 when only Yunis is there, and he can be accommodated without the need for a guest house?
> 4. Why did you buy a new fax for $470? Where are the two old faxes? Did you get permission before buying a new fax under such circumstances?
> 5. Please explain the cell-phone invoice amounting to $756 (2,800 riyals) when you have mentioned communication expenses of $300.
> 6. Why are you renovating the computer? Have I been informed of this?
> 7. General Expenses you mentioned are $235. Can you explain what you mean?...

To Ayman al-Zawahiri
From: Ezzat
Folder: Incoming Mail – From Yemen
Date: February 17, 1999
Kind brother Nur al-Din (Zawahiri)
...We don't have any guest houses. We have bachelor houses, and the offices are there too. We called it a guest house hypothetically, and we don't have any bachelors except Basil and Youssef. And Abd al-Kareem lives at his work place.

If I buy a fax and we have two old ones, that would be wanton or mad.

Communication expenses were $300 before we started using the mobile phone – and all these calls were to discuss the crises of Ashraf and Dawoud and Kareem and Ali and Ali Misra and Abu Basel and others, in compliance with the orders.

Renovating our computer does not mean buying a new one but making sure that adjustments are made to suit Abdullah's [bin Laden's] work. There were many technical problems with the computer. These matters do not need approval.

There are articles for purchase that are difficult to keep track of, so we have put them under the title of general expenses...

The first step for me to implement your advice is to resign from...any relationship whatsoever between me and your Emirate. Consider me a political refugee...[3]

The Yemen station was not unique. Internal documents on Al Qaeda computers also reveal that Zawahiri accused the London station of financial waste and irregularities and appointed a committee to investigate Islamic Jihad members in European countries, not just London, of siphoning the organization's finances. Zawahiri's Islamic Jihad also tried and failed to trick a "traitor," Abu Ibrahim al-Masri, or Nasralah, a senior lieutenant who exposed their secrets to the Yemeni authorities, and repatriate him to Afghanistan.[4] Financial woes reportedly drove Abu Ibrahim to snitch on his associates. The point is that throughout the 1990s Islamic Jihad faced insurmountable economic difficulties, which explains, in the opinion of some of Zawahiri's former associates, his unholy alliance with the bin Laden network. What these former associates overlook, however, is that, as the internal correspondence shows, a year after Zawahiri joined bin Laden's World Islamic Front, he still could not pay the salaries of his operatives or have their computers upgraded. In other words, money was not the only factor in Zawahiri's shift from localism to globalism.

The Struggle Over the Leadership of the Afghan Arabs

There is much more to Zawahiri's radical change of mind than the financial dependency hypothesis promoted by some of his associates. The story behind his transformation is much more complex than that and has to do with his overall relationship with bin Laden and the operational setbacks suffered by Islamic Jihad at home in Egypt and abroad. Zawahiri was not a passive or pliant partner, and he did have other options. Several points are worth highlighting about the bin Laden–Zawahiri relationship. To begin with, Zawahiri's financial dependence on bin Laden was an open secret, and it represented only one factor in their complex partnership. With the exception of the first three years of his presence in Afghanistan, 1986–9, which enabled Zawahiri to rebuild Islamic Jihad and restructure it under his leadership, the Egyptian dissident had no independent sources of income and relied almost exclusively on bin Laden.

Although bin Laden principally bankrolled Islamic Jihad and had financed its attacks inside Egypt, according to associates, from the outset bin Laden tried to convince Zawahiri to suspend these operations because he viewed them as futile and ineffective. In bin Laden's eyes, the political returns from confronting the near enemy were very low, and the costs in terms of sinking Muslim public opinion outweighed any tactical benefits that would be gained. Bin Laden was financially ungenerous with Islamic Jihad because he had other priorities, and he reckoned that targeting the far enemy would bring higher public returns on his investment by mobilizing the Muslim ummah. But neither bin Laden nor Zawahiri let this point of contention stand in the way of their strategic collaboration and close relationship.

A second, related point is that Zawahiri's reason for changing enemies and joining bin Laden's World Islamic Front against the United States was not just that his organization faced a financial crisis and he wanted to rescue it and keep it alive. His very alliance with bin Laden's Al Qaeda is what caused the demise of Islamic Jihad as an independent entity. Al Qaeda devoured Islamic Jihad and other tiny fringe groups that signed the infamous 1998 Declaration of War on America and Americans. In fact, in 2001 Zawahiri formally merged his organization with Al Qaeda and sealed its fate. If Zawahiri's goal had been to maintain the operational independence of Islamic Jihad, surely joining bin Laden's Al Qaeda brought about the opposite result. It is little wonder that many Islamic Jihad lieutenants vocally opposed Zawahiri's joint venture with bin Laden and expressed shock that their leader would take such a critical decision without consultation with them. Former jihadis and Islamists with access to Zawahiri's lieutenants talk about an open internal rebellion within Islamic Jihad, which at one point led Zawahiri to submit his resignation as emir (more on this later).

Thus it is unconvincing to argue, as some associates of Zawahiri do, that his financial difficulties forced his hand and led him to follow closely in bin Laden's footsteps, which meant shifting his operational focus away from attacking the Egyptian regime to attacking the United States. The same associates claim that Zawahiri's heart was not in it but that he had no choice, particularly if he wanted to stay in the jihad business and play a leadership role. Well, Zawahiri did have choices, and he made a deliberate and conscious decision to fully ally himself and his organization with Al Qaeda – without consulting the rank and file – to wage war against the Crusaders (Americans) and Jews. He did not bother to notify the Islamic Jihad Shura Council, the executive decision-making body of Islamic Jihad.

The irony is that Zawahiri and other jihadi emirs never tire of criticizing Muslim rulers for their authoritarian and autocratic ways, and yet the internal dynamics of jihadist networks show an abysmal disregard for transparency and institutional decision making. For example, according to evidence gathered by the U.S. Commission investigating the September 11 bombings, when at last they were told about the forthcoming attacks on the United States, most senior members of the Al Qaeda Shura Council reportedly opposed them. But bin Laden dismissed their objections and gave the go-ahead for the planes operation. In a revealing portrait of the Al Qaeda inner circle, a senior member of its Shura Council, Abu al-Walid al-Masri, writes a damning indictment of bin Laden's autocratic leadership and his dismissal of any perspective that differed from his own. According to Abu al-Walid, who anonymously published his diaries in *Asharq al-Awsat*, bin Laden never listened to the warnings voiced by both the "hawks" and the "doves" within the organization that the United States would be a "ruthless rival" that should not be underestimated in a military struggle; he never wavered from his belief that America did not possess the nerve or the stomach for a prolonged confrontation. According to Abu al-Walid, bin Laden marched head on with his eyes wide open and dragged the rank and file with him: "It was a tragic example of an Islamic movement under a catasrophic leadership. Despite their knowledge that their leader was taking them to the abyss, everyone was succumbing to his will and taking his orders with suicidal submission."[5] Although he did not take their judgment into account, at least bin Laden went through the ritual of consulting his Shura Council; Zawahiri never even discussed the issue of joining Al Qaeda with his lieutenants and cadres.

Bin Laden and Zawahiri are the norm within both the Islamist and the jihadist movements.[6] The cult of personality and charisma – not institutions, real consultation, or power-sharing – is the decisive driver among jihadis. In a way, jihadis imitated their secular ruling tormentors and fell into the same trap of asabiya (group or tribal solidarity) and personality-worship. The jihadist decision-making process is as narrow and personality-driven, if not more so, than the ruling autocratic order's. In his diaries, Abu al-Walid portrays Al Qaeda as revolving around one man – bin Laden – who enjoyed flattery and deference; some of bin Laden's young Saudi supporters would frequently tell him that "if anyone should be king, it would be him."[7] Accordingly, Abu al-Walid, who witnessed the most important moments in Al Qaeda history, notes that bin Laden's followers concluded that disagreeing with him was pointless; after heated debates, they would tell him "he is the emir" and they would obey his orders, even if they knew his decisions would have catastrophic effects: "The last months in the life of Al Qaeda (in Afghanistan at least) represented a tragic example of an authoritarian-ruled Islamic movement."[8] Mainstream Islamists, particularly the Muslim Brothers in the Arab world, suffer from a similar affliction; the old patriarchs in the Brotherhood do not tolerate any internal dissent and expect conformity.

Between 1999 and 2002 I interviewed several junior and young senior members of the Brotherhood who defected in 1996 and had tried to establish a new political party called the Wassat Party (middle way).[9] Their common fundamental complaint was that the old patriarchs who control the Brotherhood exercised complete control over the decision-making process and ran it from the top down, like a tribal fiefdom or a private corporation. Young voices were not the only ones stifled and excluded from the decision-making process; the majority of the rank and file were excluded. According to these young political activists, transparency and participation were frowned on by the old sheikhs, whose favorite motto was al-sama' wata'a (hear and obey) – total obedience.

After September 11, Islamists and jihadis finally came out and publicly criticized Zawahiri for sacrificing the interests of Islamic Jihad at the altar of his relationship with bin Laden, as well as for his desire to stay at the helm at all costs, including forfeiting his organization's primary mandate of confronting the near enemy. There was nothing mysterious, desperate, or inevitable about Zawahiri's decision to join with Al Qaeda and literally dissolve his group within the larger network. He went into the new marriage knowing full well that bin Laden paid the dowry and held the upper hand.

But given Zawahiri's larger-than-life ego and ambition and his close relationship with bin Laden, he reckoned he could easily influence his junior partner's conduct and maneuver him onto his own desired path. After all, Zawahiri possessed richer operational and theoretical experience than bin Laden, who was a recent convert to jihad and underground jihadist action, and had contributed considerably to bin Laden's religious and political education. According to Zawahiri's former associates, he saw himself as senior to bin Laden even though Al Qaeda was financially and structurally richer and larger than Islamic Jihad. Zawahiri reckoned he could tap into and benefit from bin Laden's celebrity status in the oil-producing Gulf countries, particularly Saudi Arabia, and run the show from behind the scenes. According to an insider's account, Zawahiri also hoped to use the operational skills of Al Qaeda's members to further the interests of Islamic Jihad. But, of course, the opposite occurred, and Islamic Jihad was ultimately absorbed into Al Qaeda.[10]

By the mid-1990s, notwithstanding his rhetoric to the contrary, Zawahiri knew that the war against the Egyptian government was lost.

In 1995 he sent an internal memo to cadres inside and outside Egypt sus-pending armed operations in the country. Egyptian Islamic Jihad was no longer logistically capable of sustaining its confrontation with the regime. A series of colossal blunders by Zawahiri enabled the Egyptian authorities to arrest and incarcerate hundreds of his operators and lieu-tenants. Islamic Jihad suffered a strategic setback, and Zawahiri licked his wounds and pondered his diminishing options. Although Zawahiri's memo to his cadres instructed them to suspend military attacks at home, this was because of operational necessity, not ideological conversion – at least not yet. He had hoped to rebuild his depleted ranks before reac-tivating hostilities.

Equally important, a violent storm within the jihadist movement was gathering steam. Although Zawahiri secretly suspended attacks inside Egypt, he did not formally declare an end to the hostilities, and he kept his options open. In contrast, leaders of Islamic Group in Egypt, the largest jihadist organization in the Arab world, debated whether to declare a unilateral ceasefire and terminate their armed insurrection. Zawahiri launched a propaganda counterattack in order to shift the bal-ance of power within Islamic Group against the proposed truce. A war of words between Zawahiri and his hardliner allies, on the one hand, and proponents of the peace initiative, on the other, played itself out on various jihadist Web sites and in magazines, personal letters, internal memos, and newspaper commentaries. As the ceasefire proposal gained momentum, the war of words turned into a tug-of-war, revealing deep and wide fissures among jihadis (more on this in the next chapter). It is worth mentioning that the Islamic Group, or al-Jama'a al-Islamiya, dwarfed Islamic Jihad and even Al Qaeda in size and social base. For example, the Islamic Group accounted for 90 percent of all the attacks that occurred in Egypt in the 1990s, while Islamic Jihad just 10 percent, and the Islamic Group's cadres and supporters numbered tens of thou-sands, while Islamic Jihad's numbered a few thousand. At its peak in the early 1990s al-Jama'a al-Islamiya had more foot soldiers than Al Qaeda and Islamic Jihad combined. Coventional wisdom has it that Al Qaeda's global jihad ideology is representative of all jihadis, which is false; it represents a branch of a highly diverse and complex movement, one that has undergone dramatic shifts from localism to globalism and now appears to target internal and external enemies alike.

Infighting among Egyptian jihadis did not represent a unique case. Rather, it reflected the state of disarray, defeat, and confusion in which jihadis almost everywhere found themselves. By the second half of the 1990s, jihadis and radical Islamists in Egypt, Algeria, and elsewhere were either defeated militarily by pro-Western Muslim regimes or they failed to build viable Islamic political and economic entities. The jihadist emperors were discovered to be without clothes, and Muslim publics lost faith in and turned against their revolutionary project. Jihadis' failure left them with a few unpleasant options. Their high hopes and dreams of the 1980s and early 1990s crashed on the rocks of state power and lack of public support. Never unified with formal institutional ties, jihadis now fractured further along regional, ideological, and class lines.

Algeria is a case in point. As the uprisings of Islamists and jihadis lost momentum, jihadis turned against both one another and civilians in general with a vengeance. The Algerian civil war degenerated into a multiplicity of mini–civil wars with gruesome massacres of whole civilian communities. Regardless of the intricacies of the civil strife in Algeria, one of the most pivotal Arab and north African states, by the second half of the 1990s the murderous actions of the jihadis shocked the Muslim public imagination and reinforced its skepticism and fear about the jihadist project as a whole. The damage was incalculable, and jihadis, along with their supporters outside Algeria, fretted over what could be done to prevent the bloodletting there from killing their movement. After much hand-wringing and accusing the Algerian security elements of infiltrating jihadis' factions and committing massacres in their name, a host of jihadis, including Zawahiri's Islamic Jihad, finally condemned their Algerian counterparts' descent into mayhem and terrorism. Although this partial indictment came very late, it testified to the internal turmoil and turbulence roiling the jihadist movement. Jihadis also lost the battle with government security forces and Muslim public opinion. As a result, intrajihadist squabbling and infighting intensified and undermined the public posture and standing of jihadis. The winter of discontent set in, and with it came structural decline. Religious nationalists reached the end of their ropes.

It is within this volatile context that Zawahiri's alignment with bin Laden and his shift to the transnationalist camp must be seen. It is misleading to say that Zawahiri joined Al Qaeda mainly because of a financial crisis and his increasing dependence on bin Laden. Zawahiri's alliance with bin Laden afforded him the opportunity, which had previously eluded – or not interested – him, to lead an international network with impressive human and financial resources. Here was Zawahiri's historic moment to emerge from hibernation and make a difference on behalf of the ummah. Since the battle against the near enemy had gone nowhere and brought no public dividends, taking jihad global held the promise of mobilizing Muslims worldwide and garnering public opinion support for what at the time seemed to be a dying cause.

Also important in this equation is Zawahiri's nurturing of a special relationship with bin Laden, which had endured years of hardship, exile, and power struggle. In the mid-1980s Zawahiri, a hardened, seasoned jihadi who fled Egypt, met with bin Laden first in Saudi Arabia and then in Afghanistan; bin Laden was a young wealthy Saudi with no operational background who had spent no time underground or in prison. They were two of the early Arab volunteers to arrive in Afghanistan. Unlike bin Laden, who did not possess a delineated agenda, Zawahiri wanted to rebuild and revitalize the Jihad group, which had been hit hard by Egyptian security forces after Sadat's assassination in the first half of the 1980s.

From the beginning, Zawahiri cultivated a close relationship with bin Laden, who initially worked with sheikh Abdullah Azzam, formerly of the Jordanian-Palestinian Brotherhood. More than any other contemporary figure, Azzam, considered the spiritual father of the Afghan Arabs, exercised a formative influence over bin Laden, who, as one of his associates said, "emerged from under the cloak of the Saudi Salafi call."[11] Wahhabi clerics (Wahhabism is a puritanical religious doctrine founded by the eighteenth-century evangelist Mohammed b. Abd al-Wahhab in Saudi Arabia) describe themselves as adherents of Salafism and idealize the time of the Prophet and his companions and insist that on all issues Muslims ought to rely on the Qur'an and the Sunnah (all the deeds and words of the Prophet – second in importance to the Qur'an). It is worth mentioning that traditional Salafis tend to be introverted and focused on internal Muslim affairs, not transnational relations. In Western parlance, classical Salafis, like bin Laden and his Saudi associates, were Muslim isolationists, not internationalists. They advocate a strict adherence to traditional Islamic values, religious orthodoxy, correct ritualistic practice, and moral issues, especially as they pertain to the seclusion of women.[12] Classical Salafis had much more in common with religious nationalists than with transnationalist jihadis.

In his recently published testimony, bin Laden's senior bodyguard, Nasir al-Bahri (alias Abu Jandal), who grew up and lived in Saudi Arabia until the early 1990s, recalls that the dominant Salafi current in the kingdom opposed jihad. His generation, al-Bahri adds, was not ideologically conscious of global developments and their implications to the ummah: "In the past, our work was purely charitable and all our problems were internal. We did not have a strong connection with outside events."[13] According to al-Bahri, who in the mid-1990s went to fight in Bosnia, young Saudis were intentionally kept in the dark with eyes and minds shut to prevent their politicization and radicalization:

> The Salafi current was not oriented toward jihad. The youths did not have a clear idea about the various trends of the Islamic groups until we went out for jihad. As soon as we left for jihad from the large prison called the kingdom of Saudi Arabia, large horizons of knowledge opened up for us. We began to feel that we were completely absented from what was going on in our world. ... We were brought up in Saudi Arabia on the concept of eat and remain silent. This is the prevailing concept of the kingdom's motto [two swords and a palm tree]. This means eat from the palm tree and remain silent because the two swords are there to cut off the head of anyone who acts differently.
>
> We were brought up on this thought. The Saudi government had its prestige and we were terrified by it. This, however, has changed now. It had negative results on the country and its government and people.[14]

Thus, as mentioned before, the Afghan experience and the jihad caravan in other Muslim lands transformed bin Laden and his Salafi Saudi cohort into hyperglobalists. In his recent book, *The Struggle for Islam*, Ridwan al-Sayyid, a leading Muslim specialist on Islamists' discourse, attributes this shift to the influence of the radical faction among the Muslim Brothers, including Azzam, Zawahiri, and the Egyptian contingent; Azzam possessed an internationalist outlook that defines Islam as the antithesis to the Christian West and a militant vision that does not accept separation between church and state. "The outcome of this fusion," Sayyid adds, "between these two extremist movements produced violent groups like Al Qaeda."[15]

Bin Laden and modern Saudi jihadis are a product of this recent marriage between evangelical Salafism-Wahhabism and transnationalist Islamism represented by the late Sayyid Qutb. Ridwan al-Sayyid and other Muslim scholars argue convincingly that bin Laden and Khattab, emir of the Arab mujahedeen in the Caucasus who was killed in 2002, marked a critical rupture with the traditional, introvert, ritualistic Salafi-Wahhabi current, which historically aligned itself with pro-Western states. More than anything else, the Afghan jihad years brought about a doctrinal transformation among traditional Salafi-Wahhabis, like bin Laden, and a revolutionary international sensibility that was missing. For example, bin Laden's personal guard and lieutenant, al-Bahri, recalls that initially Salafis did not buy the call to internationalize jihad and attack the United States; they were conflicted, being naturally more introvert than extrovert. According to al-Bahri's testimony, it took a while to convince Salafis and get them out of the "closed Saudi environment":

These issues generated an internal conflict within ourselves and prompted us later to think deeply of the reasons. When we went abroad and began to mix with the world of jihad, we argued about some issues until jihad against America was announced. Some members of the Salafi [Saudi] current asked in surprise: "Jihad against America?!" Some of them even said, "America knows everything about us. It knows even the label of our underwear." This was the result of the psychological defeat America planted in their hearts. Therefore, we began to concentrate on Salafi students and engaged with them in a detailed dialogue on jihad. After reaching certain convictions with them, we asked them, "Why do you not go to Afghanistan to know true jihad and what is taking place there and then you can decide about jihad?" The purpose was getting them out of the closed Saudi environment so that they would open their eyes and minds. The doors of scientific independent judgment will then be opened for them instead of depending only on what is reported to them. We used to tell them to research and discuss things with others. Some of them were convinced of the idea of going to Afghanistan. Some went to Afghanistan with the purpose of opening constructive dialogue there

about what Osama bin Laden said about jihad. Others went there to
return the young mujahedeen from there, but they were convinced of
the idea of jihad as announced by bin Laden after discussing this issue
with their leading sheikhs. An extraordinary jihadist Salafi current
had thus emerged.[16]

In this, throughout the 1980s, Azzam was a pioneer in getting bin Laden
and other Salafi Afghan veterans out of their shells – out of the "closed
Saudi environment." He set up the first guest house, or Services Bureau
(Maktab al-Khadamat), in Peshawar, Pakistan, to coordinate and facilitate the flow of Afghan Arabs from and to Afghanistan. When bin
Laden arrived in Pakistan, Azzam played host to him and took him
under his wing. Although bin Laden financed the Bureau's jihad activities, Azzam managed its operations. According to jihadis and former
associates, bin Laden was inspired by Azzam's charisma and political-
religious oratory. He sat at his feet as a student and looked up to him
as a hero. But by the second half of the 1980s, as more Arab veterans,
particularly seasoned fighters from Egyptian Islamic Jihad and Islamic
Group, joined the Afghan war, bin Laden developed new ties with their
leaders and ambitious ideas to expand jihad. He and his new associates
established an advanced training camp, called Al-Faruq, designed like
a military college to provide enlisted volunteers with methodical military training and to prepare senior officers to lead jihadist operations
anywhere.

According to al-Bahri, "The idea of establishing that military college was a global idea. Thus, if the jihad in Afghanistan were to end,
graduates of the college could go anywhere in the world and capa-
bly command battles there. Those objectives were actually achieved
through the success accomplished by the young men who had moved
to many fronts outside Afghanistan, in Bosnia-Herzegovina, Chechnya,
the Philippines, Eritrea, Somalia, Burma, and elsewhere."[17]

Victories achieved on those fronts, al-Bahri boasts, were a direct
result of the rigorous curricula taught at Al-Faruq Military College,
which were the same as at other army institutions around the world and
comprised all specializations. Equally important was the emergence of
new professionalized jihadist cadres that owed allegiance to bin Laden
and the emirs of militant Egyptian groups, particularly Zawahiri. By the

end of the 1980s Zawahiri's relationship with bin Laden had deepened, and their views on waging jihad converged, whereas bin Laden and Azzam went their separate ways. Former associates note that the new bin Laden–Zawahiri connection came at the expense of the old ties between bin Laden and Azzam and signaled the birth of a potent alliance.[18]

Zawahiri's replacement of Azzam as bin Laden's confidant testifies to the fierce personal and ideological competition and rivalry among jihadist leaders who wanted to be in charge of the Afghan Arabs and direct their journey. For example, people who knew Zawahiri say that he disagreed with Azzam's vision of jihad and the future direction of the jihadist caravan. Unlike Zawahiri, who went to Afghanistan to prepare for a final showdown with the Egyptian government and who supported the overthrow of pro-Western Arab regimes, Azzam was not an ideologue and had no local agenda; he was more interested in harnessing the resources of the Afghan Arabs and transforming them into an Islamic "rapid reaction force" to assist persecuted Muslims around the world. But he opposed expanding the Afghan jihad against Muslims, including pro-Western regimes. His main source of finance came from Saudi Arabia and members of the royal family, and he had taught in official Saudi institutions and had been affiliated with the mainstream religious establishment nurtured by the Saud family. Azzam could not just bite the hand that fed him because, unlike bin Laden – who could rely on his family's fortune – he had neither an independent financial patron nor grievances against the house of Saud.[19] As a Palestinian refugee, Azzam also hoped to use the military expertise and know-how gained in Afghanistan against Israel. In his fund-raising speeches in the United States and the Gulf, Azzam stressed the importance of the Afghan jihad to the liberation of Palestine and saw Afghanistan as a dress rehearsal for making jihad in Palestine.

Azzam's conception of jihad also differed from that of the new ideologues, including Zawahiri, by being more limited and defensive. In his sermons and writings, especially in *Al-Jihad*, the mouthpiece magazine of the Afghan Arabs, Azzam stressed that jihad becomes a personal duty (fard 'ayn) when Muslim lands are either imminently threatened or occupied by nonbelievers: "When the enemy enters the land of the Muslims, jihad becomes individually obligatory, according to all jurists, mufassirin, and muhaddithin" (interpreters).[20] Unlike Sayyid Qutb, sheikh Abdel Rahman, Zawahiri, and other revolutionaries, Azzam did not break completely with the classical canon of fiqh (jurisprudence) and held a middle position between the two camps.

Although Azzam said that his fundamental goal was to awaken the sleeping Muslim giant and the "hidden capabilities of the ummah," he hoped to do so by breeding a new generation of Islamic mujahedeen to protect the homeland and resist invaders. The emphasis is on resistance, not expansion or aggression. For example, Azzam also focused almost exclusively on the Afghan war against the Russians and opposed meddling in the internal affairs of Arab and Muslim countries, including Afghanistan. He also eschewed terrorism, targeting civilians, and taking jihad global, stating that unless directed into the right path, jihadis "could turn into bandits that might threaten people's security and would not let them live in peace." Thus the jihad caravan must be built on "Al Qaeda al-Sulbah," or a solid foundation, which he coined as early as 1987, before the end of the Afghan war. Indeed, a case can be made that Azzam conceived the idea of Al Qaeda al-Sulbah as an Islamic army ready to do battle on behalf of the ummah, not as a terrorist network as subsequently evolved under bin Laden, Abu Ubaidah, Abu Hafs, and Zawahiri. The difficulty with Azzam's jihadist stance is that he does not fit easily into either the religious nationalist camp or the transnationalist camp. He is more of an irredentist jihadi who struggles to redeem land considered to be part of dar al-islam (House of Islam) from non-Muslim rule.[21]

One wonders what Azzam would have done had he survived the Afghan jihad. In 1989, Azzam and his two sons were assassinated by a car bomb as they drove to a mosque in Peshawar. Would Azzam have followed in the footsteps of his young pupil, bin Laden, or would he have challenged his leadership of the Afghan jihadis? At the end of the Afghan war, did we have a clue about bin Laden's expansive transnationalist ambitions, even after he and Azzam established a rudimentary skeleton of an organization in Afghanistan in late 1988? Was bin Laden not on the same wavelength as Azzam? Could bin Laden have taken over the mantle and leadership of the Afghan Arabs had Azzam remained alive? Was not bin Laden a direct beneficiary of Azzam's exit from the Afghan scene, which enabled bin Laden to take over control of the organization? What was the role of the large Egyptian contingent, particularly Zawahiri's Islamic Jihad, in fueling and inflaming the rivalry between bin Laden and Azzam?

There exists no solid evidence pointing to an intrajihadist conspiracy in the Azzam bombing. In fact, in his 1996 Declaration of War Against the Americans, bin Laden blames the killing of Azzam on "the Zionist-Crusader alliance" and calls on Muslims to avenge Azzam's blood.[22] But suspicions persist among neutral observers and former jihadis alike that there was more to Azzam's assassination than meets the eye and that Zawahiri played a direct role in precipitating the final break between bin Laden and Azzam. Zawahiri reportedly undermined Azzam's position in bin Laden's eyes by spreading rumors that Azzam was an American spy. According to Osama Rushdi, a former member of the Islamic Group Shura Council, "Zawahiri said he believed that Abdullah Azzam was working for the Americans. Sheikh Abdullah was killed that same night," Rushdi told Lawrence Wright of *The New Yorker*, directly blaming Zawahiri's incitement for Azzam's murder.[23]

In his memoir, although Azzam's son-in-law and would-be-heir, Abdullah Anas, refrains from pointing accusatory fingers at his former associates, he insinuates that Azzam's assassination left the Afghan Arabs "orphaned" and leaderless and further splintered along personal and ideological lines.[24] Similarly, in his recently published diaries, Abu al-Walid reports that in the aftermath of Azzam's murder there was a period of extensive chaos, internal disputes, and strife among the Afghan Arabs, pitting Arab jihadis against one another in a struggle for supremacy as they fought to fill the power vacuum left by Azzam's removal.[25] But it was this very struggle, a struggle over the future direction of the Arab mujahedeen movement, that may have led to Azzam's murder. In his recently published testimony, Abu al-Walid hints at one of the major fault lines between the Azzam camp and the bin Laden–Egyptian camp; he said that the level of individual training of fighters had developed so much that it now included hijacking of airplanes and assassinations during a time when there was actually no urgent need for such operations.[26] From the outset, Azzam had been opposed to training mujahedeen fighters in terrorist methods and had issued a religious opinion saying that doing so would violate Islamic law. It is difficult to find out who murdered Azzam and whether bin Laden, Zawahiri, or Abu Hafs played a direct role or knew about it in advance. But one point must be made clear: bin Laden inherited the spoils of the Azzam legacy, was anointed "the king" of the Afghan Arabs, and surrounded himself with powerful Egyptian ministers, commanders, and theoreticians.[27]

Egyptians' Hegemony Over Bin Laden?

Indeed, Azzam's violent removal from the Afghan scene marked the end of one era and the beginning of another: the bin Laden–Zawahiri moment, or Egyptians' hegemony over bin Laden. It also represented a dramatic change in how jihadis interact with one another. Old comrades-in-arms, who publicly portrayed themselves as altruistic, self-less, and brotherly, brutally conspired against each other and stabbed one another in the back. For example, Anas recalled that his father-in-law, Azzam, complained bitterly to him about the backbiting and trou-blemakers, particularly Zawahiri, who talked against the mujahedeen: "They have only one point, to create fitna [sedition] between me and these volunteers."[28] Despite their denials, jihadis live on earth, not in heaven, and they possess earthly ambitions. There is nothing unique or exceptional about intrajihadist dynamics and politics; jihadis are as prone to infighting and rivalry as their secular counterparts. Rela-tions among the trio – Azzam, bin Laden, and Zawahiri – are a case in point. Zawahiri reportedly launched a successful preventive strike against Azzam and snatched bin Laden away from his camp. The coup worked because Zawahiri had much in common with the privileged but down-to-earth man of the desert, bin Laden.

Zawahiri brought vast operational, political, and conceptual skills to his alliance with bin Laden. Although he lacked the monetary wealth of bin Laden, Zawahiri came from a highly learned and prominent Egyp-tian family with deep roots in Islamic learning and Arab nationalism. He was not born rich like bin Laden, but he was privileged to access modern education and he was accepted into a vibrant social and politi-cal environment. His conversion to underground jihadist action in his teens did not prevent him from enrolling in the Cairo University medi-cal school, specializing in surgery and becoming a doctor. His first loves, though, were religion and politics, and he immersed himself in religious texts and their political interpretation and application. As his uncle, Mahfouz Azzam, recalled, "Ayman told me that his love of medicine was probably inherited. But politics was also in his genes."[29]

While in prison in Egypt in the early 1980s, Zawahiri sharpened his revolutionary credentials and, according to his cellmates, took a leading role in intrajihadist disputes and rivalries between factions of the Jihad organization and Islamic Group, the two largest jihadist groups. But unlike bin Laden, who gradually learned to enjoy the limelight and who developed a stirring oratory style, Zawahiri eschewed public exposure and preferred to remain in the background. Close associates who accompanied him during part of his journey implicitly criticize him for his awkwardness and preference for secretive, underground work. Others suggest that Zawahiri was not a natural leader, that he preferred to be led, not to lead, and that he had an overreliance on the opinions of subordinates who more often than not were wrong. There is also an agreement among former associates that the Afghan years (since 1986) changed Zawahiri, and that he rebuilt and led Egyptian Tanzim al-Jihad or Islamic Jihad and took the fateful decision, against the wishes of its rank and file, to align and merge it with Al Qaeda. With Zawahiri, the pendulum shifts from one extreme to the other; there is no middle ground.[30]

With the exception of Azzam, Zawahiri contributed the most to the radicalization of bin Laden and the deepening of his politicization and versatility in jihadist tactics. Zawahiri and bin Laden came from similar privileged backgrounds and shared a common religious and ideological sensibility and affinity, although Zawahiri possessed richer operational experience and a more complex and broader education than bin Laden. All these qualities enabled Zawahiri to develop intimate ties with bin Laden, eclipsing Azzam as the powerhouse behind the scenes. As one of bin Laden's close associates noted, by the mid-1990s Zawahiri "played a major and important role. He became the number-two man in the organization [Al Qaeda]."[31]

According to former participants and my interviews with jihadis, Zawahiri reportedly planted around bin Laden his own most trusted and competent lieutenants, who were loyal to Zawahiri and who subsequently became leading actors in Al Qaeda. The vital input of Egyptians in Al Qaeda has not received its due weight. The presence of fifteen Saudi men among the nineteen Arab hijackers in the September 11 attacks overshadowed the leadership role played by conceptualizers, lieutenants, and computer technicians, most of whom were Egyptians. The Egyptian contingent, including Zawahiri's Islamic Jihad, was the brain trust and the nerve center within Al Qaeda. In his diaries, al-Bahri noted that the majority of the leadership under bin Laden was Egyptian.[32]

Throughout the 1990s, the hegemony of Egyptians became a sore point among other nationalities, particularly Saudis, and bin Laden worked hard to recruit young people from the Arabian Peninsula to establish an ethnic and nationality equilibrium in Al Qaeda. He also wanted to dispel accusations and assure his Taliban allies that he was not a lone Saudi Arabian controlled like a robot by militant Egyptians. After his return to Afghanistan in the mid-1990s, the Saudi government tried to discredit bin Laden and to convince the Taliban to expel him by saying that he had no following in the conservative kingdom. Al-Bahri, a member of bin Laden's entourage, tells of an encounter that sheds light on the importance of the ethnic and nationality composition of Al Qaeda (it is worth quoting at length):

An official Taliban delegation headed by Prime Minister Mullah Mohammed Hassan Rabbani visited [bin Laden] on a certain feast after returning from Saudi Arabia. At the beginning of the visit they expressed a wish to be introduced to all those who were present. The brothers began introducing themselves: I am so and so from Egypt, I am so and so from Algeria, I am an Egyptian and my name is, I am from Iraq, I am from Morocco. Mullah Rabbani looked at bin Laden and said: sheikh Osama, we have not heard anyone say I am from the Gulf. The Saudis have said that you do not have with you anyone from your country, the people of the cause. They say all those around you are a group of Egyptians, not from Saudi Arabia or the Arabian Peninsula. Sheikh Osama was provoked by this comment and said: What do they mean I have no people from the Arabian Peninsula? He turned to one of our young companions who was standing by the door and said: Call our Arab brothers. More than 70 men showed up.

Sheikh Osama began introducing them: So and so from Mecca, so and so from Yemen, so and so from Jeddah, this man from Riyadh, et cetera.

The situation completely changed and the Egyptian brothers felt lost among so many people from the Arabian Peninsula. Mullah Rabbani's eyes filled with tears and he said: All these are people from the land of the two holy mosques. He assured sheikh Osama that the Taliban would always defend him and his followers despite the pressure that Saudi Arabia was putting on the Taliban movement. He told

him: As long as all these men are with you, then you have men and
do not need us. Still we consider ourselves your allies.

These words were very moving to sheikh Osama and most of the
young men who were present. This was one occasion when I saw him
show emotion. He was moved not because of personal pride or out of
a wish to be the leader of a cause merely in name. No, the cause he
embraced had become a general cause and many people joined him in
defending it. It was not Osama bin Laden's cause but had become the
cause of many people around him in that region.[33]

But the sense of brotherhood painted by al-Bahri is only a part of the
story. In response to a question about difficulties faced by Al Qaeda
members, al-Bahri lists ethnic and regional tensions and contradictions
as the most vexing and alarming to bin Laden:

Actually there were rivalries among Al Qaeda members depending on
their countries of origin … This troubled sheikh Osama and he used to
send me to them to help eliminate these regional rivalries because the
enemies of God, those who have sickness in their hearts, and infor-
mants would exploit these ignorant attitudes and try to sow divisions
and disagreements among Al Qaeda members.

I believed that if we wished to confront our strong enemy or confront the broad front that the United States wielded against us, we
needed to entrench amity among ourselves and eliminate regional
rivalries.[34]

Rhetoric aside, the sociology of jihadis does not differ much from that of
their nationalist counterparts; jihadis tend to be just as prone to political
positioning, calculation, and power struggle. The warriors of God also
unconsciously internalized nationalism and sometimes acted as members of separate tribes, although they would be shocked to be told so
because they spent a lifetime portraying themselves as the vanguard of
the ummah.

A critical point to stress is that Zawahiri and the Egyptian team
around bin Laden were vital players in the Al Qaeda network. The
most senior executive positions within the organization were held by
Egyptians, including Zawahiri; Mohammed Atef, also known as Abu
Hafs al-Masri, bin Laden's defense minister until his death in 2001; Abu
Ubaidah al-Banshiri, general field commander of Al Qaeda who established a foothold for Al Qaeda in Africa, particularly the Horn of Africa;

Seif al-Adl, who in 2001 succeeded Abu Hafs as overall military commander of Al Qaeda; Abu al-Walid al-Masri, leading theoretician; and many others. Egyptian operators also managed various sensitive committees and functions in the network, including media, training, and recruitment. Al-Bahri recalls that it was difficult to distinguish between Al Qaeda members and members of Zawahiri's Islamic Jihad because they worked together as one team: "There were coordination of operations, logistical support, and joint implementation of some operations in and outside of Afghanistan. There were Al Qaeda organization members fighting within the ranks of the Jihad organization [Islamic Jihad] and members of the Jihad organization were fighting in the Al Qaeda organization ranks."[35] Long before they officially merged in 2001, the bin Laden network and Zawahiri's Islamic Jihad functioned operationally as an integrated team. The merger formally sealed a well-cemented alliance.

The influence of Egyptians within Al Qaeda was not limited to the leaders, operators, and lieutenants. It extended to the general direction of the organization and the type and nature of its paramilitary operations. For example, former jihadis whom I interviewed are convinced beyond the shadow of a doubt that Zawahiri, and no one else, inducted bin Laden into suicide bombings, or "martyrdom operations." Zawahiri had pioneered and legitimized suicide attacks against the near enemy (Egyptian authorities inside and outside the country).[36] But to get a Salafi-Wahhabi like bin Laden to sanction suicide in the service of politics or religion is a big feat. As noted earlier, Salafis of the Wahhabi variety tend to be slaves to the religious texts and to shun ijtihad (an effort at interpretation). Given that Islam does not sanction suicide, and even forbids it,[37] either bin Laden was brainwashed or he underwent a revolutionary transformation, thanks mainly to the influence of Zawahiri, not Azzam. Azzam eschewed terrorist attacks against civilians.[38] In a way, the use of suicide bombings by jihadis represents a rupture, not continuity, with classical Islamic political thought and practice. As argued previously, Zawahiri subscribes to a takfeeri (practice of excommunication of Muslims) ideology and he converted bin Laden to this creed as well.

Some of the "spectacular martyrdom operations" carried out by the Al Qaeda network also appeared to have the fingerprints of the Egyptian contingent, particularly Zawahiri's Tanzim al-Jihad. "These are vintage Islamic Jihad," a former lieutenant in an Egyptian Jihad cell told me. In my interviews with jihadis in Egypt and Yemen, former operators of the Jihad organization went to great lengths to differentiate between "spectacular" attacks carried out by their organization and those carried out by other jihadis, including Islamic Group. They stressed that the jihad's operations were qualitatively different and designed to psychologically shock the enemy. Thus Zawahiri's model of earth-shaking suicide bombings became Al Qaeda's signature, leaving his lasting mark on its future armed operations, beginning with the 1998 attacks on the U.S. embassies in East Africa and including the September 11 suicide bombings and other attacks worldwide.

The Catalyst: America Enters Saudi Arabia

A point of qualification is in order. It is misleading to exaggerate the importance of Zawahiri on bin Laden's thinking and action and to overlook bin Laden's substantive influence on religious nationalists in general, and on Zawahiri in particular. One of this book's central arguments is that throughout the 1980s and until the mid-1990s jihadis, including Zawahiri's Islamic Jihad, attempted to overthrow the near enemy and did not consider the far enemy a priority that required immediate action. Yet by the second half of the 1990s, as Zawahiri's relationship with bin Laden deepened, Zawahiri turned his fire against what he and bin Laden called "the head of the serpent," the United States. He fully adopted bin Laden's worldview, signaling a substantive change in his thinking and operational priorities.[39] One associate, who met Zawahiri after he and bin Laden left Sudan for Afghanistan in 1996, reportedly found Zawahiri to be a changed man; he faithfully followed in bin Laden's footsteps.[40]

As mentioned previously, associates of Zawahiri mainly ascribe the shift in his conduct to a deepening financial crisis that made him fully dependent on bin Laden, as well as his isolation in Afghanistan and the military setbacks suffered by Islamic Jihad in Egypt in the first half of the 1990s. But the change from localism to globalism is much more historically and ideologically nuanced and complex than that. It was a well-known secret among jihadis in Afghanistan that bin Laden opposed Zawahiri's operations against the Egyptian regime because he thought they were costly and counterproductive. Bin Laden reportedly argued that internal strife alienated the ummah, whose support was urgently needed in the unfolding global struggle, and diverted attention and resources from the real confrontation against infidels and crusaders that was coming. On this score, bin Laden was more consistent than Zawahiri and other religious nationalists who subsequently changed camps.

Throughout the 1980s and 1990s, bin Laden was not in favor of attacking pro-Western Muslim regimes, and he exerted moral and financial pressure on Zawahiri to suspend military operations inside Egypt. This reasoning would explain why bin Laden's Al Qaeda did not launch a full onslaught against the Saudi regime until 2003 and concentrated its attacks instead against Westerners. Although he shared Zawahiri's opinion that local rulers, including the royal Saudi family, were apostates and "voiders" of Islam, bin Laden viewed them as mere agents of the American-Israeli alliance, which he said controls politics, economics, and culture in Muslim countries. This alliance, bin Laden claims, is responsible for keeping the ummah "divided" and for aborting and sabotaging any "corrective movement" to unify its ranks.[41]

Thus bin Laden ranked the main "kufr," or impiety (the United States) much higher on his threat list than the lesser kufr (Muslim rulers) and called on Muslims to make expelling "the enemy – the greatest kufr – out of the country a prime duty." In his Declaration of War Against the Americans, bin Laden also cautioned Muslims against descending into civil strife among themselves because that would weaken them further and keep them subjugated: "An internal war is a great mistake, no matter what reasons are there for it. The presence of the occupier [American] forces will control the outcome of the battle for the benefit of the international kufr."[42]

More than anyone else, bin Laden articulated the position and rationale of a transnationalist jihadi. In his eyes, the center of political gravity and power lies in Washington and New York, not in Cairo, Riyadh, Baghdad, Amman, Algiers, or elsewhere. If real change is to occur, then the far enemy must be forced to retreat in humiliation and defeat from Muslim lands. Yes, bin Laden says that local regimes "betrayed the ummah and joined the kufr, assisting and helping them against

Muslims." But they are independent in name only and do not run the show. Attacking the "lesser kufr," he adds, could also spark a fitna or sedition and play into the hands of the colonial powers. Better strike against "the head of the serpent." In this sense, although bin Laden did not possess a coherent strategy to achieve his goal, all along his definition of the enemy remained constant.

When asked whether bin Laden considered the United States his only target in the second half of the 1990s, al-Bahri, whose recently published diaries and memoir provide an insider's glimpse into the Al Qaeda inner circle, said he did and that he restricted his armed attacks to the United States. Al-Bahri recalled incidents when Al Qaeda members, who were very zealous, asked their boss if they could attack this or that apostate Muslim government. Bin Laden retorted by saying: "Leave them alone and do not preoccupy yourselves with them. They are scum. . . . When they witness the defeat of the United States, they will be in their worst situation."[43]

According to al-Bahri, who spent several important years by bin Laden's side, bin Laden did not distinguish between Muslim leaders and the Americans. He considered them one and the same, but his strategy was not to strike inside Muslim countries. On various occasions, al-Bahri noted that he heard bin Laden say, "There are some Arab countries which cannot stand the battle for even a week. If we concentrate on them we will completely defeat them and topple entire regimes. . . . I can topple the regime in two or three Arab states because these are not states in the true sense of the word and their leaders are not up to the level of responsibility."[44]

Throughout the 1990s, unlike Zawahiri and his cohorts, bin Laden never wavered on the urgency and primacy of attacking the greater kufr and postponing the fight against the lesser kufr. Al Qaeda did carry out some military operations in the Gulf against Western targets, but it never launched a systemic assault against the near enemy like the religious nationalist camp did in Egypt and Algeria. It is worth stressing that it was not until the 1991 Gulf war that bin Laden severed his ties with the Saudi royal family. He did so only after the Saudis dismissed his proposal to mobilize an Islamic army of mujahedeen along the Afghan lines to expel the Iraqi army from Kuwait and sanctioned the stationing of American troops in the birthplace of the Prophet.

Bin Laden reportedly met with a senior Saudi prince and Muslim scholars and told them, "we are ready to get the Iraqi forces out of Kuwait." He subsequently told his lieutenants he had called on the Saudi royal family to allow for the recruitment of youths and to open the door of jihad in the kingdom in order to expel the Iraqi invaders from Kuwait. According to al-Bahri, who heard his boss tell the story, "he asked the Saudi government to open the door for him. He said he was ready to prepare more than 100,000 fighters in three months. He used to say, 'I have more than 40,000 mujahedeen in the land of the two holy mosques [Saudi Arabia]. These were trained in Afghanistan.' He said he was ready to prepare them within a few days. The number of other mujahedeen outside Saudi Arabia was many times more. Had Saudi Arabia allowed that to happen, all would have participated in expelling the Iraqi forces from Kuwait, especially since Saudi Arabia enjoys a special religious status that concerns all Muslims because the two holy mosques are located there."[45]

According to al-Bahri's diaries, to reassure the royal family of the seriousness and efficacy of his proposal and to foil the entry of American troops into the region, bin Laden went to the senior clerics aligned with the government and told them, "I am ready to prepare 100,000 fighters with good combat capability within three months. If the Iraqi army has an eight-year experience of war with Iran, these mujahedeen have longer experience and they are ready to wage wars and defend you."[46]

Then Bin Laden, according to al-Bahri,

> presented an integrated military program and asked them to open training camps for the young and recruit the jobless. He also called for implanting the military spirit in their minds. He got into a heated argument with them in this regard and they were angry with him. We were surprised why Saudi Arabia rejected bin Laden's offer. We, however, understood the reason after some time [obviously, after bin Laden explained everything to them!]. We learned that it was a U.S. scheme to invade the region. That was met with an internal defeat. The Gulf states allowed foreign interference to protect themselves. We also learned that the Saudi rulers contacted the men of religion and asked them to issue fatwas about the subject. That came too late.[47]

Why was that too late? Al-Bahri quotes Saudi Arabia's most senior cleric, Sheikh Abd al-Aziz bin Baz, as saying that the ruling Saud family first requested American intervention and then asked for his fatwa to confer legitimacy on its action. According to bin Laden's narrative, the Saudi government told bin Baz, "O sheikh, if you do not issue a fatwa allowing Muslims to seek the assistance of U.S. and other foreign forces, sedition will erupt in the kingdom of Saudi Arabia. The mujahedeen will then clash with the U.S. forces, triggering sedition. Besides, the Iraqi Ba'th forces are at the door."[48] Although the religious establishment did not agree with the government, they obliged because, as bin Laden and his associates tell it, they were cowardly and feared for their lives and positions. Al-Bahri says that he heard bin Laden tell the story of a visit with bin Baz and another senior cleric, sheikh Mohammed bin Salah bin Uthaymin, for talks about the Americans' entry into the Gulf; bin Uthaymin reportedly confided in bin Laden, "'my son Osama, we cannot discuss this issue because we are afraid.' Sheikh bin Uthaymin said this while pointing to his neck as an indication that he feared beheading if he talked about that issue."[49]

The importance of this insider's narrative lies in shedding light on bin Laden's intentions and how he portrayed his breakup with the ruling and religious establishment in Saudi Arabia. Al-Bahri's diaries are extremely valuable because they provide a peek into that shadowy universe and let us read bin Laden's sales pitch to his followers. Out of this tale, bin Laden emerges as standing tall, pressuring the Saudi government to rethink its dependence on the Americans and nudging and inciting the clergy to challenge the royal family and express their dissent. In response to a question about how bin Laden reacted to the clerics' fear and skepticism, al-Bahri said that his boss "used to look at the men of religion and tell them, 'you are the men of religion and people of position. You must speak up and bravely announce your positions.'"[50] But the cards were stacked against bin Laden, al-Bahri concludes: "The Saudi leaders, however, did not give this [bin Laden's] offer any attention because they were controlled by others [the Americans] and they obeyed their orders blindly. There was no room for any discussion."[51]

Nonetheless, in the end bin Laden came out victorious, al-Bahri concludes, because he exposed the hypocrisy of the ruling and religious Saudi establishment. Equally important, bin Laden opened the eyes and minds of young Saudis to what was happening at home and abroad and to the need to question what the authorities told them: "All these things opened new horizons for the youths, broadened their mental faculties, and changed their positions."[52]

Former Saudi chief of internal security, Prince Turki al-Faisal, who knew bin Laden relatively well from the Afghan war days, confirmed that bin Laden contacted senior officials with a proposal to field an army of mujahedeen to liberate Kuwait, thus forestalling external, particularly American, military intervention. However, the official Saudi narrative stressed that bin Laden's idea was vague and could not be translated operationally; it left too many questions open. Where will the mujahedeen come from? Who will arm them, and how long will that take? Who will be in charge of that Islamic army, and to whom will it be loyal?[53]

Saudi rulers were not interested in bin Laden's offer because they did not want to gamble on an imaginary mujahedeen army that, if it were to materialize, could pose a serious threat to their throne, like Saddam Hussein's army. Their immediate concern was to deter Hussein from marching from occupied Kuwait into Saudi Arabia; their secondary concern was to help free Kuwait from Hussein's grip. The royal family had more faith and confidence in their superpower patron, the United States, than in bin Laden, an upstart jihadist who possessed no formidable armada to roll back the Iraqi tanks. Furthermore, Saudi leaders feared that an Islamic force, after having dealt with the Iraqi army, would be used to seize power within the kingdom; they could not allow the presence of some 100,000 armed jihadis in their midst.

There is no doubt that the 1991 Gulf war and subsequent events turned bin Laden against his former patrons and set him on his current journey. The snub by the royal family, coupled with its decision to invite the Americans to the kingdom, sent bin Laden into exile with injured pride and a vendetta against his former patrons.

What is worse, according to bin Laden, is that the house of Saud sanctioned the permanent stationing of U.S. troops in the land of the two holy mosques. That, for bin Laden, was the point of no return because the sanctity of Islam's holiest shrines was desecrated by the impious crusaders. Instead of faithfully discharging their duty as the guardians of the faith, Saudi rulers violated al-ahad (religious oath).[54]

In his 1996 Declaration of War Against the Americans (ironically, not against the house of Saud), bin Laden accused the Saudi regime of deceiving the ummah by claiming that the presence of the Americans was temporary, to expel the Iraqi army from Kuwait:

> It is out of date and no longer acceptable to claim that the presence of the crusaders is a necessity and only a temporary measure to protect the land of the two Holy Places. Especially when the civil and the military infrastructures of Iraq were savagely destroyed, showing the depth of the Zionist-Crusaders' hatred for the Muslims and their children, and the rejection of the idea of replacing the crusader forces by an Islamic force composed of the sons of the country and other Muslims.
>
> The King said that "the issue is simple, the American and the alliance forces will leave the area in a few months." Today it is seven years since their arrival and the regime is not able to move them out of the country. The regime made no confession about its inability and carried on lying to the people claiming that the Americans will leave. But never-never again; a believer will not be bitten twice from the same hole or snake! Happy is the one who takes note of the sad experience of the others!![55]

Although bin Laden's criticism of the Saudi regime is scathing, he calls on young Saudis to initiate guerrilla warfare to expel the occupying American enemy from the country. He refrains from advocating an internal uprising or a revolution against the local enemy, the house of Saud, and he goes to great lengths to caution his supporters and followers to avoid the trap of "an internal war."[56] Surely, bin Laden's long-term ambition was and is the overthrow of the pro-Western ruling Saud family and its replacement with a more authentic Islamic government. Both religious nationalists and transnationalist jihadis share the common goal of ridding the region of ruling apostates and reestablishing the caliphate. But unlike his religious nationalist counterparts, bin Laden viewed local regimes, including the house of Saud, as insignificant tools and agents in the hands of the Americans. He considered Saudi Arabia an occupied country and its regime incapable of forcing the Americans out. Therefore, he declared war on the United States, not on Saudi Arabia, because, as he told his cohorts, once the United States is expelled from the area, its local clients would fall like ripened fruits.

Since 2003, attacks in Saudi Arabia, Iraq, Egypt and Gulf countries have shown a marked change in Al Qaeda's paramilitary thinking and action. To what extent do these operations point to a shift away from confronting the far enemy to that of attacking the near enemy? Are the recent attacks inside Muslim countries a product of logistical necessity or ideological transformation? Has Al Qaeda decided to simultaneously take on internal and external enemies? To what extent has bin Laden reclaimed Zawahiri's previous emphasis on the near enemy? It is too early to speculate on the meaning of these developments because the situation remains in flux, and only time will tell if Al Qaeda has morphed into a new animal.

One thing is clear, however. Modern jihadis have reached a theoretical deadlock. The dichotomy of the near enemy and the far enemy has not taken jihadis where they want to be and has proved to be very costly. Where do transnationalist jihadis go from here? Although religious nationalists publicly conceded defeat and the futility of armed struggle, transnationalist jihadis have expanded and escalated their attacks against both local and external enemies. Borrowing a page from the manifesto of Sayyid Qutb, founding father of the modern jihadist movement, transnationalist jihadis seem to be waging a permanent revolution with no end in sight. It is an "eternal" armed struggle against all rebellious enemies who have usurped God's authority. Now bin Laden and Zawahiri, and their associates, do not just want to get rid of one or two pro-Western local regimes; they want to destroy the whole existing system. This tall order requires, in bin Laden's view, going after the enforcer and keeper of the status quo in both the region and the rest of the world: "We must completely topple the United States and we hope to be the ones who can topple its entire system," bin Laden told his followers.[57]

FOUR

Splitting Up of Jihadis

In the second half of the 1990s the rise of Osama bin Laden as an international star among jihadis coincided with the declining fortune of religious nationalists, who suffered a crushing military defeat at home. Although they were embattled and besieged in the early 1990s, by the end of the decade key Arab governments, particularly Egypt and Algeria, finally contained the threat from jihadis by arresting and killing most of their field lieutenants and operators. They dealt them a fatal blow and forced them to think the unthinkable – to lay down their arms and concede defeat. From the 1970s to the late 1990s, jihadis' paramilitary struggle against the near enemy did not bring them any closer to their dream of ridding the region of its ruling "renegades." On the contrary, by the end of the 1990s religious nationalists were a spent force.

Religious Nationalists Lay Down Their Arms

As a result of the destruction of jihadis as an organized movement, serious divisions appeared among their rank and file at home and abroad. For example, in 1997 scores of the top leaders of the Egyptian al-Jama'a al-Islamiya, or Islamic Group, who were incarcerated declared a unilateral ceasefire (a code word for acknowledging defeat) and called on their followers inside and outside of Egypt to stop military hostilities. This peace initiative by one of the biggest jihadist organizations in the Arab world (numbering tens of thousands and accounting for 90 percent of attacks), which had been unexpected, came as a bombshell to jihadis, particularly hardliners living in exile. Religious nationalists battling local regimes gave notice that they had reached the end of their rope and could no longer sustain the fight.

Although a few of the exiled lieutenants of the Islamic Group dissented, the majority expressed relief. Thousands of their cohorts and supporters were languishing in high-security prisons, and thousands of others had already been killed. They left behind families whose suffering knew no bounds. During my field research in Egypt in the late 1990s, I met families of imprisoned or killed jihadis who literally struggled to survive. The Egyptian authorities kept up the pressure by punishing anyone who provided financial support to them. One particular story remained with me. In 1998 the wife of an incarcerated member of the Islamic Group said she had no money to feed her several young children. For a few weeks she tried to sell her refrigerator to neighbors but without luck. People were afraid to purchase it for fear they would be accused of association with a terrorist. In fact, a neighbor finally took pity on the family and bought the refrigerator; shortly after, he was arrested by the Egyptian authorities, an Islamist attorney for the wife told me.

This was not an isolated story but part of the pattern of brutal measures taken by the security services against what they called the infrastructure of terrorism. A more apt term for this policy would be collective punishment. The government arrested not only alleged jihadis but also some of their family members and close relatives, including brothers, fathers, wives, and sisters, a very inflammatory method in traditional and socially conservative Muslim quarters. Some of these women (most women did not come forward because of the fear of social stigma involved) also confided that they were sexually abused and humiliated, again a very disturbing and alarming escalation in the confrontation between the security services and jihadis. In the first half of the 1990s if the idea informing the government's collective punishment was to break the backbone of the jihadist insurgency, the weight of evidence indicates that it poured gasoline on a raging fire and exacerbated matters.

All jihadis whom I interviewed pointed to the government's widespread crackdown and heavy-handedness in the early 1990s as an important factor that prolonged and intensified the conflict. For them, most alarming was the violation of the sanctity of their homes and bedrooms by security officials and the arrest and mistreatment of their women. More than one jihadi said that the latter measure enraged them and made them determined to exact revenge on the security services. By the mid-1990s, jihadis had fallen into a trap set for them by the regime by waging a tribal vendetta against officials, police officers, and intellectuals, thus further alienating the public.

Neither camp recognized any red lines and both camps committed atrocities, culminating in the 1997 Luxor massacre in which an Islamic Group cell apparently attacked a Luxor temple and killed sixty-eight foreigners and Egyptians. No other incident mobilized Egyptian and Muslim public opinion against religious nationalists like this bloodbath. Egyptian jihadis with whom I spoke said that the Luxor massacre represented a critical psychological setback in their struggle against the Egyptian regime. An emir of the Islamic Group confided to me, "Luxor was a belated awakening from a fight gone mad." Brutal and bloody as it was, the fight in Egypt paled by comparison with that in Algeria, where wholesale massacres became the norm, not the exception. In Algeria, it was difficult to tell who was doing what to whom.

Unlike Egypt, which witnessed a limited jihadist insurgency with a few thousand casualties, Algeria was fully engulfed by a civil war that caused more than 100,000 deaths of mostly innocent civilians. Neither the government nor jihadis observed any limits. The net result was that Algerians, like their Egyptian counterparts, got fed up with the brutal ways of the Armed Islamic Group (GIA) and its successor, the Salafist Group for Dawah and Combat, and held them responsible for the country's bloodletting. Egyptian and Algerian jihadis had lost the battle for Muslims' hearts and minds long before they lost the military fight against local authorities. It is little wonder that by the end of the 1990s Egypt and Algeria succeeded in breaking the backbone of the jihadist movement.

At any rate, the 1997 ceasefire initiative by the Islamic Group leaders was met with a particularly hostile reception by Zawahiri and other jihadist hardliners. Ironically, the opposition to the religious nationalists' peace offer came from those militants who resided in exile in Afghanistan, Yemen, European countries, and elsewhere. There was broad support for the initiative among jihadis at home, which was understandable because they were at the front lines facing the brunt of the government's fire. Led by Zawahiri, exiled voices rejected their cohorts' ceasefire proposal, and some questioned its credibility and legitimacy because those who signed it were not free. A big debate ensued among jihadis about whether incarcerated leaders should be obeyed. But underlying the war of words was an internal turmoil roiling the jihadist movement as a whole. Military defeat deepened the divisions within the religious nationalist camp and sparked a tug-of-war between accommodationists and confrontationalists. While the former were represented by the so-called historical leaders – founders of al-Jama'a al-Islamiya and leading members of its Shura Council, most of whom were imprisoned – and a few of their counterparts in Islamic Jihad, Zawahiri and his cohorts launched a counteroffensive from their base in Afghanistan.

Zawahiri clearly recognized the significance of al-Jama'a's ceasefire initiative because it had the stamp and signature of its top leaders, including the "blind sheikh" Abdel Rahman (jailed in the United States), who was highly respected by the rank and file. Zawahiri also feared that the proposal could hand a strategic victory to his nemesis, the Egyptian regime, by neutralizing the biggest bloc of jihadis, splintering them and weakening them. The future of the jihadist movement was at stake. Zawahiri tried to undermine the ceasefire initiative by appealing to al-Jama'a's military commander, Rafa'i Ahmad Taha (alias Abu Yasir), who was a hardliner who reportedly opposed his leaders' peace offer. Between 1997 and 1999 Zawahiri dictated several impassioned letters to Taha, asking if the media reports on the ceasefire initiative were correct:

> There are many frightening thoughts going through my mind at present. Did you all agree on this policy [of nonviolence]? What is the strategy vis-à-vis the government? Have you reached an agreement with the authorities? If so, what are the details? Why wasn't it publicised? Does the accord include some secret clauses? Would the secret be known to the government but concealed from [jihadis]? If an agreement has been concluded, what is the government permitting you to do?[1]

Zawahiri pressed Taha further to see if he should take the media reports seriously: how unanimous is al-Jama'a's decision to stop violence? Is the Egyptian government aware of any disagreement among your ranks, if it exists? If media reports are incorrect, Zawahiri asked anxiously, why have you been silent on this important issue? Why won't you issue a clarification since, on other matters, such as the World Islamic Front, you have been very vocal in your opposition? What is the balance of power between those who oppose the ceasefire initiative and those who support it? Zawahiri urges Taha, a like-minded ideologue in al-Jama'a, to make his voice heard and implores him to impress on his imprisoned bosses at home the danger and futility of their new adventure; Zawahiri even incited Taha to challenge the wisdom of the leaders' decision. He warns Taha that the initiative contradicts al-Jama'a's proud legacy of steadfastness and sacrifice and, if one is to believe media reports, the initiative would represent "a serious setback" to both al-Jama'a and the jihadist movement. "Beware of losing both in this world and thereafter," Zawahiri warns his counterpart. "Your loyalty must be to God and His Prophet. Righteousness will be your salvation in this world and the next."[2] To convince Taha that he means well and that the letter was written in a positive spirit, Zawahiri concludes by urging him to visit the Brothers in Afghanistan for consultation:

> In conclusion, I urge you to come and visit with us. It is very impor-
> tant that you consult with all the Brothers. I hope you have faith
> in me to receive this letter with an open heart and mind. May
> God give you success, nurture you, and guide you. May He help you
> to cling firmly to what is right, until the day when you will meet
> Him and He will forgive all your sins. Peace and God bless you.
>   Your loving brother, Abu al-Muizz [Zawahiri][3]

Although initially, in 1997, Taha expressed his dissent from the al-Jama'a consensus by publicly supporting the Luxor massacre, his was a lone rejectionist voice within the Group. Al-Jama'a's "historical leaders" ordered him to tow the Group's line or resign. They publicly reprimanded him for making personal statements contradicting their stated position. Zawahiri should have known better because Taha was not in a strong position to challenge al-Jama'a's senior leadership. For example, in July 1998, Taha was forced by al-Jama'a's leadership to issue a public retraction, saying that attacking the United States was not a priority for his Group and that he was not a signatory of bin Laden's World Islamic Front. Zawahiri's exercise was designed to drive a wedge between al-Jama'a's imprisoned leaders and those in exile, like Taha, and to sow dissent. But he was fighting an uphill, losing battle because the majority of religious nationalists, not just in Egypt but also in Algeria, had already recognized the futility of battling local regimes; their will to power was shattered.

Having failed to get a satisfactory response from Taha, Zawahiri took an unprecedented step and addressed a letter directly to al-Jama'a's leaders and signed his real name (that was unusual because Zawahiri used various aliases and never put his real name on official business; obviously, he felt very strongly about this issue and wanted to make a point). The letter is informative and fascinating because it reveals Zawahiri's broader intentions and goals and the changes that had occurred in his thinking. This letter and other important primary documents were recovered from computers from Al Qaeda's main office in Kabul, which had been used by Zawahiri and his associates, that were looted by Afghanis immediately after the city fell. These documents were acquired by *The Wall Street Journal* and by the Arabic-language newspaper *Asharq al-Awsat*. Both *The Wall Street Journal* and *Asharq al-Awsat* ran a series of articles highlighting salient features (I will refer to these documents as "Zawahiri's Secret Papers").[4]

In his letter to the al-Jama'a imprisoned leaders, Zawahiri explains that he did not write until a year after their ceasefire initiative because he was waiting for the right opportunity to present itself.[5] (This was not true because he had written to Taha more than once but Taha never responded.) Zawahiri notes that although the jihadist movement is young and facing internal and external enemies with a powerful armada, it has come a long way and become a power to be reckoned with on the local and international scenes, thanks to its tenacity and sacrifice. The ceasefire initiative, added Zawahiri, "will not see the light of day" and will not produce any practical or symbolic results for jihadis; far from it, it exposed divisions within al-Jama'a and a "flaw" in its decision-making process. Zawahiri implies that the Islamic Group suffered from incoherence, internal disunity, and management problems. Again, Zawahiri exaggerates. With the exception of Taha, no major voice within al-Jama'a opposed the ceasefire initiative. Once the leadership publicized their decision, the ceasefire held without any major incident. They left no doubt in anyone's mind that they fully controlled their organization and there was no parallel competing leadership. Even the revered Abdel Rahman endorsed the ceasefire offer from his U.S. prison cell.

But Zawahiri's real concern was with the psychological and political effects of the ceasefire offer on jihadis: "The jihadist movement showed itself to be weak because the political translation of this initiative means capitulation." "The initiative," Zawahiri adds, "also showed that some forces in the jihadist movement are prepared to collaborate with the government individually, thus enabling the latter to manipulate each of them separately."[6] He gently reprimands his counterparts by saying that their decision raises serious questions about the purpose and future of the jihadist movement as a whole: "If we stop [fighting] now, then why did we start in the first place? Why do our brethren in prisons propose something without coordination with their counterparts outside? Does that position apply to inciting people to perform jihad against Americans? And does it apply to Israel as well? There is no doubt that this initiative undermined the image of the incarcerated leaders in the eyes of the youths and came as a violent shock."[7] He indirectly accuses the Islamic Group leadership of collusion with the Egyptian authorities.

Zawahiri reminds the Islamic Group chiefs that they represent a powerful symbol for all jihadis, including himself, and that they should be concerned about their legacy and contribution to the jihadist movement, particularly bin Laden's World Islamic Front, or Al Qaeda. The latter has escalated the fight against "the biggest of the criminals, 'the Americans,'" Zawahri reassures his audience, "to drag them for an open battle with the nation's masses without stopping its confrontation with the Egyptian government."[8] It is worth mentioning that Zawahiri's letter was written a few months after the announcement establishing the World Islamic Front and less than a month before the Front's bombings of the U.S. embassies in Kenya and Tanzania. Obviously, from the outset, the fundamental goal of bin Laden and Zawahiri, as stated in their secret communication with other jihadis, had been to pit the ummah against the leader of the Western world, the United States, and to unleash a clash of religions and cultures. The letter was also designed to internationalize the conflict with local governments and turn it into a clash of civilizations. The change of tactics, bin Laden and Zawahiri reckoned, would resonate in Muslims' imaginations and could reverse the military-political misfortunes suffered by jihadis since the mid-1990s.

Zawahiri concluded his letter by stressing that "the Islamic Front for Jihad against Jews and Crusaders is a correct step in the right direction, and that this is a Front which we have hoped you would join in because it is a move designed to strengthen the mujahedeen and provoke their enemies."[9] Again, Zawahiri's reference to the Islamic Group must be contextualized because the latter had already dealt a blow to bin Laden and Zawahiri by forcing Taha, who was present at the ceremony announcing the creation of Al Qaeda, to subsequently disclaim being a member of it. After the attacks on the U.S. embassies in east Africa, senior leaders of the Islamic Group publicly repudiated Al Qaeda and distanced themselves from it.[10]

Jihadis' Civil War

Al-Jama'a's olive branch represented a threat to the ambitions of bin Laden and Zawahiri because it exposed the existence of divisions and internal rivalries between religious nationalists and transnationalists. It also showed that Al Qaeda did not speak for all jihadis. In his memoir published after September 11, which he began to write in 2000, Zawahiri devotes an entire chapter to the ceasefire initiative and criticizes those who were behind it for either abandoning the struggle or being treacherous. In particular, he reserves his harshest criticism for a former associate of the Islamic Group, Montasser al-Zayat, who in the early 1980s served time with Zawahiri in prison in the Sadat assassination case and who has since become the best-known attorney defending Islamists and jihadis in Egyptian trials. He raises questions about Zayat's role in the ceasefire initiative and accuses him of working with the Egyptian security apparatus. Zawahiri claims that the Egyptian security apparatus granted only Zayat access to the incarcerated leaders of al-Jama'a and that they used him as a front to misinform and mislead the Group's operatives at home and abroad.[11]

Zawahiri's conspiratorial approach is designed to discredit the peace proposal advanced by the al-Jama'a leadership and paint it as part of a deal between the ambitious Zayat and the security services. He does not tell readers how and why Zayat succeeded in selling the government's viewpoint to the imprisoned jihadis who had authorized Zayat to be a conduit with their free associates. Zawahiri draws a caricature of Zayat, who is portrayed as having played tricks on Islamic Group leaders and leading them on the wrong path. But the truth is that Zayat, who is vain and enjoys the limelight, was just the messenger. Zawahiri refrains from directly addressing the merits and arguments behind the ceasefire proposal, and when he partially does, he exposes the vulnerability of his own case.

For example, he cites a top leader of al-Jama'a, Karam Zuhdi, as saying "if military operations have not achieved the Group's goals all those past years, we must find another modus operandi." Instead of examining the logic of Zuhdi's stance, Zawahiri asks if that means that the Group has abandoned the armed struggle, including the incitement to wage jihad, inside and outside Egypt. Is the alternative, he disapprovingly inquires, to urge the government, as the advocates of the ceasefire have done, to accept their initiative and involve leaders of political parties in mediating among them. Zawahiri sarcastically asks what has become of jihadis who now plead with secular governments to allow them to work toward establishing Islamic states.[12] Zawahiri also chastises his counterparts for proposing a ceasefire while jihadis were being hunted down by American intelligence services and shipped to Egypt to be tortured and persecuted. He tried to pressure his counterparts in the religious nationalist camp to turn their guns against the United States. By the late 1990s a pronounced shift could be discerned in Zawahiri's exchange with his own associates and other jihadis: operationally, the far enemy began to take priority over the near enemy. Zawahiri's correspondence is full of references to the "enemies of Islam," the forces of arrogance, and the coming battle against Americans and Jews.

Zawahiri's memoir and correspondence also show that the official birth of Al Qaeda in the second half of the 1990s, as opposed to its conceptualization in the late 1980s, coincided with an internal upheaval that tore the jihadist movement apart. In Egypt, Algeria, and elsewhere, jihadis had just begun to question the very premises that informed their words and deeds, particularly the utility of waging jihad against "impious" Muslim rulers, in the last two decades. They entertained laying down their arms and rejoining society. Zawahiri's secret letter to the al-Jama'a leaders gives us a bird's-eye view of the emerging tensions and contradictions among old comrades who had joined ranks against the near enemy and who now went their separate ways. In his effort to convince al-Jama'a to persevere and continue the fight, Zawahiri writes that internationalizing jihad is key to shuffling the military-political cards and tipping the balance of power in the jihadis' favor.

Thus, taking jihad global would put an end to the internal war that roiled the jihadist movement after it was defeated by local Muslim regimes. "The solution" was to drag the United States into a total confrontation with the ummah and wake Muslims from their political slumber.

But what bin Laden's deputy did not recognize was that the al-Jama'a senior leaders had already made up their minds about the peace initiative. They viewed the battle as strategically lost, and they felt that the costs of continuing the fight could not match any likely benefits. Their rank and file at home were exhausted and needed breathing space to heal their wounds. There was fresh thinking: is the conception of jihad against the near enemy licit in terms of Islamic law? How high are the costs to the ummah? Are not there other nonviolent ways, such as al-da'wa (call), to Islamize society?

Implicit in these questions is a utilitarian, rational calculation that differs from what doctrinaire jihadis, who view loss and gain in absolute religious terms, think. The latter say this: "since we are fighting to make God's word supreme, our death and sacrifice will ultimately expedite this process and we will be rewarded in the afterlife. Martyrdom on the battlefield will not signify our end but a new beginning. Listen to bin Laden address young Muslims by citing Allah and His messenger: 'and do not speak of those who are slain in Allah's way as dead; nay [they are] alive, but you do not perceive' (al-Baqarah; 2:154)."[13] Similarly, in his letter to Taha, Zawahiri warns him to be loyal first and foremost to "God and His Prophet" because "righteousness will be your salvation in this world and the next."

While in the late 1990s jihadis in many Muslim lands began to question their dogma and ideology, in Afghanistan bin Laden and Zawahiri decided to fully internationalize the struggle by attacking Americans and their Western allies. Al-Jama'a wanted nothing to do with the new unholy alliance against the West; Zawahiri's pleas fell on deaf ears. By the spring of 1999 leaders of al-Jama'a at home and abroad formalized their unconditional ceasefire with the Egyptian government and called off their war. The rift and divide between the two camps – religious nationalists and transnationalists – deepened and widened. Despite early efforts by a few elements within the two blocs to play down their political, ideological, and personal disagreements, their ships were sailing in opposite directions. Since then they have substantively differed and bickered over armed tactics and strategy and politics in general. The struggle within has proved to be as costly and far-reaching as, if not more costly and far-reaching than, the confrontation between jihadis and "impious" rulers. The two camps have waged an open vendetta against one another, particularly since September 11 (see the next chapter for further details).

Since September 11 a tendency has existed among Western commentators to lump all jihadis together in one category and to overlook important subtleties, nuances, and differences among them. Al Qaeda represents just one violent current in a diverse and complex movement. Of all jihadis, the transnationalists, like bin Laden, Zawahiri, and their associates, are the most controversial and the least rooted within the jihadist movement, which since its inception in the 1970s has been more locally, rather than globally, oriented. Transnationalists are not only new to the game but they have also engendered an internal tug-of-war that is still unfolding.

For example, many people do not realize that the overwhelming majority of jihadis did not join Al Qaeda and that Zawahiri was one of the few prominent jihadis to do so. Although jihadis from many countries added their names to the statement announcing the formation of bin Laden's World Islamic Front, they belonged to tiny fringe factions, and leading jihadist and Islamist organizations were noticeable for their absence. No heavyweights like al-Jama'a al-Islamiya or the military wing of the Islamic Salvation Front (FIS) signed on, and many members of Zawahiri's Tanzim al-Jihad also opposed the shift to globalism. Although all these absentees shared bin Laden and Zawahiri's enmity against Western and American foreign policies, they did not join in the new crusade against the United States and were not tempted by Al Qaeda's utopian rhetoric; they remained on the sidelines. After suffering military defeat at home by the second half of the 1990s, tens of thousands of jihadis, including the top leadership, were languishing in prisons in Egypt, Algeria, and elsewhere; those who had been released from prison were burned out and took time off to think things over before making their next move.[14]

In 1999 and 2000 I met dozens of these released jihadis and had long conversations with them. They all sounded elated to be free and told horror stories of their prison years. They all gave the same answer to my question of what their next step would be: "We are enjoying our freedom and families. We need time to recover." After spending many hours with these former prisoners, I believe that they were genuinely exhausted and had adopted a wait-and-see attitude for the future. They did not sound enthusiastic about rejoining the fight against the near enemy or embarking on a more ambitious adventure against the far enemy, as Zawahiri and bin Laden incited them to do. This salient point tends to be glossed over, and all jihadis are portrayed as being synonymous with Al Qaeda. That is precisely what bin Laden, Zawahiri, and their associates want us to believe: that they speak for and represent the entire jihadist movement, but this is simply untrue.

What many Western pundits and bin Laden and Zawahiri do not say is that there was no swell of support among religious nationalists, let alone Muslim publics, for Al Qaeda. Far from it: Zawahiri faced a rebellion within his own organization for adding his signature to the formation of the World Islamic Front without consulting his lieutenants and operators, most of whom favored continuing the fight against the near enemy. They also believed that the new strategy – opening a second front against the sole surviving superpower and its Western allies – was unwise and endangered the very survival of their organization.

Private communication between Zawahiri and his associates reveals widespread opposition within the Tanzim to the bin Laden–Zawahiri joint venture. Tanzim al-Jihad's head of the so-called Islamic law committee in Yemen criticized what he considered Zawahiri's discarding of his responsibility to Egypt, and he asked why Zawahiri had not gone to "Egypt to perform the work there that he says he supports so much." He reminded Zawahiri that bin Laden had a "dark past" and "black history" and therefore he "could not be trusted."[15]

One of the revealing portraits that emerges out of Zawahiri's private communication with the Tanzim's rank and file is their entrenched suspicion and mistrust of bin Laden. Even the few who supported joining Al Qaeda expressed misgivings about how bin Laden had previously dealt with their organization – promises he had not kept and other lies he had told. The correspondence is littered with criticism of bin Laden's past conduct and warnings against Tanzim al-Jihad abandoning its top operational priority (the struggle against the Egyptian government) and being seduced by bin Laden, who was known as "the Contractor." For example, a warning sent by a Tanzim lieutenant in Yemen to Zawahiri said the alliance with bin Laden had caused "continuous catastrophes." He added, "if you keep receiving messages through the Contractor's system a big and a huge disaster will occur."

What is striking about these internal portraits gleaned from Al Qaeda computers is that Zawahiri's men expressed no admiration or affection toward bin Laden and even insinuated that their boss could fall under the former's spell and no longer be independent. They seemed to mistrust bin Laden and were worried about the future of their organization and its very survival.[16]

Multiple sources confirm that Zawahiri's move to join Al Qaeda inflamed internal rivalries among Tanzim al-Jihad operators, who first learned about it from the media. The correspondence between Zawahiri and his followers was so embittered that both sides accused each other of "treachery," and Zawahiri expelled two leading members of his group in London. According to Hani al-Sibai, a former leader of the Jihad group, when Zawahiri called an emergency meeting demanded by angry members, there was so much opposition and resistance to the joint venture with bin Laden that Zawahiri threatened to resign: "The members were shocked that their leader joined [Al Qaeda] without asking them. Only a few, who could be counted on the fingers, supported it."[17] Zawahiri, Sibai notes, did not convince those present that targeting America would reinvigorate and unite jihadis; many voiced concerns and warned of dire consequences, although they said they had no choice but to join because they were stranded in Afghanistan and Yemen and were being hunted by the Egyptian security services with nowhere to go. They felt they were in the same boat with Zawahiri, associates say, and that they could not easily disembark. As to Zawahiri's threat to resign, those at the meeting in Afghanistan knew it was a "game" designed to unnerve them.

Although they rejected his resignation and insisted on his emara, or leadership, the seeds of discord were sown within Zawahiri's homogeneous organization. Tariq Anwar, who attended the meeting, provided an insider's account of the prevalent bitter atmosphere (recovered from the Al Qaeda computers in Kabul). He reported that Zawahiri had repeatedly threatened to resign; had denounced his own brother, Mohammed (accused of squandering funds); and had revealed that financial accounts for two years were missing. Everybody agreed this was a disaster, according to Anwar, a veteran associate of Zawahiri. "I expected some members to start wrestling each other. I always felt this entity may dissolve in seconds."[18]

In other words, that gathering of Islamic Jihad did not put an end to the entropy and winter of discontent among its members. According to Sibai, the overwhelming majority of Islamic Jihad operators residing outside Afghanistan were more security-conscious than Zawahiri and insisted on keeping the fight focused on the near enemy instead of the far enemy ("the original kufar" or infidels, Jews and Americans).[19] They kept up the pressure on Zawahiri to distance himself from bin Laden and to maintain their organization's independence from Al Qaeda.

In 1999 and 2000 I interviewed former members of the Jihad Group in Egypt, all of whom expressed bewilderment at Zawahiri's declaration of war on the United States. The consensus was that taking jihad global would endanger the very survival of Zawahiri's organization, after it had already suffered heavy blows from the Egyptian authorities. Most of all, these former jihadis were surprised by Zawahiri's dramatic shift in priorities and his deference to bin Laden because, they said, there existed little support within Tanzim al-Jihad for the new adventure.

Clearly these jihadis with whom I talked sounded as critical of America and its foreign policies as Zawahiri, but they justified their opposition to internationalizing jihad in terms of costs and benefits, not on moral grounds. They pointed out that the infrastructure of Tanzim al-Jihad inside Egypt had been dismantled and lay in ruins. Between 1993 and 1998 almost a 1000-strong cadre of operatives had been incarcerated by the Egyptian government, thanks to operational blunders committed by Zawahiri and his top aides. As a result, Zawahiri had already taken a tactical decision to suspend military operations in Egypt and called on his followers to observe a "truce" and assess what went wrong and why senior lieutenants had fallen into the government's hands.[20] How then could Zawahiri turn around, former associates critically inquired, and declare war on the West? "It goes against common sense and military doctrine. That was a kiss of death," a jihadi who in the 1980s spent several years in an Egyptian prison, told me.

America Joins the Fray

Indeed, before the ink had dried on Zawahiri's signature joining the World Islamic Front, the high costs to his men and organization became apparent. The United States no longer pretended to be neutral in the unfolding bloody struggle between its ruling Muslim clients and militant Islamists. Although in the early 1990s American officials maintained a healthy distance between mainstream Islamists and pro-Western Arab regimes, establishing diplomatic contacts with the former, by the second half of the decade they threw caution to the wind and fully sided with their ruling allies. America's active intervention on behalf of its friends tipped the balance dramatically in their favor.

But the configuration of forces had already shifted in favor of authoritarian Muslim rulers and against religious nationalists. America's belated decision to join the fray on the side of its allies reveals its over-reaction to the so-called Islamic threat insofar as it constitutes a real danger to the tenure of power of specific regimes in the Middle East.

Egypt and Algeria are two examples that spring to mind. Scores of Egyptian jihadis whom I interviewed acknowledged they had no chance of actually constituting themselves as an alternative or ruling order in Cairo; they said they were not equipped socially and politically or even intellectually to construct a functioning Islamic polity. The assassination of Sadat was more of an operational fluke than a well-delineated, long-term strategy to replace the entrenched secular order with an Islamic entity, more than one jihadi told me. From the early 1990s until 1997 jihadis carried out attacks, most of which were skirmishes that did not represent an existential threat to the Egyptian state. Yet the U.S. government was extremely rattled by manifestations of Islamist activity and jihadis' violence. Although it may have been nasty and murderous for those on the receiving end, the jihadist challenge did not really constitute the vanguard of either social revolution or a skillfully executed coup within the political class and state administration and bureaucracy. Jihadis' violence was highly costly in human and material terms but they could not have captured the Egyptian state; that would have been a tall order for the whole Islamist movement, not just jihadis.

Equally, in Algeria the civil war was just that and not a question of jihadis versus the secular state because the ruling elite was fragmented and cultivated Islamists and others in their curiously violent internecine games. An argument can be made that far from posing a viable alternative to the existing order, the jihadist phenomenon was in some respects its creation. The main point to stress is that many Western powers, including the United States, bought into the claim made by Arab rulers that the jihadist challenge posed as potent a danger as Soviet communism; American officials viewed jihadis' clash with their local ruling allies through the lens of the Cold War struggle, or more precisely as some kind of Central American Cold War, and they acted accordingly. Similarly, in the 1980s the Cold War mentality distorted the lens of U.S. policy makers and led them to ally themselves with the very militant Islamists whom they would consider a "security threat" a decade later.

When asked if U.S. strategies in the Arab world were shaped by the Cold War mentality, Thomas Kean, chairman of the National Commission on Terrorist Attacks Upon the United States – more commonly known as the 9/11 Commission – best expressed America's predicament:

> I think we're moving past it, but it's still a problem. We still always fight the last war. That was a problem with 9/11. When the planes attacked, we vectored our Air Force planes out to sea because we were looking for attacks coming from the ex–Soviet Union.[21]

To be fair, the Cold War mind-set was not the only factor that made the United States take sides in the unfolding internal struggle in the Muslim world. In a way, bin Laden and Zawahiri forced the United States to become more entangled in the region's shifting sands. For example, the 9/11 Commission reviewed more than 2.5 million pages of documents and interviewed more than 1200 individuals, including nearly every senior official from the Bush and previous administrations who had any responsibility related to the September attacks, and concluded that until 1996 hardly anyone in the U.S. government understood that bin Laden was an inspirer and organizer of the new terrorism; as late as 1997, even the CIA's Counterterrorist Center continued to describe him as an "extremist financier."[22] All that changed with the bin Laden–Zawahiri 1998 Declaration of War on the Americans, which pitted the United States against all jihadis, not just transnationalists who had been attacking U.S. interests since the early 1990s.

The Clinton administration had begun to construct an ambitious approach to confront the entire Al Qaeda network. In a 1998 commencement speech at the Naval Academy, President Clinton said:

> First, we will use our new integrated approach to intensify the fight against all forms of terrorism: to capture terrorists, no matter where they hide; to work with other nations to eliminate terrorist sanctuaries; to respond rapidly and effectively to protect Americans from terrorism at home and abroad.[23]

The new approach gained urgency after the attacks on the U.S. embassies in east Africa. The U.S. government fixed responsibility on bin Laden and his associates and struck militarily at an Al Qaeda camp in Afghanistan. In his memoir, President Clinton wrote that the goal was "perhaps to wipe out much of the al-Qaeda leadership."[24] Other American officials also told the 9/11 Commission that the strike's purpose was to "kill" bin Laden and his chief lieutenants, who were supposed to gather for a meeting at Khost, Afghanistan, to plan future attacks. Although the strike missed bin Laden and his senior aides, it marked the beginning of a sustained campaign to "immediately eliminate" any significant threat to Americans posed by the bin Laden network.[25] According to then–Secretary of State Madeleine Albright, Clinton specifically authorized the use of force to "kill" or "capture" bin Laden and his top aides.[26]

Likewise bin Laden and his senior aides arrived at a similar conclusion; correspondence stored in the Al Qaeda computers in Kabul shows that America's limited military retaliation reinforced bin Laden and Zawahiri's belief that all-out onslaught on the United States would help their cause. Shortly after the U.S. missile strike, Zawahiri used bin Laden's satellite phone to call a Pakistani journalist, Rahimullah Yusufzai, who met with Taliban and Al Qaeda leaders many times, saying he and bin Laden were safe and adding, "The war has only just begun."[27] Both camps came to a similar conclusion, although Al Qaeda had the determination and the advantage of patiently plotting to kill civilians, not just American military personnel. Bin Laden, Zawahiri, and their associates became consumed with exacting revenge on America and satisfying and expanding their base of support.

In his memoir, Richard Clarke, then–Counterterrorism Coordinator at the White House, cites President Clinton as asking his senior national security team (one week after the attacks on the U.S. embassies) to develop an overall plan to make the destruction of Al Qaeda "one of our top national security objectives and an urgent one." Clinton stressed that although retaliation is needed, "we gotta get rid of these guys once and for all."[28] At a meeting with the heads of the CIA, the FBI, the Justice Department, and others at the White House fifteen months after the embassy attacks, Clinton's National Security Advisor Sandy Berger could not have been more graphic: "I spoke with the President and he wants you all to know . . . this is it, nothing more important, all assets. We stop this fucker."[29] Clinton confirms his advisers' accounts by writing that after the attacks on the U.S. embassies in east Africa, "I became intently focused on capturing or killing him and with destroying al-Qaeda."[30]

Clarke, who describes himself as having been "obsessed" with Al Qaeda, said he and his colleagues at the White House got the message. They were resolute: "if al Qaeda could issue fatwas declaring war on us, we could do the same and more to them." The top priority, Clarke added, was to "eliminate the organization."[31] What that meant, according to Clarke, who coordinated American strategy toward Al Qaeda during the pivotal period from 1998 to 2001, was breaking up Al Qaeda cells worldwide, finding its money, training and arming its enemies, and eliminating all its leaders, not just bin Laden.[32]

Therefore, by the end of the 1990s a full-fledged confrontation between the United States and the bin Laden network was being fought on multiple levels. To suggest that on September 11 the U.S. government was caught napping does not mean it was unaware of Al Qaeda's menace and did not wage a hidden war against the network and its supposed allies and associates. For example, the CIA began a covert campaign to capture jihadis and pressed its partners to either incarcerate wanted fugitives or repatriate them to their home countries. CIA operatives had raided jihadist cells in Baku and Tirana and captured senior figures in Zawahiri's Tanzim al-Jihad. There were arrests in Azerbaijan, Bulgaria, Italy, Britain, Germany, Albania, and Uganda. The

9/11 Commission report says that several suspects were shipped to an Arab country, which it does not name (although it is known to be Egypt). Washington's new active intervention inflicted fatal blows on Egyptian jihadis, particularly Zawahiri's close confidants and followers. The United States and France also lent a helping hand to the Algerian government in the civil war against jihadis. Russia, Britain, and other European countries tightened the grip on jihadis' activities in their territories.[33]

After 1998 European, African, Latin American, and former Soviet Muslim countries extradited dozens of operatives of Tanzim al-Jihad and the Islamic Group to Egypt, which represented a major breakthrough in the Mubarak government's struggle against jihadis. These extraditions and arrests disrupted jihadis' paramilitary and political operations and weakened them further. According to the Egyptian authorities, these extradited fugitive chiefs provided valuable details about the inner workings of jihadist groups and their complex networks of support inside and outside of Egypt. For example, following the 1998 arrests in Baku and Tirana, more than 100 members of Zawahiri's Tanzim went on trial in Cairo, and Zawahiri and his brother Mohammed, who managed Al Qaeda's computer and media system, were sentenced to death in absentia. Particularly damaging to Zawahiri's group was the capture and repatriation to Egypt of his right-hand man and secret-keeper, Ahmad Salama Mabruk, who ran a cell in Azerbaijan. Mabruk knew the code names, telephone numbers, and hiding places of Tanzim al-Jihad's leading operators and reportedly revealed all under torture. Egyptian security services fell on a treasure trove of militants who had remained underground waiting to be activated. Ironically, Mabruk did not think much of bin Laden and strongly opposed both the alliance with Al Qaeda and taking jihad global. He left Afghanistan in protest and bitterly and vocally criticized Zawahiri's close relations with bin Laden. According to Sibai, Mabruk was one of the two associates that Zawahiri expelled from the Tanzim in June 1998. In less than a year, a seasoned cadre of operatives (hundreds) were put out of commission for good. That handicapped Tanzim al-Jihad's capacity to conduct military operations in Egypt. Former jihadis whom I interviewed acknowledged that by 1999 Zawahiri lost most of his human assets in Egypt and no longer possessed a functioning, let alone effective, network there.[34]

The Merger: A Way Out of the Bottleneck

Tanzim al-Jihad lieutenants held Zawahiri accountable for the irreparable damage inflicted on their organization by the Egyptian government assisted by Western intelligence services, particularly the United States. They said that Zawahiri's formal alliance with bin Laden made the American authorities obsessively hunt down members of Tanzim al-Jihad who were residing in Europe and help dismantle its secret cells in European capitals. Equally important, Zawahiri's joint venture with bin Laden did not bring financial stability to the hard-pressed operators, who could not make ends meet. As mentioned previously, documents obtained from the Al Qaeda computers in Afghanistan reveal a bleak picture whereby Zawahiri cut members' salaries in half, and his penny-pinching led to constant complaints and infighting among associates. For example, an operative pleaded desperately: "I am almost broke. The money I have may not last until the feast. Please send money or bring it to us as soon as possible." Another pinched activist was told to find a house for just $30 a month. Several operators resigned after being ordered by Zawahiri to tighten their belts further and "stop all expenses unless it is an emergency."[35] Obviously, bin Laden was not as generous as some members had hoped and others had feared. Not only was there no marked improvement in the well-being of the operatives, but their conditions actually worsened, according to the documents gleaned from the Al Qaeda computers.

In the summer of 1999 the combination of financial and operational difficulties led to an internal mutiny against Zawahiri, forcing him to step down as leader of Tanzim al-Jihad. A veteran lieutenant, Tharwat Shehata, who replaced him at the helm, wanted to return the organization to its original mandate of targeting the near enemy. The odds were against Shehata, however. Former associates say that the old guard around Zawahiri in Afghanistan resisted Shehata and tried to undermine him at every opportunity by questioning his fitness to lead. Since 1986 Zawahiri had painstakingly rebuilt Tanzim al-Jihad from scratch and surrounded himself with loyal associates. Shehata inherited a splintered and bleeding organization, a shadow of its former self, which desperately needed cash and restructuring. Those who knew Shehata said he could not overcome the forces arrayed against him. He could neither redirect the Islamic Jihad ship back to the old harbor nor find the money to meet the current needs of its members. Shehata had little choice but to hand the steering wheel back to Zawahiri, who resumed control of Tanzim.[36]

Far from ending acrimony and the war within Islamic Jihad, the latest convulsion at the top sealed its fate. A bulletin (stored on one of the Al Qaeda computers in Kabul) that went out to members to try to explain what occurred, sheds light on the internal tensions tearing the organization apart: "The heart is full of pain, sorrow and bitterness. . . . There is a new problem and a new dispute every day." The report claimed that Shehata was unfit to lead because he had attacked Zawahiri as a "liar, a sinner and a cheat," had thrown stones at an accountant and called him a homosexual, and had pushed others "to the brink of explosion." Some members who were upset with Shehata's misconduct, the bulletin added, "left the city to avoid meeting or even seeing" him.[37]

But once back in the driver's seat Zawahiri did not take stock of what had gone wrong and why former associates, who had been loyal, either left the organization or rebelled against his dictatorship. He moved with full speed to consolidate his control over Islamic Jihad and formalize his alliance with bin Laden. Again, the documents obtained from Al Qaeda computers provide a glimpse of his tactics and state of mind. As soon as he regained leadership of the organization, Zawahiri sent a note to his colleagues (addressed specifically to a senior lieutenant in charge of an underground cell, alias Abu Mohammed al-Masri) proposing a formal merger with Al Qaeda as "a way out of the bottleneck." Using the language of global commerce Zawahiri wrote that the merger could "increase profits," bring more dividends for jihad, and reduce the risks from "international monopolies" – the CIA and Egyptian security services. It is worth quoting the letter in full to show the internal struggle that was occurring within the organization:

To: [Abu Mohammed al-Masri]
[An alias used by Abdullah Ahmad Abdullah]
From Ayman al-Zawahiri
Date: May 3, 2001

The following is a summary of our intentions: We are trying to return to our previous main activity [probably the merger]. The most important step was starting the school [Al Qaeda], the programs of which have been started. We also provided the teachers [mujahedeen] with means of conducting profitable trade [jihad] as much as we could. Matters are all promising, except for the unfriendliness of two teachers [dissidents], despite what we have provided for them. We are patient.

As you know, the situation below in the village [Egypt] has become bad for traders [jihadis]. Our Upper Egyptian relatives [Islamic Group] have left the market [armed struggle], and we are suffering from international monopolies [hunted by Western and intelligence services]. Conflicts take place between us for trivial reasons, due to scarcity of resources. We are dispersed over various cities. However, God had mercy on us when the Omar Brothers Company [the Taliban] here opened the market for traders and provided them with an opportunity to reorganize, may God reward them. Among the benefits of residence here is that traders from all over gather in one place under one company, which increases familiarity and cooperation among them, particularly between us and the Abdullah Contracting Company [bin Laden and his associates]. The latest result of this cooperation is ... the offer they gave. Following is a summary of the offer:

Encourage commercial activity [jihad] in the village to face foreign investors [Americans and their allies]; stimulate publicity; then agree on joint work to unify trade in our area. Close relations allowed for an open dialogue to solve our problems. Colleagues here believe that this is an excellent opportunity to encourage sales in general, and in the village in particular. They are keen on the success of the project. They are also hopeful that this may be a way out of the bottleneck to transfer our activities to the states of multinationals and joint profit. We are negotiating the details with both sides ... [38]

Zawahiri concluded his letter by urging colleagues to spread the word among sympathizers and welcoming all those who want to participate in Al Qaeda's training camps in Afghanistan, although he said they would have to cover their own expenses, at least temporarily. He also impressed on them the need to think of ways to reactivate military operations against Westerners and Israelis inside Egypt.[39]

Although some members welcomed Zawahiri's sales pitch "as long as it leads to stimulating profitable trade" and "ends the state of inertia we are in now," others were not enthusiastic. They accused Zawahiri of steering the Tanzim ship in dangerous waters and, instead, favored continuing the fight against the Egyptian regime rather than confronting the United States and its Western allies.[40] It is useful to quote one of the responses to Zawahiri's letter to highlight the deep gulf separating the religious nationalist bloc from the transnationalists like Zawahiri within Tanzim:

To: Ayman al-Zawahiri
From Unknown
Folder: Letters
Date: Summer, 2001

Dear brother Abdullah al-Dayam:
[Another alias for Zawahiri]

... I disagree completely with the issue of sales and profits. These are not profits. There are rather a farce of compound losses. I believe that going on in this is a dead end, as if we were fighting ghosts or windmills. Enough of pouring musk on barren land.

I don't believe that we need to give indications of how this unplanned path will fail. All we need to do is to estimate the company's assets since the beginning of this last phase, then take inventory of what remains [probably bin Laden's lack of generosity since Zawahiri joined bin Laden's Islamic Front in 1998]. Count the number of laborers in your farms [probably cells and new recruits] at the mother's area [probably Egypt], then see if anyone has stayed. Consider any of the many projects where you enthusiastically participated. Did any of them succeed [probably Tanzim al-Jihad's failure to carry out attacks inside Egypt], other than the Badr external greenhouses [probably operations against America], which enjoyed limited success?

All indicators point out that the place and time are not suitable for this type of agriculture [probably merger with Al Qaeda and taking jihad global]. Cotton may not be planted in Siberia, just as apples cannot be planted in hot areas. I am sure you are aware that wheat is planted in winter and cotton in summer. After all our efforts we haven't seen any crops in winter or summer [probably no results].

This type of agriculture is ridiculous. It's as if we were throwing good seeds onto barren land.

In previous experiments where the circumstances and seeds were better we made losses. Now everything has deteriorated. Ask those with experience in agriculture and history [probably referring to the dismantling of Tanzim al-Jihad cells in Egypt and European countries after the formation of the World Islamic Front].[41]

Despite the warnings and protests of leading associates within Tanzim, Zawahiri pushed ahead with plans to merge with Al Qaeda: "Stop digging problems from the grave," he pleaded in a letter to followers that was stored on a computer in Kabul, dated May 2001. Bin Laden, he added, had a "project" that needed their support. "Our friend has been successful and is seriously preparing for other successful jobs. . . . Gathering together is a pillar for our success."[42] Zawahiri sent another memo to colleagues: "Brothers, the competition has escalated. We cannot stand idly by as observers. We cannot wait. Events are happening quickly."[43] In an undated note, a writer using a common alias for bin Laden made his own pitch to a Tanzim al-Jihad lieutenant, Abdullah Ahmad, to whom Zawahiri had appealed earlier: "We all support this project and believe that it will provide a way out."[44] To the dismay and fear of many of his colleagues, in the spring of 2001 Zawahiri incorporated his organization with Al Qaeda under a new "company" name: Qaeda al-jihad. In June 2001 Qaeda al-jihad issued "Statement No. 1" (found on an Al Qaeda computer in Afghanistan) that threatened the "Zionist and crusader coalition" that "they will soon roast in the same flames they now play with."[45] Tanzim al-Jihad, originally established to struggle against the near enemy, ceased to exist and was replaced by Al Qaeda, whose fundamental mandate and mission are to target the far enemy.

Three points are worth stressing about the internal correspondence between Zawahiri and his colleagues. First, it provides an intimate view into Tanzim al-Jihad's inner circle and workings and shows how its military setbacks in "the village" (Egypt) precipitated internal upheaval and led Zawahiri to seek salvation by joining bin Laden's global jihad caravan. Second, the documents obtained from Al Qaeda's computers, along with other primary sources, flesh out the stiff opposition that Zawahiri faced in his attempt to redirect the Tanzim journey. There existed little support among his leading associates, including the two most senior figures, Mabruk and Shehata, for taking jihad global and consummating a marriage with bin Laden's Al Qaeda. Their hearts and minds remained focused on Egypt, not on the United States, and, unlike Zawahiri, they did not undergo an ideological transformation and were not taken in by bin Laden. Although Zawahiri had finally merged his group with Al Qaeda, he did it by fiat against the wishes of a critical constituency.

Finally, the merger did not end the civil war within Tanzim al-Jihad, although it was briefly silenced by the new, bigger war with the United

States and its allies. Former associates of Zawahiri say that scores of Tanzim al-Jihad members stayed on the sidelines, and several key lieutenants resigned in protest. If Zawahiri's goal was to stop internal bickering and rivalries, as he implied, he tactically succeeded in doing so. But in the process he fed entropy and endangered, as his colleagues had warned him, the very existence of the organization. Former jihadis agree that with the exception of Zawahiri and some loyal operatives scattered in a few hiding places, Tanzim al-Jihad has lost its infrastructure and operational underground cells both inside and outside of Egypt; it is leaderless, with most of its members either incarcerated or having given up altogether. "It is a defunct organization," a knowledgeable Islamist said, although the attacks against tourists in Egypt since 2004 raise serious questions about how "defunct" Tanzim al-Jihad really is. The spectacular, coordinated, and suicide nature of the bombings, coupled with the strategic choice of the targets, carries the fingerprints of Zawahiri's Tanzim. We have to wait and see if Zawahiri has reestablished a foothold in Egypt and succeeded in recruiting new cells. The signs are alarming.

Unlike Zawahiri, who upped the ante, his counterparts in al-Jama'a al-Islamiya, by far the biggest jihadist organization in the Arab world, reached a dramatically different conclusion. As mentioned previously, defeat at home motivated Islamic Group leaders to lay down their arms and begin to question the utility of the armed struggle against the near enemy. Also, from the outset they recognized the danger inherent in attacking the United States and bringing its wrath and power on the jihadis' heads. Indeed, after bin Laden and Zawahiri declared war on America, jihadis in general, not just Al Qaeda operatives, were targeted by American and European intelligence services, and some were grabbed and sent home, including Islamic Group members. Although it was not their war, they were caught in it when the U.S. embassies in Kenya and Tanzania were attacked. Islamic Group leaders acknowledged that bin Laden and Zawahiri's "biggest mistake" was to translate their anti-American diatribe into violent deeds against American diplomats and citizens. The Islamic Group said they wanted nothing to do with Al Qaeda and were not a "party" to any military campaign confronting Americans.[46]

Other leading jihadist groups elsewhere also did not join Al Qaeda and kept their distance from its global struggle. I spent two years, 1999–2000, interviewing former jihadis, Islamists, activists, and civil society leaders in the Middle East and abroad. There was a general agreement among those involved that Al Qaeda did not have a future and possessed no power base outside Afghanistan that could sustain it in the long term. Few had taken the Al Qaeda network seriously, and most dismissed it as an overambitious venture built and financed by bin Laden, a multimillionaire dissident Saudi, to force his former patrons, the royal family, to recognize his political influence and grant him power. Some Yemeni associates of the Afghan war years told me that bin Laden had a big chip on his shoulder from being turned down by the ruling Saud house in the 1990–1 Gulf war. Since then, he had nursed his grievances and felt he needed to redeem his injured pride. On the whole, jihadis and Islamists did not think very highly of bin Laden's jihadist credentials and viewed him more as a personal-political phenomenon than a religious-sociological one.

Others said that the Americans, by targeting bin Laden, turned him into a "star" and a "hero." My questions about bin Laden's World Islamic Front went mostly unanswered or were thrown back at me: "forget about bin Laden; he is a small player," a former member of the Jihad Group advised. Another asked skeptically: "why are Americans too obsessed with this insignificant network?" In fact, before the 1998 attacks on the U.S. embassies in Kenya and Tanzania few American officials understood, let alone obsessed about, bin Laden's network. However, after the attacks on the embassies, Clinton administration officials recognized the new danger and called for the elimination of the bin Laden organization, although they did not assign it a top priority on their policy agenda. Bush aides, as Richard Clarke noted in his illuminating memoir, were much less concerned about Al Qaeda's threat than their Clinton administration predecessors were and ranked it even lower.

On this, the U.S. foreign policy establishment and non–Al Qaeda jihadis were in agreement. Less than a year before September 11 non–Al Qaeda jihadis did not appreciate the operational and political weight of Al Qaeda and the danger it posed to the international community, including the ummah. In the late 1990s the dominant question among the bulk of jihadis outside Afghanistan was how to convince local governments that they were sincere in their desire to terminate their armed campaign and that they had rethought their previous stance on waging jihad. The big debate on Arab television stations and on the editorial pages of leading newspapers centered on whether to trust jihadis and give them an opportunity to prove themselves. There was hope in the air that the prolonged and costly confrontation between religious nationalists and secular authoritarian rulers was over, and that the religious nationalists had lost the battle. From Egypt to Algeria and from Yemen to London, jihadis engaged in a heated debate over how far to go in acknowledging past errors and charting a new paradigm.

The winds of change had finally reached the jihadist universe, or so we thought. I sat in on meetings between former jihadis who openly debated the utility of offering one-sided concessions to the authorities. They discussed the legitimacy of participation in the political process and engagement with secular political parties and forces. Incarcerated jihadis also engaged in major revisions of words and deeds. In 2000 I interviewed Montasser al-Zayat, a well-known attorney defending Islamists and jihadis in Egyptian trials, who said his clients had written books of revisions and that he would make them available to me if I could publicize them. Although I declined the offer because I am not a publicity agent, Zayat and his clients were attempting to get the word out regarding the new thinking taking place within the jihadist movement. They had to break through the wall of official and societal hostility and convince their foot soldiers to abide by the ceasefire. It was not easy because of widespread suspicion of jihadis at home and abroad.

Nevertheless, it appeared that the majority of the religious nationalists had embarked on a nonviolent journey. There was no return to the old violent days of the early 1980s and 1990s. Al Qaeda's tirades seemed to be divorced from the dominant jihadist reality, a lone voice in the Afghan wilderness. Operationally, Al Qaeda did represent a security menace but it possessed no mass following and no theoretical repertoire of ideas. The transition from localism to globalism marked a rupture in the jihadist historical doctrine and practice.

Why We Underestimated Al Qaeda

And yet, on September 11, bin Laden, Zawahiri, and their associates were heard loud and clear. They have proved to be much more lethal, durable, and adaptable than had been expected. Why did some of us, even researchers who work on social and political fringe movements, underestimate Al Qaeda's operational reach and its capacity to carry out spectacular military operations along the lines of September 11? First, we measured efficacy with numbers. Although Al Qaeda represented a tiny minority within the jihadist movement, it possessed a formidable human armada. We should have recognized that an organization's strength depends on its ideological cohesiveness and asabiya, or tribal solidarity, the charisma of its leaders, and the dedication and commitment of its members, not just on the number of its members. Al Qaeda also proved to be very professional in its approach to militancy, particularly on intelligence-gathering, meticulous planning, organizational structure, and security. In this regard, Al Qaeda, which comprised thousands of die-hard loyalists willing to commit suicide, constituted an effective paramilitary force to be reckoned with.

Next, we underestimated bin Laden's mobilizational skills and charisma as well as his determination to exact revenge on "the enemies of God." He infused Al Qaeda with raw tribalism coupled with religious messianism that resonated with the imagination of young zealous Muslim men, particularly from the Arabian Peninsula. Although the Egyptian contingent within Al Qaeda served as the brain and nerve center of the organization, Saudis and Yemenis comprised the foot soldiers. Bin Laden spent considerable energy and resources recruiting young men from his homelands, Saudi Arabia and Yemen, to balance the dominant role of Egyptians in Al Qaeda's top echelons and to build a loyal base of support. It is little wonder that on September 11 fifteen of the nineteen hijackers were Saudis. The memoir of bin Laden's personal bodyguard, Nasir Abdullah al-Bahri, points to a concerted effort by bin Laden to indoctrinate young Saudis and Yemenis and entice them to join his network. Al-Bahri said his own group, made up of dozens of Saudis and Yemenis, joined bin Laden's network en masse after bin Laden personally waged "a kind of media campaign directed at us in an attempt to convince us of the justification for his call for jihad against America."[47]

Bin Laden's recruiting techniques were successful and brought him a small army of young Saudis and Yemenis, along with other nationalities, who formed the backbone of Al Qaeda's striking force. Those zealous Saudis and Yemenis would do anything for him and for the cause – including die. Khalid Sheikh Mohammed, who supervised the

September 11 planes operation, estimates that in any given camp in Afghanistan, 70 percent of the mujahedeen were Saudis, 20 percent were Yemenis, and 10 percent were from elsewhere.[48] Diaries by former associates and pre–September 11 training videotapes widely disseminated among Saudis and Yemenis provide a clear picture of how bin Laden used propaganda most powerfully and effectively. The core of his message was that the "Land of the Two Holy Places," Mecca and Medina, the spiritual heart of Islam, had been occupied by the infidel Americans and Jews. He used fiery religious symbolism to shock the sensibilities of young Saudis and inspire them to journey to Afghanistan and train for the coming war against the United States, the new occupier of Muslim holy lands. In one training tape, standing in front of a wall-sized map of the world, symbolizing the scope of the problems and solutions he wanted his audience to be conscious of, bin Laden cried: "The wounds of the Muslims are deep everywhere. But today our wounds are deeper because the crusaders and the Jews have joined together to invade the heart of dar al-islam [the House of Islam]: our most sacred places in Saudi Arabia, Mecca and Medina, including the Prophet's Mosque, and the al-Aqsa Mosque and Dome of the Rock in Jerusalem [al-Quds]."[49]

Driving that point home, the tape begins with interspersed images of American troops in Saudi Arabia, coupled with former U.S. presidents visiting, socializing, and fraternizing with Saudi leaders. With his voice thundering in rage, bin Laden laments that Saudi rulers allow American troops, including Jewish and Christian male and female soldiers, to roam freely on the land where the Prophet Mohammed was born and the Qur'an descended: "This land is exceptional because it is the most beloved by Allah. How could it be that the Americans are permitted to wander freely on the Prophet's land? Have Muslim peoples lost their faith? Have they forsaken the Prophet's religion? Forgive me, Allah, I wash my hands of these [Muslim] rulers!"[50]

To magnify the shock effects, the viewer is bombarded with graphically bloodied and horrifying images of Palestinian, Iraqi, and other Muslim children. Bin Laden angrily asks, "Where is the Muslim ummah and its one billion believers? The ummah sees and hears that the Qur'an is being defamed, burned, and used by the Jews as disposable tissues, yet it stands idly by . . ." He pleads with Muslims to rise up and avenge the wrongs committed against their brethren: "The only way to destroy this atheism is by jihad, fighting, and bombings that bring martyrdom. Only blood will wipe out the shame and the dishonor inflicted on Muslims."[51]

This inflammatory ideological fuel powered the September 11 suicidal airplane hijackers. In the 1990s we focused on the primary, big jihadist movements in Egypt and Algeria and overlooked bin Laden's frantic and systemic efforts to build a jihadist empire in Afghanistan. He tailored his message and recruiting tactics to the Saudi and Yemeni youths who were inspired by both the messenger and the message. America's military intervention in the 1990–1 Gulf crisis and its fateful decision to permanently station troops in Saudi Arabia were catalysts in the fracturing of the geostrategic alliance between Wahhabis-Salafis, on the one hand, and Western powers, on the other, that had been inaugurated after World War II. Bin Laden's genius lies in channeling and redirecting the anticommunist fervor of Wahhabis-Salafis against the West, particularly the United States. It was a big feat to puncture a hole in the historical relationship that was half a century old. Bin Laden did it over the heads and against the wishes of the Saudi ruling and religious establishments.

In his diaries, al-Bahri provides a first-hand account of how in 1996 bin Laden spent days trying to recruit him and scores of his colleagues. He says that he was initially skeptical of bin Laden's efforts and rejected his offer to become a member of Al Qaeda; but bin Laden would not take no for an answer, and for three days he tried to convince al-Bahri to join the jihad caravan against the United States. "Throughout the three days," al-Bahri recalls, "sheikh Osama continued to talk to us and to put to us the issue of the Arabian Peninsula and U.S. occupation of it. Of course, we were convinced there was a U.S. presence and a U.S. occupation, but our view was different from his view, in light of the fatwas of sheikh Abd al-Aziz bin Baz (former mufti of Saudi Arabia) and sheikh Mohammed Salih bin-Uthaymayn, who issued fatwas on the permissibility of calling on the assistance of unbelievers."[52]

By the end of the third day, al-Bahri notes, he and his young colleagues saw the light: "His strong argument opened to us distant and wide horizons about the issue and about the situation of the ulema in Saudi Arabia, the situation of the existing alliance between the Saudi regime and the Islamic Salafi movement..." So when finally bin Laden called and asked if he had made up his mind, al-Bahri, known as Abu Jandal, said: "'I will not hide from you, sheikh, that what you said is convincing and that you are putting forward a clear case, but it is clear to me you do not have anyone from the people of the land itself, that is, from the people of the Arabian Peninsula, whose cause this is.' He said to me: 'What you say is true. Most of the brothers around me are Egyptians, Algerians, and North Africans. That is why I invite you to join our caravan.' I had believed that sheikh Osama had missed such a fact, but I discovered that he concentrated a great deal on the people of the Arabian Peninsula, especially on the people of Hijaz [the western province of Saudi Arabia where Mecca and Medina are located]."[53]

After al-Bahri and his group from Saudi Arabia and Yemen agreed to join with the Al Qaeda network, al-Bahri writes that each of them swore baiya, or fealty, to bin Laden secretly.[54] Al-Bahri worked closely with bin Laden as a trusted lieutenant and personal bodyguard from 1996 until the end of 2000, a critical period in the rise of bin Laden's network. Al-Bahri draws a fascinating sociological picture of bin Laden and his organization; anyone who wished to be a formal member of Al Qaeda had to pay homage to his personage. This new portrait sheds further light on Al Qaeda, a secret society with only one man who initiates members and knows their names and codes. At least since his 1991 estrangement from the Saudi royal family, bin Laden built a network of operatives who were blindly loyal to him. This fact could explain bin Laden's concentration on recruiting young Saudis and Yemenis who looked up to him as their hero and who, by their very presence, diluted the powerful influence of the Egyptians within the network. In his diaries, a senior member of the Al Qaeda Shura Council, Abu al-Walid, writes disapprovingly that some of bin Laden's young Saudi operatives worshipped the ground on which he walked; they would frequently tell him that if anyone should be "king," it would be him. Bin Laden was their king.[55]

In fact, inside accounts tell of bin Laden, who acquired a mythic reputation and was a cult personality among a loyal crowd of jihadis; the jihadis admired bin Laden's austerity and courage for turning his back on a life of wealth, luxury, and comfort. Those traits, which bin Laden nourished, captured the imagination of young Muslim men, mostly Arab, who reviled the political and moral decadence and corruption of the

Arab ruling elite. They found in bin Laden a heroic, fatherly figure who inspired them to sacrifice their lives for an idea and a cause. For example, what inspired a young recruit, like al-Bahri and his colleagues, was bin Ladin's down-to-earth attitude, modesty, and simplicity. Al-Bahri approvingly quotes bin Laden as often saying to his followers: "We want a simple life."[56]

It is worth quoting at length from al-Bahri's diaries to give the reader an inside sociological view of how and why bin Laden captivated the imagination of young followers:

> Imagine a man with the kind of resources he had, the cause he embraced, and his stature as a leader, sitting with us and eating rice and potatoes. I remember that at one period, we used to eat dried bread and water only. Sheikh Osama used to take hard bread, dip it in the water and eat it, saying: may God be praised. We are eating but there are millions of others who wish they could have something like this to eat.
>
> So we never really felt afraid as long as we were with that man. We ate with him, walked with him. Our love for sheikh Osama springs from the fact that we went hungry together and were filled together. We felt afraid with him and felt safe with him. We wept and rejoiced with him. We were joined by a common destiny. We lived a full life with him without discrimination. The man was very simple in all his dealings and in everything in his life. Nevertheless, he bore the nation's concerns and he did that very cleverly.
>
> Our life with sheikh Osama, his honorable character, tolerance, and easy dialogue with others caused us to become very attached to him. He was consistently very generous with others. No one ever came to ask for financial assistance and was rebuffed. I remember in this context that we once passed through a very difficult financial situation. An Arab brother who wished to travel abroad came and explained his difficult circumstances to him. Sheikh Osama went into the house, came out with whatever money his family had, which was around $100, and gave it to the man.
>
> I was aware of the sheikh's financial situation and said: "Abu Abdullah, why did you not leave a part of that money for us? Those who are staying here are more deserving than those who are leaving." He replied: "Our situation is not hard. God will send us money. Do not worry. Our livelihood will come to us." For five days after this incident we had nothing to eat except pomegranates which grew around

his house although they were not yet ripe. We ate raw pomegranates with bread, three times a day. I believe that God raised Osama bin Laden to a high status because despite his great wealth, he was very modest, attached only to what rewards God would give him, and his preference for the afterlife over this world.[57]

When asked about bin Laden's wealth and how he could have reached a situation of absolute poverty, al-Bahri offered a revealing response: "Sheikh Osama dealt with money from a special perspective. He preferred that he and his followers should live very economically and poorly so that they could learn to bear hardships and overcome crises, no matter how extreme. For this reason he followed a path of austerity and renunciation of worldly goods as an educational method that enhances people's ability to endure. Many other jihadist organizations were infiltrated with the help of money and luxury. This happened because their numbers lived in luxury and could not face hardship." And did this austere style of living also extend to his family, the interviewer retorted? "Yes," al-Bahri answered, "he treated his family and children in the same way."[58]

Regardless of whether this inside narrative accurately captures life in bin Laden's camps, it definitely shows that the Saudi millionaire successfully fostered an image of modesty, austerity, and simplicity. His followers, as al-Bahri notes, identified with him and felt at home in his presence. They related to him as a "father," an "uncle," and a charismatic icon. I and other researchers who in the 1990s worked on jihadist movements had no appreciation of the symbiotic relationship that had existed between bin Laden and his men. It was a relatively small, but highly dedicated, army of Saudi and Yemeni operators fully committed to bin Laden, unlike Egyptian jihadis whose loyalty was not absolute. We focused on the big picture and evolving trends in the jihadist movement but lost sight of a powerful actor who had been nursing his grievances, biding his time, and setting up the building blocks of a jihadist empire. While the Egyptian contingent provided a bureaucracy, structure, and ideas, young Saudis and Yemenis were the ones who mainly carried out the military operations. At the helm of the empire stood bin Laden, "a whole nation embodied in one man," as his mentor, sheikh Abdullah Azzam, reportedly said before his assassination – and as has since been repeated as an article of faith by his followers.

Finally, we missed the signs of bin Laden's obsession with exacting revenge on the Americans and inflicting massive civilian casualties. The logic of revenge and will to power overwhelmed his rationality and humanity. So determined and impatient to carry out the September 11 planes operation was he that a close associate heard him remark, "I will make it happen even if I do it by myself."[59] We also overestimated the effect of U.S. deterrence after the Clinton administration had taken measures to weaken Al Qaeda and keep it off balance. Far from deterring bin Laden, Zawahiri, and their cohorts, Washington's calculated response emboldened them to up the ante. They welcomed the coming war with the United States and expected Afghanistan to turn into a graveyard for the Americans, if and when they invaded, like it did for the Russians. As Zawahiri put it after the 1998 missile strike on an Al Qaeda camp in Afghanistan, "The war has only just begun." Three years later Al Qaeda took the war to the American heartland in New York and Washington.

FIVE

The Aftermath

The War Within

Although on September 11 Al Qaeda took its war to America and successfully flexed its military muscles by carrying out spectacular and coordinated attacks, success for Al Qaeda remains a distant dream, if not an illusion. It is arguable whether bin Laden possessed a strategic vision or a blueprint for the morning after. Debating the issue won't take us far because we cannot get into bin Laden's head. A more fruitful approach is to measure Al Qaeda's success or failure against its own expectations as stated in public pronouncements and internal messages. Taking stock of Al Qaeda's rhetoric and reality provides a balance sheet of breakthroughs and setbacks and enables us to critically reflect on the long-term viability of the bin Laden network.

Three sets of questions deserve special scrutiny. The first has to do with the impact of Al Qaeda's actions on the jihadist movement as a whole. To what extent have the attacks on the United States reinvigorated the jihadist movement and arrested entropy? Has the globalization of jihad stopped the internal rivalries and struggles that have roiled jihadis since the late 1990s, or has it exacerbated them further? Has gathering and merging together, as Zawahiri advocated, offered "a way out of the bottleneck" and ensured "success"? How did the majority of jihadis outside Afghanistan react to September 11? Did they join Al Qaeda's war against the far enemy, or did they attack bin Laden and Zawahiri for "declaring war on the entire world" without considering the international configuration of forces that would oppose them? In what ways has Al Qaeda evolved and devolved since the United States launched its "war on terror"? Has Al Qaeda morphed from a centralized global organization into an amorphous, diffuse, decentralized, and locally inspired and focused network? Are we witnessing a devolution of Al Qaeda or another metamorphosis, a mutation within the organization? Have September 11 and its aftermath widened the gap between mainstream Islamists and jihadis? How did mainstream Islamists cope with the reverberations of September 11?

The second set of questions ask to what extent Al Qaeda's call for war against the Americans has resonated with ordinary Muslims. Have bin Laden and Zawahiri succeeded in inciting Muslims to take arms against the Western powers? Have they dragged the United States, as they dreamed, into "an open battle" with the ummah, and have they brought about a clash of cultures and religions? How did the Muslim religious, political, and intellectual classes respond to the challenge posed by Al Qaeda? Did any of them join the fight? Or does a consensus exist among Arab/Muslim ulema, critics, and civil society leaders on the futility and nihilism of Al Qaeda's venture? Is there any attempt at deconstructing Al Qaeda's discourse and ideology?

The last set of questions focus on the American war on terror. How effective has the expansion of the "war on terror" been? Has it played into the hands of transnationalist jihadis like bin Laden and Zawahiri and given their network a new lease on life? Can the war against Al Qaeda be won on the battlefield, or would that require broader socioeconomic engagement with Muslim civil societies as well as addressing the structural crisis of governance and political economy in the Arab world? Have military preemption and cultural insolence undermined the struggle against militancy in general? To what extent does obsession with militarism and triumphalism and empire among a segment of the U.S. foreign policy elite feed and sustain confrontationalists in the Muslim world? What are the fundamental challenges facing accommodationists in both camps in trying to regain the initiative and silence the drums of war of cultures?

Jihadis' Responses

In general, outside Afghanistan the initial reaction of jihadis to September 11 was disbelief and deep skepticism about the identity of the perpetrators of the attacks. The overall sentiment expressed to me in conversations with several former jihadis is that Al Qaeda, a fringe organization in Afghanistan, did not have the operational reach or means to launch such complex military operations inside America; these former jihadis could not comprehend how nineteen young Arabs could escape the scrutiny and alertness of the U.S. intelligence services, infiltrate the airline security system, and hijack several planes and crash them into the World Trade Center and the Pentagon, highly sensitive and secured targets. In this, the reaction of jihadis was no different from that of the Arab and Muslim public at large, critical segments of which still hold this view.

Two weeks after September 11 I traveled to the Middle East to attend a panel on the future relations between the United States and the Arab world in light of the latest developments. Most striking to me was the widespread skepticism of almost everyone I met about the identity of who was behind the attacks. From airport workers to taxi drivers to bank managers to university students, I got a common question: "How could a few young Arab men fool the CIA?" Enamored of American power and the CIA legend, ordinary Arabs and Muslims did not believe that Al Qaeda could be responsible – and in fact found the whole thing unbelievable. Instead, many believed conspiracy theories circulating on various Western Web sites that pointed an accusing finger at the Israeli intelligence service, Mossad, or even at rogue elements within the U.S. government itself. Although illogical, the attitudes of Arabs and Muslims were not unique but were shared by some Westerners and Asians. It took a while – and bin Laden, Zawahiri, and their cohorts privately boasting about their feat and publicly taking responsibility – for some to recognize Al Qaeda's fingerprints on the September 11 crime scene.

Despite their initial skepticism, non–Al Qaeda jihadis in general did not heed bin Laden and Zawahiri's call and join the fight against the United States. Far from rushing to defend their transnationalist brethren, religious nationalists also dreaded the coming war and decided not to take sides. One of the major miscalculations made by bin Laden and Zawahiri was an expectation that attacking the United States would bring estranged jihadis back into the fold as well as mobilize the ummah against pro-Western Muslim rulers and their superpower patron – the United States; they had expected a Muslim response similar to that to the Russian invasion and occupation of Afghanistan. The goal was to generate a major world crisis – prompting and provoking the United States "to come out of its hole," as Seif al-Adl, Al Qaeda's overall military commander, wrote in a 2005 document, and attack Muslim countries – which would reinvigorate and unify a splintered, war-torn jihadist movement and restore its "credibility" in the eyes of the ummah and beleaguered people elsewhere.[1] At the heart of this thinking lies the idea advanced by Sayyid Qutb: that only an Islamic "vanguard" can rid Muslim society and politics of jahiliya (ignorance of divine authority) and restore hakimiya (God's sovereignty) to earth. What has changed is the nature of the enemy; although Qutb stressed the need to confront internal ghosts, bin Laden and his transnationalist crew thought that attacking the United States would galvanize the ummah and help it "wake from its slumber."

For example, Al Qaeda's 1998 attacks on the U.S. embassies in Kenya and Tanzania and the subsequent American missile strikes had brought high "profits" to the "Abdullah Contracting Company" (bin Laden's network) and turned bin Laden and his network into jihadi stars. His network's ranks swelled with new recruits, and internal dissension was silenced. The embassy bombings marked a turning point for bin Laden and his associates and greatly advanced their cause. In bin Laden and Zawahiri's eyes, striking inside America would bring a bigger bonanza in terms of new recruits and would make them jihadi megastars, particularly if the sole superpower confined its response to limited retaliation (as bin Laden and Zawahiri expected), not the full-scale invasion of Afghanistan that did result.

When the United States invaded Afghanistan, Al Qaeda found itself alone facing the brunt of the American armada. Rather than the expected major flow of seasoned jihadis and fresh volunteers to the Afghan theater, there was just a trickle of volunteers. America's Afghan war was dramatically different from Russia's. When Russian troops invaded Kabul, the calls for jihad echoed from almost every corner and mosque in Arab and Muslim lands. Tens of thousands of Muslim men, including jihadis, flooded into Afghanistan to resist the Russian occupation. They had the blessings of the religious and the ruling establishment. In contrast, there was a deafening silence when the United States declared war on the Taliban and Al Qaeda. Although many Muslims criticized America's impulsiveness and reliance on force, they stopped short of calling for jihad against the United States. No religious authority lent his name and legitimacy to repeling the U.S. troops. In response to an inquiry from the most senior Muslim chaplain in the U.S. army, a group of leading Islamic scholars issued a fatwa on 27 September 2001, declaring that American Muslims were obliged to serve in the armed forces of their country, even when the United States was at war with a Muslim nation. Yusuf al-Qardawi, one of the leading conservative Islamic scholars – who has been highly critical of American foreign policies – lent his name and prestige to this fatwa.[2] The very same Qardawi subsequently stated that killing the American occupiers in Iraq is legitimate.

This is a salient point because the responses of Muslims to both September 11 and the overthrow of the Taliban tend to be overlooked and drowned out by their subsequent vocal condemnation and opposition to the expansion of the U.S. "war on terror," particularly the American-led invasion and occupation of Iraq. Although Islamic scholars did not sanction America's military assault on Afghanistan, neither did they call, as they did in the 1980s, on young men to travel there and fight the Americans. Bin Laden and Zawahiri faced a difficult battle in their efforts to incite a large pool of recruits to come to their defense because they lacked legitimacy and a credible religious cover. Equally important, they possessed no social base of support outside of Saudi Arabia, Yemen, and, to a much smaller extent, Pakistan, from which they drew most of their foot soldiers. These pro-Western countries made a calculated decision to join the U.S. war against Al Qaeda and to crack down on Al Qaeda's adherents and supporters.

But Al Qaeda's grand failure lay in its inability to tap into the natural base of tens of thousands of like-minded jihadis – religious nationalists – who live throughout the Muslim landscape. Since September 11 attention among Western analysts and Western security services has focused on Al Qaeda's sleeping cells and sympathizers. Little has been said about the other huge pool of religious nationalists who, if they had joined the Al Qaeda network, could have qualitatively escalated and expanded the theater of military operations and increased the security risks multifold. Had bin Laden and Zawahiri succeeded in coopting and enticing the deactivated army of religious nationalists into the Al Qaeda network, they could have replenished its depleted ranks and fielded lethal

190 • The Far Enemy

brigades in many parts of the world. The current clash would have been deadlier if more jihadis had joined the fray.

This goes to the heart of whether Al Qaeda speaks for and represents the bulk of jihadis or is a fringe creature born out of the internal mutations and multiple internal struggles that have roiled the jihadist movement since the late 1990s. Before September 11 bin Laden and Zawahiri launched an ambitious campaign to control the movement and change its direction. Unable to rally the disparate factions and put an end to internal rivalries and entropy, they plunged into a confrontation with the United States, hoping that it would serve as a galvanizing and unifying experience. Al Qaeda's gamble did not pay off, however. Neither the ummah nor the bulk of jihadis were on the same wavelength as Al Qaeda. Surely, if Al Qaeda cannot speak for most jihadis, its claim to be the vanguard of the ummah does not carry much weight.

After withstanding initial shock and self-enforced silence, the chiefs of the main jihadist groups in the Middle East and elsewhere went public and pinned the blame squarely on bin Laden and Zawahiri, holding them personally accountable for endangering the very survival of their movement. Instead of expressing solidarity with their besieged and entrapped associates in the Afghan-Pakistani border area, the chiefs publicly blamed Al Qaeda for the problems being faced by other jihadist groups. Since the end of 2001 jihadis of different persuasions, both transnationalists and religious nationalists, have engaged in a bitter public quarrel revealing deep and wide rifts that separate them from one another. This intrajihadist tug-of-war has hardly been noticed, let alone critically examined, in the West, particularly in the United States.

Three points are worth highlighting. First, jihadis, who usually hibernate underground and tend to be highly secretive, for the first time exposed their dirty laundry in public and provided an authentic view into the war raging within their movement. As the walls of secrecy collapsed, so did the pretense of solidarity and altruism. Like secular activists, jihadis are political animals with huge egos and ambitions; they live on earth, not in heaven, and they are socialized into a subculture of authoritarianism and the cult of personality. Secondly, the public bickering among jihadis, fleshed out in the following pages, has showed the depth of existing fault lines and the new trends and shifts that have occurred among the different factions. The debate sheds light on how jihadis have coped with the September 11 earthquake and its aftershocks and what lessons, if any, have been learned. Finally, the response of jihadis to Al Qaeda is a useful barometer to measure the relative weight of the latter within the jihadist movement as a whole. For example, since September 11, has Al Qaeda made inroads into the religious nationalist camp? Has it appealed to and tapped a new pool of fighters? Has the bin Laden transnationalist organization been overshadowed and superseded by regional branches and affiliates, such as Al Qaeda in Iraq, Saudi Arabia, Yemen, Euorpe, and elsewhere, with local concerns and targets? Does this recent transformation affect Al Qaeda's armed tactics and operational reach against the far enemy, or is the decentralization and devolution of Al Qaeda a product of military necessity and adaptation to new conditions?

Since September 11 more than a dozen books, memoirs, and diaries written by leading jihadis, some of whom have played pivotal roles in the jihadist movement, have presented a devastatingly comprehensive critique of Al Qaeda. Far from being marginal or on the fringe, these jihadis, who know those in the Al Qaeda inner circle, are former associates of bin Laden, Zawahiri, and their cohorts and had previously fought with them against common enemies – "impious" Muslim rulers and godless communism. Their critique is important because it comes from within the movement, not from outside it. It lays bare the pretensions and assertions of bin Laden and Zawahiri regarding their war against the far enemy, and it offers a dramatically different alternative for overcoming the existential crisis facing the jihadist movement. Jihadis' critiques of Al Qaeda illuminate the cumulative social and political upheaval that has occurred within the movement in the last ten years, particularly since September 11, and the desperate efforts by religious nationalists to find a way out of the bottleneck into which bin Laden and Zawahiri have squeezed them.

In a nutshell, the core of the jihadis' critique is a direct assault on what the religious nationalists view as the shortsightedness and colossal miscalculations of bin Laden and Zawahiri. Although these veteran militants are highly critical of America and its foreign policies, they say that killing American civilians has proved to be disastrous for the Islamist and jihadist movements, and for the ummah as well. In their view, attacking the United States empowered the hardliners in the U.S.

foreign policy establishment and enabled them to unleash America's unrivaled power against Muslim countries, particularly Afghanistan and Iraq. They also say that pro-Western Muslim rulers now feel emboldened to crack down harder against all Islamists and former jihadis, not just Al Qaeda operators. I will present a broad sample of these writings, coupled with interviews I conducted, to give the reader a representative flavor and sense of jihadis' responses to September 11 and the subsequent developments.

Fault Lines Within Al Qaeda

Some of bin Laden's inner circle have publicly criticized his "catastrophic leadership" and his underestimation of American willpower. The Arabic-language newspaper *Asharq al-Awsat* obtained and published a rare critical document about bin Laden titled "The Story of the Afghan Arabs: From the Entry to Afghanistan to the Final Exodus with the Taliban," written by a senior member of the Al Qaeda Shura Council who is considered a leading theoretician in the organization and who witnessed and participated in the most important moments of the drama.[3] Although the editors did not disclose his name at the request of the former jihadis who negotiated the publishing deal, the author is Abu al-Walid al-Masri, one of the most veteran Afghan Arabs; he was based in Qandahar, and he supervised *The Islamic Principality*, a newsletter regarded as the mouthpiece of Mullah Omar, the deposed Taliban ruler.[4]

Abu al-Walid knew Mullah Omar and bin Laden well and worked closely with both; his account sheds light on the entangled relationship between the two militants, particularly on bin Laden's disdain of Mullah Omar's advice and his accommodation for the hawks within his organization at the expense of the doves. But this important testimony, based on Abu al-Walid's notebook, shows bin Laden in a highly negative light, managing Al Qaeda like a tribal fiefdom. For example, ignoring the advice of many of the hawks and doves around him, bin Laden, according to Abu al-Walid, thought that the United States was much weaker than people imagined and that it would not withstand two or three of Al Qaeda's painful blows. Bin Laden's evidence of this was the U.S. Marines "fleeing" Lebanon in 1983 when their headquarters in Beirut was blown up and the clashes in Somalia, which led the U.S. forces to leave in a "shameful disarray and indecorous haste." But Abu al-Walid admits that after September 11 matters "took an opposite turn compared to what bin Laden had imagined. Instead of buckling under his three painful blows, America retaliated and destroyed both the Taliban and Al Qaeda."5

Al Qaeda members knew better but they did not dare to challenge bin Laden; Abu al-Walid says they told bin Laden: "You are the emir, do as you please!" Such a view, Abu al-Walid adds, is not only wrong but dangerous:

> It encourages recklessness and causes disorganization, characteristics which are unsuitable for this existential battle in which we confront the greatest force in the world, the USA. It is therefore necessary to consider the real nature and the size of this battle as well as preparing for it in a way that takes into account its danger and, consequently, mobilizing the mujahedeen and the Muslim masses for an extended and a long-term battle that requires great sacrifices. It was necessary to prepare for the worst scenario that could come of this battle rather than dreaming of an easy victory. This shortcoming definitely led to our defeat as we were prepared materially and psychologically only for an easy short-term battle, this is exactly what happened.6

Abu al-Walid is more critical of bin Laden for stifling internal debate and hampering open and effective decision making than for underestimating America because that is what ultimately caused underestimation of the battle and led to the military defeat. According to Abu al-Walid, the final stages of Al Qaeda's existence in Afghanistan represented "a tragic example of an Islamic movement managed by a catastrophic leadership. Every one knew that their leader was leading them to the abyss and even leading the entire country to utter destruction, but they continued to bend to his will and take his orders with suicidal submission."7

This powerful indictment by a senior member of bin Laden's inner circle shows restiveness and bitterness among Al Qaeda's top-echelon leadership after suffering crippling blows since September 11. At certain points Abu al-Walid's firsthand account takes personal stabs at bin Laden by talking about his "extreme infatuation" or "crazy attraction" with the media in general and the international media in particular; Mullah Omar and other Taliban officials often impressed on bin Laden

the need to refrain from giving interviews to the international media
and involving them in uneccessary conflicts with the world community.
Their underlying message to bin Laden, according to Abu al-Walid, who
worked closely with Mullah Omar, was that bin Laden was one of them
but should not speak to the media. But bin Laden was "obsessed" with
the media, Abu al-Walid writes, particularly the international media,
and Mullah Omar could not restrain or silence him; bin Laden was prepared to sacrifice Afghanistan and Mullah Omar at the altar of his public
relations campaign.[8]

Abu al-Walid draws a picture of bin Laden as being self-centered and
manipulative, more concerned with his own media image than with the
stability and security of his Taliban hosts; his motto was: "let them go
to hell as long as I can have my cup of tea." It is little wonder that
the arrival, or rather the return, of bin Laden to Afghanistan 1996,
Abu al-Walid argues, represented one of the biggest challenges facing
the Taliban movement at a time when it had not consolidated its control over the entire country; bin Laden overburdened the Taliban rule
and made them more enemies than they could afford, particularly Saudi
Arabia, a generous financial patron, and the world community.

According to Abu al-Walid, who witnessed the internal debates
among the Taliban mullahs, a group composed of hawks resented bin
Laden's conduct and believed that he was deciding Afghanistan's foreign policy, and that his controversial media statements cost the Taliban
a great deal in American, Pakistani, and official Arab support; these
hawks advocated the mass expulsion of the Afghan Arabs, who became
a local and international liability to the Taliban. Another anti–bin
Laden faction among the hawks, who were opposed to his presence in
Afghanistan, advanced a conspiratorial theory and claimed that he had
been sent by the Americans as a ploy to destroy the Taliban emirate.
Both factions, Abu al-Walid narrates, wanted to rid Afghanistan of bin
Laden and the crises associated with the Afghan Arabs.[9]

But Mullah Omar, undisputed dictator, did not listen to his aides'
recommendation, even though bin Laden did not obey his orders; he
felt, Abu al-Walid notes, gratitude for the sacrifice given by the Arab
mujahadeen contingent during the Afghan war, and he hoped that bin
Laden would heavily invest in development and reconstruction in the
war-torn Islamic emirate, as he did in Sudan in the first half of the

1990s. In fact, Mullah Omar used to order his young ministers to travel long distances to meet with bin Laden and ask for technical advice and financial support. Implicit in this firsthand account is that Mullah Omar appears to have been greatly impressed by his Arabian guest and to have fallen under his spell. Although he gently implored bin Laden to keep a low media profile, he did not threaten him or try to force him. Abu al-Walid describes the first "historical meeting" between the two militants, to which he was a witness, in 1997; for two hours Mullah Omar "pleaded" with his guest to stop contacting the international media but bin Laden argued that he should be permitted to speak with the media and make the case for the liberation of the holy places as well as calling on Muslims worldwide to support the Taliban financially and invest in their Islamic emirate. But when Mullah Omar disagreed, bin Laden did not take no for an answer. He persisted with his argument; at the end of the meeting Mullah Omar stood up and told bin Laden, "do not be upset. You are a Mujahid [Islamic fighter]. This is your country and you are welcome to do whatever you like."[10]

Abu al-Walid laments that bin Laden interpreted Mullah Omar's last comment as a carte blanche to do as he wished; he did not take into account the interests of Afghanistan and the harm his words and deeds would bring to the country. Abu al-Walid, who had close ties with both Mullah Omar and bin Laden, blames bin Laden for entangling the Taliban in regional and international conflicts against its will and bringing about the final destruction of the Islamic emirate; the Taliban was defeated and Afghanistan was lost because of bin Laden's reckless conduct, which culminated in the attacks on the United States. What fuels Abu al-Walid's anger against bin Laden is that bin Laden "was not even aware of the scope of the battle in which he opted to fight, or was forced into fighting. Therefore, he lacked the correct perception and was not qualified to lead." He cites an old Arab proverb to explain the "catastrophe" caused by bin Laden in Afghanistan and beyond: "Those who work without knowledge will damage more than they can fix and those who walk quickly on the wrong path will only distance themsleves from their goal."[11]

Abu al-Walid sounds highly critical of bin Laden for abusing the hospitality of his hosts, the Taliban, and bringing the temple down on their heads; but he is curiously silent on the destructive role played by Mullah

196 • The Far Enemy

Omar in hastening the fall of his emirate. Abu al-Walid, who was a pro-
tege of Mullah Omar and managed one of his propaganda newsletters,
insinuates that after Al Qaeda's 1998 bombing of the U.S. embassies
in East Africa, Arab radicals warned the Taliban leadership that their
decision not to extradite bin Laden to the Americans amounted to a
declaration of war on the United States; time and again after 1998
Mullah Omar was told by his senior aides and foreigners alike that bin
Laden's terrorism could explode and destroy the Taliban's weak foundation. And how did Mullah Omar react to the multiple warnings from
friends and foes? According to Abu al-Walid, Mullah Omar made his
point crystal clear: "I will not hand over a Muslim to an infidel."[12] Well,
that said it all. Mullah Omar's decision sealed his regime's fate and he,
not bin Laden, was fully responsible for what befell Afghanistan. Mullah
Omar was the Taliban's undisputed ruler, and he offered refuge and protection to the bin Laden network, which had carried out several spectacular terrorist activities over the years; restraining bin Laden's tirades
was the least of the challenges faced by Mullah Omar and his advisers.

But Abu al-Walid's critique of bin Laden's character and ego shows
how he became a prisoner of his own public relations rhetoric and hyper-
bole. According to Abu al-Walid, bin Laden enjoyed the limelight and
exaggerated his strength and capabilities, including creating a big media
buzz about weapons of mass destruction (WMD). A fascinating section
in Abu al-Walid's book deals with the debate between the "hawks" and
the "doves" within Al Qaeda regarding the merits of acquiring WMD:
the hawks argued that obtaining WMD could serve as a deterrent to
America's overwhelming power, a balancing act in the military struggle against the United States; in contrast, the doves advocated placing
limits on how jihadis wage the struggle and confining local conflicts
to their geographical borders and settings. The doves, Abu al-Walid
writes, opposed the expansion of the struggle lest jihadis lose international sympathy and invite brutal military retaliation; as to WMD, the
doves warned that jihadis were in no position to match the destructive
power of the U.S. nuclear armada. On the other hand, the hawks dismissed world, particularly Western, public opinion as inherently hostile
to Islam and Muslims and claimed that acquisition of WMD, regardless
of how primitive, could deter the United States from carrying out "geno-
cide" against Muslims. The whole debate about WMD was theoretical

because, according to Abu al-Walid, Al Qaeda did not possess the means, materials, capability, or know-how. Bin Laden did not side with either the hawks or the doves because he did not view the matter as pressing; however, he publicly boasted about Al Qaeda's WMD potential and made it seem that the organization was on the verge of a breakthrough. What bin Laden overlooked, according to Abu al-Walid, is that he supplied ammunition to his enemies, the Americans, who exaggerated Al Qaeda's threat to the international community: a "propaganda bubble blown by bin Laden, bursting in his face."[13]

Abu al-Walid's public criticism of bin Laden has been echoed by other senior members of Al Qaeda who considered bin Laden a publicity hound. According to internal letters found on the Al Qaeda computers in Afghanistan, two leading senior operatives sent bin Laden a memo via Zawahiri voicing alarm at his obsession with public relations and the media despite the stated wishes of Mullah Omar. In the late 1990s Mullah Omar reportedly grew annoyed with bin Laden's high media profile, and many feared that he would expel the Afghan Arabs from the country. The Syrian operatives urged Zawahiri to convince bin Laden to get his act together:

> To: Osama bin Laden
> From Abu Mosab al-Suri and Abu Khalid al-Suri
> Via: Ayman al-Zawahiri
> Folder: Incoming Mail – From Afghanistan
> Date: July 19, 1999
> ... The strangest thing I have heard so far is Abu Abdullah [bin Laden] saying that he would not listen to the Leader of the Faithful [refers to Mullah Omar in his hoped-for capacity as head of a new Islamic emirate based in Afghanistan] when he asked him to stop giving interviews ... I think our brother [bin Laden] has caught the disease of screens, flashes, fans, and applause ... Abu Abdullah should go to the Leader of the Faithful with some of his brothers and tell them that ... the Leader of the Faithful was right when he asked you to refrain from interviews, announcements, and media encounters, and that you will help the Taliban as much as you can in their battle, until they achieve control over Afghanistan ...[14]

In his book, Abu al-Walid exposes bin Laden and brings him down to earth. It is not a pretty picture; the emir of Al Qaeda is found without clothes. Abu al-Walid's demystification of bin Laden will likely resonate with militant activists because it comes from within Al Qaeda's highest circles and draws on close experiences and activities of the Taliban movement and the bin Laden network. Abu al-Walid documents the rise and fall of the two organizations and the fatal errors committed by bin Laden that brought the temple down on jihadis' heads; more than any other actor, bin Laden emerges as the central villain who did not confront the hawks in the organization and who became infatuated with his own rhetoric. As to lessons learned from this catastrophe, Abu al-Walid says that "The fundamentalists finally discovered from their experience in Afghanistan something of which they remained oblivious for several centuries: that absolute individual authority is a hopelessly defective form of leadership, an obsolete way of organization that will end in nothing but defeat." His final verdict is that bin Laden's autocratic style was responsible for plunging jihadis into an unequal confrontation with America (and Israel), which, in his opinion, is "beyond present capabilities of the whole Islamist movement."[15]

But the problem, according to Abu al-Walid, is much bigger and more complex than bin Laden's authoritarian decision making; it is the very intellectual bankruptcy and paucity of original ideas of the jihadist project:

> It may be that the Islamic movement had already suffered from an intellectual as well as an organizational defeat before it even started its battle against America (otherwise known as the Great Satan). Jihad is a bigger and a more serious issue that should not be left to the jihadist groups alone. Jihad is more than just an armed battle. Narrow-minded mentalities towards the issues such as religion and politics are incapable of developing their conflict with America, which represents the pinnacle and height of "devils" intellectually and militarily.[16]

It does not occur to Abu al-Walid to question his own complicity, along with that of other associates, or to ask why they acquiesced in bin Laden's "suicidal" schemes. Surely, the Shura Council, of which Abu al-Walid was a full member, could have applied the brakes on bin Laden's recklessly speeding train. The so-called doves could have either gone public with their dissent or resigned. But the differences between the hawks and the doves within Al Qaeda were more cosmetic than substantive and more tactical than paradigmatic. Sociologically, however, it is not surprising that dispersal and defeat unleashed a torrent of internal criticism of bin Laden, Zawahiri, and other close associates, particularly Al Qaeda's late defense chief, Abu Hafs. At the height of his power, bin Laden was seen as "a whole nation embodied in one man." But as military setbacks accumulate, more and more jihadis try to distance themselves from his crashing train. Though his account has many weaknesses, Abu al-Walid's critique marks the beginning of the deconstruction of bin Laden and his close aides from within his own organization.

Another striking feature of this criticism is acknowledgment of disarray and defeat. This is not a simple matter because it goes against jihadis' notion of calculating loss and gain. Militants like bin Laden, Zawahiri, and their associates believe that the power asymmetry with the United States is of little consequence because they are armed with faith – God is watching over them so they will ultimately prevail. In a rare interview after the United States began bombing Afghanistan, when asked if he was confident of victory, Mullah Omar retorted, "yes, because Allah is on our side." Similarly, in his letters and speeches to his followers in Iraq, time and again Abu Musab al-Zarqawi, emir of Al Qaeda there, has underscored the inevitability of victory because of divine intervention on the side of the mujahedeen. Zarqawi has urged his fighters to ignore those "hypocrites" and doomsayers who maintain that the powers that be will not allow them to prevail and establish an Islamic polity and caliphate; he told them that God would help Muslims conquer Rome and grant them victory: "We pray God to conquer the White House, the Kremlin, and London."[17]

However, many jihadis both within and outside of Al Qaeda concluded that the war is lost and that bin Laden and his hawkish aides had promised heaven but delivered dust. New fault lines appear to have emerged among transnationalist jihadis, mirroring those between them and religious nationalists. As the Al Qaeda military crisis deepens, so do the internal fault lines. The war within could be more fatal to bin Laden's network than the war waged against it by the international community.

Al-Jama'a Al-Islamiya's Critique of Al Qaeda

Al-Jama'a al-Islamiya, the largest jihadist organization in the Arab world, has presented a comprehensive and provocative critique of jihadism in general and transnationalist jihadis in particular. Since early 2002 imprisoned leaders of al-Jama'a have published eight books, which they describe as self-criticism and in which they renounce their previous militant ideas. They also advance a new paradigm based on peaceful engagement with state and society. The first four books, collectively called *tashih al-mafaheem* or *The Correction of Concepts*, comprise a remarkable exercise in ideological revision, which has been in the making since the Islamic Group's historical leaders proposed the 1997 ceasefire initiative. The four books go beyond the ceasefire proposal into a repudiation of the past and an acceptance of society's rules. The ideological revision represents a revolutionary rupture with and departure from doctrinaire jihadist theory and practice. The imprisoned leaders said that they take full responsibility for the outbreak of violence in Egypt that began in the early 1980s and they renounce the resort to jihad against a Muslim ruler who does not apply the Shariah. In a radical reversal of essential jihadist doctrine, these leaders said that jihad is a collective duty determined by qualified and representative ulema (Islamic scholars) and the prerogative of the state; it is not a personal obligation that may be activated by a dissident leader. Jihad, the imprisoned leaders added, is regulated by a complex set of rules that cannot be left to the whims of individuals like themselves and their associates. Equally important, they used the Shariah to construct an Islamic "constitution" for jihad that unequivocally forbids killing Muslim and non-Muslim civilians under any conditions, as well as tourists in Muslim lands.[18]

In subsequent interviews with the Egyptian weekly *Al-Mussawar* and with *Asharq al-Awsat* in 2002 and 2003, Karam Zuhdi, head of the Majlis al-Shura (Consultative Council), and Nageh Ibrahim, the Islamic Group's theoretician, conceded that their organization erred in attacking the Egyptian authorities and bestowing on itself the right to declare jihad. Zuhdi, who was one of the founding fathers of the Islamic Group and who spent twenty-two years in prison in the Sadat assassination case, went further, saying that international conditions militate against the application of the Shariah in many Muslim countries. He even apologized for Islamic Group's armed conflict with the state, which he described as fitna (sedition) and for killing Sadat. He also apologized for the deaths of all security forces killed since 1981, referring to them as "martyrs." Asked what he would do if he could go back to Sadat's time, Zuhdi said that he would have "intervened to prevent his murder." And would he consider Sadat a martyr? "Yes," he answered. "Sadat is a martyr."[19]

Here is Zuhdi, the leader of a militant organization, publicly insinuating that the application of Islamic law is no longer feasible because of mitigating external factors. Zuhdi would have been accused of apostasy by former associates had he made such a provocative statement a few years ago. A few of his colleagues who support the ceasefire have criticized him and other imprisoned lieutenants for absolving the Egyptian government of responsibility for the violence and for labeling Sadat a martyr. They also said that the blanket apology by the "historical leaders" is counterproductive because it gives the impression of being extracted under duress (more on this debate later). But they did not say anything against Zuhdi's statement that jihad against Muslim rulers, even those who do not apply the Shariah, is illicit.[20]

In the last ten years religious nationalists have come a long way, although they still have far to go. Long periods of imprisonment and defeat on the battlefield have served as a catalyst for the ideological revision or reversal of a long-held jihadist belief in the legitimacy of the armed struggle against impious rulers. Like their 1997 ceasefire initiative, which marked a turning point in the insurgency in Egypt, Islamic Group leaders have begun debating old doctrinaire conceptions of jihad and takfeer (the practice of excommunication of Muslims). It is a long and difficult journey fraught with uncertainties and risks, but the end result could transform the jihadist movement into one of nonviolence and integrate it into the political process.

Of the eight books published by Islamic Group leaders, two deal specifically with Al Qaeda and the war with the United States. The first, authored by Mohammed Essam Derbala and reviewed and approved by the leadership, is titled *Al Qaeda Strategy: Mistakes and Dangers* (2003), and the other, authored by Nageh Abdullah Ibrahim, is titled *Islam and the Challenges of the Twenty-First Century* (2004).[21] Both were serialized in the Arabic-language newspaper *Asharq al-Awsat*, and both received wide publicity in the Arab world, although they were hardly mentioned in the Western media. Western commentary gives more prominent coverage to militant anti-Western voices than to the substantive debates and ideological revisions taking place within the Islamist and jihadist movements. Although the former are wrecking international peace, the latter promise a new beginning and hold a key to reconciliation. The Islamic Group leaders have also been interviewed by the Arab press, further exposing their views on Al Qaeda and the harm its actions have inflicted on the ummah.

Of all Islamist and jihadist organizations, the Islamic Group presented the most systematic and devastating critique of Al Qaeda, using the Shariah to puncture another hole in the doctrinaire jihadist legitimization of attacking the Americans. For example, in his book, Derbala makes extensive use of religious texts to show that Al Qaeda's attacks on Americans violated Islamic law, which "bans killing civilians" of any religion or nationality. Islamic Group's imprisoned leaders denounce Al Qaeda for preaching that American and Muslim interests would never meet and that "the enmity is deeply embedded and the clash is inevitable." They cite several cases in the 1990s when the United States helped to resolve international conflicts with results that benefited Muslims: American military and financial assistance in the Afghan war tipped the balance in favor of the mujahedeen against the Russian occupiers; in 1990 to 1991 the United States helped Kuwait and Saudi Arabia expel Iraqi forces from Kuwait; in 1995 American military intervention put a stop to the persecution and massacre of Bosnian Muslims by Serbs, which had caused tens of thousands of casualties; and in 1999 the United States led a NATO military campaign to force Serbia to end its ethnic cleansing in Kosovo.[22]

All these examples clearly show, Islamic Group leaders assert, that American and Muslim interests do meet, and that throughout the 1990s Al Qaeda failed to peacefully exploit and benefit from positive developments in the international system and U.S. policies toward Afghanistan; history also testifies that there is nothing inevitable about a clash of cultures or religions because Islam is a universal religion that is not isolated in a ghetto but is fully integrated with other civilizations.

The leaders also argue that bin Laden's advocacy of war between dar al-iman and dar al-kufr is not only misguided but also is based on misreading reality and the ummah's capabilities: "The question is, where are the priorities? Where are the capabilities that allow for all of that?" Instead of this suicidal approach, the leaders of Islamic Group call for a genuine dialogue and engagement with the West based on mutual respect and recognition of one another, as well as on peaceful interaction and nonaggression.[23]

Although, on the whole, over the last sixty years U.S. policies toward Arabs and Muslims have been "negative" and "oppressive," Derbala writes, armed confrontation is not the solution. Far from deterring the United States, Derbala adds, "Al Qaeda boosted the anti-Islamic wave in America and the West" and widened the cultural gap between Muslims and Westerners. Derbala, serving a life sentence in prison for his role in the 1981 Sadat assassination, refutes bin Laden and Zawahiri's assertion that the West is waging a crusade against Islam and Muslims. "Some claim that there is a crusader war led by America against Islam. However, the majority of Muslims reject the existence of crusader wars," he said, adding that "religious motives" may influence American policy toward Muslim nations, "but these are not crusader wars." In fact, "interests remain the official religion of America, and those interests determine its international relations," Derbala writes. Thus, "Al Qaeda's policy," he adds, "helped crusading and anti-Muslim forces in America and the West to advocate a total war against Islam."[24]

Derbala accuses Al Qaeda of mastering "the art of making enemies" rather than following Prophet Mohammed's example of "neutralizing enemies." Al Qaeda declared war against the whole world, he writes contemptuously, and tried to ignite a clash of civilizations without possessing the means to wage – let alone prevail in – a global struggle. Equally important in his view is that bin Laden and Zawahiri recognize that jihad must not be undertaken without an honest assessment of costs, benefits, and difficulties: "Al Qaeda has to understand that jihad is only one of the Muslims' duties. Jihad is a means, not an end." Making jihad for the sake of jihad, as Al Qaeda has done, is counterproductive because it produces the opposite of the desired results; for example, it brought about the downfall of the Islamist Taliban regime in Kabul and enabled the killing of thousands of young Muslims. Surely, the ummah is much worse off, Derbala points out, because of Al Qaeda's foolish conduct.[25]

Derbala warns bin Laden and Zawahiri against the pitfalls of violating the Shariah and waging "illegitimate jihad" because that means superimposing their own views over those of the Prophet. Derbala comes close to calling the Al Qaeda chiefs apostates, an ironic way of using their own rhetoric against them. But bin Laden and Zawahiri could still cut their losses and those of the ummah, Derbala concludes, if they swiftly step back from the brink of the abyss; otherwise, they would meet a similar fate to that of the Algerian Armed Islamic Group (IGA), a criminal gang that has forsaken Islam.[26]

A year later, in 2004, the Islamic Group released a book by Nageh Abdullah Ibrahim, *Islam and the Challenges of the Twenty-First Century*, which built on Derbala's critique and developed it further. Ibrahim's book goes beyond Al Qaeda and calls for the renewal of Islamic discourse to meet the existential challenges facing Islam and Muslims and to demolish myths held by militants for decades. Ibrahim, serving a life sentence with Derbala, writes that September 11 and its reverberations exposed the need for Muslims to face reality and make the difficult decisions necessary for them to catch up with the rest of humanity. Muslims, Ibrahim adds, can no longer afford to postpone reforms because the world is moving ahead quickly, leaving them further and further behind: "Standing still would mean suicide."[27]

According to Ibrahim, the renewal of Islamic discourse and thought would enrich the education of young Muslims and make them less vulnerable to "conspiracy theory," which is being used to explain historical developments and international affairs. "Conspiracy theory," Ibrahim writes, "retards the Arab and Muslim mind by holding it back and keeping it from taking off and restricting its ability to resolve problems." Instead of viewing international relations as based on state interests and power relations, this theory, Ibrahim adds, views everything through the lens of conspiracy and holds the West accountable for "all of our tragedies and neglects our own strategic errors." In his opinion, it is their own strategic errors, not the West, that are the real villains, which explains the decline of the ummah. He holds Islamists and nationalists responsible for trafficking with conspiracy theory and leading young Muslims astray. Ibrahim cites several examples in which Muslims explain events through conspiracy theory. For example, many Arabs and Muslims believe that in 1990 the United States sucked Saddam Hussein into Kuwait to weaken Iraq so that the United States could control the oil fields in the Arabian Peninsula; many perceive the 1973 Arab–Israeli war as a great victory that restored Arab honor and dignity; and many claim that the Israeli Mossad plotted the September 11 attacks on the Americans so that the United States would strike back at Muslims.[28]

In addition to ridding Muslims of conspiracy theory, the renewal of Islamic discourse, Ibrahim notes, would discredit the theory of "the inevitability of confrontation" with either Muslim rulers or Western powers. It is worth mentioning that in the late 1980s the Islamic Group distributed a document titled "The Inevitability of Confrontation," which legitimized armed struggle against the Egyptian regime.[29] Ibrahim concedes that he and his associates committed a strategic error by adopting this theory and making it synonymous with jihad. The result was loss of human lives, suffering, and military defeat. More alarming was that Algerian armed Islamist groups excommunicated state and society alike and acted like the Khawarji (a Muslim sect that rejected the authority of the fourth caliph, Ali bin Abi Talib, and rebelled against rulers because they abused their wealth and power and did not faithfully apply the Shariah). Ibrahim gently critiques Sayyid Qutb, who is considered the spiritual father of the modern jihadist movement, for confusing literary theory with Islamic law. He stresses that Qutb was a literary writer, not an Islamic scholar, and that his contribution belongs more in the literature field than in the fiqh (Islamic jurisprudence).[30]

Although Islamists and jihadis have not debated, let alone deconstructed, Qutb's ideas yet, the Islamic Group has begun the process. It would be critical for religious nationalists, including the Islamic Group, to engage with Qutb's thought and attempt to demystify the man and subject his ideas to critical scrutiny. More than any other individual, Qutb exercises tremendous moral and intellectual influence over young activists. As argued previously, Qutb's conception of permanent revolution against internal and external enemies informs the rhetoric and actions of most jihadis, including bin Laden and Zawahiri and their associates, and supplies them with a justification. Bin Laden and Zawahiri are classic Qutbists, and a critique of Qutb's ideas, such as al-jahiliya, al-hakimiya, and permanent revolution, would be essential to debunk their religious pretensions and rationalization of eternal jihad.

Ibrahim and his imprisoned colleagues appear to be aware of the need to lay certain terms and tenets to rest in order to pull the rug out from underneath transnationalist jihadis. In *Islam and the Challenges of the Twenty-First Century*, they stress the danger of taking particular concepts out of their historical context, investing them with religious symbolism, and applying them to the present. They cite their own experience, an obsession with the so-called theory of the inevitability of confrontation, which led them into a costly armed clash with the state. Although Ibrahim says their intentions were good and just (applying the Shariah), their actions did more harm than good; they lost sight of the high costs to society and the ummah. He asks, "is armed conflict the ideal way to apply the Shariah? Is fighting the only way to free prisoners and resolve Islamists' problems? All these inquiries raise one question: Does the justice of a cause imply the inevitability of armed confrontation?" No, Ibrahim says, because more harm may be caused by fighting than by showing restraint and patience; reality and societal harmony take precedence over the ideal of justice. Jihad also is a collective duty that cannot be triggered except by a legitimate authority when all necessary requirements are met.[31]

The cases of Egypt and Algeria, Ibrahim writes, show clearly the pitfalls of activating jihad without taking into account conditions at home and abroad; far from achieving its desired goals, the jihadist movement was dealt a strategic blow, losing public sympathy and support. According to Ibrahim and his Islamic Group colleagues, a decade of armed clashes with the near enemy did not bring them any closer to establishing an Islamic state; far from it, jihadis are in a state of disarray and decline. Ibrahim argues further that the setbacks suffered by the jihadist movement have weakened its immune system and left it vulnerable to hostile forces; its very survival is at stake. The lesson learned is that obsession with jihad at the expense of other important issues can be fatal. Fateful decisions, like war and peace, must also be based on a correct reading of reality and the existing balance of power. Patience and compromise are virtues, not weaknesses as some think, and the common interests of society and the community must be given priority. Had

Egyptian and Algerian jihadis been patient and cool-headed, Ibrahim advises, they would be in better shape, and the nation and Islam would be stronger as well.[32]

Similarly, Ibrahim and other imprisoned Islamic Group leaders fault Al Qaeda for ignoring reality and living in its own bubble. They go after bin Laden with a vengeance, accusing him of shutting his eyes and ears and blindly plunging forward, bringing the temple down on his own head and the ummah's as well. The problem with bin Laden, they note, is that he violates a basic principle of Islamic tradition and historical realism in general: measuring one's strength relative to others, particularly real or imagined enemies. Not so with bin Laden, Ibrahim says sarcastically, who marches on armed only with faith, as if faith divorced from strength could tip the balance of power in his favor; Islamic experience proves that belief and faith are wedded not only to material strength but also to justice and tolerance. What this means is that Islam, Ibrahim adds, respects the rights and humanity of non-Muslims; bin Laden violates all that, even while preaching the value of piety and faith. His split personality manifests itself, according to Ibrahim, in his ambition "to fight the entire world simultaneously, though he does not possess real power and cannot find a shelter or a government to assist him; nevertheless, he wants to fight America on September 11, the Russians in Chechnya, and India in Kashmir, as well as carry out military operations in Muslim lands in Saudi Arabia, Yemen, Morocco, Indonesia, and elsewhere."[33]

Ibrahim says that had bin Laden paid adequate attention to his humble capabilities, he would have refrained from declaring war on the world, but the issue is bigger than that because bin Laden has lost touch with reality, rationality, and religious precepts. As a result, Ibrahim adds, Al Qaeda caused the downfall of two Muslim regimes – in Kabul and Baghdad – and Arab states have faced the brunt of the American armada. In short, Al Qaeda is no longer an intact, cohesive organization because it confuses myth with fact and entertains strange ideas. Ibrahim compares Al Qaeda with the Saddam Hussein regime and implies that bin Laden could bring about the destruction of his network like Hussein did to the Iraqi state.[34]

There is nothing positive or flattering in the Islamic Group's critique of bin Laden, who is seen as a suicidal adventurer. Of all the critiques of bin Laden, the Islamic Group's is the most authentic and comprehensive. Derbala, Ibrahim, and their imprisoned colleagues condemn bin Laden and Zawahiri's religious justification for attacking the Americans. For example, Ibrahim reminds bin Laden and his associates that throughout history, Islam has practiced, not just taught, "peaceful coexistence" as a permanent way of life; in Islam "religious coexistence" is a strategic, not a tactical, good, particularly when Muslims migrate to foreign lands and are welcomed by inhabitants. What makes the crime of the September 11 suicide bombers uniquely un-Islamic, Ibrahim writes, is that the U.S. government let them in as guests but, instead of coexisting peacefully with their hosts, they stabbed them in the back. Ibrahim bemoans the bombers' religious ignorance, because if they had read the Sunnah, they would have taken "peaceful coexistence" to heart. Thus bin Laden and Zawahiri are portrayed as sinners and manipulators sending young men who did not know they were flouting a fundamental tenet of Islam on a suicide mission.[35]

Like Derbala, Ibrahim stresses the significance of understanding the function of jihad in Islam: "It is essential to know that armed struggle or jihad was never an end in itself, and Islam did not legislate fighting for the sake of fighting or jihad for the sake of jihad." According to the Islamic Group's incarcerated leaders, Islam cannot be reduced to one duty, jihad, while overlooking other "prophetic" choices such as al-solh, or truce-making, which was often practiced by Prophet Mohammed throughout his life. The leaders argue that by neglecting al-solh as a "strategic choice," the jihadist movement made grave errors that endangered its survival. It is worth mentioning that the two books by Derbala and Ibrahim highlight a series of strategic errors committed by jihadis since the late 1970s, which helps to explain the difficult situation they now face. Ibrahim writes that had the Taliban regime, the Algerian Islamic Front (FIS), and the Islamic Group enacted truces and looked for reconciliation with state and society, they would have escaped their current predicament and gained in strength: "Should not Islamists [jihadis] in Saudi Arabia, who carried out the May 2003 bombings, have made al-solh their choice and closed ranks with the Saudi public and their government and assisted them against post-9/11 dangers instead of assisting the entire world against the biggest and most important Islamic state that applies the Shariah and tends toward upholding religion."[36]

The internal critique by al-Jama'a's imprisoned leaders goes beyond the jihadist movement to touch on sensitive topics like the Arab–Israeli conflict. For example, the leaders are critical of the late Palestinian and Syrian presidents Yasir Arafat and Hafiz al-Assad, respectively, for not heeding the advice of their Egyptian counterpart, Anwar Sadat, in the second half of the 1970s and negotiating a truce with Israel; if they had done so, they would have achieved a much better settlement than their countries will ever get. Look at the weak negotiating position of Syria and Palestine now, they say, thanks to Arab rulers' shortsightedness and obstinacy.[37]

Two points must be made. First, ironically, al-Jama'a, along with the Jihad Group, reportedly assassinated Sadat because he had signed a peace treaty with Israel. They felt he betrayed the Arab cause by ending the state of war with the Zionist enemy. Now they are critical of the Palestinians and Syrians for not imitating Sadat and making peace with Israel. For this, the Islamic Group will be savagely condemned by Islamists, leftists, and Arab nationalists, not to mention transnationalist jihadis and some of their religious nationalist counterparts as well. Many will dismiss the Islamic Group's stand as being extracted under duress or as an attempt to appease the Egyptian regime. Second, Ibrahim mentions solh, or truce-making, not salam, or peace-making. Did he endorse reaching a short-term, technical ceasefire, rather than a peace treaty, with the Jewish state, even though Sadat signed a peace agreement? Did Ibrahim use solh to lend legitimacy to his argument because the Prophet enacted solh with hostile tribes? Either way, the Islamic Group's stand on Israel marks a dramatic departure by Islamists and jihadis, even though it is not representative of Arab political opinion; it forces Islamist critics to think the unthinkable: to start a conversation between mainstream and radical Islamists.

In interviews with *Al-Mussawar* and *Asharq al-Awsat* in his prison cell, Karam Zuhdi offered a more pointed critique of Al Qaeda. He said that bin Laden and Zawahiri misunderstood the changed international alignment after the end of the Cold War and the replacement of the bipolar system with a unipolar U.S.-dominated system. Al Qaeda, Zuhdi added critically, refused to recognize that the United States emerged as the unrivaled world power and took it upon itself to challenge America's global supremacy by dragging it into a confrontation with the ummah. But the ummah neither possesses the capabilities to resist an

American-led alliance nor desires to do so. Built on shaky foundations, Zuhdi asserts, Al Qaeda's strategy cared less about the means and costs and "became obsessed with killing Americans, Christians, and crusaders without distinctions."[38]

In conclusion, the Islamic Group's imprisoned leaders raise a critical question: "what is the alternative to all this mayhem?" What is to be done? They suggest that the United States should pursue a more just foreign policy, that Muslim states should empower their citizens – freedom and democracy for everyone – and that jihad should be activated against foreign aggressors and occupiers. To their credit, they put much more emphasis on internal reforms than on foreign affairs, although foreign affairs were seen as important; they also seemed to appreciate that the problems and dangers facing Muslims can only be resolved by strengthening state-society relations and freeing citizens of their political bondage. There was not even a hint in their pronouncements that placed blame for the decline of the ummah on the enemies of Islam, as bin Laden, Zawahiri, and their associates claim.

How Important Is Al-Jama'a's Critique?

Al-Jama'a's powerful and, at times, personal critique of Al Qaeda testifies to the depth and intensity of the war among jihadis. I devoted more space to al-Jama'a because of its historical weight within the jihadist current and the comprehensiveness of its critique. The central thesis of al-Jama'a's imprisoned leaders is that Al Qaeda did not just err but also misinterpreted and distorted Islamic texts to advance its own transnationalist agenda. These jihadis, who led the fight against the Egyptian regime throughout the 1990s and who spent years behind bars, had been the hardliners within al-Jama'a and so they cannot be dismissed as inconsequential or unrepresentative of a critical jihadist constituency. It would also be simplistic and misleading to claim that Zuhdi, Derbala, and Ibrahim attacked Al Qaeda because the Egyptian regime ordered them to do so.

In contrast with their transnationalist counterparts, as this book has shown, since 1997 the attitudes of the religious nationalist camp, like the Islamic Group, have evolved in opposition to armed struggle as a tool of political action. The Al Qaeda chiefs, not Islamic Group leaders, are swimming against the current of the times and the dominant trend within the jihadist movement. Religious nationalists represent a broad, diverse segment, perhaps even the largest constituency, among jihadis. Although Islamic Group leaders might have discredited their collective self-criticism by appearing to shed their history and disavow their previous actions, their ideological revision represents a natural, though radical, progression. The prison years helped; so did September 11 and the pressures and promises by the Egyptian government. When questioned by an interviewer about the sudden dramatic change in the Islamic Group's position, Zuhdi retorted that the collective self-criticisms represent a "corrective revolution," not an intellectual revolution against previous ideas. He said that he and his imprisoned colleagues had been reassessing their position on jihad since 1997 and that the evolution of their new vision was a product of "maturity and studying reality with care."[39]

Indeed, understanding the nuanced views of religious nationalists, including the Islamic Group, requires a recognition of the historical and sociological influences that shaped their words and deeds. The baptism of fire and defeat forced the Islamic Group to change against its will. There is nothing mysterious about the 180-degree turn in its journey; the Group faced reality and came to terms with it. The more interesting, critical question, as I have argued throughout the book, is why did some of their transnationalist counterparts dismiss reality and open a second front against the far enemy? In addition, can religious nationalists be trusted, and is their change of heart genuine? We do not know what is in their hearts; it is futile to speculate about that. We do know, however, that since the late 1990s religious nationalists have scrupulously abided by their proposed unilateral ceasefire and have engaged in internal debates that have culminated in a rejection of the armed struggle. Regardless of what one thinks of the Islamic Group's "ideological revisions," it has refrained from using violence and has deactivated its paramilitary cells; it has not carried out a single military operation since the late 1990s. Challenged to prove that the Islamic Group would honor its peace commitment, Zuhdi stressed that in 1997 his organization laid down its arms and conceded that it had made mistakes and that it has embarked on a new journey: "this development is a proof of our moral courage and the sincerity of our new outlook."[40]

Skeptics may ask what is to prevent religious nationalists from resorting to violence and terrorism if new opportunities arise. The truth is that jihadis' violent actions have engendered widespread societal and governmental suspicion and left them with few friends. Muslims do not trust them, nor do Westerners. These local jihadis must prove – by deeds and by words – that they made a clean break with the past and that their "ideological revisions" are real, a product of moral, religious, and political reality, not just of military necessity.

By the same token, it would be counterproductive to set the bar too high and hold religious nationalists to a higher standard than other political forces. That would send the wrong message and imply that regardless of what they say and do, religious nationalists would not be given the benefit of the doubt and be integrated into society. This would drive them into the deadly embrace of their former hardliner counterparts and play into the hands of bin Laden and Zawahiri. Opening up the political space and empowering all nonviolent voices will go a long way to stealing the thunder away from the militants and providing an outlet for mainstream, moderate Islamists, which would dissipate the need for jihadism. Equally important, the normalization of Arab and Muslim politics would be the yardstick by which to measure the authenticity of jihadis' self-criticism. In this, the burden lies with authoritarian Muslim rulers to loosen their iron grip on state and society and give citizens breathing room.

Muslim and Western officials should listen closely to intrajihadist debates and the ideological revisions undertaken by religious nationalists. Lumping all jihadis together with Al Qaeda is conceptually false and politically shortsighted. For example, al-Jama'a's critique of Al Qaeda represents a breath of fresh air that should be encouraged, not belittled, because it is a potent force that might resonate with some of Al Qaeda's wavering operators; it also serves as a warning to young Muslims who are taken in by the rhetoric of bin Laden and Zawahiri and now Zarqawi. By taking a public stand and making their voices heard, religious nationalists level the playing field with the transnationalists and dispute the latter's ownership of the jihadist movement.

Although bin Laden, Zawahiri, and their associates may try to plant doubts in Muslims' minds and suggest that the Islamic Group's imprisoned leaders said what they did under duress, they cannot question the leaders' jihadist credentials. Zuhdi, Derbala, Ibrahim, Osama Hafez, Assem Abdel-Maged, and the rest who blessed the ideological revisions, were founding fathers of an important wing of the jihadist movement who paid their dues in blood and sweat. Some of them had supplied the intellectual ammunition that fueled the militant passions and actions of subsequent generations of jihadis. For example, in the late 1970s, while they were students at Asyut University in Upper Egypt, Ibrahim, Derbala, and Abdel-Maged, who were in their early twenties at the time, authored a manifesto titled "Chapters from the Charter of Islamic Political Action," which became al-Jama'a's operational constitution and served as a major legitimizing source for jihadis' violence.[41]

Thus al-Jama'a may even claim ownership of the jihadist movement and change its direction and destination, shed its paramilitary character, and resurrect its original goal of spreading al-da'wa (religious call). Unlike the al-Jihad group, which was founded as a collection of underground militant cells, from the beginning al-Jama'a was dedicated to preaching and spreading al-da'wa. It converted to wholesale violence and terrorism in the early 1990s, and now its leaders say they want to revive its early mission. Regardless of whether they succeed, there is no ambiguity on where they stand on the major issues of the day, particularly their opposition to armed struggle against both the near enemy and the far enemy. Although they have not defined what they mean by an Islamic state, let alone constructed an Islamic intellectual paradigm on state-building, they have debunked the idea that a paramilitary organization is doctrinally qualified to declare and wage jihad against government or society, asserting that jihad is a collective, not an individual, duty.

The critical questions, then, are how will their main audience – jihadis – receive the ideological revisions, and will they be convinced that their attacks on internal and external enemies were illicit aggression, and not legitimate defensive jihad? Asked if al-Jama'a's initiative has made any progress among jihadis, Zuhdi, the overall chief, answered in the affirmative and claimed that it has begun to influence many in Egypt and other countries, but he provided no evidence. Although it is exceedingly difficult to measure the influence of al-Jama'a's collective self-criticism on jihadis, it has encountered stiff resistance not just from transnationalists, like Al Qaeda, but also from other religious nationalists. The religious nationalists support its peaceful approach, but they also bitterly criticize what they call the imprisoned leaders' wholesale "collective repentance," "intellectual collapse," and unwarranted attacks against all jihadis who resort to the use of force. Those critics and hardliners are skeptical about al-Jama'a's ability to fill the vacuum left by Al Qaeda and the transnationalists in general because its ideological revisions do not provide a credible alternative.

Critiquing Al-Jama'a's Critique

Hani al-Sibai, whom the Egyptian government accuses of being a leader of Tanzim al-Jihad and sentenced to life in prison in absentia, criticized the collective revisions by al-Jama'a's founding fathers as unauthentic and suspect, conceived in an unhealthy environment (prison). He attacked al-Jama'a's leaders in the strongest possible terms and accused them of opportunism, intellectual poverty, and vacillating like a pendulum from one extreme to the other; for example, they killed Sadat and now they say he is a martyr. Sadat, Sibai adds angrily, "who was the biggest agent for the Americans and Zionism, in their view, has become a martyr. They justified this in the name of religion. Before they had said they reviewed the ideas of Islamic scholars to rationalize their military operations; now in their revisions, they said they also reviewed the ideas of Islamic scholars. . . . How do we trust a group that overnight changes its color from black to white and then white to black? How are we to take its revisions seriously? What I want to say is that this initiative was born in a corrupt environment, the prison environment, and what is founded on corruption would be corrupt."[42]

Nothing will come of their so-called ending-violence initiative, claims Sibai, who resides in London and has emerged as the unofficial voice of jihadis who subscribe to armed struggle, because neither the Egyptian public nor jihadis would buy into it. He dismissed the initiative as a plot hatched by Egyptian security services and signed by al-Jama'a's leaders, and he even predicted a rebellion by the rank and file. In a one-page interview with *Al Hayat* and other Arabic newspapers, Sibai challenged al-Jama'a's leaders "to take a courageous decision and dissolve their group and apply to the ministry of social services to turn it into a charitable society and choose a new name for it."[43]

The implication is that by renouncing its previous ideas and actions, al-Jama'a ceased to be a jihadist organization and can no longer belong to the jihadist club. Sibai does not elaborate on what the membership requirements are in this exclusive club; he does not provide any evidence to support his assertions or flesh out the real sources of his anger: Does it have to do with al-Jama'a's criticism of transnationalist jihadis, particularly Al Qaeda and Tanzim al-Jihad? Sibai reprimands the imprisoned leaders for exploiting the difficult conditions in which Al Qaeda leaders find themselves and attacking them and their policies. Was Sibai outraged by al-Jama'a's apology for killing Sadat and calling him a martyr? Or was it that al-Jama'a's imprisoned leaders indirectly equated "jihad" with "violence" and warned all other jihadis against resorting to armed struggle because al-Jama'a would expose them? Was it al-Jama'a's total volte-face and lumping of all past jihadist actions with the stain of violence? Or could it be the combination of all this that incensed Sibai and led him to go public with his accusations against al-Jama'a's imprisoned leaders?

Whatever fueled Sibai's anger, his countercritique of al-Jama'a's revisions was shared by other jihadis, including a few of al-Jama'a's leaders residing in exile. For example, Osama Rushdi, formerly in charge of al-Jama'a's media or propaganda committee and a member of its consultative council (Holland granted him political asylum), leveled criticisms similar to those of Sibai against his former associates, but in a milder tone. He accused Egyptian authorities of using coercive police tactics to extract "collective repentance" from al-Jama'a's imprisoned leaders in order to demystify their aura in the eyes of their followers and destroy them politically and symbolically. Osama Rushdi, who from the outset supported the 1997 ceasefire initiative, says that the Egyptian regime does not appreciate that humiliating and manipulating the imprisoned leaders will not bring lasting peace because dissatisfied young activists may ignore their elders and resort to violence. Like Sibai, Rushdi claims that the Egyptian authorities were not interested in allowing al-Jama'a to peacefully participate in the political process and spread the religious call; instead, they forced the imprisoned leaders to publicly repent. But "collective repentance" not only undermines the credibility of the historical leadership, it "could lead to the renewal of violence."[44] Rushdi reminds his associates that it is one thing to alter the means – the armed struggle – but it is unacceptable to give up the end – applying the Shariah. He gently admonishes his associates for their total retreat: "what is the reason for al-Jama'a's continued existence after all these reversals?"[45]

It is worth mentioning that neither Sibai nor Osama Rushdi supports Al Qaeda's strategy and the globalization of jihad (more on their views of Al Qaeda later). They also support al-Jama'a's ceasefire initiative and oppose the reactivation of jihad against the near enemy. Their disagreement with al-Jama'a, they say, revolves around the latter's capitulation to the Egyptian regime, as well as its disowning of its jihadist past. They want to preserve the credibility and integrity of their movement, be taken seriously by Muslim governments, and be fully integrated into political life. What Sibai and Osama Rushdi and like-minded associates do not appreciate is that jihadis possess few options and are at the mercy of the powers that be. Most of them are either incarcerated or hibernating deep underground and on the run. In the eyes of Muslim rulers, who in the last two decades fought and defeated jihadis on the field of battle, surrender, not compromise and reciprocity, is the only acceptable solution. Imprisoned for more than two decades, al-Jama'a's leaders were in no position to negotiate a better deal with the Egyptian regime. They could have resisted whatever offers were dangled before them by the security services, but a negative stance, as they learned the hard way, would have taken them nowhere. It is much easier for Sibai and Osama Rushdi – who live comfortably in the West, as some of their imprisoned associates pointed out disapprovingly – to demand steadfastness from their hard-pressed colleagues; they could afford to do so.

But the countercritiques of al-Jama'a by Sibai, Osama Rushdi, and others raise a legitimate question with important implications: did al-Jama'a's imprisoned leaders miss an opportunity to provide a credible, peaceful alternative to Al Qaeda jihadis that would keep dissatisfied activists from joining paramilitary cells? Did they miscalculate by retracting everything they had believed in and conceding that they were wrong? In its effort to preempt the Bush administration from linking Egyptian jihadis with Al Qaeda, did the Mubarak government, using carrots and sticks, force al-Jama'a's imprisoned leaders to cut the umbilical cord with the jihadist movement as a whole? Or did al-Jama'a's leaders take a conscious decision to sever their previous links with doctrinaire jihadism and to refocus on al-da'wa?

The controversy surrounding al-Jama'a's critique of Al Qaeda, coupled with the countercritique of al-Jama'a by other jihadis, highlights a critical point: there exist multiple internal wars tearing the jihadist movement apart. Sibai – a religious nationalist who denies being a leader of Tanzim al-Jihad and who opposed taking jihad global – launched a powerful onslaught against al-Jama'a and publicly demanded its dissolution. On the one hand, as this book has shown, at the end of the 1990s a bloody war pitted transnationalist jihadis against religious nationalists, and since September 11 this has intensified and escalated into open public warfare. On the other, religious nationalists are also engaged in an intense struggle to shape the future of their movement. As the debate between al-Jama'a and other similar-minded jihadis reveals, the lines of agreement and disagreement are not well demarcated among religious nationalists. They do not seem to agree on a common political platform, even though they all now eschew violence, and they do not offer a convincing, credible way out of the bottleneck. There is considerable fluidity, confusion, and disarray within their ranks, testimony to the fracturing of the movement as a whole.

At this stage, it is difficult to envision how and if jihadis will ever be able to rescue their movement from terminal decline and decay. In the case of Al Qaeda jihadis, they are waging war on behalf of the Muslim masses, most of whom do not support the jihadist movement. But there is also a danger that existing fault lines among jihadis could deepen further and cause mutations, which could lead to limited localized and globalized forms of warfare like what has been experienced since September 11 in Indonesia, Turkey, Saudi Arabia, Pakistan, Spain, Kuwait, Egypt, Iraq, Madrid, London, and elsewhere. With the exception of Iraq, which appears to be developing a jihadist base, or a second generation of Al Qaeda militants, driven by resistance to the American-led invasion and occupation, these countries have witnessed variations of localized militant activities without overall supervision or control by the parent organization, Al Qaeda.

The vacuum created by the dismantling of Al Qaeda's centralized command and control structure is being filled by small semiautonomous local affiliates and factions, which according to the 2004 Joint Report by the U.S. State Department and the National Counterterrorism Center, are inspired by Al Qaeda and carry out attacks using its ideological label but "with little or no support or direction from al Qaeda itself." The 2004 and 2005 bombings in Madrid and London are cases in point. Because of this trend, "an increasing percentage of jihadist attacks are more local, less sophisticated than the 9/11 bombings, but still lethal."[46] Although Al Qaeda provides general operational guidelines at the strategic level and helps out with allocation of financial resources, at the tactical level the various branches, franchises, and cells act independently. However, a new generation of young jihadis, driven by local agendas and inspired by the Al Qaeda ideology, appears to be emerging (more on this later).

Leading Former Jihadis Join the Onslaught Against Al Qaeda

Regardless of the internal turmoil within the jihadist current, a plurality of jihadis critique the despotic decision making of bin Laden, Zawahiri, and Zarqawi, which is responsible for the misfortunes that have befallen the movement as a whole. Al-Jama'a's imprisoned leaders were not the only jihadis who condemned Al Qaeda's internationalization of jihad. For example, Montasser al-Zayat – the best-known attorney defending jihadis and Islamists in Egyptian trials who, by virtue of profession and ideology, is privy to intimate details of jihadis' inner circles in Egypt and elsewhere – has published two memoirs in Arabic titled *Ayman al-Zawahiri as I Knew Him* and *Islamic Groups: An Inside-Out View* that are highly critical of Al Qaeda's globalist ideology and paint an unflattering portrait of bin Laden and Zawahiri.[47] Both books generated considerable publicity and debate in the Arab world and provoked jihadis and Islamists alike.

The importance of Zayat's critique lies in narrating and analyzing from within the changes that have occurred in the jihadist movement in the last three decades. In particular, he critically examines the role played by Zawahiri in dramatically shifting the focus and ideology of Tanzim al-Jihad away from the near enemy to the far enemy; Zawahiri did so, as the book has shown, against the wishes of many Tanzim members. Zayat also wrote the book to clear his own name and reputation and to prove his authentic jihadist credentials after Zawahiri, in his memoir, questioned Zayat's loyalty and commitment to the cause and accused him of having suspicious connections with the Egyptian authorities. As mentioned previously, the controversy stemmed from Zayat's active promotion of al-Jama'a's 1997 ceasefire initiative among jihadis, including Zawahiri's followers and counterparts. It is worth examining Zayat's *Ayman Zawahiri* at length because it reflects the dominant views of religious nationalists in general and of freelance jihadis who act as intellectual referees among competing and rival factions.

Zayat raises an important sociological point by saying that by themselves social and economic variables are inadequate to explain Islamic resurgence and the rise of jihadism; class analysis fails to capture various currents of political Islam, which, in his view, aim to create an Islamic renaissance. Islamism, Zayat asserts, is rooted in an idea, a belief in the grandeur of Muslim civilization. He writes that bin Laden and Zawahiri are not the only aristocrats-turned-jihadis. Many of his imprisoned clients were successful businessmen and professionals, Zayat writes; the jihadist movement defies Marxist theories of class conflict and stratification.[48] Although well-to-do jihadis exist, Zayat does not mention that their numbers and importance pale when compared with the disfranchised multitudes. Surely, the attraction to Islamism and jihadism by this huge underclass constituency is a product of a deepening developmental and governance crisis in Arab and Muslim societies.[49] But Zayat's point sheds light on the political sociology of jihadis. It does seem that jihadism can be seen as a very self-conscious, and thus to some degree intellectual, endeavor, as can questions of identity. In this respect, it appeals to a certain social constituency, including the intelligentsia, professionals, and college students, and, some might argue, the more transnational any aspect of jihadism becomes, the more likely it is to recruit from among these sectors – or from among those who aspire to be included in these sectors.

Zayat, however, is less concerned with sociological analysis than with evening the score and landing punches against Zawahiri. His critique, which is damning, can be summarized in eight points:

1. Zawahiri spent his adulthood underground plotting to overthrow the Egyptian regime.
2. He aimed at infiltrating the military as the most effective and least costly method to seize power.
3. He believed the struggle against the near enemy was more vital and urgent than that against the far enemy.

4. He was radicalized further during his prison years in Egypt because of abuse and torture.

5. While in Afghanistan Zawahiri rebuilt Tanzim al-Jihad and consolidated his control over it.

6. Zawahiri's complex relationship with bin Laden marked a watershed in his thinking and action.

7. In the late 1990s Zawahiri faced a grim predicament as a result of defeat on the home front in Egypt and debilitating financial woes.

8. Zawahiri joined bin Laden's 1998 World Islamic Front to fight Americans and their allies without consulting the Tanzim's rank and file and without taking into account the repercussions on the jihadist and Islamist movements and on the ummah.

Zayat portrays Zawahiri as a reckless opportunist with no moral scruples; he contends that Zawahiri merged his organization with Al Qaeda because that enabled him to continue to play a leading role in the jihadist movement after suffering crippling blows from the Egyptian authorities. Selfish and ambitious reasons, not ideology, Zayat notes, propelled Zawahiri to jump on bin Laden's bandwagon and to reinvent himself after loss of influence among his countrymen; it is no wonder that Zawahiri not only joined bin Laden's Islamic Front but also informed the world of his own pivotal role in planning its paramilitary operations. For example, only hours after the 1998 attacks on the American embassies in Kenya and Tanzania, Zawahiri released a statement taking full responsibility for targeting U.S. interests. He was desperate, Zayat adds, to prove his centrality and relevance, notwithstanding the exorbitant costs to his supporters and coreligionists.[50]

Zayat's narrative, based on conversations with hundreds of jihadis, takes Zawahiri to task for opening a second front against a far more superior enemy, the United States. How could Zawahiri commit such a fatal strategic error, he sarcastically wonders, and disregard deeply embedded beliefs regarding the primacy of establishing an Islamic state in Egypt? Zayat cannot find a rational explanation for Zawahiri's abrupt shift other than miscalculation and egoism; unlike his counterparts in the Islamic Group, Zawahiri could not concede defeat and shut down his jihadist shop. Although Zayat does not mask his contempt and condescension toward the inexperienced bin Laden, he says that bin Laden was at least more consistent with and faithful to his followers than Zawahiri because all along he had been struggling to expel the Americans from the Persian Gulf, particularly Saudi Arabia.[51]

Embellishments aside, Zayat's *Ayman Zawahiri* paints an authentic portrait of the metamorphosis of this revolutionary from an unabashedly Egyptian religious nationalist to a wholeheartedly pan-Islamist. In Zayat's eyes, Zawahiri is an overambitious, vain, and irresponsible tactician who cared less about the future of Tanzim al-Jihad than about his own image and status; he accuses Zawahiri of sacrificing the interests of the Tanzim at the altar of his unholy alliance with bin Laden. And for what? Zayat says that Zawahiri turned the Tanzim from an organization that "aimed at building an Islamic state in Egypt into a branch within Al Qaeda. He subordinated a well-established organization to a new, experimental one – Al Qaeda – which subsequently caused considerable harm to Islamist groups and activists throughout the world."[52]

To reassure his Islamist and jihadist friends that his critique of Al Qaeda is internal, not external, Zayat stresses that he shares their loathing of American foreign policy, which is, in his opinion, anti-Arab and anti-Muslim, and that resistance is a religious duty. But any effective strategy, he adds, must be informed by costs and benefits and the configuration of regional and international forces; in contrast, Al Qaeda was and is driven by a desire for revenge without regard to repercussions. According to Zayat, who has contacts with a broad spectrum of jihadis, Zawahiri and bin Laden had underestimated the magnitude of the American reaction to September 11; they thought the United States would limit its retaliation to air strikes as it did after the attacks on its embassies in East Africa.[53]

Jihadis whom Zayat consulted expressed anger at bin Laden and Zawahiri for entangling the entire Islamist movement in a very costly confrontation with the sole surviving superpower. The world no longer distinguishes between Al Qaeda and nonglobalist jihadis; it now lumps all of them together as terrorists, thanks to bin Laden and Zawahiri, who succeeded in unifying the international community against the fundamentalist current. Who thought, Zayat asks, that European governments, which had historically granted political asylum to radical and militant Islamists, would no longer do so and would repatriate those who had resided there to their home countries to face trial and persecution.[54]

A consensus exists among Islamists and jihadis, Zayat adds, that Al Qaeda has plunged their movement into one of its gravest crises and that they cannot afford to neglect it; their very survival is at stake. According to Zayat's conversations with jihadis, the United States, along with its European and Muslim allies, has launched a total war against all militant Islamists to get rid of them as a political, not just a military, force; it is viewed as waging a total war to eliminate the Islamist menace. Zayat notes that the ability of the Islamist movement to withstand the American storm depends on the willingness of its leading members to critically reflect on what went wrong and to take stock of their previous words and deeds; there is an urgent need to begin repairing the damage inflicted on the movement by Zawahiri and bin Laden, who forced the jihadist caravan off track, and to construct a long-term strategy in order to resist the onslaught by the new imperial power.[55]

Zayat, an activist-turned-celebrity who built a power base by virtue of his connections with jihadis worldwide, particularly in Egypt, does not lay out a blueprint to help militant Islamists overcome their current predicament. His conclusion is vague and general and lacks specific daring remedies. Although Zayat's diagnosis is that militant Islamists suffer from terminal cancer, instead of recommending immediate surgery or chemotherapy, he prescribes pain killers. There is a major disconnect between Zayat's diagnosis and his remedial action. For example, he urges militant Islamists to unify their ranks and elevate the Palestinian question to the top of their priorities because it is a winning card. Obviously, Zayat wants his Islamist colleagues to jump on the Palestinian bandwagon like their secular counterparts. But he does not elaborate on how embracing the Palestinian cause would rescue the sinking jihadist ship. He hardly addresses the structural problems that lie at the heart of the sociological crisis facing jihadis, like the feasibility and applicability of building a viable Islamic state to which he remains deeply wedded. Zayat and other Islamists have not yet developed a comprehensive politico-economic program that goes beyond ideological slogans and identity politics. As mentioned previously, the Islamist movement as a whole suffers from a paucity of original ideas on governance and political theory.

Despite the shortcomings of Zayat's prescriptions and solutions, it is refreshing to read his straightforward critique of Al Qaeda and his reporting that a majority of jihadis renounce the use of violence in the service of religion and politics. Like other jihadis' critiques of Al Qaeda, Zayat's reinforces the existence of deep fault lines among their ranks. It is unconvincing for a hardliner cleric like Omar Mahmoud Abu Omar, also known as Abu Qatada, to claim that Zayat is only moti‑ vated by revenge and that his book is a "deviant case"; Abu Qatada is a Palestinian preacher who has lived in Britain since 1993 – he is accused of being the spiritual counselor of Mohammed Atta and is under house arrest under a new British law introduced after September 11 that permits the detention without trial of foreigners deemed a danger to national security. After the 2005 London attacks, the British govern‑ ment has struck a deal with Jordan to repatriate Abu Qatada there. He holds a Jordanian passport and was sentenced in absentia by a Jordanian court.[56] The critical question is not whether Zayat was motivated by revenge but rather if his narrative is credible and consistent. Although Zayat is self-promoting and at points inflates his importance, his critique tallies with those of other jihadis and is historically consistent. Equally important, Zayat's is informed by close encounters and conversations with hundreds, if not thousands, of jihadis and the internal debates that have occurred among jihadis over the last three decades.[57]

Abu Qatada, who had boasted of being a fan and supporter of Al Qaeda and who had multiple links with some of the most extremist transnationalist and religious nationalist jihadis, is much less credible and has much more of a vested interest in Al Qaeda than does Zayat. Although after his arrest by British authorities Abu Qatada distanced himself from Al Qaeda and denied any terrorist links, internal mes‑ sages obtained from the Al Qaeda computers in Kabul to and from Abu Qatada indicate extensive contacts with operatives in Afghanistan. The correspondence shows that Abu Qatada offered his computer skills to veteran jihadis in Afghanistan and gained their "trust" and gratitude. The champion of global jihad, as Abu Qatada is fondly remembered, also introduced and recommended activists who wanted to join the jihad caravan there.[58]

For example, in a recent personal testament posted on fundamentalist Web sites after news reports that Al Qaeda's leader in Iraq, Abu Musab al-Zarqawi, had been injured, Seif al-Adl, the military commander of the parent organization (who is thought to be incarcerated by Iran), said that when Zarqawi and his brothers arrived in Pakistan after their release from a Jordanian prison in 1999, they did not need any introduction and were welcomed with open arms, thanks to Abu Qatada, who had publicized Zarqawi's jihadist ideas in his journal, *Al Menhaj*, published in London: "It was in this journal that we first read the letters of Abu Mohammed al-Maqdisi [Zarqawi's spiritual and intellectual mentor], the letters of al-Zarqawi, and their historical defense before the prosecution [in Jordan]. Abu Qatada always reminded us that we had active brothers in Jordan who were expected to have a promising future in spreading al-da'wa."[59]

Regardless of whether Abu Qatada was an honest preacher with "a big mouth and a big belly," as he said, with no relationship to Al Qaeda, or an active member, he had politically supported its project and remains infatuated with its ideology. As recently as 2004 he called Zawahiri "al-hakim," or the wise man of the jihadist movement, and dismissed Zayat's critique as nothing but "evil analysis."[60] But far from being unique, Zayat echoes dominant sentiments among jihadis. Hani al-Sibai wrote a foreword to Zayat's book, reiterating the main points raised in the book, but in a more measured tone. Sibai also praised Zayat's balanced narrative and, anticipating detractors like Abu Qatada, stressed that the Islamist attorney is a dedicated son of the jihadist movement, thus endowing his account with revolutionary legitimacy. Jihadis must not refrain from debating and critiquing one another, added Sibai, who considers himself the official historian of the jihadist movement. He added that engaging in self-criticism is also necessary because the alternative is stagnation and decay; not to do so would doom jihadis to repeat the same mistakes, a clear reference to Al Qaeda and Zawahiri's Islamic Jihad.[61]

In 2004 Sibai published his own diaries, serialized in *Al Hayat*; they documented major watersheds and turning points in the history of the jihadist movement, particularly al-Jama'a al-Islamiya and Tanzim al-Jihad.[62] Sibai's memoir is bluntly critical of Al Qaeda and its globalization of jihad. When he first read the announcement of bin Laden's World Islamic Front, Sibai wrote, he could not believe his eyes; he thought the whole thing was fabricated. But after he investigated and found out that the World Islamic Front was authentic, he confided that he thought it was an "unnecessary propaganda move, senseless, and literally and doctrinally awkward." "The Front," Sibai added, "was disastrous to Islamic Jihad in particular and to Islamist movements in general."[63]

Like Zayat and other Islamist critics, Sibai said the decision to shift operational priorities and attack the United States was unwise and not based on critical and empirical analysis and broad consultation with the rank and file; many senior jihadis with whom he had conferred about the World Islamic Front expressed shock that they had not been informed or consulted in advance. They said they found out about it when it was reported in the Arabic-language newspaper Al-Quds al-Arabi. Sibai's sources told him that even Zawahiri had not read the 1998 fatwa declaring war on the Americans and their allies before it was made public, a shocking discovery to Sibai and his colleagues. How could Zawahiri join in such a dangerous adventure without informing and consulting the organization's Shura Council, asked Sibai. As the previous chapter has shown, the Council had overwhelmingly opposed the new global alliance with bin Laden, a man who did not gain their confidence because he did not come to their rescue in their hour of need. According to Sibai and as Chapter Four fleshed out, Egyptian jihadis had already decided to keep their distance from bin Laden; they could not understand why Zawahiri would autocratically overrule their decision and fully align – and then submerge – Tanzim al-Jihad with Al Qaeda.[64]

Sibai rehashes all the previously stated reasons for Zawahiri's partnership with bin Laden, particularly financial dependency and tightening of the security noose around Zawahiri and his men. The Taliban and bin Laden, Sibai adds, offered Zawahiri and his associates protection and refuge; it was an alliance of necessity, not of choice or ideology. According to Sibai, who talked to Zawahiri's senior aides, the latter rationalized the decision to join bin Laden's network by saying "we all function under the banner of the Taliban regardless if we were members of Al Qaeda or not."[65] But there were few buyers of Al Qaeda among Zawahiri's lieutenants, Sibai said.[66]

According to Sibai, many Tanzim members who opposed joining Al Qaeda had hoped to stay with their families in Afghanistan and remain independent without publicizing their differences with Zawahiri; they did not want to be associated with Al Qaeda's assault on America and its Western allies. But September 11, the subsequent American war, and the overthrow of the Taliban shattered their plans and decimated their ranks. It is no wonder, Sibai acknowledges, that the very survival of Tanzim al-Jihad is in doubt; its shrinking number of human assets exists in Egyptian and American prisons or are scattered in the mountains and caves on the Afghan-Pakistan border. Zawahiri's gamble on Al Qaeda appears to have endangered the very existence of the Tanzim.[67] Since 2004 Egypt has been rocked by several major sophisticated attacks. Although it is difficult to say if Zawahiri has breathed new life into his organization in Egypt, the spectacular, coordinated nature of the bombings does have the markings of Zawahiri's Tanzim. It is likely that Zawahiri could have infiltrated the 100,000 or so Bedouins who live in northern Sinai. The Egyptian government and the Bedouins have a strained relationship.

Like Sibai, Yasir al-Sirri, another alleged leader of the Tanzim who took refuge in London after being sentenced to death by an Egyptian military court, publicly condemned Al Qaeda and the globalization of jihad, although Sirri is not as forthcoming and transparent as Zayat, Sibai, Osama Rushdi, and others. The crux of the jihadis' critique lies in that bin Laden, Zawahiri, and their associates diverted the jihad caravan from its correct historical path (the near enemy) into a difficult foreign terrain. They plunged the Islamist and jihadist movements into an uneven and unequal fight with the most powerful nation on earth.

But with the exception of al-Jama'a's imprisoned leaders, who stressed moral and ethical considerations in their critique of Al Qaeda, on the whole, jihadis' critique of Al Qaeda is more utilitarian and pragmatic and focuses on the asymmetry of power and the balance of forces between the ummah and its enemies; power relations take precedence over moral variables. In his rebuttal of Al Qaeda, Osama Rushdi comes close to coupling the moral with the political and calling on fellow jihadis to be self-critical.

In several interviews with the Arab media, Osama Rushdi drives a point home: although Al Qaeda justified its attacks on the United States in religious terms, it has nothing to do with Islam. Islam does not sanction killing civilians or violating legal and moral percepts, he adds, because that would threaten international harmony and coexistence. Osama Rushdi says he opposes not only Zawahiri and bin Laden's internationalization of jihad but also their notion of "blessed terrorism," which goes against the strict rules and regulations set for activating and waging jihad. He poses a critical question for Al Qaeda members: will they respect the rules established by the Shariah for pursuing jihad? If so, Osama Rushdi urges them to reflect on their erroneous ways and correct them before it is too late.[68]

Although Rushdi says it is easy to criticize American foreign policy, he prefers to address his message to transnationalist jihadis whom he holds accountable for the current crisis: "Does hostility to America justify utilizing all means to attack it and harm its citizens regardless of their legitimacy and the inherent benefits and costs? Do the ends justify the means in this struggle, or should the means be as justifiable as the end?" Osama Rushdi concludes his critique of Al Qaeda by bluntly warning his colleagues that the greatest threat facing the jihadist movement lies in its self-inflicted "wounds" and "errors" and the lack of institutional, political, and legitimate religious experiences; for too long jihadis and Islamists neglected institution building and offered "blind obedience to the charismatic leader who surprises his companions with abrupt decisions to the extent that they find out about them in newspapers," a direct reference to the fateful decisions taken by bin Laden and Zawahiri.[69]

One of the consistent themes that emerges out of jihadis' critiques of Al Qaeda is that "charismatic" or "autocratic" leadership must be replaced by institutional, transparent decision making, where shura or consultation is obligatory, not voluntary. A common thread runs through all the critiques: bin Laden, Zawahiri, and a few senior aides monopolized all decisions and did not seek, let alone listen to, the diverse views within the organization. Although these jihadis, who are critical of Al Qaeda, may prefer a broader and more encompassing decision making, they cannot be called democrats; their pronouncements exhibit an antidemocratic bias, and some of them underscore that shura or consultation is not democracy.

Thus Al Qaeda is not the only jihadist organization that was autocratically led. As this book has shown, the jihadist and Islamist movements are usually micromanaged by strongmen who demand obedience. At the risk of generalization, the cult of personality is a structural infliction in the Arab and Muslim body politick that infects both the rulers and the opposition. The inner workings of both mainstream and militant Islamists tend to be more autocratic than that of their ruling tormentors. Measuring the compatibility between democracy and political Islam must await the democratization of the internal Islamist decision-making process, even though few mainstream Islamist groups, which aim to build their envisioned Islamic state via constitutional or electoral means, have well-established internal democratic mechanisms, like Jama'at-i-Islami of Pakistan.

Al Qaeda's Counteroffensive

The comprehensive survey and analysis of jihadis' responses to Al Qaeda and the globalization of jihad do not bode well for the transnationalists; the news is far from encouraging for bin Laden, Zawahiri, Seif al-Adl, Zarqawi, and their associates. The ideological revisions and self-critiques that have been taking place within various parts of the movement provide fascinating sociological profiles and portraits of jihadist currents and personalities. They also clearly show that transnationalist jihadis possess no mass following within the movement as a whole and are poor cousins of the jihadist family.

As this chapter indicates, the dominant response by jihadis to September 11 is an explicit rejection of Al Qaeda and total opposition to the internationalization of jihad, rather than heeding its call and taking up arms against the camp of unbelief. Privately, former jihadis confide that they are furious with Al Qaeda, whose actions appear "senseless" and "self-destructive," supplying ammunition to their tormentors – Muslim rulers – to strike harder against the Islamist movement. I have not heard a single former jihadi praise Al Qaeda or support its tactics, although many think that the United States exaggerates the network's power and reach for cynical foreign policy reasons. A critic might question the significance of their attack on Al Qaeda because they can no longer be classified as real jihadis. Well, those voices are not isolated or newcomers to the jihadist current; they represent the dominant, traditional wing within the movement. When Sibai, Rushdi, Derbala, Abu al-Walid, and others criticize Al Qaeda, their views resonate among the rank and file.

There is a general realignment within the jihadist current against, not in favor of, Al Qaeda and global jihad. (Iraq seems to have given birth to a second generation of transnationalist jihadis; more on this in the next chapter.) This is a significant point to highlight because if jihadis do not take Al Qaeda's bait, what constituencies would? If seasoned and committed jihadis stay on the sidelines, where could Al Qaeda recruit and replenish its rapidly depleting ranks? As the book has shown, jihadis did not just remain neutral in the unfolding struggle between transnationalists and the international community; they publicly and actively campaigned against Al Qaeda. They have waged a public relations campaign to distance themselves from being associated with Al Qaeda and to discredit bin Laden and Zawahiri by accusing them of violating jihad's basic tenets.

Instead of coalescing and closing ranks against "the enemies of Islam," as bin Laden and Zawahiri had hoped, transnationalists and religious nationalists are pitted against one another in a brutal war of words that exposes the wide gulf separating them. Since the late 1990s the fissure has widened and deepened, not narrowed, and September 11 put to rest any possibility of bridging the gulf. In this, Al Qaeda is the real loser because it desperately needs loyal allies and revolutionary legitimacy; its supposed natural partners not only deny it recognition but also indirectly join its enemies and attack it with a vengeance. Religious nationalists' disavowal of Al Qaeda represents a major blow to its credibility and long-term durability and exposes its minuscule weight within the jihadist movement.

In diaries, memoirs, and video- and audiotapes, Zawahiri, bin Laden, and their spokesmen launched a counterattack and appealed to the Muslim masses to join their global jihad over the heads of the religious establishment and former jihadist associates. In 2003 Zawahiri put out another book with a religious title, *Al Walaa wa Al Baraa*, or *Loyalty to Islam and Disavowal to Its Enemies*, in which he reminds Muslims that although he is on the run and in hiding, he felt that the dire situation facing the ummah "compelled" him to write this testament. Zawahiri chose a recognizable religious term, *Al Walaa wa Al Baraa*, to drive the point home to Muslims that they must make a choice between Islam and its enemies; it is one or the other, with no third alternative, a direct response to those critical voices who reject this simplistic dichotomy.

The last few decades, Zawahiri writes, "have witnessed an intense struggle between impious forces, domination, and arrogance and the Muslim ummah and its jihadist vanguard, culminating in the two blessed raids on New York and Washington and the subsequent new crusading campaign declared by Bush against Islam, or what he termed the war on terror."[70]

More than *Knights Under the Prophet's Banner*, which he began writing in 2000 and completed after September 11, *Al Walaa wa Al Baraa* delivers a specific message to Muslims regarding the importance of loyalty to Islam and the danger of neglecting this duty, especially during these momentous times. He also warns Muslims to be wary of those "enemies who are waging a misleading intellectual and moral campaign, paralleling that of the crusading military campaign, whose aim is to maintain the unjust status quo."[71] In his view, "the worst fitna [sedition] in this century threatening tawhid [monotheism, or the principle of the absolute unity of God] and Islamic doctrine is not being loyal to believers and hostile to infidels."[72] Zawahiri's *Al Walaa wa Al Baraa* is another effort to regain the edge in the battle of Muslim public opinion and to cast doubt on those former associates who criticized Al Qaeda's global jihad. How dare those who claim to be Muslims and "guardians and defenders of the Shariah," he adds mockingly, adopt the terms and references of secularists and impious rulers and call for recognition of Israel?[73]

In his memoir, Zawahiri disdainfully dismissed al-Jihad members who found fault with his project, as "the hot-blooded revolutionary strugglers who have now become as cold as ice after they experienced the life of civilization and luxury, the guarantees of the new world order, the gallant ethics of civilized Europe, and the impartiality and materialism of Western civilization." In *Al Walaa wa Al Baraa*, he broadens his net to include anyone who deals with secular governments and accepts the existing order. He seems to be indicting and excommunicating large sectors of Muslim society. It is difficult to see how Zawahiri could win Muslim hearts and minds when he lectures and reproaches believers for dealing with "the rotten reality." Al Qaeda's reaction to its Muslim critics has become more volatile and abusive, a clear sign of desperation and escalation of the war within. In a way, the internal tensions and contradictions roiling the jihadist movement bear a strong resemblance to processes that tore the European revolutionary left apart at various times in the 1960s, '70s, and '80s. There is nothing unique about Islamism and jihadism, even though their members portray themselves as apolitical and puritan; they have much more in common with nationalists and leftists than they realize or acknowledge.

Indeed, the Al Qaeda chiefs cannot be blamed for being anxious about the future of their organization – and for their own survival as well. The global war has not gone as well as they had expected. The United States has proved to be a much tougher and resilient adversary than the former Soviet Union, and the ummah has not awkened from its slumber. There has been a trickle of recruits here and there but no flood of volunteers along the Afghan lines. Bin Laden's global jihad is not seen as defensive as was that against the Russians in Afghanistan in the 1980s or against the Americans in Iraq now (it is no wonder that Iraq has emerged as a pivotal theater for Al Qaeda leadership, a major turning point in their global jihad). According to Abu al-Walid, long before September 11 close aides to bin Laden had concluded that the United States was "a savage" and "dishonorable" foe and that it would not show mercy to its enemy if he falls but would make sure that he is finished.[74] They were correct on one point: the Bush administration has made the dismantling of Al Qaeda and other militant networks a top strategic priority. The goal is what Bush's top adviser on terrorism, Frances Fragos Townsend, once called "decapitation strategy," that is, to capture and kill Al Qaeda leaders.[75] Bin Laden, Zawahiri, and Abu Hafs should have heeded their aides' warning that once they take war to the United States, they would face the brunt of American power; they underestimated the magnitude of the U.S. military response.

The American war strategy against Al Qaeda began to evolve just hours after the September 11 attacks. Addressing a joint session of Congress nine days later, on 20 September, President Bush noted that the new war went beyond bin Laden and his organization: "Our war on terror begins with Al Qaeda, but it does not end there. It will not end until every terrorist group of global reach has been found, stopped, and defeated." In October 2001 a new policy directive signed by Bush went into effect: the United States would strive to eliminate all terrorist networks, dry up their financial support, and prevent them from acquiring weapons of mass destruction. The goal was the "elimination of terrorism as a threat to our way of life."[76]

Although after the fall of the Taliban the Bush administration's appetite expanded and got distracted by plunging into the shifting sands of Iraq, the global coalition against Al Qaeda and other militant groups remains on track and has taken a heavy toll on jihadis worldwide. The global coalition put together by the United States immediately after September 11 is deadly effective, notwithstanding the fact that bin Laden, Zawahiri, and a few of their top aides have not been apprehended yet and have proved to be adaptable and resourceful.[77]

Although multilateral efforts, particularly by Muslim states, have not received widespread publicity, they have led to the most important breakthroughs against Al Qaeda. From Pakistan to Spain and from Indonesia to Saudi Arabia, thousands of alleged Al Qaeda suspects and sympathizers have been incarcerated. Many of bin Laden's field lieutenants and operatives have been captured by Pakistan, Yemen, the United Arab Emirates, Syria, Malaysia, Thailand, and other nations and handed over to U.S. authorities. This global alliance, not just the U.S. military campaign, has played a key role in tightening the noose around Al Qaeda's neck. It is not convincing to argue, as some observers do, that the Bush administration invaded Iraq to force Arab and Muslim states to crack down harder on Al Qaeda and secure their full cooperation in the U.S. war on terror. Soon after September 11 Muslim governments, including Sudan, Syria, Libya, and even Iran, which were not on good terms with the United States, pursued Al Qaeda diligently and aggressively, according to American intelligence officials; they had a vital interest in neutralizing Al Qaeda because they felt directly threatened by the militant network. Bin Laden and Zawahiri, as former associates point out, succeeded in uniting the world, including the ummah, against their global jihad.

As Zawahiri and bin Laden's recent pronouncements indicate, their constant appeals to Muslims to rise up and join the fight have largely fallen on deaf ears. Neither the ummah nor the army of deactivated jihadis seems prepared to take up arms and defend Al Qaeda. The opposite is true; the religious establishment and Islamists questioned the authority and utility of Al Qaeda's call for global jihad, denying it legitimacy and fresh recruits.

Al Qaeda's grand failure stems from misreading not just America's military response to September 11 but also the mood and response of the ummah. The ummah may empathize with Al Qaeda's grievances against the international order, particularly Western powers, but it is unwilling to go to war to rectify injustice. I would argue further that Al Qaeda has finally succeeded in mobilizing the ummah not against the camp of disbelief, but rather against bin Laden and his cohorts. Many Muslim scholars and civil society leaders have called on the ummah to develop a culture of resistance, an effective immune system, against the new plague called global jihad.

The critical question is not whether Muslims sympathize with bin Laden's rhetoric of victimhood but if they are ready to shed blood to support it. The answer is not really. A senior experienced jihadi leader warned bin Laden not to take Muslims' emotional empathy seriously because of the difficulty of translating that operationally: "their hearts are with you but their swords are against you." Public sympathy, he added, cannot overcome reality and the asymmetry of power; it swiftly dissipates and turns into hostility as military failure looms on the horizon.[78] Bin Laden and Zawahiri's hope of mobilizing and awakening the ummah out of its political slumber did not materialize. Worse still, more and more Muslims, including former jihadist associates, now view Al Qaeda as a losing, not a winning, horse, and they are reluctant to gamble on it.

This does not mean that some young Muslims will not be seduced by Al Qaeda's ideology and carry out terrorist acts in its name. The bombings in Madrid, London, Egypt, and elsewhere testify to Al Qaeda's continuing ability to incite and inspire uprooted young Muslims, including European-born men, to kill on its behalf and the ummah's. Sporadic acts of violence and terrorism will likely continue for the forseeable future; there exists no magic bullet to put the global jihad genie back in the bottle. But this alarming trend should not blind us to the fact that Al Qaeda is besieged and isolated in Muslim lands, and its high expectations have crashed on the rocks of Islamic reality. Far from generating popular Muslim support, the returns on Al Qaeda's operations have been mostly negative. The struggle within will ultimately determine the future of global jihad. It is no wonder that the expansion of the U.S. "war on terror" has been counterproductive and has even prolonged the agony of the beast – Al Qaeda. The United States is fighting the wrong war, one that has overlooked the imperative of nourishing and consolidating, not exacerbating further, coalitions and alliances with Muslim social and political forces that could hammer a final deadly nail in the coffin of Al Qaeda and its global jihad ideology.

Conservative Islamists and Ulema Against Al Qaeda

Like former jihadis, leading mainstream Islamists – Muslim Brothers, independents, and clerics – condemned Al Qaeda's attacks on the United States as harmful to Islam and Muslims, not just to Americans. For example, Hassan al-Turabi – formerly head of the Islamic National Front and now People's Congress, in Sudan, who in the early 1990s hosted bin Laden, Abu Hafs, Abu Ubaidah, Zawahiri, Seif al-Adl and their families and cohorts in Sudan and welcomed them as fellow revolutionaries – wrote from his prison in Khartoum three full-page essays in the Arabic-language newspaper *Al Hayat* in which he criticized Al Qaeda's killing of American civilians as morally wrong and politically counterproductive. "Intelligent mujahedeen," Turabi said, "must exercise restraint and refrain from initiating war and must limit operations to military, not civilian, targets."[79]

Although Turabi is very critical of U.S. foreign policy and has gained a high profile among radical Islamists for being vocally anti-imperialist and an advocate of Islamic unity, he said that there was no justification for attacking America and unleashing its military might against Arabs and Muslims. The same Turabi, who had offered bin Laden's network protection and political refuge and was the intellectual driving force behind the Sudanese military regime, reprimanded his former pupils for ignoring the moral limits and constraints stipulated by Islamic law when engaging in jihad, as well as the need to be cognizant of the international balance of power. Like the majority of Muslim scholars, Turabi defines jihad as a just war theory, a defensive collective obligation regulated with checks and balances, not as offensive or preemptive aggression against noncombatants. His subtle critique of Al Qaeda amounts to a repudiation of its actions, if not its ideology, and, unlike other mainstream Islamists, he stops short of directly and personally taking his former associates to task for the misfortunes they inflicted on their victims at home and abroad.[80]

That would be too much to ask from Turabi, who is not known for his consistency or intellectual integrity, even though he portrays himself as a religious scholar and moralist. In 1989 he conspired with General Omar al-Bashir and army officers in Sudan who carried out a coup d'etat, seizing power and establishing an Islamic dictatorship. Far from turning Sudan into an example of the compatibility between Islam and democracy, as Turabi, the Sorbonne-educated theoretician of the military junta, had promised, political opposition was brutally suppressed, and a reign of tyranny descended on the Arab-African state. Turabi became synonymous with the dismal failure of political Islam and militancy; Sudan was seen as a pariah state regionally and internationally, thanks to Turabi, who dreamed of establishing an international Islamic Comintern based in Sudan. In the early 1990s Sudan provided a safe haven to various jihadist groups, including Egyptians, North Africans, Saudis, Yemenis, and Chechnyans, which roamed freely in the country and plotted against their own governments. By the mid-1990s the United States and its regional allies had exerted considerable pressure on the Sudanese government to expel bin Laden and his entourage from the country. In 1996 Turabi and the military obliged and ordered bin Laden and his associates to leave Sudan immediately, which they did.

Ironically, bin Laden and Zawahiri do not buy the Western image of Turabi as an authentic revolutionary; they suspect him of being an overambitious politician influenced by corrupting Western ideas. In his memoir, bin Laden's personal bodyguard Nasir Abdullah al-Bahri, says that his boss blamed Turabi for his expulsion from Sudan:

> So the ruling Islamic Front in Sudan, under the leadership of Dr. Hassan Turabi, asked sheikh Osama to leave the country. For bin Laden, al-Turabi was always a nuisance, although he was an Islamic thinker, contrary to President Omar Hassan al-Bashir, who displayed all the good Sudanese qualities of courage and help. He would not accept the pressure because he considered bin Laden his guest and a refugee in his country. As for al-Turabi, it seems that his studies at the Sorbonne and his previous political background had a great impact on him. So al-Turabi became the tool to pressure sheikh Osama to leave the country.

Bin Laden praises General Bashir, the military dictator of Sudan, and disparages Turabi, an "Islamic thinker," who could not be trusted. Asked if Turabi played any role in convincing the Bashir regime to expel bin Laden and his entourage, al-Bahri noted accusingly:

> Al-Turabi himself exerted a great deal of pressure on sheikh Osama to make him leave Sudan. He visited him for three consecutive days, holding long meetings and heated discussions with him, until late at night, to convince him to leave Sudan. Sheikh Osama tried to convince him of the opposite: that there was no need to expel him, that they had not committed any armed acts against Sudan, and that there was no other country ready to receive them. But al-Turabi told him that he had two options: either to keep silent or to leave the country. He was very determined that bin Laden leave the country. That was when sheikh Osama decided to leave Sudan. He said: as long as many young men have been detained and imprisoned in Saudi Arabia and the Sudanese want me to keep silent, I will leave Sudan. He made arrangements with the Sudanese to leave the country with his followers and moved to Afghanistan.

And how was the personal relationship between bin Laden and Turabi? Al-Bahri said his boss did not care much for the Sudanese Islamist, who felt threatened by bin Laden's rising stardom within the jihadist movement worldwide:

> Yes, there were some sensitivities between them. Their biggest problem ... was sheikh Osama's practical program and his success in defeating the American forces in Somalia, in cooperation with the Somali Islamic groups. They also defeated the American troops in Sudan [what troops?], where Sudan was supposed to be the Americans' entrance to their control over Somalia and the whole Horn of Africa. That was why bin Laden's success in defending Sudan was a sensitive spot, which caused al-Turabi's jealousy. Al-Turabi relies mainly on theories. Maybe he was afraid sheikh Osama would take over the leadership of Sudan someday in the future, at his own expense, especially because bin Laden was at that point looking at Sudan as the backbone of the international Islamic movement, as an important extension of the Islamic movement in the Horn of Africa and East Africa, in general.

So much for Islamist and jihadist brotherhood and solidarity. In bin Laden's eyes, Turabi's "jealousy" explains the decision to expel him from Sudan. Whether that is true or false, that was how bin Laden, a Salafi, perceived Turabi, whose roots were in the Muslim Brotherhood. Behind a façade of Islamic solidarity lie clashes of personalities, petty quarrels, and personal ambitions. Islamists and jihadis are no different from other political actors except that personalities play a pivotal role in their politics and dynamics. More than their secular opponents, they failed to create formal institutions and fell victim to "autocratic" charisma. It would not be an exaggeration that you could study and write the history of the Islamist and jihadist movements through the lenses and actions of dozens of patriarchical leaders.

Turabi was not the only Islamist leader who criticized Al Qaeda's globalization of jihad and killing of American civilians. The spiritual founding father of Lebanon's Hizbollah, Sayyed Mohammed Hussein Fadlallah, challenged Al Qaeda's claim that its attacks on the United States could be religiously sanctioned. In dozens of interviews and lectures since September 11, Fadlallah, considered one of the most prominent and prolific radical Shiite clerics, called Al Qaeda's bombings "suicide," not "martyrdom operations" and thus said that they were doctrinally illegitimate. Fadlallah does not mince any words about being staunchly opposed to U.S. foreign policy.[81] However, in interviews and writings he consistently argued against killing American citizens, who are not responsible for their country's international policies – and may even oppose them: "We must not punish individuals who have no relationship with the American administration or even those who have an indirect role."[82]

In his disagreement with Al Qaeda, Fadlallah stresses several critical points. First, he says that Americans are neither synonymous with their government nor accountable for its policy. Second, he says there exists no clash of cultures with the West, but rather a "struggle against arrogance," a reference to American hegemony. Third, Fadlallah reminds bin Laden and his cohorts that "civilized Islam" does not condone launching preemptive strikes against citizens of nonbelligerent nations like the United States, even though its foreign policies inflict harm on Arabs and Muslims. Fourth, as his interlocutor noted, although he refrains from calling bin Laden and Zawahiri agitated or hyper-Sunnis who committed atrocities against Shiites in Afghanistan, Fadlallah said that bin Laden does not understand or appreciate political reality, which, in his view, could explain some of his misguided actions, particularly the September 11 attacks.

Fifth, Fadlallah argues that Al Qaeda did not consider the costs and benefits and that the costs were much higher than the benefits; nor did Al Qaeda care about potential damage to the ummah. Finally, he rejects the comparison between the Al Qaeda attacks on the Americans and those by Palestinians on Israelis in the occupied territories. Palestinians are justified in carrying out "martyrdom operations" against military and civilian targets in Israel, he adds, because Israel occupies Muslim lands and oppresses believers; the Palestinians are defending themselves against the powerful Israeli military apparatus in which all citizens serve. For him, "martyrdom" is the most effective deterrent. Fadlallah, who denies terrorism charges leveled against Hizbollah, also argues that in the early 1980s Hizbollah was justified in targeting Westerners in Lebanon because they directly aided the Israeli occupation of the country; in contrast, the Shiite cleric notes that Al Qaeda's suicide bombings against Americans cannot be religiously or politically sanctioned: America neither directly occupies Muslim territories nor oppresses and kills Muslims. In his eyes, there are more effective nonviolent ways to resist hostile U.S. policies than to attack Americans.[83]

Fadlallah's critique is controversial and requires critical scrutiny, a task beyond the scope of this book. But his debunking of bin Laden and Zawahiri's notion of transnationalized jihad is worth highlighting because he is one of the most prominent radical clerics opposed to American foreign policy, and he is highly respected across the broad spectrum of Sunni and Shiite Muslims. In the 1980s his defiance of, and some say incitement against, the United States earned him revolutionary laurels among Arabs and Muslims. He has a large audience that transcends tiny Lebanon. Thus Fadlallah's critique of Al Qaeda has particular resonance for youths.

Bin Laden and Zawahiri are in deep trouble when a revolutionary cleric like Fadlallah unequivocally repudiates their tactics and calls on believers to exercise restraint and not be driven by irrational anti-American sentiments. This shows the extent of Al Qaeda's isolation and fringe status even within the radical religious camp. If Al Qaeda cannot coopt this constituency, who can it coopt? The religious establishment? Al Qaeda has no real friends or supporters there. For example, sheikh Mohammed Sayyed Tantawi, a reformist and the Grand Imam of Al-Azhar, the oldest Islamic learning institution, was one of the first clerics to condemn Al Qaeda and dismiss bin Laden's jihad credentials as "fraudulent." On September 13, 2001, one of the leading Muslim scholars, Yusuf al-Qardawi, issued a fatwa that condemned Al Qaeda's "illegal jihad" and expressed sorrow and empathy with the American victims: "Our hearts bleed because of the attacks that have targeted the World Trade Center, as well as other institutions in the United States."[84] Qardawi, who has a huge Muslim audience and is widely listened to and read, wrote that the murders in New York cannot be justified on any ground, including "the American biased policy toward Israel on the military, political, and economic fronts."[85]

Leading religious scholars and clerics, including the muftis of Saudi Arabia, Egypt, and elsewhere, echoed Qardawi's condemnation of Al Qaeda and declared their opposition to all those who permit and engage in the killing of noncombatants. They stressed the defensive, not offensive, function of jihad in Islam and that it is a collective, not an individual, duty that could only be activated by the community, not by amateurs. There was no sympathy within the religious establishment for Al Qaeda, which threatened its very authority; rather, the reverse was true. Immediately after September 11 an outpouring of sympathy for America and anger at Al Qaeda colored religious pronouncements and statements by Islamic scholars.[86] After September 11, even those militant clerics in Saudi Arabia, Yemen, and elsewhere who had been supportive of bin Laden distanced themselves from Al Qaeda and found themselves on the defensive.

Following September 11 Al Qaeda met with stiff resistance from the religious establishment, and that resistance has recently turned into active interventional opposition because of Al Qaeda's natural propensity to commit errors, particularly its attacks inside Muslim countries. Conservative clerics have become more vocal in their criticism not just of Al Qaeda but of militancy in general, although neofundamentalists remain deeply entrenched in Al-Azhar and other institutions of higher learning.[87] Sheikh Abdul Mohsen bin Nasser al-Obeikan of Saudi Arabia is a case in point. Obeikan, a prominent conservative Salafi, who in 1990 opposed the stationing of American troops in the kingdom, utilizes the airways and print media to warn young Muslims against militant ideologies, like Al Qaeda. He says he takes this responsibility very seriously, and "I am ready to debate at any time anyone who defends Al Qaeda or justifies its actions."[88] Far from being unique, sheikh Obeikan represents a new phenomenon among conservative religious scholars, who now appreciate the danger posed to Muslims by Al Qaeda and publicly oppose it.

Two questions arise: how effective is the religious establishment's opposition to Al Qaeda, and does it make a difference and dissuade young Muslims from joining Al Qaeda's global jihad? And has the religious establishment offered an alternative or a blueprint to that of militants? When prominent religious scholars, like sheikhs Tantawi, Qardawi, and Nasir al-Din al-Albani, a Salafi from Saudi Arabia, publicly condemn Al Qaeda's terrorism, Muslims take their opinion seriously. But it would be simplistic to exaggerate the effects of the religious on the unfolding internal struggle in the Muslim world; it is under siege, and it faces a two-pronged onslaught by Muslim rulers and militants alike.[89]

As long as the religious leadership lacks institutional independence and is not structurally reformed, it will continue to be seen as an extension of the ruling establishment and will be unable to counterbalance militant Islamists who claim to be the guardians and defenders of authentic Islam. Senior clerics, including those at Al-Azhar, are appointed by governments and in a way are salaried bureaucrats who serve at the behest of Muslim rulers. It is no wonder they no longer carry moral weight and influence in the eyes of young Muslims; they are tainted by their close association and connection with the ruling elite.[90] In addition, although mainstream clerics condemned transnationalist jihadis; they have neither articulated a systematic critique of their ideologies nor offered a convincing alternative that appeals to activists and dissenters. For the purpose of this book, however, the input of the religious authority is not as critical as those of jihadis and militants whose views and positions I have examined at great length. Nevertheless, a flavor of the religious authority's overall stance shows Al Qaeda's predicament and the broad spectrum of the internal forces arrayed against it.

Articulating a Response: The Modernist Islamist and Intellectual Elite

If Al Qaeda could not find buyers within the conservative religious establishment, how did it do among enlightened, modernist, and radical

Islamists? Dismally. Like their conservative counterparts, modernist or reformist Islamists found fault with Al Qaeda's notion of waging offensive jihad against civilians to preempt and punish an imagined enemy instead of legitimately defending the homeland against occupiers. Tariq al-Bishri, a jurist and historian, said that September 11 marked a dramatic departure from the historical pattern of nationalist resistance movements in the Muslim world. This pattern, according to Bishri, who views American policy as unambiguously hostile to Arabs and Muslims, had restricted the liberation struggle to resisting imperial encroachment and aggression on national frontiers; in contrast, the attacks in New York and Washington dangerously expanded the conflict by targeting the sole surviving superpower and killing its citizens. Bishri argues that if Arabs and Muslims appeal to the moral conscience of the international community to condemn injustices inflicted on them, it is incumbent on them to refrain from falling into their enemy's trap by harming innocent civilians. Echoing a dominant theme expressed by Arabs and Muslims, Bishri writes that attacking the United States did more material and moral harm than good to the ummah and empowered their enemies.[91]

Although Bishri said the killing of Americans was wrong, he sounded skeptical of the U.S. case against Al Qaeda and demanded concrete, not just circumstantial, evidence before indicting the organization. Bishri reflected sentiments widely shared by Arabs whose skepticism sheds light on the sad state of relations between the United States and Muslim societies today. Although they reject Al Qaeda's terrorism, Islamists of all political and ideological persuasions perceive the United States as waging an indirect war against Muslims and that the latter have little choice but to resist American and Israeli aggression. In fact, Bishri, considered one of the leading enlightened Islamists, titled his book *The Arabs in the Face of Aggression*; in it he accuses the United States of being aggressive against Muslims in Palestine, Afghanistan, and Iraq, and he calls on the masses to defend their culture and nation: "The U.S. that expressed animosity against us in Palestine for the last fifty years is the one we face today in Afghanistan. It is the same hostile power which built military bases in the Gulf, laid siege to countries, and imposed sanctions."[92]

As shown, there exists among Arab and Muslim public opinion widespread anger and resentment against U.S. foreign policies, particularly on Palestine, Iraq, and, to a lesser extent, Afghanistan. It is

242 • The Far Enemy

difficult to predict the potential fallout and repercussions of that on the stability of pro-Western Middle Eastern regimes and American interests given the high ideological mobilization and powerlessness among Arabs and Muslims. For example, what operational forms would this resistance take, and how would it manifest itself on the ground? American officials may take comfort in the fact that former jihadis, conservative and radical Islamists, and the religious establishment parted company with Al Qaeda, but they can afford to neglect Muslim societal opposition to U.S. foreign policies only at their own peril.

Many young Muslims at home and abroad are being nourished on an anti-American and -British foreign policy diet, one that can be easily exploited by transnationalist jihadis, like bin Laden, Zawahiri, and Zarqawi. Once again, hideous as they were, the Madrid and London attacks must be understood within this ideologically fertile soil that attracts young uprooted men, some of whom are second-generation European Muslims, to militant causes; in their eyes, their imagined ummah is besieged and under threat. Foreign policy grievances, coupled with social and cultural, as opposed to purely economic, marginalization supply the fuel that ignites terrorist activities worldwide.

Ahmed Kamal Abu al-Magd, a prominent liberal Islamist legal authority, went beyond Bishri and deconstructed Al Qaeda's project. In a critical essay titled "Terrorism and Islam and the Future of the International System," Abu al-Magd laments that in the minds of many Westerners Islam has become synonymous with terrorism and that this great religion has been reduced to a "security problem." Although Abu al-Magd lists historical and cultural reasons for Westerners' misperception of Islam, he specifically holds militant Islamists and jihadis accountable for poisoning the minds of the West and intensifying hostility to Muslims.[93]

Abu al-Magd does not make any distinctions between moderate and militant jhadis because they all, in his view, are slaves to two doctrines – isolationism (fiqh al-uzlah) and underground action (fiqh al-amal al-sirri). They have isolated themselves from society, have contempt for its laws, and consider themselves morally superior to other Muslims; jihadis' moral superiority complex has led them down the underground path in order to overthrow the status quo. There is no denying, Abu al-Magd adds, that jihadist groups, tiny as they are, represent an important "subculture" in the world of Islam and within the Islamist universe and that they must be understood as representing a rupture and discontinuity with Muslim society, as well as a deviation from and a rebellion against mainstream Islam; this subculture has caused significant damage to Muslims at home and abroad.[94]

Abu al-Magd argues convincingly that jihadis' violent actions speak much louder than any public relations campaign designed to improve the image of Islam and Muslims internationally; as long as jihadis kill in the name of Islam, Muslims will continue to suffer. Abu al-Magd is one of the few enlightened Islamists who brilliantly vivisects the internal sources behind jihadis' extremism and calls on the ulema to actively counterbalance jihadis. Remaining silent in the face of degeneracy and abuse of Islamic doctrine, Abu al-Magd warns, will play into the hands of militants and reinforce the world's hostility to Islam and Muslims; he does not mention Al Qaeda by name because he views the organization as an extension and mutation of the jihadist movement as a whole.[95]

Al Qaeda's top captains – bin Laden, Zawahiri, Abu Hafs, and a few others – will likely be remembered in Arab/Muslim history more for their "catastrophic leadership," as a senior member of the Al Qaeda inner circle wrote, than as legitimate champions of Islam. Commenting on the "insanity" of the Arab condition after September 11, Adonis, a leading Arab liberal poet, wondered aloud, "could the fire that we lit to resist invaders devour us?"[96] Ridwan al-Sayyid, trained at Al-Azhar and a well-regarded Muslim scholar, chastised jihadis for their xenophobia and obsession with identity at the expense of universal values and engagement with the world:

> We need to explain [what happened and why] to the United States and the American people because we want to participate in this world. But we also need to make sense [of what happened] to ourselves because we are humans. If we are shocked by the dehumanization of Palestinians, what a group of us committed against American civilians was no less dehumanizing. Although we could use Palestine to rationalize [9/11] to America and the world, we cannot lie to ourselves and to one another. What occurred was big and dangerous.[97]

The "crime" that was perpetrated in New York and Washington, al-Sayyid wrote, is "an Arab scandal, a shame, evidence of the Arabs' failure to reform Islamic religious and political systems as well as the Arabs' failure to build a normal and healthy relationship with the rest of the world." He added that Muslims should act against terrorism to preserve their humanity and that just condemning those heinous activities is not enough. Arabs and Muslim must be proactive and take the lead in putting the genie back in the bottle.[98]

Contrary to received wisdom in certain Western circles, Adonis and Sayyid, two literary and cultural critics, are the rule, not the exception, among Arab and Muslim writers and scholars. The dominant commentary by the serious Arab press and literary community, if not sensational satellite television stations, is an utter rejection of bin Ladenism and a consistent plea for rationality and cultural engagement. There exists no fascination with or attraction to global jihad among public intellectuals and commentators. Far from it, they fear that bin Ladenism is another dead-end utopia with no future.[99] Arab philosopher Sadik al-Azm aptly put it thus:

> Despite current predictions of a protracted global war between the West and the Islamic world, I believe that war is over. There may be intermittent battles in the decades to come, with many innocent victims. But the number of supporters of armed Islamism is unlikely to grow, its support throughout the Arab Muslim world will likely decline, and the opposition by other Muslim groups will surely grow. September 11 signaled the last gasp of Islamism rather than the beginnings of its global challenge.[100]

One of the reasons for misunderstanding the responses of Arab and Muslim opinion makers to September 11 is that although they condemned Al Qaeda, they held American policy responsible for prolonging the predicament of Palestinians, Iraqis, and other Muslims. Unlike their Western counterparts, Muslim civil society leaders also draw direct links between unjust U.S. policies and increasing anti-American sentiments in the area, although they concede that Al Qaeda and other militants use and abuse popular anger to advance their nihilistic agenda. In American eyes, the responses of Arabs and Muslims also appeared confusing and mysterious because of the deafening silence of the majority and the gut satisfaction expressed by ordinary Arabs and Muslims to September 11. No one better expressed this emotional shamateh, or taking pleasure in the suffering of others, than Azm:

> Yet it would be very hard these days to find an Arab, no matter how sober, cultured, and sophisticated, in whose heart there was not some room for shamateh at the suffering of Americans on September 11. I myself tried hard to contain, control, and hide it that day. And I knew intuitively that millions and millions of people throughout the Arab world and beyond experienced the same emotion.
>
> But I didn't understand my own shameful response to the slaughter of innocents. Was it the bad news from Palestine that week; the satisfaction of seeing the arrogance of power abruptly, if temporarily, humbled; the sight of the jihadi Frankenstein's monsters, so carefully nourished by the United States, turning suddenly on their masters; or the natural resentment of the weak and marginalized at the peripheries of empires against the center, or, in this case, against the center of the center?[101]

Opposition to American foreign policy cannot, on its own, explain shamateh and the gut reaction of Arabs and Muslims. There exists a deep structural crisis in socioeconomic and political-institutional terms that generates and produces this alarming gut reaction in Muslim countries. A sense of powerlessness permeates Muslim civil society; Arabs and Muslims feel they have no major say over decisions affecting their life and that their identity and culture are threatened by forces beyond their control. Again Azm captures this feeling of marginality that, although it does not translate into operational support for militant Islamism, may partially explain the dichotomy in early Arab reactions to September 11:

> In the marrow of our bones, we still perceive ourselves as the subjects of history, not its objects, as its agents and not its victims. We have never acknowledged, let alone reconciled ourselves to, the marginality and passivity of our position in modern times. In fact, deep in our collective soul, we find it intolerable that our supposedly great nation must stand hopelessly on the margins not only of modern history in general but even of our local and particular histories.[102]

The structural crisis also accounts for the unwillingness of the silent majority to speak out against militants who claim to speak in its name.

Mastering the Art of Making Enemies

Nevertheless, the evidence presented in this book shows clearly that Al Qaeda failed to make major inroads into Muslim society and to build up a critical social constituency that would supply it with fresh recruits and political refuge. The evidence also points to an intense internal struggle that is shaking the jihadist movement to its very foundation. The social forces arrayed against Al Qaeda represent a broad spectrum of ideological currents, ranging from former militant Islamists to leftists and nationalists. Mainstream Islamists and the religious establishment have also taken a public stance against the bin Laden network. Fault lines have emerged within Al Qaeda itself, revealing rivalry and turmoil. To its credit, Al Qaeda united all social forces against its global jihad. One of the major criticisms leveled against bin Laden and Zawahiri by former jihadist associates is that they have mastered the art of making enemies – internal and external.

The struggle among jihadis that began in the second half of the 1990s greatly intensified after September 11. Al Qaeda now faces a two-front war: within and without. I would argue that the war within will ultimately prove to be the decisive factor in determining the future of Al Qaeda. With this in mind, I have illuminated and examined the tensions, rivalries, and contradictions among various factions, as well the responses of leading social forces to September 11 and Al Qaeda in general.

It is doubtful if Al Qaeda can withstand a prolonged war of attrition within and without and survive intact. In fact, the multiple internal wars among jihadis call into question the very future of the jihadist movement as a whole, not just of transnationalists like Al Qaeda and its new local affiliates in Saudi Arabia, Yemen, and elsewhere. We are likely to witness further mutations, fragmentations, and violent spasms in the foreseeable future but it is unlikely that the jihadist movement can be reconstituted systemically and structurally as it was in the 1970s, 1980s, and 1990s; that phase, as this book has argued, ended with a shattering military blow to religious nationalists in the late 1990s. Al Qaeda could be seen as a last effort to bankroll the jihadist enterprise and infuse it with new capital. But "the Abdullah Contracting Company" is almost bankrupt with few willing creditors left.

However, it would be shortsighted to write Al Qaeda's obituary because the global organization has shown itself to be highly adaptable and resourceful. After the United States attacked Afghanistan, bin Laden and his aides scattered operatives and lieutenants throughout the Middle East, North Africa, Asia, and Europe; they also built tacit understandings and informal alliances with fringe factions in the Middle East, East Asia, and Africa, like Ansar al-Islam and Zarqawi's al-Tawhid wa al-Jihad in Iraq; Algeria's Salafist Group for Dawa and Combat; Jama'a al-Islamiya in Indonesia; the Islamic Movement of Uzbekistan; the Libyan Islamic Fighting Group; and the Salifiya Jihadi, a Moroccan network that has allegedly carried out suicide bombings in Casablanca; and other groups. With the erosion of Al Qaeda's formal command and control structure, forward movement has devolved to regional affiliates and branches, which have increasingly taken matters into their own hands with little centralized operational planning by the parent organization.

For example, the 2005 and 2004 attacks in Egypt, London, and Spain, respectively, as well as earlier ones in Saudi Arabia, Turkey, and Morocco, indicate that semiautonomous local cells now carry out operations spontaneously in Al Qaeda's name. For example, a few days after the terror blasts in London, the British police said that a team of four British-born men in their late teens and early twenties had carried out the deadly attacks; British officials now believe the attackers were suicide bombers, which would be the first in Britain.

Although it is still early to make definite conclusions about the London blasts, three points are worth highlighting. The attacks were carried out by an independent cell composed of young Muslims born in Britain with no prior military or operational experience or training with Al Qaeda, even though British authorities are confident that the four men had help from highly trained bomb makers with "a clear Al Qaeda link." Second, the migration of suicide bombings to European cities (American cities are not immune) marks a major turning point in the radicalization and militarization of some uprooted second-generation European Muslims enticed by Al Qaeda's message and ideology. Third, the identification of three of the bombers as British citizens with Pakistani roots, along with the alleged involvement of ethnic Pakistanis in other plots in Europe, shows that Arabs possess no monopoly on global jihad and that segments of the Muslim communities in Europe are deeply disaffected with the status quo.

Defusing the crisis of uprooted migrant Muslim communities in Europe must be given a high priority by governments and civil societies; they must be fully integrated into the continent's social fabric and made to feel at home. Unlike their European counterparts, American Muslims do not feel ghettoized and culturally excluded, although they face different challenges.

A consensus exists among analysts that since 2002 Al Qaeda has been transformed into a far more "amorphous, diffuse and difficult-to-target organization than the group that struck the United States in 2001."[103] In a stark 2004 annual report to the Senate Intelligence Committee, George J. Tenet, then–director of central intelligence, said that far-flung groups increasingly set the agenda and are redefining the threat facing the United States; they are not all creatures of bin Laden, and so their threat is not tied to his. They have autonomous leadership, choose their own targets. and plan their own attacks.[104] What this recent development suggests is "a less top-down, more grass-roots-driven al Qaeda."[105]

In a rare interview with Asharq al-Awsat, the Moroccan widow of an Al Qaeda lieutenant, Abd al-Karim al-Majati, who was killed in 2004 in a shootout with the Saudi security forces and who is accused of planning the Madrid train bombings, unintentionally provided a glimpse of the transformation of Al Qaeda. She said it was logistically difficult for her husband to play an active role in the Madrid operation and attacks in Morocco because he came to Saudi Arabia after he left Afghanistan in 2001 and subsequently joined Al Qaeda on the Arabian Peninsula (a local Saudi affiliate):

> Now Al Qaeda operates along autonomous cells, each separate from one another, and there exists no centralized or hierarchical structure like other groups. Accordingly, operatives in Spain carry out operations there, and operatives in Turkey plot operations in Turkey and so on and so forth. ... When I heard about the killing of my husband in Saudi Arabia, I was not surprised because I had left him there, and when Saudi security forces raided the house in which he was in, he had two choices: either to surrender or to die. He chose the latter.[106]

But the new tactics of Al Qaeda's local affiliates are a double-edged sword that has turned Muslim public opinion violently against the militants. After the London and Egyptian blasts in 2005, there was widespread condemnation throughout Arab and Muslim lands and considerable soul searching. Equally important, the attacks by Al Qaeda regional networks inside Muslim countries do not portend well for the parent organization. The irony is that from the outset bin Laden had opposed attacks on Muslim regimes (the "lesser kufr") and instead preferred to wage jihad on the "greatest kufr" (the United States and its Western allies); he had played a key role, as this book has shown, in convincing Zawahiri to shift operational priorities and join his global jihad. Five years later bin Laden is not heeding his own earlier warnings and is waging war against both the greatest kufr and the lesser kufr, knowing full well the strategic defeat that was suffered by religious nationalists at their home fronts in the 1990s.

Saudi Arabia is a revealing case because it is bin Laden's homeland and it supplied Al Qaeda with the largest contingent of operatives; it was supposed to be a breeding ground for Al Qaeda militants and a bastion of support for bin Laden. But in May 2003 Al Qaeda on the Arabian Peninsula, a local network, carried out a triple suicide bombing in Riyadh and targeted a compound inhabited mostly by Arab and Muslim expatriates, not exactly an infidel target. Most of the casualties in Riyadh and the subsequent bombings in Turkey, Morocco, and Egypt were Muslims, not foreigners.

Far from endearing Al Qaeda and its affiliates to Arabs and Muslims, these attacks on soft targets were universally condemned by opinion makers and Islamists. Clerics in Saudi Arabia and other Muslim lands "cursed" Al Qaeda and demanded that young men, who blindly follow the terror organization, repent by desisting from terrorism and turning themselves over to local authorities.[107] The Saudi authorities clamped down hard on militants and radical clerics who support them. The combination of a high-profile religious, media, and military campaign has dealt Al Qaeda "significant setbacks" on the Arabian Peninsula and has left militants both operationally weaker and politically marginalized.[108]

Although Al Qaeda retains local affiliates in Saudi Arabia, Yemen, Jordan, Pakistan, and elsewhere, they are shrinking by the hour and bleeding profusely from the blows of the security services with substantial logistical support from the United States. Equally important, returns from local networks are not very high for Al Qaeda, and one could argue that the political and social costs outweigh any military or public relations benefits. In the long term, regional networks are also bound to emphasize local issues and concerns at the expense of global ones and to begin to bicker with one another.

In the short term, as a franchise Al Qaeda might reap some publicity and a few recruits from attacks carried out by local networks and it could prove its military reach and potency; however, it is unlikely to exercise much influence, let alone control, over the decisions and actions of these groups. Regional affiliates might strike deals with the authorities or return to their indigenous roots and go their separate ways.

The notion of a loose franchise of affiliated networks with bin Laden and senior aides at the head of Al Qaeda's pyramid structure seems seductive and creative; bin Laden and Zawahiri might even think that supervising this loose franchise could offer them a way out of their operational bottleneck. But the odds are that internal security forces would strike regional affiliates with an iron fist, as they successfully did in the 1990s. In fact, taking the war back to the near enemy could prove to be the final straw that breaks the camel's back.[109]

SIX

The Iraq War

Planting the Seeds of Al Qaeda's
Second Generation?

As already demonstrated, on the political, moral, and operational levels, the multiple internal wars have degraded Al Qaeda's decision making and considerably reduced the flow of recruits to its ranks. In particular, four important countries – Afghanistan, Pakistan, Saudi Arabia,
and Yemen – that had provided Al Qaeda with secure bases of support and thousands of volunteers have become inhospitable and highly
dangerous. Yes, Al Qaeda can occasionally inspire a direct attack, but
its mobilizational and recruiting capacity has steadily been diminishing. But there is one promising theater, Iraq, which has provided Al
Qaeda with a new lease on life, a second generation of recruits and fighters, and a powerful outlet to expand its ideological outreach activities
to Muslims worldwide, thanks to the 2003 American-led invasion and
occupation of the country.

Statements and speeches by Al Qaeda's top chiefs, including bin
Laden, Zawahiri, Zarqawi, and Seif al-Adl, show they perceive the
unfolding confrontation in Iraq as a "golden and unique opportunity"
for the global jihadist movement to engage and defeat the United States
and spread the conflict into neighboring Arab states, including Syria,
Lebanon, and the Palestine-Israeli theater. Since the beginning of the
American occupation, Iraq has become central in Al Qaeda's ideological outreach and recruit efforts. Bin Laden, for example, characterized the Iraqi resistance or insurgency as the central battle in a "Third
World War," which the "Crusader-Zionist" coalition started against the
ummah: "The whole world is watching this war and the two adversaries; the ummah, on the one hand, and the United States and its allies
on the other. It is either victory and glory or misery and humiliation.

The ummah today has a very rare opportunity to come out of the subservience and enslavement to the West and to smash the chains with which the Crusaders have fettered it."[1] In the eyes of the Al Qaeda leadership, the war in Iraq marks the second most important development since September 11 and a "historic opportunity" to establish the long-awaited Islamic state in the region, according to a recent testament by Seif al-Adl, Al Qaeda's number 3.[2]

The weight of evidence indicates that a coalition of militants composed mainly of Ansar al-Islam, some elements of Jaish Ansar al-Sunnah, and al-Tawhid wa al-Jihad has established an operational base for Al Qaeda in Iraq under the name Al Qaeda in the Land of the Two Rivers, a reference to the Tigris and Euphrates. Although the groups maintain separate paramilitary entities, they reportedly coordinate joint armed operations; they have taken responsibility for some of the deadliest attacks against Iraqis whom they accuse of being collaborators with the Americans.[3]

An important recent testament by Seif al-Adl, who inherited Abu Hafs's defense minister position in Al Qaeda and who is reportedly held by the Iranian authorities, sheds light on how Zarqawi and his close associates, long before the American-led invasion of Iraq, left Iran for northern Iraq to link up with Ansar al-Islam and attempt to set up shop in the Sunni-dominated areas in central Iraq in preparation for the coming war. Al-Adl's statement, published in a book on Zarqawi that includes other critical primary documents, reveals that when the United States attacked Afghanistan Al Qaeda dispersed its members and associates into neighboring states, including Iran; Zarqawi, who was not officially part of Al Qaeda but was an associate who shared its overall ideology and agenda, evacuated his followers to Iran, and after deliberation decided to go with his group to Iraq. Al-Adl writes that Al Qaeda's lieutenants were convinced that the United States was bound to miscalculate and invade Iraq to overthrow its government, and that they must play a leading role in resisting the American invaders. Here was Al Qaeda's "historic opportunity," al-Adl acknowledges, to establish the long-awaited Islamic state in the region and end decline, defeat, and injustice; all along Zarqawi's goal was to reach the Sunni-dominated region and establish a foothold there, store weapons, and recruit loyal fighters to enable him to sustain the fight against the Americans when

they invaded. That was not easy because there was no operational relationship between the Saddam Hussein regime and Al Qaeda. Al-Adl
confirms that Al Qaeda had no connection with Hussein and that the
Americans manufactured the whole thing to facilitate and legitimize
their invasion and the destruction of the Hussein regime. According to
al-Adl's firsthand account, one of the difficulties faced by Zarqawi was
evading Hussein's security services and linking with antiregime Islamist
elements in the north, Baghdad, and central Iraq.

Seif al-Adl draws a picture of Zarqawi as a very determined man
whose mind was made up to go to Iraq and open a front there because it
was easier for him and his followers to fit in and assimilate in Iraqi society given their similar physical traits and dialects (they come from the
Levant – Jordan, Syria, and Palestine): "The aim was to reach the Sunni
areas in the center of Iraq and then to start preparations to combat the
American invasion. It was not a random choice; it was a well-studied
one." According to al-Adl, Zarqawi headed to northern Iraq with just
dozens of fighters because under pressure from the United States the
Iranian government had arrested or extradited hundreds of Al Qaeda
operatives into their native countries, including 80 percent of Zarqawi's
men. The crackdown by the Iranian authorities on Al Qaeda, al-Adl
reports angrily, was devastating and "put us off balance and disrupted
75 percent of our plans." Zarqawi left Iran hastily with his few remaining men and embarked on his current violent journey.[4]

Al-Adl's account is consistent with other personal testaments by
Zarqawi's former associates with whom he communicated after he left
Iran for northern Iraq. Although he began with humble resources,
Zarqawi gradually and steadily built an operational infrastructure that
has proved to be durable despite suffering painful military blows by
U.S. raids and counteroffensives. He and his Syrian aides (former members of the banned Muslim Broterhood and other Syrian Islamists who
joined his training camp in Herat, Afghanistan, near the Iranian border) concentrated diligently on recruitment efforts in Syria, Jordan,
and Palestine and on fund raising from sympathetic wealthy Syrian
businessmen in Europe. In the Zarqawi network, the Syrian connection is as important as the Jordanian one, particularly as his trusted
lieutenants from his native homeland, Jordan, were killed at a rapid
pace and had to be immediately replaced. Until very recently, Zarqawi's

second-in-command was a Syrian named Suleiman Khaled Darwish (also known as Abu al-Ghadiyah); he was reportedly killed in a U.S. bombing raid near the Iraqi-Syrian border in 2005. While the overwhelming majority of operatives in the bin Laden network came from the Arabian Peninsula, Egypt, and North Africa, Zarqawi relied on men from Bilad al-Sham, or the fertile crescent – Jordan, Syria, Palestine, and now Iraq, Saudi Arabia, Yemen, and other Gulf sheikdoms and North African states.

Another point highlighted by Seif al-Adl (whom bin Laden and Zawahiri entrusted to deal with and assist Zarqawi and his men in establishing a semiautonomous force in Herat after Zarqawi returned to Afghanistan in 1999) was that Zarqawi wanted to maintain operational independence from Al Qaeda. From the outset, al-Adl says that Zarqawi had some disagreements with the bin Laden network over tactical, not doctrinal or strategic, matters. Doctrinally, Zarqawi saw eye-to-eye with Al Qaeda but he "was not fully pleased with the network's modus operandi. He criticized Al Qaeda for not being fierce enough to deal more violent and more painful strikes to the enemy."[5]

Personal testaments by al-Adl, Abu Mohammed al-Maqdisi, Zarqawi's spiritual mentor, and other close associates paint a picture of Zarqawi as an ultramilitant who was more hardliner than the hardliners within Al Qaeda (which is difficult for many people to believe); he was more interested in action than in preaching and indoctrination and had an impulsiveness and recklessness that disturbed his cohorts and caused them harm and suffering. He was in a hurry to destroy the atheist system worldwide, not just in Jordan, and to replace it with hakimiya (God's sovereignty).

In important testimony Abu al-Montasser Billah Mohammed, with whom Zarqawi jointly established his first group, Al-Tawhid, in 1993, said what he remembers most about Zarqawi is his haste and recklessness:

> The hastiness of brother Abu Musab was a problem for me. He wanted everything to be done quickly. He wanted to acheive all of his ambitions in a matter of months, if not hours. Such haste posed one of the most dangerous threats to our call. Abu Musab made decisions unilaterally at the wrong time and place. More tragically, the majority of brothers used to agree with him.[6]

Zarqawi's "hastiness" and "recklessness" cost Abu al-Montasser several years in a Jordanian prison and brutal torture sessions. He said he learned his lesson:

> When Abu Musab got out of jail [in 1999], he visited me at home and asked me to open a new chapter with him, work together, and perhaps travel to Afghanistan. I welcomed him as a guest, but I refused to work with him again in any way in view of his narcissism, not to mention other traits. Abu Musab left my house and never returned again. It was the last contact between us.

Abu al-Montasser did not have a grudge against Zarqawi and was not the only associate to blame him for causing harm and injury to cohorts. For example, al-Maqdisi painted two illuminating portraits of his disciple in which he reiterated Abu al-Montasser's charges:

> The lack of experience foiled several attempts by Abu Musab and frustrated the organizational action that he attempted to establish in Jordan. Subsequently, these unsuccessful attempts resulted in the imprisonment of many young men. Some of them were sentenced to life in prison on charges of involvement in three attempts. In the last two experiences, the enemy won huge funds that Muslims, their call, and jihad needed badly. I used to follow their news and give them advice, but they never listened until it was too late.
>
> It was sad to know that these organizational mistakes and security weaknesses took place again in Afghanistan. Abu Musab did not learn from our experiences at home. He was not successful in choosing the right individuals with organizational expertise, despite the availibility of financial resources.[7]

Al-Maqdisi was referring to Zarqawi's 1999 return to Afghanistan when he refused to join Al Qaeda and decided to go independent; he laments that Zarqawi lacked "flexibility" and could not be part of a team. Al-Maqdisi, who more than anyone else molded the views of Zarqawi, insinuates that his pupil is a one-man show and his supersize ego demands "utter allegiance" from subordiantes, a tendency that "attracts ignorant people who are not qualified for many missions and whose flaws shocked us many times," a veiled reference to Zarqawi's shortsighted "jihadist decisions" in Iraq.[8]

Like Zawahiri's prison experience in Egypt in the early 1980s, Zarqawi's in the 1990s hardened his views further and set him on a violent orgy. His Jordanian biographer, Fu'ad Hussein, who in the 1990s spent time with Zarqawi in prison and who talked to his closest friends and associates, writes that Zarqawi's prison experience "was the most significant phase in the development of personality," more important than his participation in the Afghan jihad years at the end of the 1980s: "The prison left a clear mark on al-Zarqawi's personality, which grew more intense. In his opinion, policemen, judges, and government members of all ranks were supporters of the regimes, which he believed were taghuts (illegitimate tyrants) who should be fought."[9] Hussein reports an encounter with Zarqawi in prison when Zarqawi told what happened to him when he was detained in solitary confinement for eight and a half months; Zarqawi told him he lost his toenails as a result of the infections caused by severe torture: "I realized then," Hussein added, "that al-Zarqawi would leave Jordan for good immediately if he was released from jail."[10]

Upon his release from prison, Zarqawi did leave Jordan, carrying with him his wounds, bitterness, and rage against the whole world, not just the Jordanian regime that allegedly tortured him. When he arrived in Afghanistan in 1999, Zarqawi was eager to do battle against the global forces of athesim and injustice, particularly the United States and Israel, sooner rather than later. Zarqawi also found fault with bin Laden's relatively tolerant views on the Shiites and the Saudi regime; Zarqawi brands the Shiites and the Saudi royal family infidels. His companions say he found fault with Al Qaeda because it was not as proactive and aggressive as he liked; forced to flee Afghanistan to Iran under American fire, Zarqawi met with his lieutenants and informed them that he had decided to go to Iraq because he expected it to be a battlefield against the Americans.

Regardless of the veracity of this congratulatory narrative and the supposed strategic foresight of Zarqawi, the American war in Iraq and the subsequent disorder and chaos have made his dream come true. There he was, with no more than 30 fighters, his admirers assert proudly, ready to take on the head of atheism. What they forget to mention is that armed with a blanket takfeeri (excommunication of believers) ideology, Zarqawi has played God and labeled whole segments of Iraqis as kufar and apostates. There hardly exists a societal group that escapes his wrath and takfeer – be it the Shiites, the Kurds, the "silent" and "defeatist" ulema, the new Iraqi authorities, or the Sunnis who are willing to participate in the nascent political order. Zarqawi has waged war against the overwhelming majority of Iraqis with no appreciation of the bloody, complex history and structure of modern Iraqi society. In this he does not differ much from the Al Qaeda chiefs who declared war against the world, except that Zarqawi is also fighting the ghosts of his past.

It is no wonder that initially even bin Laden was reluctant to agree to a merger between al-Tawhid wa al-Jihad in Iraq and Al Qaeda because of Zarqawi's excessive sectarianism and bloodletting; Zarqawi not only excommunicates believers but also justifies collateral killing of Muslims "in order to ward off a greater evil, namely, the evil of suspending jihad," according to a recent statement by his organization.[11] Bin Laden reportedly was not in favor of civil strife between Shiites and Sunnis lest it distract from the focal confrontation against the Americans. Although as a militant Salafi, bin Laden harbors anti-Shiite views, he sees Iraq as a pivotal front in his global jihad and has called on Muslim Iraqis and non-Iraqis of all ethnic and linguistic backgrounds to cooperate and oppose the pro-American order installed in Baghdad; he has also applied similar disregard for ethnic, sectarian, and ideological differences in issuing condemnations of Iraqis who collaborate with the coalition forces, including Arabs as equally guilty parties:

> The Iraqi who is waging jihad against the infidel Americans or Allawi's [former prime minister Ayad Allawi] renegade government is our brother and companion, even if he was of Persian, Kurdish, or Turkomen origin. The Iraqi who joins this renegade government to fight against the mujahedeen who resist occupation, is considered a renegade and one of the infidels, even if he were an Arab from Rabi'ah or Mudar tribes.[12]

But by the end of 2004 and despite their early reservations, Zarqawi and bin Laden found common ground, and their interests converged. In an October Internet statement, Zarqawi announced that he was changing the name of his group to Al Qaeda in the Land of the Two Rivers, and he declared his allegiance to bin Laden, saying he considered bin Laden "the best leader for Islam's armies against all infidels and apostates." The statement noted that the two had communicated and agreed to join forces against "the enemies of Islam." Two months later, in an audiotape broadcast by Al-Jazeera satellite television, bin Laden personally endorsed Zarqawi as his deputy and anointed him the emir of Al Qaeda in Iraq; he praised Zarqawi's "gallant operations" against the Americans and said that Zarqawi and those with him are fighting for God's sake: "We have been pleased that they responded to God's and his Prophet's order for unity, and we in Al Qaeda welcome their unity with us."[13]

Bin Laden's blessing of the new alliance with Zarqawi put to rest any doubts about Al Qaeda's presence in Iraq. Why formalize the connection? According to internal testimony by associates, as Zarqawi gained international notoriety and stardom among militant Islamists, he came under pressure by operatives to swear fealty to bin Laden and merge with Al Qaeda.[14] A formal association with the parent organization would also confer revolutionary legitimacy on Zarqawi and turn him from a mere field commander in Iraq into a global jihadi on a par with the masters, Abdullah Azzam, bin Laden, Abu Hafs, and Zawahiri; this could also bring a new crop of jihadist volunteers – and funds – into Iraq. For example, Zarqawi's union with Al Qaeda, his Jordanian biographer says, provided him with a permanent and systematic influx of human, financial, and logistical resources; before the merger was formally sealed, pro–Al Qaeda fighters, particularly from the Arabian Peninsula, began to arrive in Iraq and join Zarqawi's units, and wealthy Arabs contributed generously to his cause, which strengthened his network. This windfall, more than anything esle, prompted Zarqawi to pledge his "full allegiance" to bin Laden.[15]

In the case of bin Laden, Iraq has become an open front in the global war against the United States and its allies, and Zarqawi, who leads the jihadist contingent there, had offered him leadership on a silver platter. The global war is not going well for bin Laden, and Iraq presented him, as he said, with a "golden and unique opportunity" to expand the confrontation against the United States and convince his jihadist cohorts and Muslims worldwide that Al Qaeda is still alive despite crippling operational setbacks in Afghanistan, Pakistan, Saudi Arabia, Yemen, and elsewhere. By appointing Zarqawi emir of Al Qaeda in Iraq, bin Laden can take credit for military successes there and rejuvenate his battered base; equally important, he aims at broadening his network's appeal to Arab and Muslim masses who feel strongly about the American occupation of Islamic territories. Therefore, bin Laden has recently positioned himself as a defender of occupied Arab lands, particularly in Iraq and Palestine, and he hopes to reverse Muslims' hostile views of his global jihad. He could also build on military success in Iraq to attack Western nations and apostate Muslim rulers. Bin Laden has reportedly enlisted Zarqawi to plan potential attacks on the United States.[16]

The 2005 attacks in London and Egypt indicate that Al Qaeda's centralized decision making is still functioning, though it is greatly degraded. The back-to-back, spectacular, suicidal nature of the attacks, coupled with the choice of the targets, suggests overall direction by Al Qaeda's top leadership, although local affiliates could have organized and carried out the sophisticated attacks.[17]

The critical question: what is the significance of Zarqawi on the Iraqi resistance or insurgency, and is he as pivotal – enemy number one – as the U.S. government contends? Or is Zarqawi an "imaginary" threat invented by the United States, as some Sunni leaders with links to insurgents assert? American officials, including President Bush and Vice President Dick Cheney, portray Zarqawi as the world's most dangerous and prolific terrorist, preaching and practicing jihad, and ascribe to him "mythic invulnerability." The U.S. military has made him its number one target, implying that to capture and kill such a figurehead would be a considerable symbolic and moral boost in the war against Al Qaeda.[18] On the other hand, Zarqawi's biographer Hussein claims that by exaggerating Zarqawi's military strength and blaming most attacks in Iraq on foreign terrorists led by Zarqawi, the United States has unwittingly turned him into a "hero and symbol" of resistance in the eyes of the Arabs: "Every Arab and Muslim who wished to go to Iraq for jihad wanted to join al-Zarqawi and fight under his leadership."[19] Although at the beginning of the American occupation, Zarqawi controlled fewer than 30 fighters, according to Hussein, it is currently estimated that he has thousands of followers, thanks to the U.S. media and government ingenuity.

Several points should be highlighted. First, it is difficult to accurately assess the precise military strength and weight of Al Qaeda in

260 • The Far Enemy

Iraq in relation to various components of the Iraqi insurgency or resistance. The Iraqi resistance is highly complex, diverse, and decentralized, with a broad spectrum of ideological orientations and perspectives. Although a consesus exists that more than 90 percent of the fighters are homegrown Iraqis inspired by nationalist and religious sentiment, foreign fighters reportedly play a bigger role than their small number would imply because of their spectacular suicide bombings against Iraqi security forces, Shiites, and Sunni Kurds. A related point is that while American and Iraqi authorities estimate the number of Arab fighters under Zarqawi at about 1000, his biographer, who has access to Zarqawi's inner circle, claims that Zarqawi has built a force of at least 5000 full-time fighters bolstered by a vigorous network of 20,000 homegrown supporters.[20] The numbers vary wildly and cannot be verified, but one point must be reiterated: the number of foreign militants represents a small percentage – perhaps one in ten – of the total indigenous Iraqi fighters. Nonetheless, Al Qaeda in Iraq has proved to be deadly effective and has become a power to be reckoned with.

There are also credible reports that homegrown radicalized Iraqis, including members of Ansar al-Islam and Jaish Ansar al-Sunnah, have carried out joint suicide bombings with their Arab counterparts. In fact, in June 2005 Al Qaeda in Iraq posted a statement on a jihadist Web site known for carrying its messages that said that it has formed a unit of potential suicide attackers who are exclusively Iraqis, an apparent bid to deflect criticism that most suicide bombers in Iraq are foreigners.[21] An Iraqi suicide squad is another alarming sign that more Sunni Iraqis are being radicalized by the American occupation and are willing to join with foreign militants to kill Americans and fellow Iraqis.

On the other hand, fighting has been reported between homegrown Iraqi fighters and foreign militants. It is very difficult to know what is happening within the inner circles of the Iraqi resistance and insurgency; it is splintered and fragmented along political, religious, ideological, and even criminal lines. Al Qaeda in Iraq is just one component – the deadliest – in a highly complex military equation. But more Arab and Muslim voices are being heard condemning Al Qaeda in Iraq and Zarqawi and calling on Iraqis and Arabs to reject and oppose its ideology and murders. For example, the reformist Grand Imam of Al-Azhar, sheikh Mohammed Sayyid Tantawi, has called on the international community, including Arab and Muslim states, to put an end to terrorism in Iraq and to punish Zarqawi and his men for killing civilians, which violates Islamic precepts. Tantawi has insisted that members of Al Qaeda that are convicted of murder must be sentenced to death and that they must be vigorously pursued and brought to justice.[22] Imprisoned Egyptian leaders of Islamic Jihad and Tanzim al-Jihad (they have split with Zawahiri) and of Islamic Group released two separate statements in which they strongly criticized Zarqawi for killing civilians, including diplomats and government employees, and accused his organization of trying to "annihilate" the Shiites, not to "liberate" Iraq.[23] Those are strong words from two former Sunni jihadist organizations.

Zarqawi is in real trouble, given that his spiritual mentor and ideological father, al-Maqdisi, has publicly opposed his terrorism against civilians. In several interviews with Arabic-language newspapers and the Al Jazeera television network, al-Maqdisi has said that violence that does not differentiate among women and children, civilians, soldiers, and American troops is wrong: "The kidnapping and murder of relief workers and neutral journalists have distorted the image of jihad. They make the mujahedeen look like murderers who spill blood blindly."[24] There are very few exceptional cases, al-Maqdisi noted in his review of the ulema's writings, where the killing of civilians is sanctioned; on the whole, however, it is forbidden.

In two recently released testaments from prsion, al-Maqdisi tries to strike a balance between criticizing Zarqawi's mass killing of Muslims and praising his resistance against the Americans. But al-Maqdisi's message comes out loud and clear; he warns his pupil against extremist tactics that could alienate both friend and foe and play into the hands of the enemy. The Shiites and Kurds, al-Maqdisi advises Zarqawi, who reportedly read and digested most of his mentor's jihadist writings, are not the enemy; the American occupiers are. Zarqawi must neither excommunicate the Shiites, his spiritual mentor warns, nor attack them because it is religiously forbidden to do so. Al-Maqdisi also reminds his pupil that "martyrdom operations" should be carried out only under stringent conditions as a secondary, not as a primary, tool; he says that Zarqawi used to subscribe to this thinking when he was in Herat, Afghanistan, and al-Maqdisi wonders why Zarqawi has become liberal in the use of suicide bombings in Iraq. Al-Maqdisi warns Zarqawi not to lose sight of the nature and character of the struggle in Iraq, because Iraqis know what is best for their country; he reminds Zarqawi to know his place and avoid leveling threats against other nations and people lest Iraqis and the whole world turn against him and his fighters. Finally, al-Maqdisi dropped a metaphorical nuclear bomb on his disciple by saying that today spreading al-da'wa of tawhid (affirmation of the oneness of God) peacefully in the world is more important and effective than going to fight in Iraq, Afghanistan, and other theaters; waging jihad will devour the mujahedeen and dissipate and squander their effort.

Explicit in al-Maqdisi's fatherly advice is the urgent need for Zarqawi to refrain from mass killing of Muslims and to reassess his "indiscrimiate attacks which distort the true jihad."[25] Time and again al-Maqdisi cautions his pupil against taking hasty decisions and relying on unsound advice; although gentle, al-Maqdisi's criticism is direct and blunt and cannot be dismissed by Zarqawi and his apologists as a deviation. After all, al-Maqdisi is considered the mufti or the godfather of the Salafi-Jihadi current that has inspired a host of jihadis like Zarqawi and many others. It is no wonder that al-Maqdisi's public criticism of Zarqawi has reportedly caused considerable displeasure and disquiet among Zarqawi and his loyal crowd and has revealed the existence of deep fissures and fault lines within the jihadist network. Zarqawi might not care about Tantawi's learned opinion, but he surely can only afford to ignore internal critiques, like al-Maqdisi's, at his own peril.

Therefore, following al-Maqdisi's interview with Al Jazeera, Zarqawi released a statement in which he directly responded to his mentor's controversial points and gently scolded him for going public with his criticism. Firstly, Zarqawi wrote that he has always believed in the utility and efficacy of "martyrdom operations," even before fighting in Iraq. Secondly, Zarqawi did not elaborate on the legitimacy of killing civilians except by saying that he is very careful to avoid killing both Muslim and non-Muslim civilians. Thirdly, he claimed he was not the one who fired the first shot; he says the Shiites did by attacking Sunni Iraqis and "raping their mosques and homes," as well as by joining the "crusading" American occupation. Zarqawi did not address al-Maqdisi's concern against excommunicating all Shiites, even though he is on record labeling Shiites as infidels and calling them "monkeys" and their religion "an affront to God."

Despite his deference of tone to his "sheikh," Zarqawi could not restrain his anger at al-Maqdisi's call on young Muslims to spread al-da'wa rather than make jihad in Iraq and Afghanistan: "How could Abu Mohammed issue such a fatwa?" Zarqawi wrote disapprovingly. The real disaster afflicting Muslims, Zarqawi added, is refraining from going to Iraq and defending honor and religion, and he stressed that he will continue waging jihad there regardless of the costs. To silence al-Maqdisi, Zarqawi said that his fatwa would help "Bush and his mercenaries" out of the Iraq trap after they had suffered serious military blows; al-Maqdisi's media appearances and letters also pleased Islam's enemies. Zarqawi concludes his statement by advising his spiritual guru to be extra careful before issuing fatwas and to first learn the facts and ascertain that his information is accurate, a strong rebuke.[26]

Aware of the storm that is gathering both internally and externally, informed Arab sources indicate that Zarqawi and his crew have increasingly fertilized their network with Iraqis and that Zarqawi now surrounds himself with several Iraqi lieutenants, including Abu Maysara al-Iraqi and Abu al-Dardaa al-Iraqi, former army officers. Abu Maysara, the group's purported spokesman, has emerged as a critical player in its internal politics. When in May 2005 rumors circulated over the fate of Zarqawi, Abu Maysara micromanaged the media campaign and challenged reports about potential successors to Zarqawi, letting it be known that he was in charge. But according to a recent statement by Seif al-Adl, Al Qaeda's military commander, Zarqawi's likely successor would be a Syrian physician, Suleiman Khaled Darwish (known as Abu al-Ghadiyah), Zarqawi's confidant and right-hand man who has worked closely with him since the Afghan days. In June 2005 there were unconfrmed reports that Abu al-Ghadiyah was killed in a U.S. air raid.[27] But the main point is the following: if Al Qaeda in Iraq develops a home-grown base with a large Iraqi contingent, as seems to be the case, that would spell trouble for the war-torn country and prolong its predicament; it could also imply that Zarqawi's fate is no longer as significant as American officials say it is. He could easily be replaced by senior associates who are vying with one another to lead the network and continue the fight.

A related point is that the expansion of the American "war on terror," particularly the invasion and occupation of Iraq, has radicalized a large segment of Iraqi society and Arab public opinion and played directly into the hands of Al Qaeda and other militants. "Our policies in the Middle East fuel Islamic resentment," U.S. Vice Admiral Lowell E. Jacoby, director of the Defense Intelligence Agency, told the Senate Select Committee on Intelligence in 2005. Far from hammering a deadly nail in the coffin of terror, as Bush had stated, Iraq appears to have become a recruiting tool, if not yet a recruiting ground, for militant jihadist causes and anti-American voices. A consensus exists among American, European, and Arab analysts (and the American intelligence community) that Iraq has replaced Afghanistan as the training ground for the next, or second, generation of "professionalized" jihadis and that it provides them with the opportunity to enhance their technical skills. A new classified assessment by the Central Intelligence Agency says that Iraq may prove to be an even more effective training ground for militants than Afghanistan was in Al Qaeda's early days, because it is serving as a real-world laboratory for urban combat. A small group of Arab fighters trained in Iraq has already made its violent debut in Kuwait and Saudi Arabia. Prince Nayef bin Abdul Aziz, Saudi Arabia's interior minister, echoed the CIA warning by saying that he expected militants who return from fighting in Iraq to be worse than Afghan war veterans, who have been largely blamed for the violence in Saudi Arabia since 2003. Iraq is gradually replacing other theaters as a forward base for the new jihad. Today, a large concentration of active jihadis exists in Iraq, not in Afghanistan, Pakistan, Yemen, or Saudi Arabia. According to a 2005 report by the National Intelligence Council, the CIA director's think tank, "The al-Qa'ida membership that was distinguished by having trained in Afghanistan will gradually dissipate, to be replaced in part by the dispersion of the experienced survivors of the conflict in Iraq."[28] This report took a year to produce and includes the analyses of 1000 U.S. and foreign specialists; it represents the conclusions of American intelligence, which cannot be dismissed as politically and ideologically biased and antiwar.

According to a study by the conservative London-based International Institute for Strategic Studies (IISS), the Iraq war has swollen the ranks of Al Qaeda and "galvanized its will" by stirring radical passions among Arabs and Muslims. In a major report on terrorism, the foreign affairs committee of the British House of Commons said that "Iraq has become a 'battleground' for Al-Qaeda, with appalling consequences for the Iraqi people." It added, "However, we also conclude that the coalition's failure to bring law and order to parts of Iraq created a vacuum into which criminal elements and militias have stepped." The crisis, including increasing civilian casualties, the horror of the abuse of the Iraqi prisoners, and the cultural clash between occupier and occupied, is a welcome development for bin Laden and his associates, who have exploited it to justify their global jihad against America and its allies. The American war in Iraq was a god-sent opportunity for bin Laden and Zawahiri. America's imperial endeavor has given them a new opening to make inroads, if not into mainstream Arab hearts and minds, into a large pool of outraged Muslims from the Middle East and elsewhere and uprooted young European-born Muslims who want to resist what they perceive as the U.S.-British onslaught on their coreligionists.[29]

In the wake of the 2005 London blasts, reporters raided the neighborhoods where the four British-born bombers had lived, searching for answers to a lingering question: why are second-generation British Muslims, whose parents slowly but steadily climbed the social ladder, rejecting the country in which they were born and raised? The bombers left no political will or testament to provide a glimpse into why they did what they did. But the war and suffering in Iraq have figured prominently in the answers given by some of their peer group. For example, Sanjay Dutt, 22, and his friends have grappled with why their friend Kakey, better known to the world as Shehzad Tanweer, had decided to kill his countrymen: "He was sick of it all, all the injustice and the way the world is going about it. Why, for example, don't they ever take a moment of silence for all the Iraqi kids who die?" "It's a double standard, that is why," answered a friend, also 22.[30]

"We've got to look at the reasoning behind these things" said Saraj Qazai, a 25-year-old Muslim boutique owner in London, implying that he understands – even if he doesn't approve of – the logic behind their deeds, adding: "There's no denying it's payback for what's happened in Iraq and Afghanistan. You've been bombing people for the last two to four years, so you are going to get a backlash. England is a great country and we love it to bits but do we love this government? No. There were

24 Muslims killed in Iraq today; there will be more tonight and more tomorrow."[31]

It would be simplistic to reduce the cause of the London bombings to the rage generated by the American- and British-led invasion of Iraq. More factors were involved in driving the four young men to commit mass murder. But the answers given by their peer group shed light on the mood and temperament of uprooted young British-born Muslims (and European Muslims in general) and on how militants could use the war in Iraq to incite or recruit young men to commit suicide; the answers also show that Iraq now competes with Palestine in the political imagination of Muslims worldwide. In a July 2005 report, the respected British Royal Institute of International Affairs concluded that backing the United States in the war in Iraq has put Britain more at risk from terror attacks. Although the British government understandably rejected the report's conclusions, analysts argue that Britain has suffered by playing "pillion passenger" to the United States.[32] Public opinion polls in Britain echo and second these findings.

It is no wonder that Zarqawi has become a viable asset to bin Laden and Zawahiri, who had previously kept their distance from him. According to Seif al-Adl, when Zawahiri returned to Afghanistan in 1999, his bosses did not meet with him, let alone welcome him with open arms, and al-Adl says he lobbied hard to get permission to assist Zarqawi in setting up a tiny training camp in Herat. Since the onset of the Iraq conflict, however, things have dramatically changed. In the eyes of the Al Qaeda chiefs, Zarqawi is a field commander who keeps the cause of global jihad alive after having been dealt a near fatal blow after September 11. A testament to Zarqawi's importance is that American military and intelligence commanders now view him as being more operationally dangerous than bin Laden himself. Some European defense analysts claim further that Zarqawi, through senior associates in Syria, Italy, and Spain, has taken over most of Al Qaeda's remaining European network; they imply that he is Al Qaeda's de facto chief. A high-level internal review within the U.S. government has been launched to reassess the nature and character of the threat facing the United States in light of recent developments, particularly in Iraq. Top government officials are increasingly turning their attention to Zarqawi's Iraq and away from bin Laden's Al Qaeda to anticipate what one called "the bleed out" of hundreds or thousands of Iraq-trained jihadis back to their home countries throughout the Middle East and Western Europe: "It's a new piece of a new equation," a former senior Bush administration official said.[33]

Although it is difficult to assess his real military strength, Zarqawi is not a figment of the American imagination; his terrorist operations have killed thousands of innocent Iraqis. Al Qaeda in Iraq has claimed responsibility for hundreds of attacks, and Zarqawi's lieutenants have given interviews to Arab newspapers and elucidated their broader goals, which are similar to those of its parent organization, bin Laden's Al Qaeda. One of his operatives told an Arab journalist, "We are fighting in Iraq but our sights are on other places, like Jerusalem."[34] As Zarqawi's biographer concluded after extensive interviews with his senior associates, Zarqawi views Iraq as one pivotal battle in a prolonged struggle that aims at expelling the Americans from the Middle East, reestablishing the caliphate (the Muslim state dissolved with the fall of the Ottoman Empire after World War I), and liberating occupied Muslim lands, particularly Palestine.[35]

Although Zarqawi's personality remains a mystery, there is nothing mysterious about the extremist jihadist ideas he has operationalized in Iraq. After news of Zarqawi's injury surfaced in May 2005, Seif al-Adl posted a personal testament on several jihadist Web sites (cited previously) in which he describes his farewell with Zarqawi:

> When Abu Musab was saying goodbye before going to Iraq, there was an added dimension to him. It was the focus on taking revenge on the Americans for the crimes he had seen them commit in Afghanistan with his own eyes. The grudge and hostility al-Zarqawi held against the Americans was enough to create new aspects to his personality. I cannot write about this new character as I have not met him since he left Iran [to Iraq]. But from what I have heard about him, it seems that he has become an experienced leader who is able to manage the conflict with the Americans and the Israelis.[36]

The truth is far more complex than Seif al-Adl's apologist and self-serving testimony; Zarqawi's success does not lie in managing the conflict with the Americans but rather in killing Iraqis. His main targets are Iraqi Shiites, who have received the brunt of his terrorism. Although we know that Zarqawi exists, we know little else about the structure of his organization and its operational capabilities. But we clearly know that homegrown Iraqis represent the overwhelming number of fighters and have led the resistance. The unfolding Iraqi struggle is political because many Iraqis are deeply divided over the future direction of their country and the American military presence. The future of Zarqawi and his associates will ultimately depend on the Iraqis' willingness and ability to compromise and establish an inclusive, independent government that is capable of securing the peace; their umbilical cord is tied to the unfolding political and military struggle in Iraq.

Finally, it is misleading to say that only militants of the Al Qaeda variety have joined the fight against the American order in Baghdad. More alarming is that throughout Arab lands the U.S. invasion of Iraq has turned into a recruiting device against perceived American imperial policies; it has radicalized both mainstream and militant Arab and Muslim public opinion. Many young Arabs whom I met in cities and villages across the region say they would welcome an opportunity to go to Iraq and resist the Americans. Far from being Al Qaeda–type fanatics, these young men had not been politicized before the American-led invasion and had not joined any Islamist, let alone paramilitary, organization. They perceive the American war and military presence in Iraq as an alien encroachment on the ummah, which, in the eyes of their religious leaders, is not justified.

Based on my field research, I would argue that if it was not for logistical and technical reasons and difficulties, the flow of potential Muslim volunteers from the Middle East and Europe into Iraq would exceed that into Afghanistan under the Russian occupation in the 1980s. Many young men cannot afford the bus, taxi, or airplane fare to take them to the Syrian border, the most accessible and preferred route into Iraq. Arab local security services keep a close watch on the movements of young men to Iraq's neighboring countries. Pressed by the United States to stop insurgents from crossing its border into Iraq, the Syrian regime claims that it has apprehended more than 1300 militants from the Middle East and Europe, most of them from the Gulf, and repatriated them to their countries of origin, although the Bush administration is unconvinced that Damascus has fully secured its border.[37] Other recruits are traveling through Turkey into Iran and crossing into Iraq – often through unpoliced areas along Iraq's vast border.

Although the majority of foreign fighters come from countries in the Persian Gulf, mainly Saudi Arabia and Yemen, many others are from North African countries, Syria, Lebanon, Egypt, Sudan, and Jordan. Moreover, scores of young Muslims from European countries, mainly France and Britain, have already fought in Iraq, with a larger pool of potential recruits searching for ways to get there. Investigative reports in Arab, European, and American newspapers have cited several European officials and academics who voiced their concerns about Iraq becoming a recruiting tool and destination for hundreds of uprooted Muslims. There exists a broad representative sample of recruits from many countries, including both militant Islamists and zealous young men. The problem, however, is that the latter will most likely be ideologically transformed by their experience in Iraq, as their counterparts were in Afghanistan. The baptism of blood and fire, coupled with socialization with hard-core jihadis, will make them vulnerable to militancy. According to emerging evidence, fighters returning from Iraq have already been implicated in violent actions in their native countries.[38]

Will the tragic phenomenon of the Afghan Arabs be replaced by that of the "Iraqi Arabs"? This possibility cannot be disregarded because although the number of Arab fighters is reported to be in the low thousands, it could quadruple if Iraq descends into full sectarian strife or if neighboring countries open a wider crack in their vast porous border with Iraq. A recent assessment by the CIA concluded that since the American invasion, Iraq had in many ways assumed the role played by Afghanistan during the rise of Al Qaeda during the 1980s and 1990s for militants from Saudi Arabia and other Muslim countries.[39]

Final Thoughts

Instead of acknowledging structural flaws in their decision to invade Iraq and drawing appropriate lessons, President Bush and his senior aides never tire of reminding the American people and the world that Iraq is now "the central front in the war on terror." They also indirectly insinuate that they created more enemies with serious risk to U.S. security. Defense Secretary Donald Rumsfeld reportedly confided to his subordinates that more militants are joining the fight than the United

States is "capturing, killing, or deterring and dissuading" in Iraq and Afghanistan, an indirect reference to the high costs of the American-led invasion of Iraq. Bush's current and previous chiefs of intelligence, Porter J. Goss and George Tenet, respectively, have told Congress that radical anti-Americanism and the deadly expertise used by Al Qaeda have spread to other Sunni Muslim extremists, who are behind a "next wave" of terrorism that will endure "for the foreseeable future with or without Al Qaeda in the picture." As mentioned previously, the American intelligence community is seriously concerned about Iraqi Sunni elements supplying the next generation of jihadis.[40]

Despite all this overwhelming official evidence, there is little recognition, let alone acknowledgment, among Bush administration officials that the expansion of the war against Al Qaeda has damaged America's image, reputation, and standing in the Muslim world as well as threatened international peace. This is well documented with hundreds of surveys, polls, and reports, and it has given militancy a new lease on life.[41] One of this book's major findings is that contrary to the received wisdom, the dominant response to Al Qaeda in the Muslim world was very hostile, and few activists, let alone ordinary Muslims, embraced its global jihad. By the same token, a broad representative spectrum of Arab and Muslim opinion makers and Islamists utterly rejected bin Laden and Zawahiri's justification for their attacks on America and debunked their religious and ideological rationale. Al Qaeda faced a two-front war, internally and externally, with the interior front threatening its very existence.

This book has highlighted Al Qaeda's internal predicament and limited options and the cumulative repercussions of the civil war within the jihadist movement. In addition, Al Qaeda has suffered crippling military blows from outside, thanks mainly to efforts by the multilateral coalition put together by the United States immediately after September 11. On the internal and external fronts Muslims have played a fundamental role in isolating Al Qaeda and have contributed significantly to the multiple wars being waged against the militant network.

Of all these struggles, bin Laden and his transnationalist cohorts have lost the war of ideas – the struggle for Muslim minds. That was a critical achievement overlooked by American commentators and policy makers, who turned their attention to Al Qaeda and like-minded militants and overlooked the fault lines among jihadis and the vast societal opposition to global jihad. Had they tuned in closely to the internal struggles roiling Muslim lands, they would have had second thoughts about the military expansion of the so-called war on terror and would have realized that Al Qaeda is a tiny fringe organization with no viable entrenched constituency. Had they listened carefully to the multiple critiques of Al Qaeda by Muslim scholars and opinion makers, they would have had answers to their often-asked question: where are the Muslim moderates? Had they observed the words and deeds of former jihadis and Islamists, they would have known that the jihadist movement has been torn apart and that Al Qaeda does not speak for or represent religious nationalists – or Muslim public opinion.

American commentators and policy makers would also have realized that the internal defeat of Al Qaeda on its home front – the Muslim world – was and is the most effective way to hammer a deadly nail into its coffin. The United States and the international community could have found intelligent means to nourish and support the internal forces that were opposed to militant ideologies like the bin Laden network. The way to go was not to declare a worldwide war against a nonconventional, paramilitary foe with a tiny or no social base of support and try to settle scores with old regional dictators. That is exactly what bin Laden and his senior associates had hoped the United States would do – lash out militarily against the ummah. As Seif al-Adl recently put it, "The Americans took the bait and fell into our trap."[42]

The American invasion of Iraq is a case in point; on the popular level, it alienated most of the important political secular and religious Muslim groups that had rejected and opposed Al Qaeda's global jihad. The invasion also blurred the lines among mainstream, liberal, and radical politics in the Arab world and squandered much of the empathy felt by Muslims for the American victims and America itself after September 11. Liberal Arab writers and artists often maligned for their pro-Western stance denounced America's "imperial hegemony." Adonis, a leading Arab liberal poet, expressed the sentiments of his generation:

> What is the goal of American policy toward the Arabs? It aims at keeping the Arabs behind history and without future.
>
> For every free and liberal thinker in the world, America's imperial policies endanger anguish which transcends his private passion and pain.
>
> It creates civilizational agony for man and humanity.[43]

Those strong words by Adonis testify to the moral and personal anguish felt by Arabs who, while intrinsically and philosophically disposed to the West, are enraged by U.S. militarism and aggression. Distinguished Islamic institutions and moderate clerics urged Muslims to join in jihad and resist the American invasion of an Arab country. For example, Al-Azhar, the oldest institution of religious higher learning in the world of Islam, issued a fatwa advising "all Muslims in the world to make jihad against invading American forces." Sheikh Tantawi of Al-Azhar ruled that efforts to stop the American invasion are a "binding Islamic duty." Tantawi, one of the first Muslim scholars to condemn Al Qaeda, is often criticized by ultraconservative clerics as a pro-Western reformer.

Another prominent Egyptian-born cleric, sheikh Qardawi, who had forcefully denounced bin Laden and his associates, accused the Bush administration of declaring war against Islam and behaving like "a god." Fighting American troops is "legal jihad" and "death while defending Iraq a kind of martyrdom," Qardawi stated. In an interview on Al Jazeera, Qardawi sanctioned attacks on Iraqi civilians who commit the "crime" of assisting "the enemy"; he was earlier quoted to have sanctioned the murder of American civilians in Iraq. Although Qardawi later denied that he had made the remarks about American civilians and claimed that his words were taken out of context, the controversy illustrates the dramatic erosion of U.S. support in the Arab world and the dissipation of Muslim sympathy for America after September 11; equally important, it reflects the deepening cultural and religious divide between "imperial" America and Muslim civil societies.[44]

In the eyes of Arabs, Iraq now competes with Palestine as an open, bleeding wound, and Muslim writers and opinion makers compare the Israeli occupation of Palestine with the American occupation of Iraq.[45] Palestine and Iraq have also become a rallying cry for Islamists and religious nationalists, as well as for transnationalists whose recent diatribes are full of pointed references to the suffering of Palestinians and Iraqis. After Israel assassinated sheikh Ahmad Yassin, the spiritual leader of Palestinian Hamas, bin Laden, in a recording broadcast on Arab television networks, vowed revenge: "We vow before God to take revenge for him from America for this, God willing." American policy ignores the "real problem," which is "the occupation of all of Palestine," he added, as if America, not Israel, carried out the assassination.[46] Internally besieged and in its final throes, Al Qaeda's new propaganda emphasis on Iraq and Palestine is designed to tap into the reservoir of accumulated Muslim grievances against American policies and to garner political and material backing, which had been lacking.

I do not mean to imply that Al Qaeda's global jihad is fueled by the Palestine and Iraq fire, or by foreign policy for that matter. The birth and evolution, or rather mutation, of the jihadist movement, as this book has shown, stem largely from a deep structural, developmental crisis facing the Arab world, in both socioeconomic and institutional terms; it is a crisis of governance and political economy, not of culture or foreign policy. At the heart of this structural crisis lie entrenched authoritarianism and a vacuum of legitimate political authority fueling the ambitions of secular and religious activists. Zawahiri and bin Laden belong to a long line of revolutionaries who have tried to fill the authority vacuum by promising the disfranchised and oppressed Muslim masses moral salvation and political deliverance. They are not the first – and will not be the last – to do so unless effective institutional solutions are brought to bear on deepening sociopolitical and economic problems that have wrecked Arab and Muslim societies.

From the outset the modern jihadist movement was a revolt against the autocratic political and social order at home, not against the global order. Until the late 1990s, religious nationalists led the jihadist caravan and determined its course and destination. The rise of Al Qaeda was more of a mutation than a natural evolution of jihadism, and the shift to globalism masked an inverted orientation and propensity toward localism. We should not be fooled by the rhetoric of global jihad because lying just under its surface is a powerful drive to capture the state at home. In fact, one of the arguments advanced in this book is that the shift to transnationalism must be understood as a product of the strategic defeat of religious nationalists on their home fronts. Therefore, jihadis' attacks on America were a desperate attempt to reinvigorate their declining movement, even though, as the book notes, they had possessed deeply entrenched anti-Western attitudes and an obsession with identity and authenticity.

However, it would be misleading to overlook the links and connections among domestic, regional, and international politics. Redressing the hemorrhaging Palestine and Iraq question will go a long way to taking the wind out of the jihadis' sail and reducing regional tensions that are providing the fertile environment for militant ideologies. For some time there may remain a jihadist threat after the resolution of local conflicts, but resolving these conflicts will remove an effective recruiting tool from the militants' arsenal and a durable source of anti-Western sentiments.

Although this book has not dwelt on the Israeli-Palestinian conflict because until recently it did not figure very prominently on the jihadist movement's agenda, it indirectly highlighted its pivotal role in the responses to the transnationalists by opinion makers, ulema, Islamists, and former jihadis. More importantly, the Palestine tragedy continues to inspire young activists and fuel their rage. I have not met an Islamist or jihadi who does not mention Palestine as an example of Western injustices inflicted on Muslims. Deep down, bin Laden and Zawahiri might care less about the plight of the Palestinians, but many of their foot soldiers and operatives have been moved and influenced by it.

By the same token, the United States cannot effectively defeat Al Qaeda if it militarily preempts its enemies under the guise of the "war on terror" and lumps its foes as terrorists or part of the "axis of evil." I spent some time on the American-led invasion of Iraq to highlight the dangers inherent in this indiscriminate approach, which has backfired and revived Al Qaeda after it had fallen into a coma. The American invasion of Iraq has supplied bin Laden and his associates with ammunition to use against the United States and to tap into an Arab sense of victimhood, marginality, and helplessness. Young Muslims unconnected to Al Qaeda but enraged by the U.S. occupation of Iraq can apparently be nudged by militants to target and kill Americans and their European and even Muslim allies.

Equally important, the invasion of Iraq has changed the conversation among Muslims on the one hand, and between Muslims and Westerners, on the other; before, the debate in the Muslim world had revolved around the culpability of Al Qaeda and its illicit use of jihad against American civilians. Since the invasion, the debate has focused on the illegality and brutality of U.S. military actions and the illicit killing and abuse of Iraqis; bin Laden, Zawahiri, and Zarqawi have tried to join the debate and position themselves as vanguards of the ummah who will expel the American occupiers from Iraq, like they did the Russians from Afghanistan in the 1980s, and thus gain credibility. Although so far there are few Muslim buyers, Al Qaeda in Iraq has an effective operational capability and has become an important factor in the Iraqi equation. Political and military developments in Iraq will likely determine whether the new lease on life given to Al Qaeda by the American military presence is a short respite, rather than a second life.

This book will avoid the common tendency to offer policy recommendations; the narrative and analysis speak for themselves in terms of the real strength of Al Qaeda and its fringe status, not only within Muslim societies but also within the declining jihadist movement. The ideology of global jihad has not grown deep roots among either Muslim activists or a majority of jihadis; it is a tiny fringe within a small movement. I do not underestimate the menace that Al Qaeda represents to the international community, but it must be kept in perspective; it is more of a security nuisance than a strategic one, and its most glaring weakness, as this book has noted, is that it was rejected by leading social and political groups, including activists and Islamists.

But one point must be made clear: the war against transnationalist jihadis cannot be won on the battlefield in either Afghanistan or Iraq; this is not a conventional war in which two armies confront each other and emerge victorious or vanquished. One of the arguments advanced in the book is that the most effective means to put Al Qaeda out of business is to complete its encirclement and siege internally; there is overwhelming evidence pointing in that direction: bin Laden and his associates have lost the war for Muslim minds. Muslim public opinion has become more vocal in its condemnation of Al Qaeda, and more Islamic scholars have become proactive in standing up and resisting bin Laden and his cohorts' ideology of hate. The internal struggle against Al Qaeda is fully rejoined.

The United States and its Western allies can contribute significantly to Al Qaeda's internal encirclement and siege by reaching out to the large "floating middle" of young Muslim opinion and listening closely to their fears, hopes, and aspirations. A strategy of institutional partnership with Muslim civil society requires more than redressing foreign policy; there is an urgent need to address socioeconomic grievances and respond to the vacuum of legitimate authority in the region. Instead of expanding the "war on terror" and embarking on new military ventures, American policy makers would be better served to exert systemic pressure on their Arab and Muslim ruling allies to structurally reform and integrate the rising social classes into the political space. In this, old Europe is well equipped to serve as both a bridge between the old world and the new and a check on America's imperial hubris and militant impulses among Muslims.

There are limits, however, to what America and Europe can do to reduce social discontent in the world of Islam. Arabs and Muslims must take charge of their own political destiny not just by condemning bin Ladenism, as they have done, but by seizing the initiative and charting an alternative progressive and humanist path; many are already engaged in an intense struggle against patriarchy, political tyranny, and militancy. Only Arabs and Muslims, with help from the international community, can transform their society and gain freedom.

Organizations Cited

Al-Azhar, the oldest learning religious institution in the world of Islam, based in Egypt

Al-Faruq Military College, a training base established by bin Laden in Afghanistan

Al Qaeda, leading transnationalist jihadist organization led by Osama bin Laden and Ayman al-Zawahiri

Al Qaeda in the Land of the Two Rivers (Mesopotamia), a coalition of militants composed mainly of Ansar al-Islam, some elements of Jaish Ansar al-Sunnah, and al-Tawhid wa al-Jihad

Al Qaeda on the Arabian Peninsula, a local affiliate in Saudi Arabia

Algerian Armed Islamic Group (GIA), now seems to be defunct and superseded by the Salafist Group for Dawa and Combat

Algerian Islamic Salvation Front (FIS) and its armed wing, AIS, the largest paramilitary organization that confronted the Algerian regime in the 1990s

al-Jama'a al-Islamiya, Egyptian Islamic group, one of the largest jihadist organizations in the Arab world

al-Jihaz al-Sirri, or secret apparatus, an underground paramilitary unit established within the Muslim Brotherhood (dissolved)

al-Takfeer wal-Hijra (Excommunication and Hegira, or the Society of Muslims), Egyptian group led by Shukri Mutafa, an agronomist, in the first half of the 1970s (now defunct)

al-Tawhid wa al-Jihad, led by the militant Jordanian, Abu Musab al-Zarqawi, now subsumed under Al Qaeda in the Land of the Two Rivers (Mesopotamia)

Ansar al-Islam in Iraq, a militant Islamist group composed mainly of Sunni Kurds

Directorate for Inter-Services Intelligence (ISI), Pakistan's military intelligence service

Harakat ul-Ansar, militant jihad group in Kashmir

Hizb al-Tahrir, or Party of Liberation, its stated goal is to rebuild the caliphate, the Muslim state that dissolved with the fall of the Ottoman Empire

Hizbollah, or Party of God, in Lebanon

International Institute for Strategic Studies (IISS), London-based

Islamic Army Shura, composed of bin Laden's Al Qaeda Shura and representatives of other independent jihadist groups from various Muslim countries

Islamic Movement of Uzbekistan

Islamic National Front, now People's Congress, in Sudan, led by Hassan al-Turabi

Jaish Ansar al-Sunnah, composed mainly of former army officers in the disbanded Iraqi military with nationalist and Islamist loyalties

Jama'a al-Islamiya in Indonesia

Jama'a al-Jihad, or Egyptian Jihad Group (assassinated Egyptian President Anwar Sadat along with al-Jama'a al-Islamiya)

Jama'at-i-Islami of Pakistan

Kashmiri Harakat ul-Ansar

Khawarji, a Muslim sect that rejected the authority of the fourth caliph, Ali bin Abi Talib, and rebelled against rulers because they abused their wealth and power and did not faithfully apply the Shariah

Libyan Islamic Fighting Group

Maktab al-Khadamat, sheikh Abdullah Azzam's Services Bureau

Military Technical Academy group, Egyptian group led by Salah Sirriya in the 1970s

Mossad, Israeli intelligence service

Muslim Brotherhood, the most powerfully organized mainstream Islamist movement, with local branches in the Arab Middle East and Central, South, and Southeast Asia

National Commission on Terrorist Attacks Upon the United States (more commonly known as the 9/11 Commission), chaired by Thomas Kean

National Intelligence Council, the CIA director's think tank

Palestinian Hamas

Palestinian Jihad

People's Congress in Sudan

People's Democratic Party, Communist party in Afghanistan

Political Security Organization, Yemen's intelligence agency

Qaeda al-jihad, a union between bin Laden's Al Qaeda and Zawahiri's Tanzim al-Jihad formally announced in 2001

Royal Institute of International Affairs, London-based

Salafist Group for Dawa and Combat, Algerian group that superseded GIA

Salafiya Jihadi, a Moroccan jihadist network

Saudi Hizbollah, a militant organization implicated in terrorism

Taliban, former rulers of Afghanistan

Tanzim al-Jihad or Islamic Jihad, Egyptian group led by Ayman al-Zawahiri that merged with Al Qaeda

Wassat Party, an Egyptian middle way party composed of mainstream Islamists and democrats

World Islamic Front for Jihad against Jews and Crusaders, the official name of Al Qaeda

People Cited

Prince Nayef bin Abdul Aziz, Saudi Arabia's interior minister

Abdullah Ahmad Abdullah, a lieutenant in Tanzim al-Jihad or Islamic Jihad (led by Zawahiri)

Abu Jandal, alias of Nasir Ahmad Nasir Abdullah al-Bahri, bin Laden's personal bodyguard and lieutenant who performed sensitive missions for Al Qaeda from 1996 to 2000

Omar Mahmoud Abu Omar, also known as Abu Qatada, a Palestinian preacher who has lived in Britain since 1993, accused of being spiritual mentor for Al Qaeda in Europe, held under house arrest under a new British law introduced after September 11 that permits the detention without trial of foreigners deemed a danger to national security

Abu Yasir, alias of Rafa'i Ahmad Taha, a leader of Egyptian al-Jama'a al-Islamiya (Islamic Group)

Dr. Abdel Aziz bin Adel Salam, known as Dr. al-Sayyid Imam, former emir of Tanzim al-Jihad and one of the most militant jihadist theoreticians

Adonis, a leading Arab liberal poet

Makram Mohammed Ahmad, Egyptian editor-in-chief of *Al-Mussawar*

Sheikh Nasir al-Din al-Albani, a senior Saudi Salafi cleric

Madeleine Albright, secretary of state under President Clinton

Ayad Allawi, former prime minister of Iraq

Abdullah Anas, a senior veteran of the Afghan jihad, an Algerian and a son-in-law of Abdullah Azzam

Yasir Arafat, late president of Palestine

Hafiz al-Assad, late president of Syria

Mohammed Atef, known as Abu Hafs al-Masri, a founder of Al Qaeda and its military commander until his death in Afghanistan in a U.S. air raid

Mohammed Atta, leader of the September 11 hijacking team

Salman al-Awdah, hardliner Saudi cleric whose sermons and writings influenced bin Laden and his cohorts

Sadik al-Azm, progressive Arab philosopher

Abdullah Azzam, spiritual leader of the Afghan Arabs, formerly of the Jordanian-Palestinian Brotherhood

Mahfouz Azzam, uncle of Ayman al-Zawahiri

Nasir Ahmad Nasir Abdullah al-Bahri, known also as Abu Jandal, a senior personal bodyguard of bin Laden

Abu Ubaidah al-Banshiri, a founder of Al Qaeda and general field commander until his death in a ferryboat accident on Lake Victoria in 1996; established a foothold for Al Qaeda in Africa, particularly the Horn of Africa

General Omar al-Bashir, current president of Sudan

Sandy Berger, Clinton's national security advisor

Abu al-Montasser Billah Mohammed, jointly established Al-Tawhid with Zarqawi in 1993

Ramzi Binalshibh, a middleman between bin Laden and the September 11 hijackers

Sheikh Abd al-Aziz bin Baz, Saudi Arabia's most senior cleric, former mufti of Saudi Arabia

Osama bin Laden, emir of Al Qaeda

Sheikh Mohammed Salih bin-Uthaymayn, a senior Saudi cleric

Tariq al-Bishri, an Egyptian jurist and historian

Zbigniew Brzezinski, Carter's national security advisor

George H. W. Bush, former president of the United States

George W. Bush, current president of the United States

Jimmy Carter, former president of the United States

Richard Clarke, former counterterrorism coordinator at the White House

Bill Clinton, former president of the United States

Abu al-Dardaa al-Iraqi, former Iraqi army officer, an aide to Abu Musab al-Zarqawi

Suleiman Khaled Darwish, known as Abu al-Ghadiyah, Zarqawi's closest aide, a Syrian physician (reportedly killed in a U.S. raid in Iraq in 2005)

Mohammed Essam Derbala, a leader of al-Jama'a al-Islamiya who played a pivotal role in the Sadat assassination

Jamal Ahmad al-Fadl, an Al Qaeda operative from Sudan who in 1996 defected to the United States because of financial disagreements with the organization

Sayyed Mohammed Hussein Fadlallah, spiritual founding father of Lebanon's Hizbollah, Iranian-born Lebanese religious scholar

Prince Turki al-Faisal, former Saudi chief of internal security

Dr. Ayman Faraj, an Afghan veteran

Mohammed Abd al-Salam Faraj, ideologue of al-Jihad organization, coordinated the 1981 assassination of Sadat

Porter J. Goss, director of the CIA

Kamal al-Said Habib, former emir of an al-Jihad cell, played a key operational role in the assassination of Sadat

Sheikh Mir Hamzah, of the Jamiat ul Ulema e Pakistan

Jad al-Haq, former grand mufti of Egypt

Hassan Hudaibi, late leader of Egyptian Muslim Brotherhood

Fu'ad Hussein, Zarqawi's Jordanian biographer

Saddam Hussein, former president of Iraq

Nageh Abdullah Ibrahim, a leader of al-Jama'a al-Islamiya and its theoretician, played a pivotal role in the Sadat assassination

Lowell E. Jacoby, U.S. Vice Admiral, director of the Defense Intelligence Agency

Ziad al-Jarrah, a 9/11 pilot hijacker

Thomas Kean, chairman of the National Commission on Terrorist Attacks Upon the United States (more commonly known as the 9/11 Commission)

Ayatollah Ruhollah Khomeni, late leader of the Islamic Revolution in Iran

Abu Abdullah Lubnani, alias for Wadih El Hage

Ahmad Salama Mabruk, Zawahiri's right-hand man and secret-keeper, ran a cell in Azerbaijan before his capture and extradition to Egypt

Ahmed Kamal Abu al-Magd, a prominent liberal Islamist legal scholar

Abd al-Karim al-Majati, Al Qaeda lieutenant, accused of planning the Madrid train bombings, killed in 2004 in a shootout with the Saudi security forces

Abu Mohammed al-Maqdisi, Zarqawi's spiritual and intellectual mentor and leader of the Salafi-Jihadi current (imprisoned in Jordan on charges of terrorist incitement and conspiracy)

Abu Hafs al-Masri, alias for Mohammed Atef, a founder of Al Qaeda and its defense minister, one of bin Laden's closest aides before he was killed in a U.S. air raid in Afghanistan

Abu Ibrahim al-Masri, or Nasralah, a traitor of Zawahiri's Tanzim al-Jihad

Abu al-Walid al-Masri, one of the most veteran Afghan Arabs, leading theoretician of Al Qaeda and a member of its Shura Council

A. Abul A'la Mawdudi, leading Pakistani cleric and theoretician

Abu Maysara al-Iraqi, former Iraqi army officer and an aide to Zarqawi

Hosni Mubarak, current president of Egypt

Shukri Mustafa, leader of the al-Takfeer wal-Hijira

Mullah Omar, the deposed Taliban ruler

Abdelgahni Mzoudi, a close friend of Mohammed Atta, who led the September 11 suicide team

Abd al Rahim al-Nashiri, mastermind of the 2000 bombing of the USS *Cole* in Yemen and former head of Al Qaeda operations in the Arabian Peninsula

Gamal Abdel Nasser, president of Egypt from 1954 to 1970

Sheikh Abdul Mohsen bin Nasser al-Obeikan, a prominent Saudi Arabian conservative Salafi and a critic of Al Qaeda

Essam al-Qamari, a lieutenant in al-Jihad organization, played a key role in the assassination of Sadat

Sheikh Yusuf al-Qardawi, an influential Egyptian-born conservative cleric who works in Qatar

Sayyid Qutb, founding father of the modern jihadist movement (hanged by Egyptian authorities in 1966 for his alleged subversive preaching and plotting)

Fazul Rahman, of the Jihad Movement in Bangladesh

Sheikh Omar Abdel Rahman, former emir of al-Jama'a al-Islamiya, known as the "Blind Sheikh" in the United States

Ronald Reagan, former president of the United States

Osama Rushdi, a former leader of al-Jama'a al-Islamiya, in charge of its media or propaganda committee (Holland granted him political asylum)

Anwar Sadat, president of Egypt from 1970 until his assassination in 1981

Jihan Sadat, wife of the late Anwar Sadat

Sahih al-Bukhari, the most reliable authority on Hadith (Prophetic traditions)

Ali Abdullah Saleh, current president of Yemen

Seif al-Adl, overall military commander of Al Qaeda (reportedly held by the Iranian government)

Ariel Sharon, current prime minister of Israel

Tharwat Shehata, a veteran leader of Tanzim al-Jihad who briefly replaced Zawahiri at the helm

Khalid Sheikh Mohammed, a terrorist operator-entrepreneur, who supervised the September 11 attacks on the United States

Yasir al-Sirri, an alleged leader of Tanzim al-Jihad who took refuge in London after being sentenced to death by an Egyptian military court

Salah Sirriya, a Palestinian Islamist who in the early 1970s assembled a group of young Egyptian college students to carry out a coup d'etat and kill Sadat by seizing control of the Military Academy in Heliopolis in the Cairo suburbs, which failed

Hani al-Sibai, a senior Islamist leader who resides in exile in Britain (the Egyptian government accuses him of being a leader of Tanzim al-Jihad and sentenced him to death)

Samir Saleh Abdullah al-Suwailem (known as al-Khattab), Saudi commander of the Arab mujahedeen in the Caucasus

Rafa'i Ahmad Taha, also known as Abu Yasir, former military commander of Egyptian Islamic Group

Ibn Taimiyyah (1263—1328), ultraconservative medieval Islamic scholar whose ideas have influenced jihadis considerably

Ali bin Abi Talib, the fourth Muslim caliph

Sheikh Mohammed Sayyed Tantawi, Grand Imam of Al-Azhar, a reformist

George J. Tenet, former director of the Central Intelligence Agency (CIA)

Frances Fragos Townsend, Bush's top adviser on terrorism

Hassan al-Turabi, head of the Islamic National Front, now People's Congress, in Sudan

Mohammed b. Abd al-Wahhab, founder of Wahhabism in Saudi Arabia

Sheikh Ahmad Yassin, the late spiritual leader of Palestinian Hamas

Rahimullah Yusufzai, Pakistani journalist

Abu Musab al-Zarqawi, emir of Al Qaeda in Iraq

Ayman al-Zawahiri, bin Laden's deputy and Al Qaeda's leading theoretician and ideologue

Montasser al-Zayat, attorney defending Islamists and jihadis in Egyptian trials, former member of al-Jama'a al-Islamiya

Karam Zuhdi, a top leader of the Islamic Group, former head of its Shura Council

Aboud al-Zumar, a lieutenant in the al-Jihad organization, played a key role in the 1991 assassination of Sadat

Notes

PROLOGUE

1. For a good survey, see Gilles Kepel, *Jihad: The Trail of Political Islam*, translated by Anthony E. Roberts (Cambridge, Mass.: Harvard University Press, 2002); Gilles Kepel, *Muslim Extremism in Egypt: The Prophet and Pharaoh*, translated by Jon Rothschild (Berkeley and Los Angeles: University of California Press, 1984); Guenena Neamatalla, *The Jihad Organization: An Islamic Alternative in Egypt* [in Arabic] (Cairo, 1988); Emmanuel Sivan, *Radical Islam: Medieval Theology and Modern Politics* (New Haven, Conn., and London: Yale University Press, 1985); Ahmed Rashid, *Taliban: Militant Islam, Oil and Fundamentalism in Central Asia* (New Haven, Conn.: Yale University Press, 2000); Peter L. Bergen, *Holy War, INC: Inside the Secret World of Osama Bin Laden* (New York and London: Simon and Schuster, 2001).

2. See the primary documents written by jihadis and collected by Rifaat Sayed Ahmed (ed.), *The Militant Prophet: The Rejectionists*, vol. 1 [in Arabic] (London: Riad El-Rayyes Books, 1991); Rifaat Sayed Ahmed (ed.), *The Militant Prophet: The Revolutionaries*, vol. 2 [in Arabic] (London: Riad El-Rayyes Books, 1991).

3. Two qualifications are in order. First, the book examines the internal dynamics of the jihadist movement and compares and contrasts jihadis' ideas with their actions in order to highlight points of coherence and consistency or tensions and contradictions. It relies mainly on two primary sources – personal interviews I conducted with jihadis and Islamists since 1999 and internal documents, booklets, diaries, and manifestos written by them since the 1970s. Only relevant, critical secondary sources were consulted. Second, although the jihadist movement encompasses a broad spectrum of nationalities and political persuasions, Egyptians have long dominated and led various jihadist and Islamist currents in the world of Islam. Their writings supplied the intellectual fuel that powers the engine of the Sunni jihadist movement and enriches its ideological constitution. For example, although Al Qaeda is led by the Saudi dissident Osama bin Laden, his Egyptian deputy, Ayman al-Zawahiri, acts as the militant network's

theoretician, articulating its ideological and operational underpinnings. (In particular, see his articles published in an Islamist newsletter, *Al-Mujahedun*, beginning with "America and the Myth of Power," no. 44 (November 1997), and his memoir released immediately after September 11: Ayman al-Zawahiri, *Knights Under the Prophet's Banner* [in Arabic], serialized by the Arabic daily *Asharq al-Awsat*, December 2001.) Since the 1940s Egypt has served as the cultural and ideological capital of jihadis, and not much of substance has been produced by Algerian, Saudi Arabian, or Afghani (Taliban) jihadis. With the exception of Pakistani and Iranian (Shiite) jihadis, particularly their two leading clerics and scholars – A. Abul A'la Mawdudi and Ruhollah Khomeini – Egyptians held a near-monopoly on jihadist theory and practice, although this situation appears to be changing with this new globalization-of-jihad wave. Accordingly, I quote widely from this rich Egyptian (jihadist) repertoire, although I also draw on the writings of other jihadis worldwide.

4. See the excellent distinctions among different jihadist contexts made by International Crisis Group Middle East/North Africa Report, no. 37, *Understanding Islamism*, 2 March 2005, pp. 14–18. See also Crisis Group Europe Report, no. 119, *Bin Laden and the Balkans: The Politics of Anti-Terrorism*, 9 November 2001; Crisis Group Asia Report, no. 80, *Southern Philippines Backgrounder: Terrorism and the Peace Process*, 13 July 2004. Palestinian Hamas and Al Qaeda are two cases in point, which ideologically come from two separate strands of Islamism. The former is a nationalist group with a well-delineated and specific agenda and social constituency, while the latter is pan-Islamist and transnational with an abstract imaginary territory and community; Hamas is a direct offshoot of the Muslim Brothers, whereas Al Qaeda is a fusion of militant Salafi-Wahhabi ideas and Egyptian Islamist currents. Although Al Qaeda's ideology is fertilized with the radical strand of the Brotherhood, that influence had existed before the organization's current transformation. Hamas also appears to have accepted participation in the Palestinian political process, unlike Al Qaeda, which is virulently antidemocracy.

5. For a critical treatment, see Raymond William Baker, *Islam Without Fear: Egypt and the New Islamists* (Cambridge, Mass.: Harvard University Press, 2003); Geneive Abdo, *No God But God: Egypt and the Triumph of Islam* (Oxford and New York: Oxford University Press, 2000); Nazih N. Ayubi, *Political Islam: Religion and Politics in the Arab World* (London and New York: Routledge, 1991); Francois Burgat and William Dowell, *The Islamic Movement in North Africa* (Austin: Center for Middle Eastern Studies, University of Texas, 1997); John L. Esposito and John O. Voll, *Makers of Contemporary Islam* (Oxford and New York: Oxford University Press, 2001); Olivier Roy, *The Failure of Political Islam*, translated by Carol Volk (Cambridge, Mass.: Harvard University Press, 1994).

6. For an informative study of the establishment and evolution of the Muslim Brotherhood, see Richard P. Mitchell, *The Society of the Muslim Brothers* [with a foreword by John O. Voll] (Oxford and New York: Oxford University Press, 1993).

7. See the succinct analysis by Rudolph Peters, *Jihad in Classical and Modern Islam* (Princeton, N.J.: Markus Wiener Publishers, 1996); Olivier Roy, *Globalized Islam: The Search for a New Umma* (New York: Columbia University Press, 2005).

8. "Statement: Jihad Against Jews and Crusaders: International Islamic Front," published by *Al-Quds al-Arabi*, an Arabic-language newspaper published in London, 23 February 1998.

9. ABC Television News interview, "Terror Suspect: An Interview with Osama bin Laden," 22 December 1998 (conducted in Afghanistan by ABC News producer Rahimullah Yousafsai).

10. "Declaration of War Against the Americans Occupying the Land of the Two Holy Places," a message from bin Laden published by *Al Islah* (London), 2 September 1996.

11. ABC Television News interview, "Terror Suspect."

12. Ibid.

13. Ibid.

14. Sayyid Qutb, *Milestones* (Cedar Rapids, Iowa: The Mother Mosque Foundation, n.d.), p. 56.

15. See Qutb, *Milestones*; A. Abul A'la Mawdudi, *Jihad in Islam* (Pakistan: Islamic Publication, 1998). For a comparative perspective, see J. Kelsay and J. T. Johnson (eds.), *Just War and Jihad: Historical and Theoretical Perspectives on War and Peace in Western and Islamic Traditions* (New York: Greenwood Press, 1991). See also Michael Waltzer, *Just and Unjust Wars* (New York: Basic Books, 1977).

16. Qutb, *Milestones*, p. 57.

17. Qutb, *Milestones*, p. 71.

18. Dr. Omar Abdel Rahman, *A Word of Truth: Dr. Omar Abdel Rahman's Legal Summation in the Jihad Case* [in Arabic] (no publisher and no date), p. 75.

19. *Ibid*, pp. 126–7, 158–64.

20. Zawahiri, *Knights Under the Prophet's Banner*, Asharq al-Awsat, 4 December 2001.

21. Ibid.

22. Ibid., 2 December 2001.

23. Ibid., 4 December 2001.

24. For an English translation, see Sayyid Qutb, *In the Shades of the Qur'an* (London: MWH, 1979).

25. Qutb, *Milestones*, p. 12.

26. Abdel Rahman, *A Word of Truth*, pp. 109–18.

27. Ibid.

28. Halmi al-Nimnim, *Sayyid Qutb and the July Revolution* [in Arabic] (Cairo, 1999), chapter 12; Ridwan Jawdat Ziyadah, "Can *Milestones* Be Considered a Foundational Fundamentalist Text?" *Al Hayat*, 26 March 2005.

29. Zawahiri, *Knights Under the Prophet's Banner*, 4 December 2001.

30. Ibid.

31. "Wife of Abd al-Karim al-Majati: We Entered Saudi Arabia with Fake Qatari Passports...," *Asharq al-Awsat*, 18 June 2005.

32. Montasser al-Zayat, *Islamic Groups: An Inside-Out View* [in Arabic] (the book was serialized in *Al Hayat* on 10, 11, 12, 13, and 14 January 2005); Montasser al-Zayat, *Ayman Zawahiri as I Knew Him* [in Arabic] (Cairo, 2002).

33. Mohammed Hafiz Diab, *Sayyid Qutb: Discourse and Ideology* [in Arabic] (Cairo, 1987); Ahmad S. Moussalli, *Radical Islamic Fundamentalism: The Ideological and Political Discourse of Sayyid Qutb* (Beirut: American University of Beirut, 1992); Nimnim, *Sayyid Qutb*, chapter 12.

34. For further elaboration, see Qutb, *Milestones*, chapter 4.

35. Mohammed Abd al-Salam Faraj, "The Absent Duty," collected by Rifaat Sayed Ahmed (ed.), *The Militant Prophet: The Revolutionaries*, vol. II [in Arabic] (London: Riad El-Rayyes Books, 1991), pp. 137–49.

36. Ibid., p. 130. Also see Peters, *Jihad in Classical and Modern Islam*, p. 162. Relying on the fatwas (religious rulings) by the ultraconservative medieval Islamic scholar Ibn Taimiyyah (1263–1328), who called on people to fight Mongol Muslim rulers for violating the faith, Faraj likewise found current Muslim leaders guilty of apostasy, a crime punishable with death. I have not met a former jihadi – or a potential one – who has not memorized Ibn Taimiyyah's fatwas by heart. Jihadis fondly refer to Ibn Taimiyyah as the "Sheikh of Islam," and they credit his fatwas with inspiring and motivating Muslims to rise up and make jihad against the infidel Tartars (Mongols). Unaware of the pitfalls of drawing historical analogies, Faraj and his associates drew a parallel historical line between the Tartar rule and today's system without regard to nuances and complexities. Jihadis borrow Ibn Taimiyyah's words, which were written more than 700 years ago, and apply them in their entirety to current sociopolitical and religious conditions prevalent in Muslim countries. Faraj, Zawahiri, bin Laden, and others do that as if Islamic history, culture, and society were frozen in time and space. They also anoint themselves as spokespersons for the 1.3 billion Muslims worldwide.

37. Faraj, "Absent Duty," in Ahmed, *The Militant Prophet*, p. 136.

38. Zayat, *Islamic Groups*, *Al Hayat*, part 2, 11 January 2005.

39. For a comparative perspective, see Mark Juergensmeyer, *The New Cold War?: Religious Nationalism Confronts the Secular State* (Berkeley and Los Angeles: California University Press, 1993).

40. Zayat, *Islamic Groups*, part 2 of 5, 11 January 2005.

41. Zawahiri, *Knights Under the Prophet's Banner*, 3 December 2001.

42. Ibid.

43. Ibid.

44. In the early 1980s Azzam, formerly of the Palestinian Muslim Brotherhood, was one of the first pioneers in the Afghan jihad; he established the first guest house (Maktab al-Khadamat), which housed and trained thousands of Arab and Muslim volunteers in Peshawar, Pakistan. Azzam's religious oratory and charisma inspired the unseasoned and wealthy bin Laden and played a vital role in his religious education. The two subsequently worked together at Maktab al-Khadamat until 1989, when Azzam and his two sons were blown up by a car bomb as they

were driving to a mosque in Peshawar. Although the two had grown apart as the Afghan war came to an end, Azzam did exercise considerable moral influence on bin Laden and jihadis in general, and he was considered the spiritual father of the so-called "Afghan Arabs." His violent death, which coincided with the end of the Afghan war, marked a watershed in the journey of Arab jihadis. It is reported that the Afghan Arabs felt "orphaned" and leaderless, and that seasoned and hardened jihadis splintered along personal and ideological lines. Some Afghan Arabs accused Zawahiri and bin Laden in Azzam's assassination, saying they wanted to inherit his leadership role and legacy and to have a freer hand in expanding jihad. Indeed, the killing of Azzam exposed serious fault lines among both jihadis and the Afghan Arabs and signaled the end of one era and the beginning of another. As the Russians retreated in defeat, bin Laden and the Egyptian contingent decided against demobilization and retrenchment and in favor of expanding jihad into new Muslim territories. See Abdullah Azzam, "Join the Caravan" [in Arabic]. For an English translation, see "Join the Caravan," http://www.relgioscope.com/info/doc/jihad/azzam_caravan_3_part1.htm; Abdullah Anas, *The Birth of the Afghan Arabs* [in Arabic] (London: Dar al-Saqi, 2002), pp. 90–1; "One of the Oldest Afghan Arabs Talks to *Asharq al-Awsat* about His Journey," *Asharq al-Awsat*, 25 November 2001. Olivier Roy, a specialist on Afghanistan, agrees that Azzam's death, which is still shrouded in mystery, was beneficial to bin Laden. Bin Laden took charge of what remained of Maktab al-Khadamat, sidelining potential rivals, with the blessings of the Pakistani and Saudi sponsors, who maintained their support for him until 1990 (the Saudis) and September 11 (the Pakistanis). See Roy, *Globalized Islam*, pp. 296–7.

45. For a critical analysis, see Steve Coll, *Ghost Wars: The Secret History of the CIA, Afghanistan, and Bin Laden, from the Soviet Invasion to September 10, 2001* (New York: The Penguin Press, 2004).

46. See Gilles Kepel, *The War for Muslim Minds: Islam and the West* (Cambridge, Mass.: Harvard University Press, 2005) and Kepel, *Jihad: The Trail of Political Islam*; also see Roy, *Globalized Islam*; Mohammed Salah, *Narratives of the Jihad Years: The Journey of the Afghan Arabs* [in Arabic] (Cairo, 2001); Kameel al-Taweel, *The Armed Islamic Movement in Algeria: From the FIS to the GIA* [in Arabic] (Beirut, 1998).

INTRODUCTION: THE ROAD TO SEPTEMBER 11 AND AFTER

1. *The 9/11 Commission Report: Final Report of the National Commission on Terrorist Attacks Upon the United States* (New York: W. W. Norton, 2004).

2. Ibid., p. 250.

3. Ibid., p. 51.

4. Ibid., p. 48.

5. *Asharq al-Awsat*, 8 and 9 December 2004.

6. *The New York Times*, 17 June 2004. It is now well known that the U.S. government has increasingly used the so-called rendition program under which the CIA transfers terrorism suspects to about a half-dozen autocratic countries, particularly Uzbekistan, Saudi Arabia, Egypt, Syria, Jordan, Morocco, and Pakistan, to be held and interrogated, or, as some say, tortured, according to human rights reports, former detainees, and some government agents involved in the detention system; these practices are not allowed under U.S. law. American intelligence officials estimate that the United States has transferred 100 to 150 suspects worldwide. *The New York Times* has published a few investigative articles on the rendition program; one of the most informative, by Don Van Natta, Jr., is on the U.S.-Uzbekistan connection: "U.S. Recruits a Rough Ally to Be a Jailer," 1 May 2005; see also Raymond Bonner, "Detainee Says He Was Tortured in U.S. Custody," 13 February 2005.

7. *The 9/11 Commission Report*, p. 48.

8. Ibid.

9. Ibid. Many of the security alerts and warnings of pending attacks issued by the United States, including the elevation of the Department of Homeland Security color-coded threat levels and the arrests of some operatives such as Jose Padilla, were based on information gleaned from these leading Al Qaeda detainees.

10. "Hunting Bin Laden," PBS *Frontline* broadcast, May 1998 (online at www.pbs.org/wgbh/pages/frontline/shows/binladen/who/interview.html).

11. I will define and delineate the meanings and positions of the two camps later.

12. The report is most useful and enlightening when it traces and documents the debates among American officials and intelligence agencies regarding the most effective measures to deal with the new threat posed by Al Qaeda. It provides the most comprehensive semiofficial account of the evolution of U.S. counterterrorism strategy and why it failed to deter, contain, and defeat the terror network. The most painful and heart-wrenching aspect of the report centers on how some victims trapped in the hijacked planes and burning buildings heroically spent their last moments helping traumatized colleagues and saying goodbyes to loved ones.

13. *The 9/11 Commission Report*, pp. 362–3.

14. Gilles Kepel, *The War for Muslim Minds: Islam and the West* (Cambridge, Mass.: Harvard University Press, 2005).

15. The Bush administration apparently no longer perceives Al Qaeda as a strategic threat because its operational ability has been severely degraded. See Susan B. Glasser, "Terror War Seen Shifting to Match Evolving Enemy," *The Washington Post*, 28 May 2005.

16. Ayman al-Zawahiri, *Knights Under the Prophet's Banner* [in Arabic] (serialized by *Asharq al-Awsat*, 12 December 2001).

17. This letter and other important primary documents were recovered from computers, which had been used by Zawahiri and his associates, that were looted by Afghanis from Al Qaeda's main office in Kabul immediately after the city fell. These documents were acquired by a *Wall Street Journal* reporter and by the

London-based Arabic newspaper *Asharq al-Awsat*. Both papers ran a series of articles highlighting salient features (throughout I will refer to these documents as "Zawahiri's Secret Papers"). Andrew Higgins and Alan Cullison, "Files Found: A Computer in Kabul Yields a Chilling Array of Al Qaeda Memos," *The Wall Street Journal*, 31 December 2001; Mohammed al-Shafi'i, "Zawahiri's Secret Papers," *Asharq al-Awsat*, part 1, 13 December 2002.

18. Zawahiri, *Knights Under the Prophet's Banner*, 12 December 2001.

19. See Montasser al-Zayat, *Ayman Zawahiri as I Knew Him* [in Arabic] (Cairo, 2002); Kameel al-Taweel, a series of four lengthy interviews with Hani al-Sibai (a senior leader of Egyptian Islamic Jihad, though he denies being an active operational member), *Al Hayat*, 1, 2, 3, and 4 September 2002; Essam Mohammed Derbala, *Al Qaeda's Strategy: Mistakes and Dangers* [in Arabic] (serialized by *Asharq al-Awsat* on 6, 7, 8, and 9 August 2003); interview with Karam Zuhdi, *Al-Mussawar*, 21 and 28 June 2002; *Asharq al-Awsat*, 15 and 16 July 2003.

20. Published in *Al-Quds al-Arabi*, an Arabic-language newspaper, 23 August 1996.

21. An interview with Osama bin Laden on ABC Television News, 22 December 1998.

22. "Declaration of War Against the Americans Occupying the Land of the Two Holy Places," a message from bin Laden published in *Al Islah* (London), 2 September 1996.

23. Ibid.

24. Zawahiri, *Knights Under the Prophet's Banner*, 12 December 2001.

25. Ibid.

26. Zayat, *Ayman al-Zawahiri*, pp. 113–36; Mohammed Salah, *Narratives of the Jihad Years: The Journey of the Arab Afghans* [in Arabic] (Cairo, 2001), chapter 5.

27. Collected by Rifaat Sayyed Ahmed (ed.), *The Militant Prophet: The Revolutionaries*, vol. II [in Arabic] (London: Riad El-Rayyes Books, 1991), p. 248.

28. Nabeel Darweesh, "Mzoudi: I Refused to Apply for Asylum in Germany…," *Asharq al-Awsat*, 29 June 2005. This was the first lengthy interview given by Mzoudi.

29. "Wife of Abd al-Karim al-Majati: We Entered Saudi Arabia with Fake Qatari Passports…," *Asharq al-Awasat*, 18 June 2005.

30. "Al Qaeda from Within, as Narrated by Abu Jandal (Nasir al-Bahri), bin Laden's Personal Bodyguard," *Al-Quds al-Arabi*, 20 March 2005.

31. "Wife of Abd al-Karim al-Majati."

32. "Al Qaeda from Within, as Narrated by Abu Jandal (Nasir al-Bahri)," 30 March 2005.

33. According to the report, some of bin Laden's senior associates were concerned that the attacks may provoke an armed American response and anger Taliban leaders and the Pakistani government, whose good graces had permitted Al Qaeda to use Afghanistan as a refuge. But bin Laden overruled their objections and reportedly said that attacking the United States would bring a bonanza to Al Qaeda by attracting more suicide recruits, eliciting greater donations, and

increasing the number of sympathizers willing to provide logistical assistance: "In his thinking, the more Al Qaeda did, the more support it would gain." See *The 9/11 Commission Report*, pp. 67, 251. See also *The New York Times*, 17 June 2004. (I will have more to say on this point throughout the book.)

34. "Al Qaeda from Within, as Narrated by Abu Jandal (Nasir al-Bahri)," 26 March 2005.

35. Ibid.

36. "The Story of the Arab Afghans," *Asharq al-Awsat*, 8 December 2004.

37. Zawahiri, *Knights Under the Prophet's Banner*, 12 December 2001.

38. "The Story of the Arab Afghans," *Asharq al-Awsat*, 8 and 9 December 2004.

39. ABC Television News, 22 December 1998.

40. Published in *Al-Quds al-Arabi*, 23 February 1998.

41. Mohammed Salah, "The Violence of Jihad Turns Outward and al-Jama'a's Initiative Proceeds Successfully," *Al Hayat*, 28 December 1998.

42. I will elaborate on these intraorganizational debates and differences among jihadis in later chapters. Between 1999 and 2000 I interviewed scores of former jihadis in Egypt, Yemen, Lebanon, Palestine, Jordan, and other Muslim countries. These interviews empirically inform my analysis throughout the book.

43. *The 9/11 Commission Report*, p. 250.

44. Another fundamental handicapping problem facing all jihadis stems from the poverty and paucity of their political theory and philosophical ideas. Unlike some modernist and enlightened Islamists, jihadis offer no intellectual blueprint or paradigm of their envisioned Islamic order.

1. RELIGIOUS NATIONALISTS AND THE NEAR ENEMY

1. It is worth mentioning that there was no uniform understanding among all shades of jihadis on the dar al-islam versus dar al-harb dichotomy. As mentioned previously, a critical mass of jihadis, beginning with Sayyid Qutb, believed that dar al-islam itself is shrouded with jahiliya (ignorance of divine guidance); therefore, in their eyes, the entire international system is dar al-harb, and some go beyond that and refer to it as dar al-kufr, or the House of Disbelief.

2. Kamal al-Said Habib, "Islamic Renewal," compiled by Rifaat Sayyed Ahmed, ed., *The Militant Prophet: The Revolutionaries*, vol. II [in Arabic] (London: Riad El-Rayyes Books, 1991), pp. 204–5.

3. For a representative sample of jihadist documents and pamphlets from the 1970s and 1980s, see Abu al-Fida, "The Philosophy of Confrontation," in ibid., pp. 293–313; "Indicting the Egyptian Political System," in ibid., pp. 273–83; Mohammed Abd al-Salam Faraj, "The Absent Duty," collected by Rifaat Sayed Ahmed, ed., *The Militant Prophet: The Rejectionists*, vol. I [in Arabic] (London: Riad El-Rayyes Books, 1991), pp. 137–49; Aboud al-Zumar, "The Path of Islamic Jihad," in ibid., pp. 110–26; "Chapters from the Charter of Islamic Political Action," in ibid., pp. 165–78.

A close reading of jihadis' writings and private conversations with jihadis suggest that Muslim society had been corrupted and subverted by a systematic campaign of secularism and westernization that was enforced by local despots. According to jihadis' logic, Muslims lost touch with the real tenets of Islam as interpreted and practiced by the salaf (pious ancestors). "Islam has become alien in its birthplace" is a standard jihadist dictum. All jihadis whom I met bemoaned this estrangement and stressed the need to re-Islamize Muslim lands in accordance with the sayings and practices of the rightful salaf. On the whole, jihadis preferred force over al-da'wa (call) to undo the wrongs and to make Islam supreme. Like their secular opponents, jihadis viewed themselves as the vanguard with a monopoly on truth and the only qualified Muslims to reclaim authentic, scripturalist Islam and to impose it from the top down by fiat.

One suspects that jihadis have contempt for fellow believers who, in their eyes, are incapable of interpreting the faith for themselves and distinguishing between right and wrong. This bourgeois-elitist attitude represents a rupture with Muslim reality and subverts an egalitarian religious culture that lacks an organized priesthood or a formalized church similar to that of Christianity. In contrast to their Christian counterparts, Muslim believers communicate directly with God without an intermediate authority. Theoretically, Islam is a revolutionary, progressive religion because it entrusts the individual believer to bypass any organized priesthood and church. Jihadis' subversion and rupture lie in their attempt to institute themselves as the new papacy in Islam, thus disinvesting and disinheriting both the individual believer and the community of believers of their independent moral agency. Instead of viewing themselves as natural inheritors of Islam's free spirit, dynamism, and renewal, jihadis aimed at enshrining a new totalitarian religious hierarchy and theocracy based on a highly selective, reactionary interpretation of the canon and forcing fellow Muslims to submit to their authority.

Moreover, jihadis displayed a pronounced hostility toward the religious establishment, which they accused of abandoning its moral responsibility as guardian of the faith and serving as an extension of secular rulers. In my interviews with jihadis, they directed their wrath as much against Muslim scholars as against impious politicians because both, they claimed, colluded to perpetuate the non-Islamic political order. As to why the ulema (Islamic scholars) would bless and confer legitimacy on ruling apostates, they had a simple answer: expediency and vested interests. Jihadis subscribed the absence of Islam from society to this mutual arrangement and the unholy alliance between the religious and political establishments. As previously mentioned, jihadis' attacks on clerics were designed to gain public legitimacy for their revolt against the status quo. By discrediting the ulema, they hoped to advance their own revolutionary project as an alternative and viable substitute. For further elaboration on the debate between the religious establishment and Islamists, see Magda Ali Saleh Rabi'i, *The Political Role of Al-Azhar* [in Arabic] (Cairo, 1992); Steven Barraclough, "Al-Azhar Between the Government and the Islamists," *Middle East Journal*, vol. 52, no. 2 (1998).

4. Faraj, "The Absent Duty," in Ahmed, *The Militant Prophet: The Rejectionists*, vol. I, pp. 137–49. For an English translation, see Johannes Jansen, *The Neglected Duty: The Creed of Sadat's Assassins and Islamic Resurgence in the Middle East* (New York: Macmillan, 1986).

5. "The Inevitability of Confrontation," in Ahmed, *The Militant Prophet: The Revolutionaries*, vol. II, pp. 244–67. An argument can be made that task 3 does entail a regional conflict because American forces were stationed in and near Muslim soil and this would have triggered a clash with the United States. Task 4 could also involve fighting Israel, as Palestine is viewed as a Muslim homeland. Theoretically, this is conceivable, but jihadis' first priority was the overthrow of local rulers, not waging a global jihad. The internationalist trend was still in its infancy.

6. Montasser al-Zayat, *Ayman Zawahiri as I Knew Him* [in Arabic] (Cairo, 2002), pp. 113–36. Although doctrinaire jihadis did not actively partake in actions in the Israeli-Palestinian theater, Palestine did figure prominently in their thinking and discourse. Jihadis whom I interviewed did mention Palestine as a "deep wound" in the heart of the ummah. Nonetheless, from the 1970s until the mid-1990s jihadis argued that Palestine could be liberated only after existing rulers in the Muslim states are overthrown and Islamic rule prevails.

7. I am not suggesting that jihadis were not aware of external threats to dar al-islam or the "glory days" of the caliphate, an institution that transcended individual national frontiers; far from it, many told me they were fully aware of their countries' subservience to great powers and the need for Muslims to unite and defend themselves. But they believed that setting up Islamic polities at home was the key to internal emancipation and everything else, including the reestablishment of a "pious" caliph. Jihadis' concentration on the near enemy also testifies to the fact that the postcolonial Muslim state is a reality and thus a target as well.

8. Had jihadis been successful in overthrowing secular Muslim regimes, would they have turned their guns against Israel and the United States? This counterfactual question is worth considering because existing evidence shows that once they capture power (Islamic Sudan is a case in point), they either dissipate their political energies in internal squabbles and bickering or learn the hard way the pitfalls of overextension.

9. "America, Egypt, and the Islamist [Jihadist] Movement," in Ahmed, *The Militant Prophet: The Rejectionists*, vol. I, pp. 179–89. Since the late 1970s various cells and groups functioning under the rubric or umbrella of the Egyptian Jihad group, since united as Islamic Jihad and now led by Zawahiri, have supplied jihadis all over the Muslim world with a comprehensive repertoire and guidelines on the legitimacy of waging jihad against internal and external enemies alike. Also, operationally, Zawahiri's Islamic Jihad was a pioneer in legitimizing suicide bombings against the near enemy and became well known for its spectacular operations against Egyptian authorities inside and outside the country. Senior members of Islamic Jihad often reminded me that although their organization was much smaller than its Egyptian competitor, Islamic Group, and other organizations elsewhere,

theirs has carried out qualitative attacks and distinguished itself on the battle-field. The weight of evidence, however, shows a dismal record of success. In his memoir, Zawahiri refers to and boasts about some of these attacks, even though they missed their designated targets and killed and injured civilian and police bystanders. Equally important, Islamic Jihad attracted highly charismatic and zealous lieutenants, including Zawahiri, Abd al-Salam Faraj, Aboud al-Zumar, Essam al-Qamari, Kamal al-Said Habib, and many others, who left their stamp on the organization and influenced the thinking and direction of the jihadist tide in Egypt and beyond. In particular, under Zawahiri, Islamic Jihad dramatically transformed itself from a purely local (Egyptian) organization into a transnational one by virtue of its alliance and merger with Al Qaeda in the late 1990s. How-ever, former Islamic Jihad members are less charitable toward Zawahiri, who they accuse of endangering the very existence of the organization and the Islamist and jihadist movements as a whole (I will discuss the intrajihadist debates in greater detail later).

10. Paul Berman, *Terror and Liberalism* (New York: W. W. Norton, 2003); Ian Buruma and Avishai Margalit, *Occidentalism: The West in the Eyes of Its Enemies* (New York: The Penguin Press, 2004).

11. "America, Egypt, and the Islamist [Jihadist] Movement," p. 189.

12. Yusuf al-Qardawi, *Fiqh of Priorities: A New Study in the Light of Qur'an and Sunnah* [in Arabic] (Cairo, 1995), pp. 168–72; Raymond William Baker, *Islam Without Fear: Egypt and the New Islamists* (Cambridge, Mass.: Harvard University Press, 2003), pp. 235–9.

13. The essay entitled "The Road to Jerusalem Goes Through Cairo" appeared in *Al-Mujahidun*, 26 April 1995, an underground newsletter published by Egyptian Islamic Jihad.

14. Mohamed Salah, *Narratives of the Jihad Years: The Journey of the Afghan Arabs* [in Arabic] (Cairo, 2001), chapter 5; Zayat, *Ayman Zawahiri*, pp. 113–36.

15. Ayman al-Zawahiri, *Knights Under the Prophet's Banner* [in Arabic] (serialized by *Asharq al-Awsat*, 12 March 2001.

16. Kameel al-Taweel, "Hani al-Sibai to *Al Hayat*: Leaders of 'Islamic Group' Shed Blood . . . and Must Step Aside," *Al Hayat*, 5 September 2003; Taweel, a series of four lengthy interviews with Egyptian Islamist, Hani al-Sibai, in *Al Hayat*, part 3 of 4, 1 September 2002.

17. Francois Burgat and William Dowell, *The Islamic Movement in North Africa* (Austin: Center for Middle Eastern Studies, University of Texas, 1997), pp. 316–33; *Le Monde*, 7 March 1995. See also *Liberation*, 22 June 1995 (*White Paper on the Repression in Algeria, Committee of Free Algerian Militants on Human Rights and Dignity*, Hoggar, Plan les Ouattes, Switzerland, 1994).

18. *The 9/11 Commission Report: Final Report of the National Commission on Terror-ist Attacks Upon the United States* (New York: W. W. Norton, 2004), pp. 59–60; Daniel Benjamin and Steven Simon, *The Age of Sacred Terror* (New York: Random House, 2002), pp. 132, 242.

19. "Al Qaeda from Within, as Narrated by Abu Jandal (Nasir al-Bahri), bin Laden's Personal Guard," *Al-Quds al-Arabi*, 24 March 2005.

20. See Richard Bulliet and Fawaz A. Gerges, eds., "A Recruiting Tape of Osama bin Laden: Excerpts and Analyses," at http://www.ciaonet.org/cbr/cbr00/video/excerpts_index.html (Columbia International Affairs Online), October 2001. Professor Bulliet and the author translated and analyzed a three-hour videotape – which for several months prior to the September 11 attacks circulated underground in the Arab world – calling on Muslims to wage jihad against Crusaders and Jews. Produced on behalf of bin Laden and prominently featuring his image, words, and ideas, this original tape was designed to recruit young Arab men to journey to Afghanistan and train for the coming war in defense of Islam.

21. "Al Qaeda from Within," 24 March 2005.

22. Ibid., 31 March 2005.

23. *The 9/11 Commission Report*, pp. 59–60.

24. Ibid., p. 60; "Al Qaeda from Within," 31 March 2005; Benjamin and Simon, *The Age of Sacred Terror*, pp. 224–5, 300–2.

25. Bulliet and Gerges, eds., "A Recruiting Tape of Osama bin Laden."

26. A qualification is in order here. The reader must recognize that this is a shadowy universe, and that it is very difficult to establish a direct line of responsibility for all of the attacks that have occurred since the early 1990s. The Khobar operation is a case in point. Although there exists a thin line between information and disinformation, Al Qaeda's fingerprints and connections could be found "everywhere."

27. Yosri Fouda and Nick Fielding, *Masterminds of Terror: The Truth Behind the Most Devastating Terrorist Attack the World Has Ever Seen* (New York: Arcade Publishers, 2003), note that Al Qaeda was formally established some time between 1994 when bin Laden was stripped of his Saudi citizenship and 1996 when he returned to Afghanistan; moreover, the 1993 and 1994–5 attacks were the work of independent freelance jihadis like Khalid Sheikh Mohammed (he had not joined Al Qaeda yet) and his nephew Ramzi Yusuf. Another work that highlights bin Laden's pre–Al Qaeda career and his establishment of the Advice and Reform Committee is Mamoun Fandy, *Saudi Arabia and the Politics of Dissent* (New York: St. Martin's Press, 1999).

28. *The 9/11 Commission Report*, pp. 60, 109.

29. Bulliet and Gerges, eds., "A Recruiting Tape of Osama bin Laden."

30. Indeed, it can be argued that the saturation of the rhetoric of Al Qaeda and bin Laden with the "occupation of the holy places" theme and the little said about the need to establish an Islamic polity make it almost seem that the goal of transnational jihadism is to expel invading U.S. forces from Muslim lands, not to establish an Islamic state. Transnational jihadis seem to give a higher priority to ridding the Muslim world of foreign forces, and the establishment of the caliphate has been put on the back burner. The logic behind this shift lies in their belief, as

Zawahiri stressed in his memoir and videotapes, that neither an Islamic state nor structural reforms will be possible without establishing "the freedom of the Muslim lands and their liberation from every aggressor." Zawahiri, bin Laden, and their cohorts concluded that Western powers, particularly the United States, are determined to undermine the Islamist movement and keep it off balance; they sound more like irredentist jihadis than doctrinaire jihadis, with one exception – their ambition is not limited to one defined national territory. But this argument misses the real point behind the shift, which is tactical, not strategic, because the goal, as Zawahiri added, remains the establishment of "a fundamentalist base in the heart of the Muslim world." Zawahiri, *Knights Under the Prophet's Banner*, 12 December 2001; Mariam Fam, "Al-Qaida No. 2 Disparages U.S. on Reform," *Associated Press*, 17 June 2005.

31. "The Story of the Afghan Arabs: From the Entry to Afghanistan to the Final Exodus with the Taliban," *Asharq al-Awsat*, 9 December 2004.

32. Ibid.

33. Ibid.

34. Ibid.

35. Ibid.

36. Like never before, the new media, particularly Arab satellite television stations, which began broadcasting in the 1990s, made Muslims aware of the suffering of one another. Satellite television has broken the geographic and political isolation of Arabs and Muslims and created a sense of belonging, of an imagined community, of being an integral part of the ummah. As *The Economist* commented, satellite coverage has sped the homogenization of Muslim religious practices, hopes, dreams, and travails. In particular, Al Jazeera, based in Qatar with an estimated audience of 40 million to 50 million regular viewers, has broken the government's monopoly on the flow of information and has had a powerful mobilizational effect on young Muslims. In interviews with young activists and former jihadis, most of them listed the new media as their major source of news and information. On the impact of the satellite dish, see "The World Through Their Eyes – Arab Satellite Television," *The Economist*, 26 February 2005; Hugh Miles, *Al-Jazeera* (New York: Grove Press, 2005).

37. "Al Qaeda from Within," 24 March 2005.

38. "Ibid., 20 March 2005.

39. Ibid.

40. Donna Abu-Nasr, "Saudi Religious Scholars Support Holy War," *Associated Press*, 6 November 2004; "Saudi Clerics Reportedly Exporting Jihad," *Associated Press*, 24 January 2005.

41. "Al Qaeda from Within," 20 March 2005.

42. Ibid.

43. Ibid.

44. Ibid.

45. Ibid.

46. Ibid., 26 March 2005.

47. Ibid., 20 March 2005.

48. Abdullah Anas, *The Birth of the Afghan Arabs* [in Arabic] (London: Dar al-Saqi, 2002), p. 36; Salah, *Narratives of the Jihad Years*, pp. 43–62, 65–84; Taweel, a series of four lengthy interviews with Egyptian Islamist, Hani al-Sibai, in *Al Hayat*, part 2 of 4, 1 September 2002. For background, see Steve Coll, *Ghost Wars: The Secret History of the CIA, Afghanistan, and Bin Laden, from the Soviet Invasion to September 10, 2001* (New York: The Penguin Press, 2004), pp. 154–5.

49. Salah, *Narratives of the Jihad Years*, pp. 43–62, 65–84; Taweel, a series of four lengthy interviews with Egyptian Islamist, Hani al-Sibai, in *Al Hayat*, part 2 of 4, 1 September 2002. See also Mohammed Abd al-Salam, "The Afghan Arabs," *Majalat al-Siyasa al-Dawliya* [in Arabic] (Cairo: Al-Ahram Centre for Political and Strategic Studies, no. 113, 1993), p. 92.

50. Fawaz A. Gerges, *America and Political Islam: Clash of Cultures or Clash of Interests?* (Cambridge and New York: Cambridge University Press, 1999).

51. Paper by the Secretary of State's Special Assistant (Francis Russell), "U.S. Policies Toward Nasser, Washington, 4 August 1956," in *Foreign Relations of the United States: Suez Crisis, 1956*, vol. XVI (Washington, D.C.: Government Printing Office, 1989), pp. 86, 142; Richard W. Cottam, "U.S. and Soviet Responses to Islamic Militancy," in Nikki R. Keddie and Mark J. Gasiorowski, eds., *Neither East nor West: Iran, the Soviet Union and the United States* (New Haven, Conn.: Yale University Press, 1990), pp. 267–70.

52. *Weekly Compilation of Presidential Documents*, U.S. Government Printing Office, vol. 16, no. 4, 28 January 1980, pp. 194–6. See also Gary Sick, "Military Options and Constraints," in Warren Christopher, ed., *American Hostages in Iran: The Conduct of a Crisis* (New Haven, Conn.: Yale University Press, 1985), p. 151.

53. Gary Sick, *All Fall Down: America's Fateful Encounter with Iran* (London: I.B. Tauris, 1985), p. 221.

54. Zbigniew Brzesinski, *Power and Principle: Memoirs of the National Security Advisor, 1977–1981* (New York: Farrar, Straus and Giroux, 1983), pp. 470–8, 485, 489. The Russian invasion also provided American officials with a respite after Khomeini made opposition to the "Great Satan" the raison d'etre of his Islamic revolution.

55. Too much was at stake – not just for the "free world," as American officials were fond of saying, but also for their bureaucratic careers and life-long investment in anticommunism – to either decline to play the game or to suspend it temporarily.

56. It is unlikely that American diplomats critically reflected on such long-term implications, although critics and skeptics would argue otherwise. American foreign policy, like American politics in general, is driven by short-term political considerations and elite interests. The rivalry with Soviet communism represented the only constant factor in U.S. policy during the Cold War. Since the 1970s the special U.S.-Israeli relationship has also become institutionalized.

Everything else was subject to the shifting political agenda and mood of the foreign policy establishment, particularly on Capitol Hill.

57. Another factor that could have influenced the official thinking in the United States was that the Afghan mujahedeen and their guests were Sunnis, not Shiites. After the Iranian revolution, a new hypothesis regarding the violent and revolutionary nature of Shiite political thought gained ascendancy in American policy-oriented academic circles. In an effort to illustrate the social upheaval in Iran, a predominantly Shiite nation, radical Shiism was compared and contrasted with mainstream status quo Sunni Islam. This ahistorical thesis could have lulled American diplomats into thinking that the Sunni jihad caravan would take a dramatically less revolutionary turn than its Shiite counterpart in Iran and Lebanon. As mentioned earlier, at this stage Sunni jihadis had not developed a transnationalist paradigm and had been reorganizing and restructuring their ranks after the operational setbacks suffered in Saudi Arabia in the late 1970s and in Egypt in the early 1980s.

58. Zawahiri, *Knights Under the Prophet's Banner*, 3 December 2001.

59. *The 9/11 Commission Report*, p. 56.

60. Ibid., pp. 55–6; Rohan Gunaratna, *Inside Al Qaeda: Global Network of Terror* (New York: Columbia University Press, 2002), pp. 16–23.

61. See his conversation with leading Yemeni religious scholars in the Yemeni publication *26 September* (no. 989), 13 December 2001; Coll, *Ghost Wars*, pp. 216, 225–39.

62. Zawahiri, *Knights Under the Prophet's Banner*, 3 December 2001.

63. Ibid.

2. THE AFGHAN WAR: SOWING THE SEEDS OF TRANSNATIONAL JIHAD

1. On the Afghan war, see Mariam Abou Zahab and Olivier Roy, *Islamic Networks: The Afghan-Pakistan Connection* (London: Hurst, 2004); Roy, *Islam and Resistance in Afghanistan* (Cambridge, UK: Cambridge University Press, 1986); John K. Cooley, *Unholy Wars: Afghanistan, America, and International Terrorism*, second edition (London: Pluto Press, 2000); Steve Coll, *Ghost Wars: The Secret History of the CIA, Afghanistan, and Bin Laden, from the Soviet Invasion to September 10, 2001* (New York: The Penguin Press, 2004). For regional links, connections, and repercussions, see Gilles Kepel, *Muslim Extremism in Egypt: The Prophet and Pharaoh* (Berkeley and Los Angeles: University of California Press, 1984); Johannes J. G. Jansen, *The Neglected Duty: The Creed of Sadat's Assassins and Islamic Resurgence in the Middle East* (New York: Macmillan, 1986); R. Hrair Dekmejian, *Islam in Revolution: Fundamentalism in the Arab World* (Syracuse, N.Y.: Syracuse University Press, 1985).

2. For a selective sample, see Mohamed Salah, *Narratives of the Jihad Years: The Journey of the Afghan Arabs* [in Arabic] (Cairo, 2001); Ayman Sabri Faraj, *Memoirs of an Afghan Arab* [in Arabic] (Cairo, 2002); Abdullah Anas, *The Birth of the*

Afghan Arabs [in Arabic] (London: Dar al-Saqi, 2002); "One of the Oldest Afghan Arabs Talks to *Asharq al-Awsat* about His Journey," *Asharq al-Awsat*, 25 November 2001.

3. In the early 1980s several Muslim states were all too eager to help those among their citizens who expressed a desire to fight in Afghanistan so as to be able to get rid of these radicals and potential troublemakers at home.

4. Graham Fuller and Ian O. Lesser, *A Sense of Siege: The Geopolitics of Islam and the West* (Boulder, Colo.: Westview, 1995); Anthony Arnold, *Afghanistan's Two-Party Communism: Parcham and Khalq* (Stanford, Calif., 1983).

5. Ayman al-Zawahiri, *Knights Under the Prophet's Banner* [in Arabic] (serialized by *Asharq al-Awsat*, 3 December 2001).

6. Al-Hijaz is the western province of Saudi Arabia where Mecca and Medina, Islam's two holiest sites, are located. He appeared to be referring to expelling the American military presence from Arabia, but U.S. forces were normally stationed in the eastern provinces. By specifying al-Hijaz, bin Laden was misleading viewers into thinking that American troops were in physical control of Mecca and Medina. Richard Bulliet of Columbia University and I translated and analyzed this three-hour-long recruitment videotape, which was made at least six months before September 11 and circulated underground in the Arab world. The tape was designed to recruit young Arabs to journey to Afghanistan and train for a war in defense of Islam against the so-called Crusaders and Jews. For the entire text and analysis, see Richard Bulliet and Fawaz A. Gerges, eds., "A Recruiting Tape of Osama bin Laden: Excerpts and Analyses," at www.ciaonet.org (Columbia International Affairs Online), October 2001.

7. Zawahiri, *Knights Under the Prophet's Banner*, 3 December 2001.

8. Ibid.

9. Ridwan al-Sayyid, *The Struggle for Islam: Fundamentalism and Reform and International Policies* [in Arabic] (Beirut, 2004).

10. Zawahiri, *Knights Under the Prophet's Banner*, 3 December 2001.

11. Ibid.

12. Kameel al-Taweel, a series of four lengthy interviews with Egyptian Islamist Hani al-Sibai, in *Al Hayat*, part 2 of 4, 2 September 2002; Montasser al-Zayat, *Ayman Zawahiri as I Knew Him* [in Arabic] (Cairo, 2002), pp. 51–86; Salah, *Narratives of the Jihad Years*, pp. 65–84.

13. Zayat, pp. 51–86; Taweel, part 1 of 4, 1 September 2002.

14. Zayat, pp. 51–86; Taweel, part 1 of 4, 1 September 2002. This modus operanda is similar to that of Hizb al-Tahrir, with the only difference being that Hizb al-Tahrir does not directly carry out the coup d'etat, but rather seeks nusrah, or support, from sympathizers within the military and civilian institutions in certain countries to overthrow incumbent regimes and then transfer authority to Hizb al-Tahrir. This sequence assumes a semblance of popular uprising by the masses. Suha Taji-Farouki, *A Fundamental Quest: Hizb al-Tahrir and the Search for the Islamic Caliphate* (London, 1996).

15. Taweel, part 1 of 4, 1 September 2002; Zayat, pp. 51–86; Montasser al-Zayat, *Islamic Groups: An Inside-Out View* [in Arabic] (serialized in *Al Hayat*), 11 January 2005. Between the two polar opposites – participation in the political process and militarily struggling to overthrow the existing order – lies the approach of Hizb al-Tahrir, which does not rule out the use of force but also engages in mass mobilization. Ironically, jihadis attack Hizb al-Tahrir for its ambivalent approach by saying that its members are all talk and no action. Similarly, modernist Islamists are a little suspicious of Hizb al-Tahrir for not being fully transparent and renouncing violence. See Kamran Asghar Bokhari, "From Islamism to Post-Islamism," *Geopolitical Weekly*, Strategic Forecasting, Inc. (18 April 2005), http://www.stratfor.biz/Story.neo?storyId=247251; Bokhari, "The Social and Ideological Roots of Jihadism: A Constructivist Understanding to Non-State Actors," *Middle East Affairs Journal*, vol. 8 (Fall 2002).

16. Taweel, part 1 of 4, 1 September 2002; Zayat, *Ayman Zawahiri*, pp. 51–86; Zayat, *Islamic Groups*, 11 January 2005.

17. Zawahiri, 4 December 2001.

18. Ibid.; Taweel, part 1 of 4, 1 September 2002; Zayat, *Ayman Zawahiri*, pp. 23–47, 51–86.

19. Lawrence Wright, "The Man Behind Bin Laden: How an Egyptian Doctor Became a Master of Terror," *The New Yorker* (24 September 2002); Zayat, pp. 23–47, 51–86.

20. Osama Rushdi, "How Did the Ideology of the 'Jihad Group' Evolve?" *Al Hayat*, 30 January 2002.

21. Cited by Zayat, *Islamic Groups*, 13 January 2005.

22. Zawahiri, 5 December 2001; Zayat, *Ayman Zawahiri*, pp. 51–86.

23. Zawahiri, 3 December 2001; Zayat, *Ayman Zawahiri*, pp. 89–110.

24. Cited by Zayat, *Islamic Groups*, 13 January 2005.

25. Zayat, *Ayman Zawahiri*, pp. 113–36.

26. Taweel, part 2 of 4, 2 September 2002; Sibai, "Introduction," in Zayat, *Ayman Zawahiri*, p. 17; Zayat, *Ayman Zawahiri*, pp. 51–86, 113–36.

27. Zayat, *Ayman Zawahiri*, pp. 89–110.

28. Zawahiri, 3 December 2001.

29. Rushdi, "How Did the Ideology of the 'Jihad Organization' Evolve?"

30. Ibid.

31. Another irony worth mentioning is that in his subsequent "seminal" two-volume work of more than 1000 pages titled *Talab al-Ilm al-Sharif* (*The Noble Quest for Knowledge*), which is regarded as the ultimate introduction to Islamic Jihad's ways of thinking and actions published in the late 1990s, Sayyid Imam developed his fatwas further and went beyond takfeer Muslims to takfeer almost all existing Islamic and jihadist groups in the Muslim world. The ultimate irony is that when Islamic Jihad leaders tried to censor some inflammatory sections before publication, Sayyid Imam broke up with his own group and poured abuse on former associates for daring to question his wisdom and knowledge; he wrote a new

introduction in which he labeled Islamic Jihad as "a criminal, corrupt un-Islamic gang," and no Muslim, he added, is allowed to belong to such a group. The moral lesson is that armed with a takfeeri ideology, Sayyid Imam could easily excommunicate whomever disagreed with him. Excommunication is an open-ended, totalitarian weapon designed to terrorize with no limits. The Yemeni authorities extradited Sayyid Imam to his homeland, Egypt, where he remains imprisoned. See ibid.; Mohammed al-Shafi'i, "Al Qaeda's Secret E-Mails," *Asharq al-Awsat*, part 4 of 4, 19 June 2005.

32. Taweel, part 2 of 4, 2 September 2002.

33. Islamists, not just jihadis, have not made the transition from being a protest movement to one providing alternative leadership and a well-delineated sociopolitical program. They suffer from a paucity of creative ideas, particularly in the field of political theory and governance and political economy. Their belief in social justice is no substitute to constructing a theory of justice broadly defined that encompasses political-economic freedoms.

34. Cited by Zayat, *Islamic Groups*, 13 January 2005.

35. Taweel, part 3 of 4, 1 September 2002.

36. I will fully examine the splitting up of jihadis later.

37. For a comprehensive perspective on the Algerian civil war that broke out in the early 1990s, see Luis Martinez and John Entelis, *The Algerian Civil War* (New York: Columbia University Press, 2000); Mohammed M. Hafez, "From Marginalization to Massacres: A Political Process Explanation of GIA Violence in Algeria," in Quintan Wiktorowicz, ed., *Islamic Activism: A Social Movement Theory Approach* (Bloomington, Ind., 2004).

38. "The Story of the Afghan Arabs: From the Entry to Afghanistan to the Final Exodus with the Taliban," *Asharq al-Awsat*, 8 and 9 December 2004.

39. "Al Qaeda from Within, as Narrated by Abu Jandal (Nasir al-Bahri), bin Laden's Personal Guard," *Al-Quds al-Arabi*, 26 March 2005.

40. Trial Testimony of Fadl, *United States v. bin Laden*, 7 February 2001 (transcript pp. 321–4).

41. Andrew Higgins and Alan Cullison, "Friend or Foe: The Story of a Traitor to Al Qaeda – Murky Loyalties in Yemen Undo the Betrayal, Who Finds Himself Betrayed – Ominous Words Before 9/11," *The Wall Street Journal*, 20 December 2002.

42. Trial Testimony of Fadl, pp. 255–8.

43. The early seeds of the jihadist movement were planted on university campuses in various Muslim countries. That should not be surprising because the university and the mosque were the only institutions that could shelter dissent. What began as a dissenting and rebellious student movement in the 1970s was transformed into radical underground paramilitary cells and networks by the end of the decade. In many ways the jihadist movement has much in common with other social and political forces in the region and beyond, including the monstrous mutations that occurred within the movement in the 1990s. Zayat, *Islamic*

Groups, 10, 11, 12, 13, and 14 January 2005. See also rejoinders and rebuttals by former jihadis of Zayat's personal portrait: Kamal Habib, "Montasser al-Zayat and the Confusion Between Personal Narrative and Critical Observation," *Al Hayat*, 3 February 2005; Mamdouh Ismail, "*Islamic Groups* Book: A Personal Perspective," *Al Hayat*, 3 February, 2005. For background, see Gilles Kepel, *Jihad: The Trail of Political Islam*, translated by Anthony E. Roberts (Cambridge, Mass.: Harvard University Press, 2002), chapter 4.

44. Zawahiri, "The Bitter Harvest, the Muslim Brotherhood in Sixty Years" (no publisher, no date); Salah, *Narratives of the Jihad Years*, pp. 43–62.

45. Ibid.

46. Zawahiri, *Knights Under the Prophet's Banner*, 10 December 2001.

47. Ibid.

48. Ibid.

49. Zawahiri, *Knights Under the Prophet's Banner*, 5 December 2001.

50. "Declaration of Jihad Against the Americans Occupying the Land of the Two Holy Mosques," a message from bin Laden published in *Al-Islah* (London), 2 September 1996. See also videotape of a private meeting between bin Laden and Saudi visitor Khaled al-Harby that supposedly took place in Qandahar, Afghanistan, and in which bin Laden and his associates boasted and speculated about the lessons of September 11. The videotape was broadcast on American television stations, including *ABC News*, on 13 December 2001.

51. In the 1990s Olivier Roy, a French sociologist and an authority on Islamist movements, published a highly critical book – *The Failure of Political Islam* (Cambridge, Mass.: Harvard University Press, 1994) – that made headlines the world over and challenged the common wisdom prevalent at the time. Roy convincingly argued that the Islamist revolution was already a spent force and, more important, an intellectually and historically bankrupt one. Islamist and jihadist movements neither possessed a concrete political-economic program nor offered a new model of society. They nourished their audience on a rich moral diet, promising heaven but delivering dust. Far from being "the solution" to Muslims' developmental crisis, the radicals' rhetoric about the Islamic revolution, the Islamic state, and the Islamic economy proved to be empty talk, serving as a cheap drug for some of the masses. Nowhere was Islamists' and jihadis' failure more apparent than in their inability to go beyond the founding texts, to be self-critical, and to overcome traditional segmentations and sectarian loyalties. Roy noted that Ayatollah Ruhollah Khomeini's revolutionary Iran, often celebrated as a pioneering Islamist project, made two mistakes. Rather than reaching out to the entire ummah, it immediately locked itself into a Shiite "ghetto" by limiting its appeal to only fellow Shiites, and it quickly reverted to an ultraconservative social model that echoed Saudi Arabia's own brand of Sunni puritanism. The only remnant of Khomeini's vision of a new pan-Islamism was the rhetoric. The radicals hoped to create a new regional order based on Islam, but the hard logic of history, power, states, regimes, and borders is much more enduring than Islamists and jihadis

acknowledge in their propaganda. Roy published these insights at the peak of the Islamist revolutionary moment in 1994. Although interesting and provocative, Roy's thesis is overstated, not least in regard to September 11 and the effects of the American-led invasion and occupation of Iraq.

3. THE RISE OF TRANSNATIONALIST JIHADIS AND THE FAR ENEMY

1. This section borrows from the following sources: Montasser al-Zayat, *Ayman Zawahiri as I Knew Him* [in Arabic] (Cairo, 2002); Zayat, *Islamic Groups: An Inside-Out View* [in Arabic] (serialized by *Al Hayat* in January 2005); Kameel al-Taweel, a series of four lengthy interviews with Egyptian Islamist, Hani al-Sibai, in *Al Hayat*, part 2 of 4, 2 September 2002; Ayman al-Zawahiri, *Knights Under the Prophet's Banner* [in Arabic] (serialized by *Asharq al-Awsat*, December 2001); "Al Qaeda from Within, as Narrated by Abu Jandal (Nasir al-Bahri), bin Laden's Personal Guard" [in Arabic] (serialized by the daily *Al-Quds al-Arabi* (March 2005); Mohammed Salah, *Narratives of the Jihad Years: The Journey of the Afghan Arabs* [in Arabic] (Cairo, 2001); Lawrence Wright, "The Man Behind Bin Laden: How an Egyptian Doctor Became a Master of Terror," *The New Yorker* (24 September 2002).
2. Although in 1987 sheikh Abdullah Azzam, the spiritual father of the Afghan Arabs, planted the seeds of a transnationalist organization called "Al Qaeda al-Sulbah" (the Solid Foundation), the bin Laden network saw the light much later, around the mid-1990s.
3. Alan Cullison, "Inside Al-Qaeda's Hard Drive," *The Atlantic Monthly* (September 2004), pp. 63–4; Mohammed al-Shafi'i, "Zawhiri's Secret Papers," *Asharq al-Awsat*, parts 2 and 7, 14 and 18 December 2002.
4. Shafi'i, "Zawahiri's Secret Papers," *Asharq al-Awsat*, part 7, 19 December 2002; Andrew Higgins and Alan Cullison, "Friend or Foe: The Story of a Traitor to Al Qaeda," *The Wall Street Journal*, 20 December 2002.
5. "The Story of the Afghan Arabs: From the Entry to Afghanistan to the Final Exodus with the Taliban," *Asharq al-Awsat*, 8 December 2004.
6. Some critics might find my claim very sweeping, as the Muslim Brothers in South Asia are known for a "democratic paradox"; they are torn between their internal workings, which are relatively democratic, and their conduct toward national politics, which is reactionary. For example, the Jamaat-i-Islami is known for upholding democratic norms internally even though their commitment to democracy at the state level is questionable.
7. Ibid., 9 December 2004.
8. Ibid.
9. In Egypt, aspirants who want to establish political parties must apply to an official committee with the power to grant or deny license. It is one method by which the government maintains its control over the political arena. As expected, the official committee refused to license the new Wassat Party on the grounds that its

platform contained "nothing new or distinctive." See Rafiq Habib in the daily *Al Shaab*, 4 April 1996. The real reason, however, lies in the government's unwillingness to recognize any Islamist-oriented political entity and permit it to participate in politics. The irony is that although the Wassat Party is composed mainly of young former members of the Brotherhood, it included non-Islamist activists, including women and Copts. Islamist members whom I interviewed put much more stress on the social and political aspects of their program than on the religious one. It was fascinating to compare my interviews with members and leaders of the Brotherhood with those of the Wassat Party. I discerned a critical difference in mind-set, openness, and engagement. The Wassat Party members sounded much more forward-looking, inclusive, and transparent than the Muslim Brothers. Traditionalist Islamists are slowly losing ground to the new Islamists, who have rebelled against the old guard's authoritarian ways and have begun to construct a more democratic Islamist paradigm. On this debate, see the important book by Raymond William Baker, *Islam Without Fear: Egypt and the New Islamists* (Cambridge, Mass., and London: Harvard University Press, 2003).

10. Taweel, a series of four lengthy interviews with Egyptian Islamist, Hani al-Sibai, part 3 of 4, 3 September 2002; Sibai, "Introduction," in Zayat, *Ayman Zawahiri*, p. 16; Zayat, *Ayman Zawahiri*, pp. 113–36; Salah, *Narratives of the Jihad Years*, pp. 65–84.

11. "Al Qaeda from Within," 20 March 2005.

12. See Madawi Al-Rashid, *A History of Saudi Arabia* (Cambridge: Cambridge University Press, 2002); Khaled Abou El Fadl, "The Ugly Modern and the Modern Ugly: Reclaiming the Beautiful in Islam," in Omid Safi, ed., *Progressive Muslims: On Justice, Gender and Pluralism* (Oxford: Oneworld, 2003), pp. 33–77.

13. "Al Qaeda from Within," 31 March 2005.

14. Ibid.

15. Ridwan al-Sayyid, *The Struggle for Islam: Fundamentalism and Reform and International Policies* [in Arabic] (Beirut, 2004); Hicham Chehab and Haytham Mouzahem, "Fusion of Islamist Movements Creates Violent Groups: al-Sayyid," *The Daily Star*, 7 September 2004.

16. "Al Qaeda from Within," 31 March 2005.

17. Ibid., 26 March 2005.

18. Zayat, *Ayman Zawahiri*, pp. 113–36.

19. Ibid.

20. See Imam Abdullah Azzam, "Join the Caravan" [in Arabic]. For an English translation, see "Join the Caravan," http://www.relgioscope.com/info/doc/jihad/azzam_caravan_3_parts.htm.

21. One account claims that in the late 1980s bin Laden broke up with Azzam over the formation of an all-Arab legion of jihadis to advance bin Laden's political ambitions and elevate his status in the eyes of his Saudi patrons. His 1990 proposal to Saudi officials to field an Islamic army of mujahedeen to expel the Iraqis from Kuwait (discussed later in the chapter) supports this line of thinking,

although there is no concrete evidence to prove this hypothesis. Nonetheless, the Afghan experience transformed this shy, low-key man of the Arabian desert into a power player whose appetite expanded significantly as the Afghan war progressed. After the Russian military withdrawal from Afghanistan, bin Laden triumphantly returned home to a hero's welcome in Saudi Arabia. He was still in the official Saudi fold and had not yet exhibited rebellious tendencies. Until the Iraqi invasion of Kuwait, he settled comfortably into his new, elevated status. The upper crust of society, including many royal princes, could not get enough of him. He became a darling of the conservative religious establishment, the moneyed classes, and royalty, who all showered him with attention and respect; they all wanted to rub shoulders with Abu Abdullah (a term of endearment) and listen to his adventures and gripping stories of the mujahedeen, who supposedly terrorized Godless communists. Bin Laden found fame and fortune at home and overnight was transformed into a star with a growing list of potential donors. Bin Laden's new notoriety must have gone to his head and inflated his already supersize ego. Why be content with old glory and past laurels, and why not build an Islamic army that could be deployed in trouble spots on behalf of Muslims worldwide? Why not copy the Afghan model and formalize this army under the command of bin Laden and his crew? Such an army could be easily assembled from many troubled spots in the ummah.

Under the supervision of Azzam, bin Laden had tested these ideas during the last years of the Afghan war and put together a rudimentary core of loyal followers and seasoned fighters who could carry out his orders. Afghan veterans tell stories of bin Laden's associates aggressively and diligently testing and recruiting fighters for membership in this potential Islamic Army, which had not been officially designated as Al Qaeda yet. Only the best of the best passed the rigorous psychological and physical tests. According to Dr. Ayman Faraj, an Afghan veteran who in the late 1980s witnessed firsthand the recruitment techniques for this Islamic Army, at the end of a long training tour, only three of fifty trainees were chosen as members in this organization. Faraj says he was astonished by the recruiters' high standards and the attention they paid to the tiniest details – from a fighter's bad temper to his potential of being a spy. Faraj was even told that the three selected recruits had to undergo more rigorous tests to determine their fitness to join this new Islamic army. Faraj implies that this recruitment process resembled that of the special forces in the American military. See Ayman Sabri Faraj, *Memoirs of an Afghan Arab* [in Arabic] (Cairo, 2002), pp. 24–41.

It is worth stressing that in the midst of the Afghan war bin Laden and his associates worked hard to build an independent power base and a paramilitary organization that could be used after the war. They had an expensive vision to transfer their armed skills and experience from Afghanistan into other theaters to advance and promote their ideological agenda. While fighting the war, they planned for the morning after. They roamed the Afghan fronts freely and recruited some of the most seasoned and fervent foreign veterans, particularly Egyptians, Saudis,

Yemenis, Algerians, Pakistanis, and Chechens. At that early stage they did not register on the American radar screen – or any other intelligence screen for that matter. They were ahead of everyone else in the game, and they set in place a new paramilitary infrastructure. For example, from the beginning, bin Laden developed a reputation for taking care of the mujahedeen, particularly Arab fighters, and of being their financial sponsor. "Abu Abdullah [Osama bin Laden] spent generously on all the necessities of jihad," one Afghan veteran recalls. Bin Laden was the emir of the Afghan Arabs and spared no cost in meeting their needs. Faraj, *Memoirs of an Afghan Arab*, p. 230.

The United States and its ruling Muslim clients underestimated the ideological fervor of the new jihadis and the transformative impact of the Afghan jihad years on young men and minds. Tens of thousands of Afghan veterans say they were dramatically changed by their war experiences, especially the hardship, suffering, and loss of life. As one put it, "for years initially I enjoyed violence but the longer I fought, the less pleasure I took in it, and then it became more of a psychological burden. At this latter stage I lost interest in life and desired death." Faraj, *Memoirs of an Afghan Arab*, p. 283.

Veterans competed against one another to see who would be martyred first and enter the promised heavenly kingdom of eternal peace. Fighters had sweet "dreams" of fulfilling their duty to God and Prophet. The seeds of martyrdom were nourished during the Afghan war years, not in Lebanon, Palestine, or Chechnya. To quote an Afghan Arab, "thousands were infected with the craze of the Afghan jihad. Who could resist the magic of jihad and martyrdom and courage and sacrifice?... Who could resist the dreams of reestablishing the caliphate... a state ruled by the Qur'an... an Islamic state encompassing Muslims from Senegal to the Philippines?" Faraj, *Memoirs of an Afghan Arab*, p. 198. Waves upon waves of veterans were socialized into this mind-set and got used to it. Many of those volunteers and seasoned fighters had become professionalized jihadis, and they subsequently joined organizations like Al Qaeda that were designed to wage "eternal" jihad. Bin Laden and his cohorts found it easy to recruit these indoctrinated veterans and to channel their fervor and rage into other fronts and enemies.

22. "Declaration of War Against the Americans Occupying the Land of the Two Holy Mosques," a message from bin Laden published in *Al Islah*, 2 September 1996.

23. Wright, "The Man Behind Bin Laden." See also Zayat, *Ayman Zawahiri*, pp. 113–36.

24. Abdullah Anas, *The Birth of the Afghan Arabs* [in Arabic] (London, 2002), pp. 90–1.

25. "The Story of the Afghan Arabs," 8 December 2004.

26. Ibid.

27. For example, relying mainly on American intelligence sources, Rohan Gunaratna contends that bin Laden was behind the 1989 assassination of Azzam in Peshawar, and that bin Laden, along with the Egyptian contingent, plotted against Azzam

and ordered his killing, using six members of the Egyptian "family." *Inside Al Qaeda: Global Network of Terror* (New York: Berkley Books, 2002), pp. 22–33.

28. Wright, "The Man Behind Bin Laden."

29. Ibid.

30. According to Yasir al-Sirri, allegedly a leader of Islamic Jihad, Zawahiri's comrades had always seen something missing in him. Zawahiri did not possess a natural sense of command and often deferred to subordinates who were his junior. Montasser al-Zayat, who spent time in prison with Zawahiri and who kept in touch with him afterward, also notes that until the early 1990s, Zawahiri shunned the limelight and did not seem interested in assuming leadership. See Zayat, *Islamic Groups*, parts 2 and 4, 11 and 23 January 2005; Zayat, *Ayman Zawahiri*, pp. 23–47; Wright, "The Man Behind Bin Laden."

31. "Al Qaeda from Within," 31 March 2005.

32. Ibid.; Zayat, *Ayman Zawahiri*, pp. 89–110, 113–36.

33. "Al Qaeda from Within," 30 March 2005.

34. Ibid.

35. Ibid., 31 March 2005.

36. Salah, *Narratives of the Jihad Years*, chapter 5.

37. Sahih al-Bukhari, the most reliable authority on hadiths (Prophetic traditions), who collected Hadith and verified them, quoted the Prophet as saying: "He who commits suicide by throttling shall keep on throttling himself in the Hell-Fire [forever] and he who commits suicide by stabbing himself shall keep on stabbing himself in the Hell-Fire." See Sahih al-Bukhari (K. Jana'iz 82:445–6), translation of Sahih al-Bukhari at www.usc.edu/dept/MSA/fundamentals/ hadithsunnah/bukhari (translated by M. Muhsin Khan, vol. 2, book 23, number 446).

38. Although Azzam wrote that the killing of civilians is permissible under extreme circumstances, it is forbidden as a rule in Islam: "Islam does not (urge its followers) to kill [anyone among the kufar, infidels] except the fighters, and those who supply mushrikeen [kufar] and other enemies of Islam with money or advice, because the Qur'anic verse says: 'And fight in the Cause of Allah those who fight you.... Fighting is a two-sided process; two sides are involved, so whoever fights or joins the fight in any means is to be fought and slain, otherwise he, or she, is to be spared.

"'That is why there is no need to kill women, because of their weakness, unless they fight. Children and monks are not to be killed intentionally.... Abusing/slaying the children and the weak inherits hatred to the coming generations, and is narrated throughout history with tears and blood, and generation after generation would be told about this. And this is exactly what Islam is against.'" See Abdullah Azzam, "Guidlelines and Rules of Jihad" (formatted and edited by Abu Suhayb), http://members.tripod.com/~Suhayb/_The-Jihad-Page.htm.

39. Hani al-Sibai, "Introduction," in Zayat, *Ayman Zawahiri*, p. 14; Zayat, *Ayman Zawahiri*, pp. 113–36.

40. Zayat, *Ayman Zawahiri*, pp. 113–36, 139–72.

41. Ibid., pp. 113–36; "Declaration of War Against the Americans"; Salah, *Narratives of the Jihad Years*, pp. 65–84.
42. "Declaration of War Against the Americans."
43. "Al Qaeda from Within," 31 March 2005.
44. Ibid.
45. Ibid.
46. Ibid.
47. Ibid.
48. Ibid.
49. Ibid.
50. Ibid.
51. Ibid.
52. Ibid.
53. In 2001 an ABC television news team interviewed Prince Faisal for several hours, a few minutes of which was aired. In the unedited version of the interview, Faisal talks in detail about bin Laden's proposal.
54. Zayat, *Ayman Zawahiri*, pp. 89–110.
55. "Declaration of War Against the Americans."
56. Ibid.
57. Ibid.

4 · SPLITTING UP OF JIHADIS

1. Mohammed al-Shafi'i, "Al-Qaeda's Secret Emails," *Asharq al-Awsat* (part 3), 14 June 2005. The precise dates of Zawahiri's letters to al-Jama'a were not very clear, but he sent the letter through a trusted operative between 1997 and 1999.
2. Ibid.
3. Ibid.
4. Mohammed al-Shafi'i, "Zawahiri's Secret Papers," *Asharq al-Awsat* (parts 1, 2, 3, 4, 5, 6, and 7), 12, 16, 17, 18, and 19 December 2002 (those articles were translated into English in 2005 under the title: "Al-Qaeda's Secret Emails"; see note 1). See Andrew Higgins and Alan Cullison's series of articles in *The Wall Street Journal*, 31 December 2001, 16 January 2002, 2 and 23 July 2002, 2 and 20 August 2002, 11 November 2002, and 20 December 2002; Allan Cullison, "Inside Al-Qaeda's Hard Drive," *The Atlantic Monthly*, September 2004, pp. 55–70. The computers were purchased by a *Wall Street Journal* reporter for $1100; they contained more than 1750 text and video files on their hard drives.
5. Shafi'i, "Zawahiri's Secret Papers," part 5, 17 December 2002.
6. Ibid.
7. Ibid.; Shafi'i, "Zawahiri's Secret Papers," part 1, 13 December 2002. See also Andrew Higgins and Alan Cullison, "Files Found: A Computer in Kabul Yields a Chilling Array of Al Qaeda Memos," *The Wall Street Journal*, 31 December 2001.
8. Ibid.
9. Ibid.

10. Some observers interpreted Ahmad Taha's presence as signaling his group's adherence to Al Qaeda. But senior leaders of the Islamic Group rebutted the charge and denied having any prior knowledge of Taha's signature. Mohammed Salah, "The Violence of Jihad Turns Outward and al-Jama'a Initiative Proceeds Successfully," *Al Hayat*, 28 December 1998; Mohammed Salah, *Narratives of the Jihad Years: The Journey of the Afghan Arabs* [in Arabic] (Cairo, 2001), chapter 5.

11. Ayman al-Zawahiri, *Knights Under the Prophet's Banner* [in Arabic] (serialized by *Asharq al-Awsat*, part 8, 9 December 2001).

12. Ibid.

13. Cited in the "Declaration of War Against the Americans Occupying the Land of the Two Holy Places," a message from bin Laden published in *Al Islah* (London), 2 September 1996.

14. By the end of the decade, Egypt reportedly held about 30,000 alleged jihadis, including family members and sympathizers. Although we have no precise numbers for incarcerated jihadis in Algeria, they numbered in the thousands.

15. Andrew Higgins and Alan Cullison, "Terrorist's Odyssey: Saga of Dr. Zawahiri Illuminates Roots of Al Qaeda Terror," *The Wall Street Journal*, 2 July 2002; Shafi'i, "Zawahiri's Secret Papers," part 2, 14 December 2002.

16. Higgins and Cullison, "Terrorist's Odyssey"; Shafi'i, "Zawahiri's Secret Papers"; Mohammed al-Shafi'i, "Zawahiri Expelled Two Jihadist Leaders . . .," *Asharq al-Awsat*, 6 June 2002.

17. Hani al-Sibai, "Introduction," in Montasser al-Zayat, *Ayman Zawahiri as I Knew Him* (Cairo, 2002), pp. 14–15; Shafi'i, "Zawahiri Expelled Two Jihadist Leaders"; Shafi'i, "Zawahiri's Secret Papers," part 1, 13 December 2002.

18. Sibai, "Introduction," in Zayat, *Ayman Zawahiri*, pp. 14–15; Higgins and Cullison, "Terrorist's Odyssey"; Zayat, *Ayman Zawahiri*, pp. 113–36, 175–208; Wright, "The Man Behind Bin Laden," pp. 81–2; Salah, "Narratives of the Jihad Years," chapter 5.

19. Shafi'i, "Zawahiri's Secret Papers," part 2, 14 December 2002.

20. Ibid., part 1, 13 December 2002.

21. "A Moment with Thomas Kean '57," *Princeton Alumni Weekly*, 23 March 2005.

22. *The 9/11 Commission Report: Final Report of the National Commission on Terrorist Attacks Upon the United States* (New York: W. W. Norton, 2004), pp. 108–9.

23. Ibid., pp. 101–2; President William J. Clinton, "Commencement Address at the United States Naval Academy in Annapolis, Maryland," 22 May 1998.

24. Bill Clinton, *My Life* (New York: Knopf, 2004), p. 799.

25. Richard A. Clarke, *Against All Enemies: Inside America's War on Terror* (New York: Free Press, 2004), p. 184; *The 9/11 Commission Report*, pp. 116–20.

26. Madeleine Albright with Bill Woodward, *Madam Secretary* (New York: Miramax Books, 2003), p. 374.

27. Higgins and Cullison, "Terrorist's Odyssey"; Higgins and Cullison, "Strained Alliance: Al Qaeda's Sour Days in Afghanistan," *The Wall Street Journal*, 2 August 2002.

28. Clarke, *Against All Enemies*, p. 184.
29. Cited in ibid., pp. 211–12.
30. Clinton, *My Life*, p. 798.
31. Clarke, *Against All Enemies*, p. 184.
32. Ibid., pp. 197–8.
33. Ibid., pp. 197–8; *The 9/11 Commission Report*, p. 127; Daniel Benjamin and Steven Simon, *The Age of Sacred Terror* (New York: Random House, 2002), pp. 261, 264.
34. It is worth mentioning that the CIA-led arrests in Albania occurred a few weeks before the attacks on the U.S. embassies in Kenya and Tanzania. On 4 August 1998 Zawahiri faxed a letter to an Arabic-language newspaper in London in which he denounced the CIA and vowed that America would soon receive a response "in the only language that they understand." Three days later Al Qaeda blew up the U.S. embassies, killing more than 220, mostly Africans. The blasts, according to court testimony in New York in 2001, were planned by Al Qaeda's military chief, Mohammed Atef (alias Abu Hafs), who was also a senior lieutenant in Zawahiri's Tanzim al-Jihad. Higgins and Cullison, "Terrorist's Odyssey"; Zayat, *Ayman Zawahiri*, pp. 113–36; Shafi'i, "Zawahiri Expelled Two Jihadist Leaders"; Shafi'i, "Zawahiri Secret Papers," part 1, 13 December 2002; *The 9/11 Commission Report*, p. 127. See also International Crisis Group Middle East and North Africa Briefing, *Islamism in North Africa II: Egypt's Opportunity* (Cairo and Brussels, 20 April 2004), p. 6.
35. Higgins and Cullison, "Terrorist's Odyssey"; Higgins and Cullison, "Files Found"; Cullison, "Inside Al-Qaeda's Hard Drive," pp. 64–5; Shafi'i, "Zawahiri's Secret Papers," part 2, 13 December 2002.
36. Higgins and Cullison, "Terrorist's Odyssey"; Cullison, "Inside Al-Qaeda's Hard Drive," p. 65; Shafi'i, "Zawahiri's Secret Papers," part 2, 13 December 2002.
37. Higgins and Cullison, "Terrorist's Odyssey."
38. According to U.S. authorities, Abdullah Ahmad Abdullah, a lieutenant in Islamic Jihad, was involved in the U.S. embassy bombings in Kenya and Tanzania and the killing of American soldiers in Somalia in 1993. Cullison, "Inside Al-Qaeda's Hard Drive," pp. 65–6; Alan Cullison and Andrew Higgins, "Terror Tour: How Al Qaeda Agent Scouted Attack Sites in Israel and Egypt," *The Wall Street Journal*, 16 January 2002; Shafi'i, "Zawahiri's Secret Papers," part 4, 16 December 2002.
39. Shafi'i, "Zawahiri's Secret Papers," part 4, 16 December 2002.
40. Shafi'i, "Zawahiri's Secret Papers," part 2, 13 December 2002; Higgins and Cullison, "Terrorist's Odyssey."
41. The letter was obtained from the Al Qaeda computer in Kabul by *The Wall Street Journal* and reproduced by Cullison, "Inside Al-Qaeda's Hard Drive," pp. 66–7.
42. Higgins and Cullison, "Terrorist's Odyssey."
43. Cullison and Higgins, "Terror Tour."
44. Ibid.

45. Higgins and Cullison, "Terrorist's Odyssey"; Cullison, "Inside Al-Qaeda's Hard Drive," p. 67.

46. Salah, *Narratives of the Jihad Years*, chapter 5.

47. "Al Qaeda from Within, as Narrated by Abu Jandal (Nasir al-Bahri), bin Laden's Personal Guard," *Al-Quds al-Arabi*, 26 March 2005.

48. *The 9/11 Commission Report*, p. 232.

49. The term *dar al-islam* comes from an Islamic legal distinction between those lands that observe Islamic law and those that do not, which are called *dar al-harb* (the House of War). Richard Bulliet and Fawaz A. Gerges, eds., "A Recruiting Tape of Osama bin Laden: Excerpts and Analyses," at www.ciaonet.org (Columbia International Affairs Online), October 2001. Professor Bulliet and the author translated and analyzed a three-hour videotape – which for several months prior to the September 11 attacks circulated underground in the Arab world – calling on Muslims to wage jihad against crusaders and Jews. Produced on behalf of bin Laden and prominently featuring his image, words, and ideas, this original tape was designed to recruit young Arab men to journey to Afghanistan and train for the coming war in defense of Islam.

50. Ibid.

51. Ibid.

52. "Al Qaeda from Within, as Narrated by Abu Jandal (Nasir al-Bahri)," 26 March 2005.

53. Ibid.

54. Ibid.

55. "The Story of the Afghan Arabs: From the Entry to Afghanistan to the Final Exodus with the Taliban," *Asharq al-Awsat*, 9 December 2004.

56. "Al Qaeda from Within," 30 March 2005.

57. Ibid.

58. Ibid.

59. *The 9/11 Commission Report*, p. 250.

5. THE AFTERMATH: THE WAR WITHIN

1. Mohammed al-Shafi'i, "Seif al-Adl: Al-Qaeda's Ghost," *Asharq al-Awsat*, 1 June 2005. See the important document by Seif al-Adl, Al Qaeda's military commander, in which he chronicles al-Zarqawi's rise in the organization in a recently released book on Zarqawi, which includes personal testaments by some of Zarqawi's closest jihadist associates; the book is serialized in the Arabic-language newspaper *Al-Quds al-Arabi*: Fu'ad Hussein, *Al-Zarqawi: The Second Generation of Al Qaeda*, parts 7, 8, and 9, 21, 22, and 23 May 2004.

2. The complete text of the fatwa appeared on www.islam-online.net/ (27 September 2001).

3. *Asharq al-Awsat* (for the Arabic text, see December 2004; for an English translation, see 29 June and 1, 6, and 10 July 2005).

4. Al-Shafi'i, "Seif al-Adl."

5. *Asharq al-Awsat*, 8 December 2004 and 29 June 2005.

6. Ibid., 9 December 2004 and 1 July 2005.

7. Ibid.

8. Ibid., 6 July 2005.

9. Ibid.

10. Ibid., 10 July 2005.

11. Ibid., 6 July 2005.

12. Ibid.

13. Ibid., 1 July 2005.

14. Cited by Alan Cullison, "Inside Al-Qaeda's Hard Drive," *The Atlantic Monthly* (September 2004), pp. 59–60.

15. *Asharq al-Awsat*, 29 June and 1 July 2005.

16. Ibid., 1 July 2005.

17. Cited by Hussein, *Al-Zarqawi*, part 4, 19 June 2004.

18. The four books, written in Arabic and widely distributed and disseminated in Egypt and the Arab world, were reviewed and approved by all of the "historical leaders" of Islamic Group. Their individual titles are *Initiative of Cessation of Violence, Shedding Light on the Mistakes Committed in the Jihad, The Ban on Narrow Positions on Religion and on the Excommunications of Muslims*, and *Advice and Clarification to Rectify Concepts of Those Who Assume Responsibility for Society* (Cairo, 2002). The books were published in 2002.

19. "*Asharq al-Awsat* Talks to the Leader of Egyptian Islamic Group Inside a Prison...," *Asharq al-Awsat*, 15 and 16 July 2003. See the series of interviews in the pro-government *Al-Mussawar*, 21 and 28 June 2002, which were lengthy and conducted personally by the editor-in-chief, Makram Mohammed Ahmad, a fact that underlined the regime's interest in Islamic Group's "self-criticism"; see Paul Schemm, "Egypt Lets the World Know that the Gamaa Islamiya is out of the Terrorism Business," *Cairo Times*, 27 June–3 July 2002. See also International Crisis Group Middle East and North Africa Briefing, *Islamism in North Africa II: Egypt's Opportunity*, 20 April 2004.

20. Mohammed al-Shafi'i, "An Islamic Group Leader Criticizes from Holland 'the Statement of Apology'...," *Asharq al-Awsat*, 22 June 2002; Kameel al-Taweel, "Hani al-Sibai to *Al Hayat*: Al-Jama'a's Leaders Shed Blood... and Must Step Aside," *Al Hayat*, 5 September 2003; Gamal Sultan, "Al-Jama'a's Revisions in Egypt Await Similar Reviews by Other Groups," *Al Hayat*, 7 April 2002.

21. Derbala, *Al Qaeda Strategy, Asharq al-Awsat*, 6, 7, 8, and 9 August 2003; Ibrahim, *Islam and the Challenges of the Twenty-First Century, Asharq al-Awsat*, 21, 23, 24, 25, 26, 27, and 28 June 2004. In August 2003 *Asharq al-Awsat* summarized *Al Qaeda Strategy*, and in January 2004 it published the entire book.

22. Derbala, *Al Qaeda Strategy, Asharq al-Awsat*, 6 August 2003 and 12 January 2004; Ibrahim, *Islam and the Challenges of the Twenty-First Century, Asharq al-Awsat*, 21 and 24 June 2004.

23. Derbala, *Al Qaeda Strategy*, *Asharq al-Awsat*, 6 August 2003 and 12 January 2004; Ibrahim, *Islam and the Challenges of the Twenty-First Century*, *Asharq al-Awsat*, 21 and 24 June 2004.

24. Derbala, *Al Qaeda Strategy*, *Asharq al-Awsat*, 6 August 2003 and 12 January 2004.

25. Ibid., *Asharq al-Awsat*, 6 and 8 August 2003.

26. Ibid., *Asharq al-Awsat*, 8 and 9 August 2003.

27. Ibrahim, *Islam and the Challenges of the Twenty-First Century*, *Asharq al-Awsat*, 21 June 2004.

28. Ibid.

29. "The Inevitability of Confrontation," compiled by Rifaat Sayyed Ahmed, ed., *The Militant Prophet: The Revolutionaries*, vol. II [in Arabic] (London: Riad El-Rayyes Books, 1991), pp. 244–72.

30. Ibrahim, *Islam and the Challenges of the Twenty-First Century*, *Asharq al-Awsat*, 23 June 2004.

31. Ibid., 23 and 27 June 2004.

32. Ibid., 23 and 27 June 2004.

33. Ibid., 24 June 2004.

34. Ibid.

35. Ibid., 26 June 2004.

36. Ibid., 26 and 27 June 2004.

37. Ibid., 27 June 2004.

38. *Al-Mussawar*, 8 August 2003; *Asharq al-Awsat*, 15 and 16 July 2003. Compare Zuhdi's hard-nosed realism with bin Laden and Zawahiri's fantasies and delusions. Although he was imprisoned and isolated for more than two decades, Zuhdi's analysis of world politics is much more nuanced and complex than that of his former associates, who were free and had considerable resources at their disposal.

39. *Asharq al-Awsat*, 15 and 16 July 2003.

40. Ibid.

41. "Chapters from the Charter of Islamic Political Action," compiled by Rifaat Sayed Ahmed, ed., *The Militant Prophet: The Rejectionists*, vol. I [in Arabic] (London: Riad El-Rayyes Books: 1991), pp. 165–78.

42. Taweel, "Hani al-Sibai to *Al Hayat*," *Al Hayat*, 5 September 2003.

43. Ibid.; Mohammed al-Shafi'i, "A Fundamentalist Calls for Dissolving 'al-Jama'a al-Islamiya'. . .," *Asharq al-Awast*, 8 August 2003; Taweel, "Hani al-Sibai to *Al Hayat*," *Al Hayat*, 5 September 2003.

44. Mohammed al-Shafi'i, "Leader of Egyptian al-Jama'a al-Islamiya Criticizes from Holland . . . ," *Asharq al-Awast*, 22 June 2002; Al-Shafi'i, "Former Spokesperson of Egyptian 'al-'Jama'a al-Islamiya' . . . ," *Asharq al-Awsat*, 8 July 2002.

45. Shafi'i, "Leader of Egyptian al-Jama'a al-Islamiya Criticizes."

46. "U.S. 'Entering a New Phase' in War on Terror," The ABC News Investigative Unit, 28 April 2005. See State Department Country Reports on Terrorism 2004 (State Department).

47. Zayat, *Ayman Zawahiri as I Knew Him* (Cairo, 2002); *Islamic Groups: An Inside-Out View* (serialized by *Al Hayat* on 10, 11, 12, 13, and 14 January 2005).

48. Zayat, *Ayman Zawahiri*, chapters 1 and 2.

49. Nazih N. Ayubi, *Political Islam: Religion and Politics in the Arab World* (London and New York: Routledge, 1991).

50. Zayat, *Ayman Zawahiri*, chapter 4.

51. Ibid., chapters 4 and 6.

52. Ibid., chapter 5.

53. Ibid.

54. Ibid.

55. Ibid.

56. Kameel al-Taweel, "Abu Qatada: Zawahiri 'Wise Man of the Jihadist Movement'..." *Al Hayat*, 12 May 2004.

57. While waiting for interviews in Zayat's office in Cairo, I observed a procession of jihadis' wives and families seeking assistance from the Islamist attorney.

58. Andrew Higgins, Karby Leggett, and Alan Cullison, "Uploading Terror: How al Qaeda Put Internet in Service of Global Jihad," *The Wall Street Journal*, 11 November 2002.

59. al-Shafi'i, "Seif Al-Adl."

60. Kameel al-Taweel, "Abu Qatada to *Al Hayat*: Narrating His Journey and Relationship with Al Qaeda," *Al Hayat*, 28 November 2002; Taweel, "Abu Qatada"; Higgins, Leggett, and Cullison, "Uploading Terror." Abu Qatada is not the only radical voice that heaps praise on bin Laden and Zawahiri. Since 2001 several books written in Arabic by Al Qaeda sympathizers have come out in defense of bin Laden, Zawahiri, and their associates and in opposition to the United States. For a representative sample, see Rifaat Sayed Ahmed and Omru al-Shubaki, *The Future of Islamist Movements after 11 September* (Damascus, 2005); Rifaat Sayed Ahmed, *Qur'an and Sword: Files from Political Islam, a Documented Study* (Cairo, 2003); Mohammed Abbas, *Yes, It Is a War Against Islam* (Cairo, 2003); Nabil Sharaf al-Din, *Bin Laden: The Taliban, the Afghan Arabs and International Fundamentalism* (Cairo, 2002). These four books are big on polemics and poor on facts. They advance no substantive arguments and are conspiratorial; borrowing a cliché from their sloganeering, they could be summarized as "long live Al Qaeda and down with USA!"

61. Hani al-Sibai, "Introduction," in Zayat, *Ayman Zawahiri*, pp. 9–19; Sibai, "Call for Self-Reflection and Assessment of the History of the Islamist Movement," *Al Hayat*, 4 February 2002.

62. See Kameel al-Taweel, a series of four lengthy interviews with Egyptian Islamist, Hani al-Sibai, *Al Hayat*, 1, 2, 3, and 4 September 2002.

63. Taweel, a series of four lengthy interviews with Egyptian Islamist, Hani al-Sibai, *Al Hayat*, part 4 of 4, 4 September 2002.

64. Ibid.

65. Ibid.

66. Ibid.

67. Ibid.

68. "Osama Rushdi, Former Media Official and Member of the Shura Council of 'Al-Jama'a al-Islamiya': Bin Laden's Speech Is Provocative and Full of Terms Only Muslims Understand," *Asharq al-Awsat*, 25 January 2002.

69. Ibid.

70. Zawahiri, *Al Walaa wa Al Baraa, or Loyalty to Islam and Disavowal to Its Enemies*, obtained by *Al Hayat*, 14 January 2003.

71. Ibid.

72. Ibid.

73. Ibid.

74. *Asharq al-Awsat*, 8 December 2004.

75. Susan B. Glasser, "Terror War Seen Shifting to Match Evolving Enemy," *The Washington Post*, 28 May 2005.

76. For the National Security Presidential Directives and development of strategy against Al Qaeda after September 11, see *The 9/11 Commission Report: Final Report of the National Commission on Terrorist Attacks Upon the United States* (New York: W. W. Norton, 2004), particularly chapter 10. The commission interviewed a wide range of Bush senior aides, including the vice president and the president himself, to shed light on policy deliberation and evolution. White House Transcript, President Bush's Address to a Joint Session of Congress and the American People, 20 September 2001.

77. Since September 11, American officials and outside analysts agree, nearly 65 percent of Al Qaeda's senior lieutenants have been killed or captured. More than 3000 Al Qaeda suspects have been arrested from Tunisia to Indonesia. Important logistical networks in Spain, Italy, Germany, Britain, Morocco, Yemen, Saudi Arabia, Pakistan, and elsewhere have been dismantled. According to U.S. intelligence officials, most of the operatives who helped plan the September 11 attacks have been accounted for, and those who have been captured have described their roles in the attacks. Al Qaeda's financial assets are being steadily frozen. In the 1990s much of the strength and growth of the organization resulted from its ability to operate from a geographical base with impunity, first in Sudan and then in Afghanistan. The training camps, safe houses, and caves were the critical infrastructure for Al Qaeda; that base is now gone. Moreover, hardly any state, regardless of its political orientation, can afford to aid or harbor Al Qaeda fugitives, a testament to the effectiveness of the multilateral coalition created after September 11. The deepening of regional and international cooperation against terrorism has netted scores of Al Qaeda operatives in Pakistan, Yemen, Morocco, Malaysia, Saudi Arabia, Indonesia, and Europe. Bin Laden's surviving operatives are forced to operate underground in a hostile world with no official refuge. The leadership is hibernating deep underground. Bin Laden reportedly appears to no longer be in regular communication with his field lieutenants, and Zawahiri is practically running the organization, according to American officials. In a 2003 report, the

London-based Control Risks Group said that Al Qaeda's network has been largely dismantled and is leaderless: "The al-Qaida organization that existed on Sept. 22 (2001)... really no longer exists, it's been largely dismantled," asserted one of the report's authors. These breakthroughs are the result of multilateral cooperation among the United States and Muslim and European countries, including intelligence sharing, joint military operations, and civil society participation. Multilateralism, not unilateralism, lies behind America's success in the fight against the Al Qaeda militants. Unfortunately, America's expansion of the war and its unilateral strategy of military "preemption" diluted the unity and cohesiveness of the global coalition and energized Al Qaeda's remnants and sympathizers. See *The New York Times*, 11 September 2003; Fawaz A. Gerges and Christopher Isham, "Sign of Weakness," ABCNews.com, 22 November 2003; "Report Evaluates al-Qaida Risks Worldwide," *Associated Press*, 11 November 2003; Christopher Isham, "Terror Tape Not Recent," ABCNews.com, 23 September 2003; Annual reports of the London-based International Institute of Strategic Studies, 2003 and 2004.

78. Derbala, *Al Qaeda Strategy*, *Asharq al-Awsat*, 12 January 2004.
79. "Hassan al-Turabi Writes from His Prison on Political Terrorism and Assesses the Attacks on America," *Al Hayat*, 18, 19, and 20 January 2002.
80. Ibid.
81. See the chapter titles of one of his books: "America Does Not Know the Meaning of Justice"; "America Searches for a Victim"; "I Accuse America of Terrorism"; and so on. Sayyed Mohammed Hussein Fadlallah, *The Unsacred Versus the Sacred: America and the Banner of International Terrorism* [in Arabic] (Beirut, 2003). In the early 1980s, American authorities accused Fadlallah, as the alleged founder of Hizbollah, of sanctioning kidnapping American citizens and attacking U.S. troops in Lebanon; likewise, Fadlallah asserts that the CIA hired Lebanese agents and tried to assassinate him. There exists a blood feud between Fadlallah and American officials.
82. Unpublished text by Fadlallah in Ahmad Ayash, *After Afghanistan: Islam – Where To?* [in Arabic] (Beirut, 2002), p. 29.
83. Fadlallah, *The Unsacred Versus the Sacred*, pp. 19–393; "Fadlallah to *Al Hayat*: There Is No Clash of Cultures with the West but a Struggle Against Arrogance," *Al Hayat*, 15 September 2002, p. 10; "Conversations and Texts by Fadlallah," in Ayash, *After Afghanistan*, pp. 11–34.
84. Qardawi's complete statement in English and Arabic appeared on www.islam-online.net (13 September 2001).
85. Ibid.
86. For example, see the important fatwa by a group of leading Islamic scholars published in Arabic and English on www.islam-online.net (27 September 2001), which received wide publicity in the Arab press. See also the fatwa by sheikh Nasir al-Din al-Albani, a Saudi Salafi, "Suicide Bombing in the Scales of Islamic Law," which appeared on www.muslimtents.com.

87. After September 11 the influence of ultraconservative clerics waned a little and Muslim governments pressured by the United States cracked down against pulpit extremism. In particular, Saudi Arabia and Yemen, two countries that supplied the bulk of Al Qaeda's operatives, dismissed hundreds of radical preachers and retrained thousands. Centrist clerics, like Tantawi, have become more visible and vocal in their condemnation of militancy and extremism.

88. Mshari Al-Zaydi, "An Interview with Sheikh Abdul-Mohsen Bin Nasser Al-Obeikan," *Asharq al-Awsat*, 24 May 2005.

89. The religious establishment found itself pressed between a rock – structural constraints imposed by rulers – and a hard place – demands by Muslim public opinion to act as the moral conscience of the nation. Before September 11, the ulema had challenged neither their official patrons nor jihadis, instead preferring the safe comfort of religious rituals. Their reluctance to do so empowered ultraconservative and militant clergymen whose sermons and audiocassettes fired the imagination of young men and drove them into jihadis' arms. Ultraconservative clerics directly and indirectly served as the spiritual gurus of militant Islamists; they became most influential and powerful and had a near monopoly on access to the media because governments relied on them to project a pious face. That contributed to the further Islamization of public space and culture in the 1980s and 1990s.

90. The existing alliance between the ruling elite and the religious establishment led to the consolidation of the authoritarian political structure and created a vacuum of legitimate political and religious authority that militants try to fill.

91. Tariq al-Bishri, *The Arabs in the Face of Aggression* [in Arabic] (Cairo, 2002), chapters 1, 2, and 3. Bishri criticized all jihadist groups who use terror to Islamize state and society because, in his opinion, they possess a distorted understanding of religion and politics.

92. Ibid., chapters 1, 2, and 3.

93. Ahmed Kamal Abu al-Magd, "Terrorism and Islam and the Future of the International System" [in Arabic], *Weghat Nazar*, vol. 34 (November 2001), pp. 14–18.

94. Abu al-Magd, "Terrorism and Islam," pp. 14–18. See also Abu al-Magd, "On Modern Religious Thought," *Weghat Nazar*, vol. 38 (March 2002), pp. 4–5.

95. Abu al-Magd, "Terrorism and Islam," pp. 14–18; Abu al-Magd, "On Modern Religious Thought," pp. 4–5.

96. Adonis, "How Do We Join the Genealogy of Light?" *Al Hayat*, 12 December 2002.

97. "The Arabs After the September Attacks: Image and Discourse," Working Paper (2001), pp. 6–7.

98. Ridwan al-Sayyid, "On the Anniversary of 9/11: What to Do with the Killings in the Name of Islam," *Al Hayat*, 11 September 2004.

99. For a representative sample of commentaries, see the daily papers, *Al Hayat*, *Asharq al-Awsat*, *An-Nahar*, *As-Safir*, *Al-Ahram*, *Daily Star*, and *Jordan Times*.

For weekly and biweekly magazines, see *Weghat Nazar, Al-Ahram Weekly, Al-Mussawar*, and *Al Wasat*.

100. Sadik J. al-Azm, "Time Out of Joint: Western Dominance, Islamist Terror, and the Arab Imagination," *Boston Review* (October/November 2004), p. 2.

101. Ibid., pp. 1–2.

102. Ibid, p. 5.

103. Glasser, "Terror War Seen Shifting to Match Evolving Enemy."

104. *The New York Times*, 25 February 2004 and 22 and 28 March 2004; Fawaz A. Gerges, "Dismantling al-Qaida?" *The Baltimore Sun*, 23 November 2003.

105. Steve Coll and Susan B. Glasser, "Attacks Bear Earmarks of Evolving Al Qaeda: Targets, Timing Both Familiar," *The Washington Post*, 8 July 2005.

106. "Wife of Abd al-Karim al-Majati: We Entered Saudi Arabia with Fake Qatari Passports … ," *Asharq al-Awasat*, 18 June 2005.

107. Al Qaeda and local affiliates belatedly recognized the political and moral fallout of killing Muslims and published a purported letter on an Islamist Web site denying responsibility for the Saudi bombings. Authentic or not, Al Qaeda's denials show confusion and disarray and a loss of centralized control by the senior leadership. Historically, the organization had taken responsibility for suicide bombings, but it had rarely released a statement saying it was not involved in a particular operation. In a subsequent attack on an Al-Khobar office housing Western oil firms in May 2004, militants tried to separate Muslims from non-Muslims and asked residents and employees if they were Muslims: "We only want to hurt Westerners and Americans. Can you tell us where we can find them here?" A purported statement by militants claiming responsibility for the attack on Al-Khobar put it crudely: "It is worth mentioning that the holy warriors were very careful not to shed any Muslim blood as they differentiated between them and the infidel crusaders." Although morally repugnant, the forced distinction made by Al Qaeda militants testifies to the predicament in which they find themselves. The attacks against the lesser kufr have alienated and estranged Muslim public opinion further, the very constituency Al Qaeda desperately needs in order to overcome the wall of opposition erected by civil society leaders and opinion makers. When asked about her husband's role in the killing of Muslims, the wife of al-Majati retorted angrily: "To say that al-Majati fought the Americans I say yes, but to say that he killed Muslims I say no and a thousand times no." "Wife of Abd al-Karim al-Majati"; Sarah El Deeb, "Tape Claims Responsibility for Arab Attack," *Associated Press*, 31 May 2004; Donna Abu-Nasr, "Saudi Commandos Free Dozens Held at Resort," *Associated Press*, 30 May 2004; "Letter: Al-Qaida Denies Bombings in Iraq," *Associated Press*, 3 March 2004. Most of Al Qaeda's letters, statements, audio-, and videotapes are made available on sympathetic Islamist Web sites or are sent to Arabic television stations, particularly Al Jazeera and Al Arabiya, or to the Arabic dailies, *Al-Quds al-Arabi* and *Al Hayat*.

108. International Crisis Group Middle East Report, *Saudi Arabia Backgrounder: Who Are the Islamists*, no. 31, 21 September 2004; Gerard Seenan, "Joining

al-Qaida? Please Think Again," *The Guardian*, 7 February 2005; Martin Sieff, "Learning from the Saudis," *United Press International*, 4 January 2005; "Al-Qaeda's Diminishing Returns in the Peninsula," The Jamestown Foundation, *Terrorism Focus*, vol. II, no. 1 (7 January 2005); Neil Macfarquhar, "Saudis Support a Jihad in Iraq, Not Back Home: Riyadh Bombing Stirs Widespread Outrage," *The New York Times*, 23 April 2004; Dominic Evans, "Two Years After Bombings, Saudi Al Qaeda Weakened," *Reuters*, 11 May 2005; "FBI Praises Saudi Crackdown on Militants," *Associated Press*, 11 May 2005; Anthony Cordesman, "Saudi Arabia and the Struggle Against Terrorism," http://www.saudi-us-relations.org/newsletter2005/saudi-relations-interest-04-11b; Abdullah al-Shihri, "Saudi Forces Kill al-Qaida Leader," *Associated Press*, 3 July 2005.

109. Michael Holden, "Al Qaeda 'To Disintegrate' in 2 Years – UK Adviser," *Reuters*, 10 November 2004. This is not meant to underestimate the security nuisance that Al Qaeda poses to regional and international security. On September 11, the organization launched a coordinated set of spectacular bombings with humble resources at its disposal; they cost only half a million U.S. dollars and nineteen young men's lives. A contingent of 500 committed jihadis organized in autonomous cells and positioned in strategic theaters around the world could spread panic and terror worldwide. The post–September 2001 attacks in Indonesia, Tunisia, Turkey, Saudi Arabia, Madrid, Egypt, London, and elsewhere are cases in point. Although degraded, Al Qaeda's nerve center appears to be alive and functioning.

6. THE IRAQ WAR: PLANTING THE SEEDS OF AL QAEDA'S SECOND GENERATION?

1. "To the Muslims in Iraq in Particular and the [Islamic] Nation [ummah] in General," *Al-Sahab* (Institute for Media Production), 27 May 2004. See also Fou'ad Hussein, "Al-Zarqawi... : The Second Generation of Al Qaeda – Seif al-Adl's Testament," *Al-Quds al-Arabi*, part 9, 23 May 2005.

2. Ibid.

3. In this section I rely on the following primary sources (I have grouped them together to avoid too many citations): Kameel al-Taweel, "Al-Zarqawi: Islamic Government in Iraq as a Way Station to Overthrow Neighboring Regimes," *Al Hayat*, 19 September 2004; Taweel, "Al-Zarqawi Present and His Followers Everywhere," *Al Hayat*, 5 September 2004; "'Emir' of the Fallujah Fighters (Abu Osama) to *Al Wasat*: Every Mujahid in Iraq Is a Member of Al Qaeda," *Al Wasat*, 3 May 2004; Taweel, "Bin Laden Fails in Afghanistan... but 'Enter Iraq Through the Zarqawi Gate,'" *Al Hayat*, 19 October 2004; "Al-Zarqawi's Absence Mixes Jihadis' Cards in Iraq," *Al Hayat*, 28 May 2005; Maamoun Youssef, "Al-Qaida Announces Iraqi Suicide Squad," *Associated Press*, 21 June 2005;

"Abu Mus'ab Al-Zarqawi: Collateral Killing of Muslims Is Legitimate," http://www.memri.org/bin/opener_latest.cgi?ID=SD91705, 11 June 2005; "The Iraqi Al-Qaida Organization: Self Portrait," http://www.memri.org/bin/opener_latest.cgi?ID=SD88405, 24 March 2005; Laura Jordan and Katherine Shrader, "Bin Laden Enlisting Al-Zarqawi for Attacks," Associated Press, 1 April 2005; Peter Bergen, "The Most Dangerous Terrorist," International Herald Tribune, 29 June 2004; "Al Zarqawi Group Vows Allegiance to Bin Laden," Associated Press, 17 October 2004; Dan Murphy, "In Iraq, a Clear-Cut bin Laden–Zarqawi Alliance," The Christian Science Monitor, 31 December 2004; Michael Holden, "Al-Qaeda 'To Disintegrate' in 2 Years," Reuters, 10 November 2004; "Purported Bin Laden Tape Calls for Boycott," Associated Press, 27 December 2004; Don Van Natta, "Who Is Abu Mussab al-Zarqawi?" The New York Times (Week in Review), 10 October 2004; Nick Childs, "Zarqawi's Insurgency," BBC News, 9 June 2005; Salah Nasrawi, "Bin Laden Seeks Transformation," Associated Press, 27 December 2004; Ghaida Ghantous, "Purpoted Zarqawi Tape Vows No Negotiations," Reuters, 29 March 2005; "Iraq's Qaeda Warns Sunnis Against Constitution," Reuters, 17 May 2005; Jeffrey Gettleman, "Zarqawi's Journey: From Dropout to Prisoner to an Insurgent Leader in Iraq," The New York Times, 13 July 2004; Donna Abu-Nasr, "Saudi Religious Scholars Support Holy War," Associated Press, 6 November 2004; Patrick McDonnell, "Confessions of a Saudi Militant in Iraq," The Los Angeles Times, 20 February 2005; "New Jihadist Confessions," http://www.memritv.org/search.asp?ACT=S9&P1=629, 12 April 2005; "Terrorism Studies Project," http://www.memri.org/bin/opener_latest.cgi?ID=SD89605, 20 April 2005; "Iraqi Qaeda Vows to Kill Sunnis Joining Government," Reuters, 24 April 2005; "Captured Iraqi Terrorist Saleh Al-Jubouri: We Got Communications Calling to Kill Americans and Iraqi Policemen from Saudi Sheik Safar Al-Hawali," Memri, 10 April 2005; Dexter Filkins, "Insurgents Vowing to Kill Iraqis Who Brave the Polls on Sunday," The New York Times, 26 February 2005; Ghaith Abdul-Ahad, "The US Is Behaving as if Every Sunni Is a Terrorist," The Guardian, 26 January 2005; Jackie Spinner and Bassam Sebti, "Militant Declares War on Iraqi Vote," The Washington Post, 24 January 2005; Matt Spetalnick, "Al Qaeda Ally Declares All-Out War on Iraqi Election," Reuters, 23 January 2005; Edward Wong, "Balking at Vote, Sunnis Seek Role on Constitution," The New York Times, 24 January 2005; David Sanger, "Bush Takes Rare Step of Debating Bin Laden," The New York Times, 29 December 2004; Sameer Yacoub, "Purported Al-Zarqawi Tape Raps Scholars," Associated Press, 24 November 2004; Bob Herbert, "Iraq, Then and Now," The New York Times, 21 February 2005; "Iraq Qaeda Says Zarqawi in 'Good Health,'" Reuters, 27 May 2005; Paul Garwood, "Claims About Al-Zarqawi Suggest Confusion," Associated Press, 26 May 2005; Jamal Halaby, "Web Posting Claims Al-Zarqawi Fled Iraq," Associated Press, 25 May 2005; Sally Buzbee, "Iraq Insurgents' Failure Raises Questions," Associated Press, 31 January 2005; Craig Whitlock, "In Europe New Force for Recruiting Radicals," The Washington Post,

18 February 2005; "World Terror Risk 'on the Rise'," *BBC News,* 19 March 2005; Martha Raddatz, "Secret Task Force Hunting Iraq's Most Dangerous Man," *ABC News,* 26 May 2005; Scott Peterson, "Pressure Builds on Iraq's Insurgents," *The Christian Science Monitor,* 26 May 2005; Nicholas Blanford and Dan Murphy, "For Al Qaeda, Iraq May Be the Next Battlefield," *The Christian Science Monitor,* 27 August 2003; Randa Habib, "Iraq New Fertile Ground for Jihad: Son of Bin Laden's Mentor," *Agence France Press,* 29 August 2005.

4. Hussein, "Al-Zarqawi... : Seif al-Adl's Testament"; Mohammed Al-Shafi'i, "Seif al-Adl: Al-Qaeda's Ghost," *Asharq al-Awsat,* 1 June 2005.

5. Hussein, "Al-Zarqawi...: Abu al-Montasser's Testament," part 2, 14–15 May 2005.

6. Ibid., part 5, 18 May 2005.

7. Ibid., "Al-Zarqawi...: Al-Maqdisi's Testament," parts 6 and 7, 19 and 20 May 2005.

8. Ibid.

9. Ibid., part 1, 13 May 2005.

10. Ibid.

11. "Abu Mus'ab Al-Zarqawi: Collateral Killing of Muslims Is Legitimate," http://www.memri.org/bin/opener_latest.cgi?ID=SD91705.

12. "To the Muslims in Iraq in Particular and the [Islamic] Nation [ummah] in General." The full text of bin Laden's message was translated by *FBIS Report* – FEA20041227000762, 27 December 2004. See Christopher M. Blanchard, "Al Qaeda: Statements and Evolving Ideology," *CRS Report for Congress,* 20 June 2005, p. 7.

13. "Al Zarqawi Group Vows Allegiance to Bin Laden," *Associated Press,* 17 October 2004; Dan Murphy, "In Iraq, a Clear-Cut bin Laden–Zarqawi Alliance," *The Christian Science Monitor,* 31 December 2004.

14. Taweel, "Al-Zarqawi"; Taweel, "Al-Zarqawi Present and His Followers Everywhere"; "'Emir' of the Fallujah Fighters (Abu Osama) to *Al Wasat*"; Taweel, "Bin Laden Fails in Afghanistan."

15. Hussein, *Al-Zarqawi,* part 3, 16 May 2005.

16. Laura Jordan and Katherine Shrader, "Bin Laden Enlisting Al-Zarqawi for Attacks," *Associated Press,* 1 April 2005.

17. Craig Whitlock, "Al Qaeda Leaders Seen in Control," *The Washington Post,* 24 July 2005.

18. Don Van Natta, "Who Is Abu Mussab al-Zarqawi?"; Nick Childs, "Zarqawi's Insurgency," *BBC News,* 9 June 2005; Raddatz, "Secret Task Force Hunting Iraq's Most Dangerous Man."

19. Hussein, *Al-Zarqawi,* part 3, 16 May 2005.

20. Ibid.

21. Maamoun Youssef, "Al-Qaida Announces Iraqi Suicide Squad," *Associated Press,* 21 June 2005.

22. Mohammed Salah, "Tantawi Considers al-Zarqawi Faction 'Mishief-Makers,'" *Al Hayat*, 5 July 2005.

23. Mohammed Salah, "'Al-Jihad' and the 'Islamic Group' Attack al-Zarqawi," *Al Hayat*, 11 July 2005; "Egyptian Islamic Group: Zarqawi Does Not Understand the Meaning of Jihad," *Asharq al-Awsat*, 11 July 2005.

24. Marwan Shahadat and Maysar al-Shumri, "Al-Maqdisi to *Al Hayat*: Bin Laden Rejected a Request by al-Zarqawi to Assign My Books to His Followers and I Advised Abu Musab to Avoid Killing Civilians and Attacking Churches and Shiites Mosques," *Al Hayat*, 5 July 2005, http://www.alghad.jo/index.php?news=31781&searchFor; Hazem Amin, "Stories from al-Maqdisi House...," *Al Hayat*, 5 July 2005; Bernhard Zand, "Zarqawi's New Strategy: Four Days of Martyrdom," *Der Spiegel*, 11 July 2007.

25. Hussein, "Al-Zarqawi...: Al-Maqdisi's Testament," parts 6 and 7, 19 and 20 May 2005.

26. Marwan Shahada, "The al-Zarqawi–al-Maqdisi Dispute...," *Al Hayat*, 5 July 2005; Mshari al-Zaydi, "Abu Mohammed al-Maqdisi: Al-Zarqawi's 'Spiritual Godfather'," *Asharq al-Awsat*, 26 July 2005; "The Recruiting Story of al-Zarqawi," *Elaph* (an Arabic-language electronic newspaper), 18 and 19 July 2005. See http://www.elaph.com/ElaphWeb/AkhbarKhasa/2005/7/76980.htm.

27. Al-Shafi'i, "Seif Al-Adl"; Maysar al-Shumri, "Al-Zarqawi's Comrade 'Abu al-Ghadiah' Killed in American Air Raids...," *Al Hayat*, 5 June 2005.

28. Douglas Jehl, "Iraq May be Prime Place for Training of Militants, C.I.A. Report Concludes," *The New York Times*, 22 June 2005; Dana Priest, "Iraq a New Terror Breeding Ground," *The Washington Post*, 13 January 2005; Dana Priest and Josh White, "War Helps Recruit Terrorists, Hill Told," *The Washington Post*, 17 February 2005; David Morgan, "Iraq Conflict Feeds International Threat – CIA," *Reuters*, 16 February 2005. "Iraq Warns Neighbors of Terror Threat," *Agence France Presse*, 10 July 2005.

29. "Iraq Now an Al-Qaeda Battleground, British Report Says," *Agence France Presse*, 29 July 2004; Faiza Saleh Ambah, "Iraq: Spinning off Arab Terrorists?" *The Christian Science Monitor*, 8 February 2005; Taweel, "Bin Laden Fails in Afghanistan"; Blanford and Murphy, "For Al Qaeda, Iraq May Be the Next Battlefield"; Craig Whitlock, "In Europe, New Force for Recruiting Radicals," *The Washington Post*, 18 February 2005; Elaine Sciolino, "France Seizes 11 Accused of Plotting Iraq Attacks," *The New York Times*, 27 January 2005; Peter Grier and Faye Bowers, "Bin Laden Tape Seeks to Stir Anger Over Iraq," *The Christian Science Monitor*, 12 September 2003; Nadia Abou El-Magd, "Alleged Zawahiri Statement Pushes Holy War," 2 February 2005; Richard Norton-Taylor, "Iraq War Has Swollen Ranks of al-Qaida," *The Guardian*, 16 October 2003; Fawaz A. Gerges, "The Bleeding of Iraq and the Rising Insurgency," *Institute for Social Policy and Understanding*, Policy Brief No. 6 (September 2004); Fawaz A. Gerges, "Understanding Iraq's Resistance," *The Christian Science Monitor*, 10 September 2003.

30. Hassan M. Fattah, "Anger Burns on the Fringe of Britain's Muslims," *The New York Times*, 16 July 2005.

31. Alan Cowell, "British Seeking Fifth Man, Thought to be Ringleader," *The New York Times*, 14 July 2005.

32. "Study: U.K. at 'Risk' for Supporting Iraq War," *Reuters*, 18 July 2005; Patrick Seale, "Europe's Home-grown Terrorists," *Agence Global*, 18 July 2005; Seale, "London Pays the Price of the Iraq War," *Agence Global*, 11 July 2005.

33. Alexis Debat, "The New Head of Jihad Inc.?," http://abcnews.go.com/International, 28 March 2005; Glasser, "Terror War Seen Shifting to Match Evolving Enemy."

34. Taweel, "Al-Zarqawi." The "Department of Indoctrination" of the Zarqawi network published an article by Abu Maysara al-Iraqi in which he discusses the identity of Al Qaeda in Iraq and outlines its aims. For a translation of the article, see "The Iraqi Al-Qaida Organization: Self Portrait," http://www.memri.org/bin/opener_latest.cgi?ID=SD88405, 24 March 2005.

35. Hussein, "Al-Zarqawi," part 3, 16 May 2005.

36. Hussein, "Al-Zarqawi . . . : Seif al-Adl's Testament," part 9, 23 May 2005; Al-Shafi'i, "Seif al-Adl."

37. Ibrahim Awed, "1300 Terrorists Caught in Syria," *Asharq al-Awsat*, 10 July 2005; Samar Azmashli, "Damascus Announces the Arrest of 34 Arabs . . . ," *Al Hayat*, 5 July 2004; "Jordan Says Syria Is a Training Ground for Jihadists," *Reuters*, 15 July 2005.

38. Hazem Amin, "Mujahedeen of the Town of 'Al Qaeda Leader in Lebanon' Accuse the Government of Dragging Them into Jihad," *Al Hayat*, 29 September 2004; "Lebanon: An Angry Funeral for Al-Kateeb in Majdal Anjar," *Al Hayat*, 3 September 2004; Mustafa al-Ansari, "Two Saudis Return from Iraq with Sad Experiences," *Al Hayat*, 14 May 2005; Ibrahim Hmeidi, "A Trans-national Network to Assist in Transporting Mujahedeen [to Iraq]," *Al Hayat*, 27 October 2004; Mohammed al-Ashab, "European Networks to Infiltrate Mujahedeen [to Iraq] . . . ," *Al Hayat*, 11 February 2005; Patrick McDonnell, "Confessions of a Saudi Militant in Iraq," *The Los Angeles Times*, 20 February, 2005; "New Jihadist Confessions," http://www.memritv.org/search.asp?ACT=S9&P1=629, 12 April 2005; "Terrorism Studies Project," http://www.memri.org/bin/_opener_latest.cgi?ID=SD89605, 20 April 2005; *The New York Times*, 25 February, 26 April, and 25 May 2004; Don Van Natta, Jr., and Desmond Butler, "Calls to Jihad Are Said to Lure Hundreds of Militants into Iraq," *The New York Times*, 1 November 2003; Craig Whitlock, "In Europe New Force for Recruiting Radicals," *The Washington Post*, 18 February 2005; Todd Pitman, "N. Africans Joining Iraq Islamic Fighters," *Associated Press*, 14 June 2005; Ahmed Al-Haj, "Yemeni Youths Seeking Martyrdom in Iraq," *Associated Press*, 20 December 2004.

39. Jehl, "Iraq May Be Prime Place for Training of Militants, C.I.A. Report Concludes."

40. "Rumsfeld Questions Terror War Progress," *Associated Press*, 22 October 2003; *The New York Times*, 1 November 2003 and 25 February, 26 April, and 25 May 2004; Fawaz A. Gerges, "Sunni Insurgency," *The Baltimore Sun*, 4 April 2004.

41. See the informative series of survey reports by the Pew Global Attitudes Project, a project of the PewResearchCenter, which has surveyed the attitudes of thousands of people worldwide toward their own countries and the United States. The various international opinion polls show clearly that the American invasion of Iraq has taken its toll on how the world, particularly Muslims, views the United States. In particular, see "America's Image Further Erodes, Europeans Want Weaker Ties: But Post-War Iraq Will Be Better Off, Most Say" (18 March 2003); "Views of a Changing World 2003: War with Iraq Divides Global Publics" (3 June 2003); "A Year After Iraq War: Mistrust of America in Europe Ever Higher, Muslim Anger Persists" (16 March 2004); "U.S. Image Up Slightly, But Still Negative: American Character Gets Mixed Reviews" (23 June 2005). All reports are posted on http://pewglobal.org/reports/. Official and semiofficial reports by the U.S. government arrived at similar conclusions. See *Report of the Defense Science Board Task Force on Strategic Communication* (Washington, D.C.: Office of the Under Secretary of Defense for Acquisition, Technology, and Logistics, September 2004); *Changing Minds, Winning Peace: A New Strategic Direction for U.S. Public Diplomacy in the Arab and Muslim World*, Report of the Advisory Group on Public Diplomacy for the Arab and Muslim World, submitted to the Committee on Appropriations, U.S. House of Representatives, 1 October 2003, http://www.state.gov/documents/organization/24882. See also Craig Charney and Nicole Yakatan, *A New Beginning: Strategies for a More Fruitful Dialogue with the Muslim World* (New York: Council on Foreign Relations, CSR no. 7, May 2005).

42. Hussein, "Al-Zarqawi...: Seif al-Adl's Testament," part 9, 23 May 2005.

43. Adonis, "Behind History, Without Future," *Al Hayat*, 4 December 2003. Another liberal columnist, Hazem Saghie, lamented the fact that Arabs and Muslims were being forced to choose between two tyrannies – the Saddam Hussein tyranny and the tyranny of the Bush administration.

44. "Al-Azhar Grand Imam: Resisting U.S. Aggression Islamic Duty," http://www.islamonline.net/english/News/2003-02/22/article14.shtml; "Those Who Die Fighting U.S. Ocupation Forces Are Martyrs: Qardawi," http://www.oislamonline.net/english/News/2003-01/28/article08.shtml; Mohammed Salah, "Al-Qardawi: Killing American Civilians in Iraq Is a Duty," *Al Hayat*, 2 September 2004; Ridwan al-Sayyid, "The End and the Means," *Al-Mustaqbal*, 7 September 2004; "Mufti of Lebanon: Jihad Is Our Weapon to Resist the Threat of American Imperialism," *Al Hayat*, 27 October 2003; Essam al-Aryan, "Can Jihad be Invoked in the Case of Iraq," *Al Hayat*, 4 May 2003; Fawaz A. Gerges, "Muslims Called to Jihad," *The Los Angeles Times*, 26 March 2003; Fawaz A. Gerges, "War in Iraq," The WashingtonPost.Com, 3 April 2003; Fawaz A, Gerges, "Fuel on Mideast Ire: Arab Moderates Are Now Joined with Radicals

Against the U.S.," *The Star-Ledger*, 30 March 2003; Michael Isikoff and Mark Hosenball, "Preaching Violence," *Newsweek*, 29 September 2004.

45. Al Jazeera, which has an estimated audience of 40 million viewers and reflects an Islamist bent, reported that more Arabs and Muslims believe there exists a "ferocious confrontation between Israel and the United States, on the one hand, and the Islamist current in all of its moderate and extremist variety, on the other." See http://www.aljazeera.net, 22 April 2004.

46. "Purported Bin Laden Tape Offers 'Truce,'" *Associated Press*, 15 April 2004.

Glossary

Afghan Arabs: veterans of the Afghan war

al-Adou al-Baeed: far enemy (United States and its allies)

al-Adou al-Qareeb: near enemy (apostate Muslim rulers)

al-ahad: religious oath

al-da'wa: religious call

al-Faridah al-Ghaibah: Absent (or Forgotten) Duty

al-hakimiya: God's sovereignty

al-jahiliya: state of divine ignorance

Al Qaeda al-Sulbah: solid base or foundation

al-sama' wata'a: hear and obey, total obedience

al-shabab: the youths

asabiya: group or tribal solidarity

caliph: pan-Islamic ruler

caliphate: centralized Islamic authority

dar al-harb: the House of War

dar al-iman: the House of Belief

dar al-islam: the House of Islam

dar al-kufr: the House of Impiety

emara: leadership

emir: prince, leader

fard 'ayn: permanent and personal obligation

fard kifaya: collective duty

fatwa: religious edict or ruling

fiqh: Islamic jurisprudence

fitna: sedition

five pillars of Islam: profession of faith, prayer, fasting, alms-giving, and pilgrimage

hadiths: Prophetic traditions

iman: faith or belief

intifada: uprising

irredentist jihadi: jihadi who struggles to redeem land considered to be part of dar al-islam

ijtihad: individual's effort at interpretation

jihad: armed struggle

jihadi: radical activist who feels estranged from the secular social and political order at home and intrinsically threatened by globalization and westernization

kufar: infidels

kufr: impiety

"Land of the Two Holy Places": Saudi Arabia

Maktab al-Khadamat: Services Bureau

mazhabiya: confessionalism or sectarianism

mujahid, mujahedeen: Islamic fighter, Islamic fighters

naksa: setback

nizam al-kufr: deviant system

salaf: pious ancestors

shahid: martyr

Shariah: Islamic law

shura: consultation

Shura Council: Consultative Council

solh: truce

Sunnah: all the deeds and words of the Prophet, second in importance to the Qur'an

takfeer: the practice of excommunication of Muslims

taqleed: emulating ancient tradition

tawhid: affirmation of the oneness of God

ulema: religious scholars

ummah: the Muslim community worldwide

uzla: withdrawal from society

Wahhabism: a puritanical religious doctrine founded by the eighteenth-century evangelist Muhammad b. Abd al-Wahhab in Saudi Arabia

Index

regional affiliates of, 217–18, 247–50,
253–9
rise of, 22, 24, 30–4, 47, 53, 55, 66–7,
101, 102, 125, 139, 151, 157,
159–61, 307–8
as Salafi, 131–2, 142–3, 236
Saudi Arabia's relationship with, 128,
145–8, 150, 176, 181, 249
Shura Council governing, 18, 19,
192, 198, 231
Somalia, U.S. withdrawal and, 53–4,
193, 313
Sudan expelling, 235–6
Taliban's alliance with, 140–1, 172,
225
Tora Bora as meeting site for, 16
ummah harmed by, 28
United States as top enemy of, 23, 24,
43, 56–7, 64–5, 74–5, 77–8, 143,
144, 149, 157–8, 160, 184, 203,
225
vision of, 185
al-Zarqawi's alliance with, 253–9,
266–7
al-Zawahiri's alliance with, 4, 33, 42,
50, 64, 66, 119–20, 121, 122,
125–6, 128, 130–1, 134–5, 138–40,
143, 167, 170–5, 193–7, 203, 212,
220–1, 287–8
bin Uthaymayn, sheikh, 146–7,
180
Binalshibh, Ramzi
as 9/11 field commander, 17–18,
19–21, 23
credibility of, 2003
al-Bishri, Tariq, 241
Blind Sheikh. See Rahman, sheikh
Omar Abdel

caliphate (centralized Islamic authority)
as jihadi goal, 10, 11–12, 25, 30, 43,
44, 47, 49, 114, 267
kufr (impiety) replaced by, 44,
114

charismatic leadership
of Azzam, 102, 139, 258–9
of bin Laden, 36–41, 102, 178–84,
198, 218, 227–8
of al-Masri, 38, 102
role of, among jihadis, 34–41, 42, 99,
101–2, 117, 126, 127, 181–4, 197,
227–8, 237
of al-Zawahiri, 36–41, 102, 139, 178,
218, 227–8, 310
Clarke, Richard, 168, 176
Cold War, 70–4, 77–8
cult of personality. See charismatic
leadership

dar al-harb (House of War), 43–4, 203,
314
dar al-islam (House of Islam), 43–4,
179, 203, 314
Darwish, Suleiman Khaled, 263
"Declaration of War"
Azzam's death and, 137
bin Laden's instructions in, 31, 137,
144, 148–9, 167
Derbala, Mohammed Essam, 201–4,
207–8, 210, 212–13, 214

Egyptian jihadis. See also Islamic
Jihad
bin Laden and, 139–43, 178, 181,
183, 287–8
defeat of, 151, 169, 206–7
jihad dominated by, 64, 139–43, 178,
181, 183, 287–8
Sadat assassinated by, 44, 46, 88, 89,
92, 100, 200–1, 203, 209, 214,
215
embassy bombings, 31, 39, 54, 157, 167,
175, 176, 188, 220, 313
external enemies. See far enemy

Fadlallah, Sayyed Mohammed Hussein,
237–8
al-Faisal, Prince Turki, 148